LIFE

Life

A Journey through Science and Politics

PAUL R. EHRLICH

Yale
UNIVERSITY PRESS
NEW HAVEN AND LONDON

Published with assistance from the Louis Stern Memorial Fund.

Yale University Press books may be purchased in quantity for educational, business, or promotional use. For information, please e-mail sales.press@yale.edu (U.S. office) or sales@yaleup.co.uk (U.K. office).

Set in Electra type by Integrated Publishing Solutions.
Printed in the United States of America.

Library of Congress Control Number: 2022935358
ISBN 978-0-300-26454-8 (hardcover : alk. paper)

A catalogue record for this book is available from the British Library.

This paper meets the requirements of ANSI/NISO Z39.48-1992 (Permanence of Paper).

10 9 8 7 6 5 4 3 2 1

For Anne: Sine Qua Non

CONTENTS

FOREWORD

Lisa Marie Ehrlich

My father frequently introduces me as his daughter by his first wife. Which is true—it's just that he is still married to his first wife: Anne Howland Ehrlich. When I was a teenager I went through a period of "Call me Svetlana," after Stalin's daughter, Svetlana Alliluyeva, who had published a memoir of her father that was not altogether complimentary. At the time, my father was on *The Tonight Show* starring Johnny Carson frequently, we were getting death threats, and his fame mostly seemed a burden. Thus, I often joked darkly that someday I would write a Svetlana-style tell-all. Instead, as I became an adult, and my dad became one of my closest confidants (right after my husband), I largely changed my views and ultimately helped him with this book.

It is not a secret that my parents were deeply involved in their research and fieldwork when I was growing up. I was an only child, born in 1955, and unlike the stereotype of the coddled poppet, I was expected to be as independent as possible. In many ways I think that has stood me in good stead, but as a child I lacked the perspective I have now. In the early sixties, academic years were spent at Stanford, where I went to public school and we lived in the faculty ghetto next door to my best friend, Susan Gere. Summers were spent at the Rocky Mountain Biological Laboratory (RMBL) at 9,600 feet in the Colorado Rockies. RMBL was kid heaven, and I had a number of good friends that I saw there each summer. It was also where I learned about basic safety around mountains, streams, and wildlife. So began experiences that made me a bit more savvy about wild places and things than the average suburban kid's, which increased even more as I grew up helping with fieldwork in virtually every major jungle in the world.

Then, in June 1965, we set sail for Australia for my dad's first sabbatical and began the fifteen-month adventure going around the globe that is described in this memoir. Most relevant to the topic of this book, it was in Australia that I first read a speech that my dad had written. Lying innocently on our coffee table, the paper was my first exposure to the issue of overpopulation, and I well remember being somewhat shocked and concerned. How come no one had told me about this before? I was ten.

Dad (and Mom) wrote *The Population Bomb* in 1968 and asked me to read it: Dad wanted to be sure it would be understandable to anyone reading at a sixth- or seventh-grade level. The book was published that same year, and it hugely changed all of our lives—at least in the short run.

But enough about me. From my earliest childhood I remember my dad working . . . a TON. I do not remember, but have been told many times, that when dad was in graduate school and I was a toddler, I thought his name was "Bye bye" because he was always leaving to go into the lab. Once he was at Stanford, he no longer went into the lab after dinner, but most nights he would retire to his den and continue working well past my bedtime. My mom also worked—for him. Until I was eight or nine, Mom would be there when I got home from school, often dissecting butterflies at the microscope in her study and drawing their genitalia. After that, I was given a house key to hang around my neck and rules about who could be in the house with me (basically, girls and not boys!). Fortunately for everyone, I was quite a reliable child.

Do not be fooled by this memoir's emphasis on adventures and socializing with friends. My parents worked hard and virtually constantly all their lives—eighty hours a week would not be an exaggeration. One does not publish some fifty books and twelve hundred articles, many hundreds of them scientific papers published in prestigious, peer-reviewed journals, as they have done, by screwing around. Nor does one win every possible award in a scientific field or get elected to virtually every major scientific academy without the deep respect of one's peers in the field. The notion that my parents are somehow unscientific mavericks, as the press sometimes—and their opponents often—depict them, is absurd.

In addition to all their work researching, writing, and teaching, my parents squeezed in a ton of socializing (probably three evenings a week once I was nine or ten, and more on trips). This speaks to their ridiculous indefatigability. Most of their trips involved field research of some description. I was often pressed into service to help (usually schlepping butterfly equipment in the field during the day and copying field notes at night). My dad would say, "The butterflies don't know it's a holiday," while I would pray for rain so we could have a day off. (On the bright side, I eventually earned enough money to buy a horse.) Even their non-fieldwork trips, such as going to Hawaii, largely consisted of writing whatever book or papers they were currently engaged in, with breaks for socializing in the evening. Dad's mother went with them on one trip to Hawaii and complained afterward that she saw them only at dinner time because they were either working all day or, she speculated, having sex! Grandma Ruth was nobody's fool.

My dad insists, as you will read, that he is not a workaholic. That may be (and it may be semantics!), but he is nonetheless the only person I have ever met who, if he has two minutes to spare before being picked up to go somewhere, will start something new. I have literally never seen him putter around. My mom is not nearly so internally driven, but she reaped the whirlwind when she married my dad, and so off she whirled with him.

This book occasionally displays my father's curmudgeonliness, not to say ability to vituperate; you will hear less about his softer side. Dad, of course, grew up in an era when men were men and women were mostly subservient. Along with that went the "Men don't show weakness" dictum, and from what I have heard (mostly from Grandma Ruth, with whom I was close until her death in 2007), her husband, Grandpa Bill, who died just before I was born, was a big proponent of this version of manliness. I have never seen my father cry—not even when his best friend killed himself. That does not mean that he has no soft side; it just means he won't admit to it. His friends and students, however, are all well aware that he is incredibly loyal, generous, and there for them. He is the opposite of the stereotypical professor who rarely credits his students. He has always made sure his students had research opportunities and got published, and he has always been quick to credit them and help them advance in their careers. This is a partial explanation of something that does come out in the book, his lifelong connections with former students as well as with mentors and colleagues and his abiding concern for their well-being. As just one example, when Steve Schneider was in Stanford Hospital for weeks fighting lymphoma, Dad visited him every single day.

Dad is the quintessential extrovert: he thrives on interaction. My mother, by contrast, is the quintessential introvert, though she is more "out there" than she used to be. I remember her telling me when I was in high school that if it were up to her, Dad and she would socialize about a tenth as much as they did. She has always had a temporizing role: "Oh, Paul, you don't really want to say that" was a frequent refrain as she read over a first draft. Inherently shy and comparatively literal-minded, Mom has often played the straight man to Dad's comic routines. She was also my shelter when I was a child and he was mad at me. My parents are truly opposite in this. Dad's energy is nearly always high—whether positive or negative. Being around him is energizing, but he can also set peoples' (and dogs') teeth on edge. My mom, at the other extreme, has a calm presence that engages the skittish, be it adults, small children, or animals.

A few more words about my mom, also to add balance: she was a gifted artist. I use the past tense because the arthritis in her hands no longer allows her to draw or paint. If you can get hold of a copy of *How to Know the Butterflies*, you will see her amazing pen-and-ink drawings. I have her beautiful oil painting of a lake in Canada hanging prominently in our home. I remember watching her paint it when I was a little girl—probably five or six. I also have a pen-and-ink drawing she did of me when I was about two; it is remarkable in its accuracy and detail. When I was little she made all of her clothes and all of mine (until I grew rebellious in my early teens and she got busier working on books). She could make her own patterns, and I would sometimes catch her doodling ideas for dresses that looked like the drawings in magazines. I once asked what she would have done if she hadn't married my father, and without hesitation she said she would have liked to become a fashion designer. It is interesting to imagine what her life would have been like in a different era. But she and my father married in December 1954, when she was barely twenty-one years old, and I was born the following November. Dad recruited her to help with his work, initially drawing and dissecting, later writing and editing, but she also became more involved on her own in environmental work, serving, for example, on boards such as Sierra Club and Friends of the Earth and working on nuclear issues. My parents' marriage, now going on sixty-eight years, is much more equal than it used to be, but like many men of his generation, my dad still relies heavily on my mom for the practical things in life. I doubt he has any idea where the dry cleaner's is or even what clothes need to be dry cleaned. And trust me, that is only one example.

The memoir you are about to read is personal. Dad dwells relatively little on his public life. He doesn't describe most of his thousands of public addresses and media appearances and interactions with celebrities, although he does address head-on some of the major controversies, such as the now-infamous confrontations with Barry Commoner. But this memoir is much more about his favorite things in life: the study of biology, doing stuff with friends, and engaging in political efforts to change what he saw as a deadly trajectory for society. To a great extent, but not entirely, those three things have overlapped. And fortunately for you, the reader, he was involved in really interesting science—often in far-flung places—and had some pretty cool, and in some cases, harrowing adventures.

PREFACE

I've been buried in life. My own, of course, but much of my life's work has focused on the lives of animals, plants, and microbes and their evolution and behavior. It has included the evolution and behavior that shapes the individual lives of my favorite mammal, *Homo sapiens*. My life also has entailed efforts to influence society to move rapidly in the direction of improving all life, and lives, by limiting human population growth, increasing racial, gender, and economic equity, and conserving our environmental life-support systems abundantly supplied with nonhuman lives. A vision for a better and more sustainable life for all the people living on the one-and-only habitable planet in our solar system has arisen naturally from my lifelong studies of butterflies and my distress at the loss of their natural habitats.

I had the good fortune to have been born in 1932. I thus have lived through the various controversies, causes, and crises that define our time, and I have been an active participant in a number of them, of course as a citizen, but also in my role as a scientist. They range from addressing the threat of nuclear annihilation and the likelihood of pandemics to conservation of habitats and the nonhuman populations they support. I was professionally involved where an understanding of environmental science and evolutionary biology could help deal with existential threats to civilization such as a sixth global mass extinction of biodiversity and the intertwined issues of overpopulation, overconsumption, climate disruption, and planetary poisoning.

How did my life as a scientist-activist in the twentieth and twenty-first centuries develop? How can luck, science, and a vision of how the world could be changed in positive ways lead to activism? What lessons might encourage scientific curiosity and political engagement, and even help to avoid some crises in the future? What were my mistakes? These are questions I'll touch on, and ones I've had a long time to think about.

I'm one of the very few remaining population biologists (a category that includes evolutionists, ecologists, animal behaviorists, and epidemiologists, among others) who have personally observed the great acceleration in both scientific and social change that have characterized much of the past century. I started in a world with a quarter of today's people, where airliners flew at less than two hundred miles an hour; credit cards, photocopying, transistor radios, commercially manufactured television sets, and cell phones didn't exist; no one had run a catheter into a human heart; and doctors didn't have antibiotics to save a life. I've ended up in a much more crowded world, with the internet, space tourism, CT scans, and dozens of colleagues and thousands of others now engaged in attempts to understand and change the world for the better. On a more negative side, I approach my end forced to see numerous routes by which civilization appears ready to destroy itself and has developed ever more technically proficient means to do so.

I was born into the Great Depression in a country in which prejudice against minorities and women was epidemic, grew up in World War II and its metamorphosis into the Cold War, and witnessed a great boom of material production, population, and consumption and the United States becoming, at least for a time, a world-dominating empire. I enjoyed a great flowering of science, civil rights, and travel and now, sadly, am observing rising fascist tendencies in the United States, among other countries, as well as increasing economic inequity and what I fear may be the first stages of a collapse of civilization as the existential threats—those endangering our very existence—are largely ignored, if not always in rhetoric, often in practice.

I've been privileged to know many of the key players in various aspects of the great environmental drama. In my professional life, they've included Theodosius Dobzhansky, Ernst Mayr, Ledyard Stebbins, E. B. Ford, and other builders of the "modern evolutionary synthesis" that transformed biology. On the broader social front I've had the opportunity to spend time with a host of politicians ranging from Tim Wirth, Dick Lamm, Jerry Brown, and Stewart Udall to Prince Philip, Oscar Arias, and Bob Carr. In addition, I got to meet a number of other public figures, some of whom, like some of the politicians, became long-term friends (and, occasionally, persistent enemies). I co-organized sit-ins to desegregate restaurants in Lawrence, Kansas, protested the Vietnam War, and was a prime mover along with American and Soviet colleagues in the nuclear winter studies and public relations campaign. I even became for a time a correspondent on *NBC News*, and over my career I have made thousands of speeches and appearances—including more than twenty with Johnny Carson on *The Tonight Show*.

For those who believe me an incurable pessimist, note that I would not write this memoir if I were certain of an approaching collapse, if I thought the crumbling of humanity's life-support systems would surely end civilization as we know it. But some degrees of disintegration at least locally, perhaps globally, clearly seem entrained as testified by the wide array of scientists and others who have looked at the current human trajectory, issued warning after warning of the need for dramatic change, and seen little evidence worldwide of the efforts required to effect that change. In any case, the whole point of my concern is to find ways to avoid such disastrous occurrences and to build a new social structure, a way of living in the natural world, in which the possibility of collapse is minimized and almost everyone has substantial well-being.

Some progress had been achieved toward those goals in the United States over the past half century, with many members of the scientific community, politicians, and the general public starting to deal with climate disruption, loss of biodiversity (the other animals, plants, and microbes with which we share Earth), and other environmental threats. It was aided during the 1960s and early 1970s by legal steps such as passage of the Clean Air and Clean Water Acts, the National Environmental Policy Act, the Endangered Species Act, and Superfund (the government program to clean up toxic wastes). That progress, faltering in the Reagan and George W. Bush years, began to be rapidly eroded in 2017 by the Trump administration and its congressional allies. That same gang of kleptocrats and their supporters were successful in reversing some of the environmental gains we as a country had made, along with other gains in areas such as racial, religious, and gender equity, while reinforcing the unhappy decades-long backsliding in the area of economic equity. The degree to which the Biden-Harris administration and those that follow it may manage to recoup those gains, much less make further progress, remains uncertain, but the needs are much greater and the time is much shorter.

One theme that runs implicitly through the book I will make explicit here: my love for the beauty of our planet and its inhabitants that I have seen while spending much of my life in Earth's wild places. Anyone who knows me will tell you that I am not inclined to gushing or sentimentality, so you will not read long passages (or even many short ones!) about the wonders of the natural world. Nonetheless, its beauty and intricacy, and the real tragedy of its accelerating loss, have driven me both to seek it out and to fight as best I've known how for its preservation. From diving on coral reefs below the sea surface to hiking above the tree line in high mountains, I've relished it all, usually in the company of my beautiful and adventurous wife, Anne, though I've always tried to mix my awe with the evidence-based approach of science. And my enjoyment of biodiversity includes my fellow *Homo sapiens*—as my interactions with mentors, colleagues, students, relatives, and friends of my own and other cultures indicate. *Homo sapiens* is a quintessentially social animal, an intricate part of nature, and I belong to that species.

This brings me to another, related major theme: the value and critical importance of a scientific approach to the world. In recent decades the question of what is scientific knowledge has loomed large in my life. With much original input from a close friend and colleague, evolutionist Richard Holm, I realized long ago that human beings could not detect a "pure" reality—the sort of invariant and immortal Forms imagined by Plato. All of reality is viewed by people through the lenses of their nervous systems and their cultures. Still, by basing conclusions on evidence, and by making science an adversary game where scientists could advance their careers by testing other scientists' ideas and, in some cases, demonstrating they were faulty, a superior understanding of the world we experience could be constructed. Its superiority lay in its ability to predict future events in the physical world (often with considerable accuracy), to enable the creation of many technologies that could be useful and sometimes even expand our sensory capacities, and even (as many social psychologists have) to make better sense of our behavior.

A third theme that runs throughout is more personal: I have always felt lucky in both my personal life and in the areas of my professional life that were not directly concerned with policy. And in setting so much of my life to paper, I have been struck by the abundance of personal and professional fulfillment I have been fortunate to attain—or, to put it another way, how many great adventures I've had as I pursued my love of biology. This is thus a cross-cutting theme: personal and professional fulfillment coexisting with deep frustration from the failure so far of concerned citizens, me included, and institutions, to derail the forces that pose existential threats to civilization, democracy, and many of the life-forms with which we share Earth. This frustration is combined with considerable sadness when contemplating what kind of world Anne and I will leave to our grandchildren and great-grandchildren, as well as our many younger friends and their families. This is my chunk of what I like to call the human dilemma—the contrast between what humanity *could* do and what it *likely will* do.

But in the area of public policy it is extremely important to understand that science can never supply *certainty*. Scientific theories and conclusions are always subject to change and open to challenge from other scientists eager to marshal evidence to demonstrate the weaknesses or errors in those conclusions or even in entire paradigms. Science never proves anything, and scientific ideas—even great theories—are subject to revision in the light of new evidence. Science now can't answer to my satisfaction many questions I and many others have puzzled over, such as the Leibnizian query, "Why is there anything at all?" or, less grandly, "How does the brain create consciousness?" But science's evidence-based approach can do a much better job of answering such questions as "Why are there so many kinds of animals?" or "Will the flying machine we've constructed stay aloft?" or "What will happen to the average temperature on land and the level of the seas if we keep adding greenhouse gases to the atmosphere?" than can any faith-based approach.

When it comes to policy, science can tell us with (generally) increasing likelihood what will happen if we do *x*, *y*, or *z*. But it is we who make the decision of what we *ought* to do, of which path, *x* or *y* or *z*, we should take. The "ought" problem is often one where science (indeed, any field of knowledge) can only help, not answer. Tommy has an earache. Ought he be given a dose of anonymycin? Real uncertainties reign in the scientific realm: Is, for example, the cause of his earache an anonymycin-susceptible bacterium? Is Tommy likely to be allergic to annamycin? Ethical uncertainties exist as well: Does the good of decreasing the odds of Tommy going deaf or dying compensate society for the bad of possibly increasing bacterial resistance to annamycin with an unnecessary anonamycin treatment (if Tommy's natural defenses likely can do the job)? Such uncertainties must plague any scientist involved in issues of public policy (indeed, in most of scholarship), but my focus throughout my life and in this book is scientific—that is, evidence-based—and always with an eye to potential uncertainties. I used to agree with Benjamin Franklin and had faith in only two certainties: death and taxes. I guess Ben can be forgiven for his faith in the second, not then knowing about offshore accounts and the lawyers for the ultrarich 0.001 percent.

Unquestionably, the luckiest aspect of both my family and professional lives was meeting and marrying Anne. That most beautiful girl on the University of Kansas campus was also smart and funny, though rather shy. Anne was a petite five foot three to my six foot two, and we've always looked a bit like Mutt and Jeff, but we were perfect complements to one another. When I would lose my storied temper, she would look up at me with her beautiful green eyes and calmly say, "Turn blue!" Thus began a marriage and intellectual partnership that is continuing in its sixty-eighth year. Over that time, she became not just a coauthor of many of my articles and books but editor of all of them. Any success I've had has been due in large part to her.

This book is a culmination of my lifelong ambition both to understand and discover new facets of the world and then have the pleasure of telling others what I've learned. In recent years, especially with the coronavirus pandemic, I have increasingly felt that the experience of doing science is not adequately shared with the general public, and in this memoir I attempt to show what one engaged scientist's experience has been like and what it reveals about the momentous time in which we are living.

ONE

The World of My Childhood

Without a doubt, aside from marrying Anne, the smartest thing I ever did was to be born in 1932. My choice of place wasn't so propitious: Philadelphia, the city of brotherly love, where I lived until I was in fifth grade. As a youngster the area made little impression on me—a city with lots of trolley cars and ethnic hatred. From an early age I was increasingly made aware that I was a "Jew boy" mixing with an array of kids of different ethnic backgrounds, many of whom slung ethnic slurs about others, if not to their faces, then behind their backs. I don't remember worrying much about it, though, except that my mother forbade me to use any such terms. I had, of course, been supremely lucky to have been born white, middle class, and male. I also was born soon enough to get a small taste of the Great Depression, since my father lost his job a few days after I appeared, and my folks talked about it as I grew up, but I remember no deprivation. My father got another job almost immediately, and as far as I know, my mother didn't then take a job to supplement the family income. (She didn't work outside the home until she became a middle-school teacher of English and Latin after my father died.) Of those Depression years I do remember the horse-drawn wagon that the huckster who sold us vegetables brought around regularly. And I remember that the milkman delivered milk in bottles (of the kind in which I later raised fruit flies) in another horse-drawn conveyance. During my grammar school days, when I went to the New Lyric Theatre on Germantown Avenue, I would enjoy a double feature: it cost nine cents, and for that I also got a newsreel, a cartoon, an episode of a serial, a crockery dinner plate, and a comic book with the cover torn off. I also remember going to Fitler School, which still exists. But I only remember its name—I was bored in school from the beginning, and until college, classes, teachers, and fellow students made little lasting impression on me, an exception being a Miss Upton who was a nice middle-school teacher, appreciated largely because of my rising testosterone titer.

We lived in the Philadelphia neighborhood of Germantown, in those days a mixed middle- and working-class area. After school, kids ran loose in their neighborhoods until dinnertime—I was with them playing games such as Red Rover in vacant lots. I did return home around 5:00 p.m. to listen to my favorite radio serials such as the adventures of *Jack Armstrong, All-American Boy,* and *The Shadow.* I did get some moral training from them—I still remember, for instance, "The weed of crime bears bitter fruit; crime does not pay. The Shadow knows!"

My first girlfriend, Ann Parker (about age eight), had a father who had worked for Atwater Kent, a pioneering radio manufacturer. The Parkers had a television—a real novelty before the war—and I remember watching a football game on it in the late 1930s. The contraption was the size of a refrigerator, but as I recall it had a screen the size of a Coke-bottle bottom.

The different training and opportunities of females compared to males entered my mind only as a dating teenager, and then only dimly. Racial issues, though, were brought to my attention earlier by my mother. It was an era when lynchings were common in the South and a Ku Klux Klan mentality pervaded the U.S. Congress. People with dark skin couldn't play anything but maids and other menials in movies, and they were banned from professional sports except boxing. When Joe Louis became heavyweight champion in 1937, it was considered normal for newspapers to talk about finding a "white hope" to replace him. We learned almost nothing about the War of the Rebellion (now bowdlerized into the Civil War or the War between the States). In college I did learn that "the North won the war but the South won the history of the war," but it wasn't until late in life that I realized how truly pervasive and sadly successful the myth of the Lost Cause has been and how the traitor Robert E. Lee mistreated his slaves and was respon-

I consider the environmental situation accompanied by three earlier generations of Ehrlichs: Bill, my father; Grandpa Abe; and "Old Grandpa" Morris. Author photo.

sible for the deaths of more American soldiers than any general of any nation in defense of the "peculiar institution" he so fervently supported.[1]

During my childhood (and subsequently), I was extremely fortunate to have the family I did. My father, William (Bill) Ehrlich, was a crackerjack shirt salesman and later became president of the New Jersey Men's Apparel Club. He was Mom's high school sweetheart in Philadelphia, a practical businessman who studied a couple of years at Penn's Wharton School, had a great sense of humor, and even when fatally ill with Hodgkin's disease generally put up with a teenage son who collected butterflies and raised tropical fishes. I always envied his ability to charm other people and regretted our lack of opportunity to get to know each other well as two adults.

My mother was intellectual, understanding, and supportive, and she spoiled me. Mom encouraged my interest in everything from stamp collecting to girls, and especially my passion for tropical fishes, butterflies, and science in general. Ruth Rosenberg Ehrlich was born in 1907 and was unusual for her generation. Valedictorian at Philadelphia's Girls' High, she went first to college at Bryn Mawr, and when she couldn't afford to continue there, she transferred to the University of Pennsylvania, where she had a scholarship, refusing to marry my father until she got her degree. Mom took me to museums and talked to me about everything; she encouraged me to read and, as I got older, to pay attention to public affairs, domestic and foreign. I was also lucky to have a mother who was so well educated and open-minded for her generation. I didn't hesitate to ask her anything, and she always tried to answer honestly. When I was little, she read to me constantly. I remember her reading from the French version of *Babar the King*, translating as she went along. As soon as I could read I was surrounded by books. I loved learning about everything from Homer Randall's *Army Boys Marching into Germany* to *Lives of the Hunted* by the wildlife artist and a co-founder of the Boy Scouts of America Ernest Thompson Seton. My mom would discuss these and anything else with me and tried hard to explain the world as she went.

Probably what I owed most to her was a direct and honest approach to sex. In her old age she could still laugh at Woody Allen's line that "sex without love is an empty experience, but as empty experiences go . . . ." On conveying the details of sex to a small child, she was very modern, answering questions honestly, but not elaborating at each stage. This led to considerable later-in-life amusement on my part. First there was the "seed becomes a baby that grows in Mama's belly" stage. I naturally inquired how the seed got there. This led to the penis-in-the-vagina-injecting-fluid routine. I went away (age five or six?) to contemplate this. Since the only fluid I'd ever seen emerge from a penis was urine, I decided my parents must "do it" in the bathtub—otherwise it would be pretty hard on sheets and mattresses.

Eventually, a month or so later, I cornered Mom with, "Isn't it cold and uncomfortable in the bathtub?" "Where did you ever get that idea?" I explained. "Oh," she replied, "it's not urine, it's a special fluid." More contemplation. "How does Pop know when it's going to be urine, and when it's going to be the special fluid?" That stopped her. "You'll have to ask your father that." Dad left the sex education of my sister, Sally, and me, as well as virtually all other child-rearing, to his wife, but he gave me a straightforward and completely accurate answer: "You just know!"

My sister, Sally, who followed me by four and a half years, wasn't quite so lucky as I was, since, among other things, she had an annoying older brother. Her main contribution to my early life was educational—she made me realize that I wasn't going to be the center of attention forever. I, however, was fortunate to watch her grow up into a competent and compassionate sister.

Just before the war (World War II; in my generation that was and always will be *the* war), when I was nine, we moved to New Jersey, first to South Orange and then to Maplewood. Those locations allowed Dad to sell shirts working out of the Empire State Building office of the Marlboro Shirt Company on the twenty-fifth floor. I loved going there with him on the Delaware, Lackawanna and Western commuter train to Hoboken, and then on the "tube" (now known as the PATH train) to Manhattan. People looked so tiny from that floor. Dad was still using that office when in 1945 a U.S. Army B-25 bomber, flying through fog, crashed into the building between the seventy-eighth and eightieth floors. It was a Saturday—a few people were unfortunately killed, but looking back now, it seems amazing that the death toll wasn't much higher. Dad wasn't at work, but the event made a big impression on me, as I had by that time become a real aviation buff, subscribing to *Flying* magazine through much of the war. I didn't imagine that, twenty years later, as a pilot, I'd publish an article in the same magazine, or of course that sixty-six years later terrorists would purposely fly airliners into two yet-to-be-built New York City skyscrapers with vastly more tragic consequences.

North Jersey was where I really became aware of the underbelly of ethnic relations in America at the time. My parents had no friends who weren't at least nominally Jewish. The better-off families usually had African American maids and lived on Orange Mountain in an area known as "The Golden Ghetto." The children in North Jersey, like those in Philadelphia, self-segregated themselves ethnically. There were more than a few episodes in which kids of one background would attempt and sometimes succeed in physically assaulting a child of another background.

When I was about ten, a couple of big Italian American kids decided to teach the Jew-boy (me) a lesson. I was rescued by an Irish American school friend, Jack Drury. The incident stuck in my mind, and more than thirty years later, when I was doing *The Tonight Show* starring Johnny Carson, I ran into Jack: he had become a friend of John's. It can be a very small world.

My parents sent me to camp most summers, although the exact chronology escapes my decaying synapses. The first I do remember was Camp Carson. It was run by the YMCA, in Lebanon County, Pennsylvania, near the Fort Indiantown Gap army base. I was in the youngest group, at age maybe nine or ten. Highlights were trying to catch my first swallowtail butterfly (*Battus philenor*) with my fingers (I missed); a pilot in a biplane trainer from the base dropping a note to his son on the camp's athletic field; climbing Big Mountain and Little Mountain on opposite sides of the valley containing the camp; having toilets named Kybos (Keep Your Bowels Open); and a group visit to Indiantown Gap, where I saw a machine gun being fired.

In my early teens I spent a few summers at a camp near Ely, Vermont, where I initially got hooked on butterfly collecting—it was part of the nature program. The program supplied me with a net so that I could actually catch swallowtail butterflies that I'd tried to hand-capture in Pennsylvania a few years before. They were killed by putting them in killing jars, which we were taught to make by putting potassium cyanide and sawdust in the bottom of a jar and sealing it in by pouring in plaster of paris. The hydrogen cyanide gas that worked its way through the plaster quickly stopped the butterfly from battering its wings, producing more perfect specimens. It was a ridiculously dangerous procedure, and I've often wondered why I've never heard of a fatality. I loved using insect pins to fasten the butterfly to a grooved spreading board, carefully arranging the wings, allowing the specimen to dry, putting a finely printed locality label on the pin below the specimen, and finally placing it in a glass-topped box with others of my collection. I could then examine the intricate markings on the wings, seeing differences between individuals of the same and different kinds (species) and trying to imagine the process that had produced them. The only part of the procedure I didn't like was the killing—and fortunately for me in my subsequent research, I marked and released alive hundreds of butterflies for each one I had to kill for scientific reasons.

At the camp I also learned to troll for pickerel and had the thrill of climbing Mount Washington (6,288 feet, I've always remembered) in nearby New Hampshire via the Ammonoosuc Ravine Trail. I also remember a huge bonfire in August 1945, to celebrate the end of what the Japanese government liked to call the "Greater East Asia Co-Prosperity Sphere." We laughingly called it that at the event.

I took up boxing at camp, largely I think, to compensate for a general lack of coordination. I tried to pitch baseball and, being tall, could produce a pretty good fastball, but there was never any telling where the pitch would go. Hiking and swimming soon became my major sporting activities and remain so to this day. I remember at the Y camp being confined to the "crib" in the lake because I couldn't swim. I could glide from the center of the crib and end up holding on to the wooden edge. Then it dawned on me that if I just lowered my legs when gliding, I could stand on the crib floor. Stupid as it sounds (it was), that knowledge immediately made it possible for me to swim using the dog paddle.

Like many boys at the time, I was surrounded at school by peer interest in team sports but wasn't particularly good at them. Though an erratic pitcher, I was a pretty good batter in softball. I had skipped a grade in school, so I was always a little small and light for football, and I was afraid of getting hurt, so I only boxed a little.

In junior high I did become a demon fan of the Brooklyn Dodgers, though. I started following the team in 1940, but I have no clear idea why (my sister, Sally, caught the same disease). Maybe it was because listening to their games was a way to entertain myself, especially when in high school I worked the evening shift at Earl B. McPeek's gas station. I certainly missed that entertainment at the worst high school job I had: working during the summer at a machine shop in Manhattan. The job consisted of carrying boxes of socket castings for shower curtain rods up a set of stairs and reaming them out with a drill press to take off the rough edges (getting coated with iron filings in the process). The work was too noisy to listen to the ball games, but it did give me a sense of what work many people less lucky than I have to endure over a lifetime, arriving home exhausted after a commute and getting up the next morning to do it all over again. But I think the main reason for becoming a fan was that being a sports enthusiast was just a cultural norm. You rooted for a baseball team, followed a football team, took vicarious pride in their successes, and were downcast if they lost. My liking for the Dodgers was only reinforced when that organization brought Jackie Robinson into the major leagues on April 15, 1947. I think many of my fellow students approved—the top football player at my Columbia High School that year was also African American. But of course, that was in the relatively liberal Northeast.

I did not end up a skeptic about supernatural beliefs because my parents had neglected to give me a taste of religion. They did, but it was a half-hearted effort on their part. When I was six or so they had sent me off to a Jewish Sunday school. I came home with a general dislike of listening to Bible stories I thought were silly when I could have been out playing instead. I knew they were silly because when I asked Mom and Pop questions such as "Where does God live?" I got wishy-washy answers like "Nobody knows" or "In heaven." When I asked where heaven was, I was treated to the same kind of evasive responses. It was a few years later that I discovered that Pop had no truck with religion and Mom didn't believe in any supernatural stuff but simply liked socializing in the Jewish temple's sisterhood.

Mom and Pop said I didn't have to go to Sunday school if I didn't want to, but if I didn't, I couldn't stay home from school on Jewish holidays. Since I had figured out that there were only a few Jewish holidays scattered through the year, but there was a Sunday every week, I closed the deal and became what I am today, identifying as Jewish only when persecution against

Jews is an issue. I never picked up those vague feelings of connection and tradition shared even by some of my most atheistic Jewish colleagues.

When I was twelve, however, my folks insisted that I be bar mitzvahed—a primitive puberty rite, I thought even then. "Why do you want me to do that?" I challenged them, pointing out that they themselves weren't believers. Mom responded, "Because your father's parents will make our lives miserable if you aren't bar mitzvahed." Like any sensible twelve-year-old, I replied, "Isn't that your problem? I'm not going through with it." Then my father said the magic words: "If you do it, you'll get a lot of money." My parents wouldn't let me buy the rifle I craved (I had learned to shoot .22s in summer camp), and I hadn't yet realized that a car would later greatly increase my chances with girls, but I was dying to get a good microscope. "How much?" I asked. Pop said, "Probably about $1,000" (a relative fortune in 1945 and not bad for a kid even today). "If I don't get that much, will you make up the difference?" Pop, a good businessman, was virtually certain I'd get more and agreed. So the deal was sealed with a guaranteed gate.

That was the background for the two thrills of my brief religious life. Just before Christmas in 1944, the Orthodox rabbi my parents had hired to teach me enough Hebrew to negotiate the rite of passage came for our tutoring session and discovered our Chanukah Bush. As was our annual custom, it was coniferous, fully decorated with even a star on top. The rabbi augured into the ceiling, my mother was extremely embarrassed (I can still picture her red-faced on the stairs of our Maplewood house), and I suppressed a belly laugh.

The second religious thrill took place the evening after my bar mitzvah. I sat up for hours opening envelopes, pulling out checks and cash, and opening packages of religious books, promptly consigned to the then-equivalent of the Goodwill pile. The take was $1,350—today's equivalent of some $17,000. Considering I had spoken for only about five minutes at the event, it was by far the best honorarium per minute I've ever earned for giving a speech. It was of course far more than I needed for the secondhand dissecting microscope I eventually would acquire. Much of the money went, some years later, toward the car I drove to graduate school in Kansas and my adventures there.

I always felt fortunate that my parents did not insist on religious belief and practices barring that one exception. Inculcating children with the views of ancient desert nomads, I came to feel, hardly prepares them to operate in the world of the twenty-first century. It often leaves them vulnerable to a host of crackpot ideas, depending on the persuasion, about anything from vaccination to racial, ethnoreligious, and gender differences. It leads many of them to live lives plagued with fears of such nonexistent threats as ghosts (over 45 percent of Americans in 2021 believed that ghosts and demons are real) or being consigned forever to torture in an imaginary place called "hell" (over 30 percent believe that is an actual place).[2] And it makes it difficult for some among them to participate cooperatively with those of other beliefs—a necessity if we're to deal with the existential threats now facing human society. A prominent example has been powerful Senator James Inhofe, a fan of coal burning, whose religion tells him that only God can change the climate.[3] That said, I've also come to recognize that the tendency of accepting some things on faith is necessarily ubiquitous and that many of the ethical, empathic people are religious. Religion, like many other cultural inventions, is not all of a piece, and there is wide variation in how people respond to what they are taught.

One event I did get to know about in my childhood, most of it spent in the pre-antibiotic era, was death. In Philadelphia, our next door neighbor's son, Sammy McCleary, a couple of years older than me, died of some infection around 1939. Billy Hassinger, a fifth-grade classmate in Fitler School, died around 1941, and my best friend, Nathan Armour, died a year later. Nathan got some nasty infection early in the war. Sulfa drugs were not available for civilians, but his father, an executive in the pharmaceutical industry, had pull. He got some sulfa, but tragically Nathan turned out to be allergic to it, and he died.

Among the well-off in developed countries now, childhood death is very rare. The situation was quite different not that long ago. Virtually every powerful American family in the 1860s, as Doris Kearns Goodwin describes in *Team of Rivals: The Political Genius of Abraham Lincoln*, for example, had lost at least one child. I had a very bad case of scarlet fever (a nasty strain of strep bacteria), which was a major cause of child deaths at the time. I was quarantined but recovered fully. Strangely, there has been a recent resurgence of scarlet fever, but no one knows why, and it remains treatable with antibiotics.

I was lucky to survive those pre-antibiotic days, but I was even luckier to be born in the United States and late enough that I couldn't be exposed to that major cause of teenage death, World War II. That was another advantage of my 1932 birth. I was old enough, however, to be fully aware of the conflict. I started getting war cards with my chewing gum in the late 1930s, showing pictures of conflict in China and, later, in Europe. I remember the bombing of Pearl Harbor—we were living in North Jersey at the time, and at first nobody knew where the hell that naval base was. We stood up in school assembly on the Monday after the attack and ritually tore the Japanese national anthem out of our songbooks (this is a memory that now leads me to wonder if it actually happened, since I have no recollection of the anthem and can't imagine why it would have been in an American grammar school songbook!). Following Pearl Harbor, of course, we all were inundated by war news in the papers and magazines, on radio, and in newsreels at the movies.[4]

Mom and Pop fortunately disabused me of both American propaganda attempts to imply genetic inferiority of the Japanese and the notion that the Japanese would easily be beaten because they supposedly couldn't innovate, only copy. In fact, as I later learned, the Mitsubishi Zero was probably the best carrier fighter aircraft in the world at the time of Pearl Harbor, and Japanese torpedoes were faster than ours, had longer range, and had one interesting characteristic that ours often lacked early on: they blew up when they hit their target. In any case, that Japan's armed forces wouldn't be beaten easily seemed simple for even a ten-year-old to figure out.

I desperately—and foolishly—wanted the war to last until I could get into it. That wasn't possible, but I did get the job during air raid drills of turning off the streetlight in front of our house by climbing a ladder and pulling down on the wire ring that shut off the gas, and I helped put Scotch tape on our windows to reduce glass splinters from the bomb blasts that never happened. I also remember collecting milkweed pods for their floss (white, fluffy hairs) to be used as stuffing in life jackets and picking up aluminum scrap to be recycled into making aircraft.

Rationing became part of everyday calculation. Gasoline rationing hit our family activities pretty hard even though my father got a little extra because he was a traveling salesman. Meat was to us the most important rationed substance; we had to save up red points, or stamps, in our ration book, if the family was to have the traditional rare roast beef on Sunday night. Once, my grandparents were invited up to Maplewood from Philadelphia for Sunday dinner. My folks had saved a lot of points and had a wonderful large roast. Grandpa said, "Wow, you must have saved for a long time to get that." Pop replied: "No, we got it from Whirlaway." Whirlaway was the name of the racehorse that had won the Triple Crown in 1941; as soon as beef rationing started, a string of horsemeat shops named Whirlaway opened to fill the meat gap. (The Triple Crown winner was too valuable at stud to eat—he didn't die until 1953.)

My father was, of course, kidding. Horsemeat is actually quite tasty if, as with beef, you get a good cut from an animal properly bred and raised. My grandparents were nevertheless appalled. Although they had left Austria in the late nineteenth century and believed in Judaism, they weren't strictly kosher. Yet in their culture horses weren't eaten, just as I wouldn't eat a rat no matter how delicious and healthy. Even though my mother (a notorious truth-teller) swore it was roast beef, my grandma and grandpa wouldn't touch it. So I got to gorge on roast beef.

TWO

A Passion for Butterflies

If I were young again, I'd start another butterfly collection tomorrow. Only sex has given me as much pleasure in a long life as has science, especially collecting butterflies and studying them, in part as a way of tackling questions in evolution and ecology. And nothing has led me to more adventures or meeting more interesting people. Compared to the experiences of my peers, what was different about my junior high and high school years was the great time I spent pursuing a hobby, a passion, really, that would become lifelong—butterfly collecting. As I've suggested, my mom not only put up with my passions but encouraged me every step of the way, helping out whenever she could as my interest in science developed. One of my fondest memories is her driving to pick me up at junior high school whenever moths or butterflies I was raising from caterpillars at home would emerge from their pupae (the resting stage or butterfly chrysalis stage in which the eating, growing machine of the caterpillar is transformed into the reproducing-dispersing machine of the adult).

I scrounged together enough money to purchase a secondhand dissecting microscope without dipping into my religious "earnings," and I learned from the literature how to remove and study the genital structures (genitalia) of male and female butterflies, sometimes key to identifying species. Males of different kinds of butterflies have often strikingly different hooklike apparatuses to hold the female during long copulations and somewhat different penises to deliver packets of sperm. The evolutionary reason for their genital diversification is still somewhat obscure. Presumably natural selection favored diversification because it helped to avoid the waste of genes that might have been involved in mating across species and thereby producing infertile hybrid offspring or no offspring at all.

Butterflies were not my only interest in the natural world in junior high and high school, but they were the main one. A close second in those years lay in another beautiful group of animals and was focused on a roomful of fish tanks—the weight of the water they held giving my parents some nervous moments (my room was on the second floor). I was entranced by the microcosms one could create in a relatively few gallons of water. I made a special effort to breed the handsome blue gouramis and the gorgeous bettas; the males of both species build bubble nests at the surface to which they lure females, embrace them (fold their bodies over them), release sperm to fertilize the eggs the females then extruded, collect the eggs in their mouths, squirt them into the nest, and then guard the nest and eventually the minute young. Great behavior for a budding biologist to watch and try to encourage! Breeding guppies (whose females have eggs fertilized internally and hatch them there, bearing their young alive), of course, was easy: I soon had multiple generations of guppies of strikingly diverse colorations.

My father was sure that with my apparently never-ending fascination with butterflies I would end up a pauper and turn out to be gay. In the 1940s, of course, being gay carried a much heavier stigma, and indeed risk, than today, even though mores have not changed nearly enough. Dad eventually changed his mind on the first when butterflies led, by the standards of those days, to quite lucrative summer jobs. And my bringing home from graduate school a gorgeous woman I'd married (he was terminally ill and too sick to go to Anne's and my wedding) would soon relieve him of his other anxiety.

My first real connection with the butterflies that so concerned Pop over my sexual proclivities occurred, as noted in chapter 1, when I was introduced to collecting them in summer camp. That reinforced my goal to become a scientist (I cannot remember ever having any other career goal). The religious stories I'd heard made no sense—but the questions religions claim to answer—for example, "Where did we come from?" "Why are there people and all the plants and other animals?" "Why are some people good and others evil?"—fascinated me. I hoped science would reveal the answers to those and many other questions that crowded my mind. Most ridiculously, my biggest worry was that such questions might mostly be answered before I had a chance to become a scientist.

My interest in science and butterflies led my parents when I was about thirteen to get me a copy of the first edition of W. J. Holland's *Butterfly Book: A Popular Guide to a Knowledge of the Butterflies of North America* so that I could identify the specimens I had begun to collect. The book was my first detailed introduction to biodiversity, and I was thrilled to learn the Latinized (scientific) names that organized butterfly diversity—it seemed to me at the time my first contact with real science. It's a pity that children today are largely spared learning those names, instead having butterflies in field guides given so-called common names on the grounds that these are easier to remember and seem less daunting. Thus one is supposed to say San Emigdio blue rather than *Plebejus emigdionis.* The original reason for the Latin labels was to allow scientists from different countries with different languages to communicate unambiguously about critters of interest. That still seems like a good idea. Even though I've worked with North American butterflies for seventy-five years and once wrote a field guide to them, I often don't know what species are being referred to when only the so-called common names are used.

I was deeply disappointed when I found out that my 1898 edition of Holland had already been superseded by a 1931 edition with additional plates. I soon acquired a copy of that edition, though, and still have it, complete with a plastic cover I fashioned and tabs a girlfriend installed to let me move easily from group to group. I got a chance to use that book extensively in 1947 when, at age fifteen, my parents let me join a traveling summer camp that toured much of the mountain West and encouraged natural history projects. My project, no surprise, was observing and collecting butterflies, but before I saw a single species on that trip I had a memorable lesson of a different sort. The DC-3 in which I was flying to reach Saint Louis, where the camp trip started, refueled at Lexington-Frankfort in Kentucky. When I went to go to the bathroom in the shabby terminal, there were the signs: "White" and "Colored." It was a shock, the first time a boy from the desegregated (at least in law) Northeast ran into official, patently obvious racism.

A thrill when I did join the traveling camp was catching my first butterfly denizen of high country, a *Parnassius*, in the Colorado Rockies. Little did I imagine that as an adult I would spend more than half a century of summers doing field research on Colorado butterflies from a cabin at the Rocky Mountain Biological Laboratory (RMBL) in the West Elk Mountains. And it was more than sixty-five years later that I discovered, in to me a most informative history book, *Butterfly People: An American Encounter with the Beauty of the World*, by William Leach, that the W. J. Holland whose books had meant so much to me was an autocrat and notorious opportunist who married money, treated collectors he hired with contempt, and bribed journals to get articles published.

When I returned from the West at the end of that summer, I got a chance through a friend of my parents to visit the American Museum of Natural History in New York and to meet Charles Michener, then curator of Lepidoptera (moths and butterflies—the latter just being day-flying moths). Mich was the first real scientist I'd ever met, and one who was an expert on butterflies and evolution to boot. I was thrilled by the opportunity to talk to him and get his advice. Mich talked me into spreading butterflies for him in exchange for specimens he gave me of exotic butterflies without locality data for my collection. More important, he launched me on a career in science, encouraging me to learn more about evolution and, especially, to join the Lepidopterists' Society, an organization Charles Remington at Yale University and Harry Clench at the Carnegie Museum of Natural History in Pittsburgh were forming of scientists and hobbyists interested in studying butterflies and moths. I was secretary of the society from 1957 to 1963; by 2015 I think I was one of just seven surviving charter members, and today I still look forward to receiving its publications. The first volume was mimeographed, but now it is printed on slick paper and loaded with beautiful color photos of butterflies and moths. (I used to think it weird that older people took some pride in being lucky enough to live long—but now I sometimes find myself with that strange feeling.)

Michener would become, in 1953, my main graduate school professor at the University of Kansas, the true beginning of a lifelong friendship. His first scientific love was bees and their evolution, and he happily more or less turned over his interest in butterflies to me after I got to graduate school. Much later, around the turn of the century, I finally got involved with the bees he was studying, learned to identify a bunch of them (they can be challenging), and we were for the first time coauthors of a paper that is now one of my favorites. We showed that if some tropical forest was left standing near Costa Rican coffee fields, the profits from coffee were higher than if all the forest was cut and coffee planted where it had been. The forest supplied habitat for bees that pollinated the coffee plants—and pollinated coffee beans are more valuable. The leader on the research was then-graduate student Taylor Ricketts; the second author was Gretchen Daily, Taylor's major professor.[1] The third author was me, Gretchen's major professor, and the fourth was Mich, my major professor. That was a dramatic example of intellectual lineage in science. Sadly, shortly after Mich and I were last in contact, he aged ninety-seven and I then eighty-three, in 2015, he died quietly in his sleep.

In my career, I later realized, I was in a way following in the footsteps of prominent nineteenth-century butterfly people, such as William Henry Edwards and Samuel Hubbard Scudder, who were champions of Darwinism and who became heroes of mine when I was a graduate student. Like Scudder, my early interest in butterflies as beautiful and diverse organisms had evolved into a fascination with much broader scientific issues. Edwards's passion for butterflies came later in life than mine, but it soon led him, too, to broader issues. Both Scudder and Edwards wrote books on North American butterflies, as would I.

Soon after first meeting Mich in 1947, I purchased, at his instigation, used copies of Theodosius Dobzhansky's *Genetics and the Origin of Species* (1937) and Ernst Mayr's *Systematics and the Origin of Species from the Viewpoint of a Zoologist* (1942). I read them from cover to cover and kept them close at hand. They were basic texts of the so-called modern evolutionary synthesis in which a handful of scientists, including Dobzhansky and Mayr, built the foundations of current evolutionary thought, blending Darwinian ideas with the rapidly expanding understanding of Mendelian genetics. Little did I know then that both would become long-term colleagues and family friends. Dobzhansky ("Doby") read the manuscript of Richard Holm's and my first evolution book (*The Process of Evolution*, published in 1963), gave us useful and supportive criticisms and, as a bonus, taught my daughter, Lisa, sometime around 1960 to ride horses at the Southwest Research Station in Arizona.[2] We went on fruit-fly collecting expeditions together when he visited RMBL and enjoyed discussing genetics, him with his pronounced Russian accent. One of his famous statements (I don't think made to me) was, "Friend Beadle tells me zat zee gene is para-aminobenzoic acid, vat ever zee hell zat is."[3]

Doby was an interesting character. He could not divest himself of his childhood ideas of religion (I carefully avoided discussing the subject with him). He put up with my heterodox ideas on speciation, even though that topic had been one factor in a nasty public falling-out he had had with his close colleague and supporter A. H. Sturtevant in the late 1930s. Sturt, whom I met briefly (I think at RMBL around 1960), was one of the great pioneering geneticists, the first person ever to map a chromosome, and his differences with Doby underline a major lesson my career has taught me: scientists are very human, and the social side of science is extremely important. I had been warned that although Doby was very tolerant of new general ideas, it was scientific suicide to point out an error in one of his papers.[4]

Ernst Mayr and I enjoyed a more than forty-year-long debate about species definitions and other topics in evolutionary biology. We remained friends despite a couple of mishaps that occurred the first time I invited him to Stanford. A lively discussion followed his seminar talk, and near the end of it, he said, "I always instruct my grad students to tell me if they think I'm mistaken." One of my graduate students, Michael Soulé, then responded, "Does that go for grad students at other universities, too?" Ernst laughed, but Vic Twitty, chairman of my department, sitting next to me, thought it a terrible insult to a distinguished visitor and said I should get rid of Michael.

Fortunately, Ernst was not offended, I disagreed with Vic, and Michael went on to found the field of conservation biology. The second incident occurred when Anne and I entertained Ernst after that same seminar. During cocktails, just as I was making a point, our cheap imitation Swedish chair disintegrated under our guest, depositing him in a heap of debris on our living room floor. Fortunately, neither his body nor his pride was injured.

Ernst was deeply concerned about the implications of human population explosion occurring over the course of the twentieth century and often wrote to me positively about *The Population Bomb* after its 1968 publication. Even when approaching the age of one hundred, he drove into Cambridge one day to have lunch with me at Harvard for a discussion of species definitions and human overpopulation. One of my most treasured possessions is a copy of *Systematics and the Origin of Species* with a beautiful inscription. Ernst's sense of humor was also much like mine. One of his famous stories was about words in New Guinea pidgin (he had done fieldwork on the birds there in his youth). He related that the pidgin for "stallion" was "horse-y-man" and for "mare" it was "horse-y-mary." Geldings, however, were denoted "horse-y-missionary." After decades of listening to me cite butterfly examples in our discussions, he was much amused when I took up bird-watching and avian research. As arguably the world's leading ornithologist, that gave him a clear advantage.

I'd like to say that the copy of Charles Darwin's *On the Origin of Species* (1859), which I purchased about the same time as I bought Doby and Ernst's books, was what had really introduced me to the science of where humanity had come from, but it didn't. I found *Origin* tough going. To be honest, it wasn't until decades later, when I read it again from cover to cover before lecturing to tourists on a trip to the Galápagos, that I really appreciated the depths of Darwin's genius. In that stretch his thinking had really matured!

That was all far in the future of my junior high and high school days. In those school years my butterfly collection grew more and more extensive; only later would I gradually narrow it down (mostly by giving specimens away) until it contained only North American representatives of one genus, the largely Arctic-alpine *Erebia*. I think I concentrated on them partly because I was fascinated by stories of Arctic exploration since reading in high school Edward Ellsberg's *Hell on Ice: The Saga of the "Jeannette"* (1938) and partly because the mostly dark brown butterflies were not a challenge for a color-blind collector.

My collection had started with butterflies and moths from around the world (much boosted by Mich's donations). As I said, in junior high, my mother used to pick me up by car for lepidoptery—especially whenever a cocoon (pupa surrounded by a silken case) I had collected in the woods yielded a big, gorgeous saturniid (silkworm) moth—most spectacularly a cecropia or promethea. Then I could kill and mount it for my collection while it was still in perfect condition. I hated the process but always justified it to myself by concluding that the specimen would die soon anyway (adult silkworms couldn't feed) and it would be immortalized in the collection. Sadly, these and many other beautiful moths of the eastern United States that I enjoyed hunting are now disappearing—from a combination of factors ranging from pesticides and parasites to streetlights that attract them and to widespread habitat destruction.

My very first paper, published in 1948 by the Lepidopterists' Society, reported that a tachinid (fly) parasite, *Compsilura concinnata*, was attacking monarch butterflies. I was raising some monarchs for the fun of it and to get perfect specimens for my collection (I still can be fascinated watching a butterfly or moth emerge from its pupa and gradually spread and dry its wings). I did not know at the time that the fly had been imported from Europe in an attempt to control plagues of two introduced European pests: brown-tail and gypsy moths. Ironically, that parasitic fly also became one of the prime suspects in the decline of the giant silkworm moths I loved. The paper contained another observation as well. I had seen that tiger swallowtail butterflies may repeatedly fly the same routes in their daily activities, which I said deserved more investigation (which it received many years later from my former student Nick Haddad and others). They have demonstrated an important role of corridors in conservation.

One of the advantages of joining the Lepidopterists' Society as a high school student was getting addresses of other butterfly collectors with whom I could exchange specimens. My very first exchange was with a kindly Californian, Bill Hammer, who sent (I think because he realized I was a beginner) a nice collection of California butterflies in return for some very common eastern species. I'll never forget the smell of PDB (paradichlorobenzene) moth crystals as I emptied the cardboard box he sent, starting with a stream of triangular butterfly envelopes labeled "*Euphydryas editha bayensis.*" Who could have predicted that a dozen years later I would begin using that butterfly, with the common name Bay checkerspot, and other checkerspots as an experimental system—a connected set of organisms and environments that would be productive to study scientifically. The ecology and evolution of the Bay checkerspot would occupy my attention and that of valued colleagues and students for more than half a century. I've studied it and its relatives to this very day, over much of the United States and even on the other side of the Atlantic, where Ilkka Hanski and his colleagues took up a study of Finnish checkerspots, which they chose as a parallel experimental system. Ilkka and I eventually summarized our results in an edited book featuring contributions by a group of wonderful checkerspot biologists.[5]

From the beginning, then, butterflies have been a central feature of my scientific efforts. Tropical freshwater fishes remained a hobby through my secondary school years but faded in importance as the time required to maintain and breed them was taken up by other projects. Years later, though, they would make a research comeback in my life in the form of beautiful tropical reef fishes in the oceans.

When the time came to apply for college, I divided the course catalogs into two piles: those of institutions that had compulsory chapel and those that didn't. I applied to none of the former and just two of the latter, Bard College and the University of Pennsylvania, and surprisingly (because I had relatively mediocre grades in high school, preferring girls to studying even then), I was accepted by both. The luck of my year-of-birth came in again: I went to college when it was relatively easy to get in, and I had parents who both wanted me to have a college education and were able to pay for a good school. I think primarily because I had many connections in Philadelphia, my hometown, I chose Penn.

In late summer 1949 I drove my 1932 Buick wreck (purchased for very little from McPeek) to Philadelphia and took up residence in Penn's Craig Hall dorm. I was still devoted to butterflies and determined to become a scientist. When the time came to declare a major, I chose zoology. Early on, though, I made a strategic mistake that neither I nor my advisers realized. Mathematics was going to be critical in the study of evolutionary biology and much of ecology and environmental science; since that only became clear later, I did not take enough courses in it—indeed, I flunked the calculus course I took in (I think) my sophomore year. I got an A when I took it over in my senior year, but a lifetime of trying to teach myself math beyond simple calculus and mostly failing is the price I paid.

College only further stimulated my interest in butterflies, and I began to see them in a larger context. I can't remember how, but I suspect it was also through the Lepidopterists' Society that I met a fellow undergraduate, Nicholas W. Gillham, who was two weeks my senior and a student at Harvard on the same sort of butterflies-science track that I was on. Though he lived far away, we managed to get together enough to coauthor a paper in 1951 describing a new butterfly subspecies. Nick and I named the subspecies after the famous collector Otto Buchholz, who had befriended us and may (in 1907) have been the first collector ever to drive West by car to hunt butterflies.

My deep interest in public policy in general, and in population issues more specifically, and their connection to the natural world developed initially in 1950, when I was a sophomore at Penn, rooming with two World War II veterans I had met in the dorms my freshman year, Ted Shoemaker and Richard Graves, along with the late Tom Hirschfeld, who was a refugee from Nazi Austria, and an odd man out, Andrew Yoggy, who was training to be a minister. The five of us rented a rundown rowhouse and declared ourselves APROCS, the Autonomous People's Republic of Chestnut Street. I read avidly, and as a group we discussed two books that had been published in 1948 and would have a huge impact on my thinking, ecologist William Vogt's *Road to Survival* and conservationist Fairfield Osborne's *Our Plundered Planet*, both of which focused on human impacts on the environment and their consequences. Osborne, a prominent and important conservationist, had unfortunately been influenced by his father's enthusiasm for the eugenics movement, and his book (as I recall) had a racist tinge. Vogt, in contrast, was a liberal conservationist and national director of the Planned Parenthood Federation of America. Both men had a global view, however, and, unusual in the 1940s and 1950s, both recognized the crucial connections between population and environmental deterioration, and as a result both favored finding ways to limit population growth.

Aside from what I was gleaning from books and discussions with roommates, I was developing growing concerns about environmental disruption; these were magnified by the increasing difficulty I was having raising butterflies from caterpillars at my New Jersey home. Overspraying with DDT for mosquito control was making plants in my neighborhood there poisonous to insects, and huge Levittown-like housing developments were being constructed nearby over large areas of what once had been seminatural habitat.

Ted, Dick, and Tom were all older and more experienced than I, more cynical, and less impressed by public opinion. I can't remember the details of our discussions, except we four were all amused by the conservatism and, at the time, the pompous religiosity of our fifth APROCS citizen, Andy Yoggy (he later became a pioneer in school integration, though). In the dorm and at APROCS I had my first experiences with broad and no-holds-barred political discussions. One of the things that impressed me most was that Dick, who was wounded by a "hold-out" Japanese soldier in the Philippines after the war was officially over and then served in the occupation of Japan, was nonetheless very sympathetic toward the Japanese people. He would later marry a beautiful and very smart Nisei woman, Teru Nakano.

The discussions we had at APROCS about topics other than population and environmental deterioration in light of the Vogt and Osborne books had a profound impact on me as well. My housemates thought there was a lot wrong with the world, and they had a deep interest in politics at the time.

Issues of East-West relations, communism versus capitalism, the use of atomic bombs, war crimes and guilt (relative to Japan was especially important to Dick and Nazi atrocities to Tom)—all were in the news and on our minds. The most important Nuremberg trials had concluded in October 1946, but the extent of wartime horrors was still being revealed.

By 1951 the Korean War was also in full swing, and I was facing the draft. Very close to APROCS was the bar of the Normandy Hotel, where we often hung out. It had a television set, and I still remember sitting there in April 1951 watching General Douglas MacArthur speaking to Congress after Harry Truman fired him from command of the U.N. forces in Korea. It was a famous incident in the battles over civilian control of the military and concluded with MacArthur's self-pitying and oft-quoted sentence: "Old soldiers never die, they just fade away."[6]

My APROCS roommates not only forced me to think broadly about the state of the world but also possibly saved my life. When I was about nineteen, I got the idea of dropping out of school, joining the army, and going to Korea to gain the independence I craved through the G.I. Bill, which was available to veterans for educational expenses (my father was paying most of my college bills). My veteran roommates luckily persuaded me it was an incredibly stupid idea (which it was).

I got other great breaks by having returned to my hometown of Philadelphia to attend Penn. My grandparents lived downtown and had been long-term customers of Tarello's Italian restaurant, one of the best in the city. We had often eaten there together, and Grandpa said that if I didn't abuse the privilege, I could eat there and they would just put the meals on his tab. Tarello's was extremely popular, and there was almost always a line at the door. Whenever I met an attractive girl, the first date was to Tarello's. We'd walk past the line, Victor Tarello would greet us at the door. "Mr. Ehrlich, it's great to see you. Louie has your usual table ready, come right in." *Very* effective.

It wasn't just Tarello's and APROCS that made these years so important to my future. Above all, it was my undergraduate work in Penn's zoology department, where Rudolf Schmieder taught. As the editor of the *Entomological News,* he encouraged my interest in butterflies and helped me persuade botanist John M. Fogg Jr., vice provost of the university, to let me leave Penn before the end of the spring semester two years in a row so that I could take part in the Arctic adventures described in the next chapter. Further, James A. G. Rehn, an orthopterist (specialist in grasshoppers, cockroaches, and the like), welcomed me at the Academy of Natural Sciences of Philadelphia as a volunteer curator of butterflies in the early 1950s, a job I did for much of my Penn years. Rearranging and identifying specimens in an assemblage untouched for years was interesting work, and it allowed Nick Gillham and me to publish another paper together, this one on the specimens Henry Skinner (a famous lepidopterist) had used to describe a bunch of new species. I think I was born with collector genes—butterflies, different tropical fishes for my community tank, books in general and natural history books in particular, netsukes, bird prints, and ethnic art—I've loved and treasured them all. The academy's collection and my duties there played right into that strange propensity.

THREE

To the Arctic

Butterflies got me a job in the subarctic, in the summer after my sophomore year, working for Canada's Defence Research Board (DRB) and Department of Agriculture under the auspices of the Northern Insect Survey. That first stint led to several later summertime expeditions to the North.

I was to do biting-fly surveys and general insect collecting over the course of several months that first summer of 1951. The whole program was set up to expand knowledge of conditions for troops operating in the Arctic and subarctic, with a view to countering the Soviets, who were expected to "come over the pole" to attack the United States and Canada. We were primed to see it as a serious, even imminent threat in those early Cold War days.

I looked forward to doing the fieldwork, but I wanted to go to the Arctic for another reason as well: to study my favorite butterfly genus *Erebia* there. I owed the summer opportunity to a fellow lepidopterist, Tom Freeman, leader of the Northern Insect Survey (NIS). I had met Tom in 1950 at the first Lepidopterists' Society meeting, held at New York's American Museum of Natural History. That, in turn, was a result of Charles Michener's good advice to join the society. Tom invited me to Ottawa, purportedly to take a look at the Department of Agriculture's extensive *Erebia* collection but, I now suspect, actually to look *me* over. My big test, I think, was going out with Tom and his colleagues "for a beer." It sounded like a great idea to me, although I wasn't thrilled by the sex segregation of the beer hall that was dictated by Ontario law in those days. The hall was decorated and smelled like a men's room. A quart bottle of Molson appeared in front of each of us, and I thought, "What the hell, I can probably drink all of that!" Little could I have imagined the parade of bottles that would follow, as the entire group became a set of middlemen between Molson's brewery and the actual men's room. It was high-alcohol beer (5 percent compared to the 3.2 percent I was accustomed to) and the details of the evening (and subsequent evenings) have slipped away. But I apparently passed the test, as Tom offered me a job for the coming summer field season.

In that first summer with the survey, I was based at Hay River, on the south shore of Canada's Great Slave Lake in the Northwest Territories. I flew from Ottawa to Edmonton in a Royal Canadian Air Force DC-3 ferrying gasoline in fifty-gallon drums (what a stink!) and then took a bus through Peace River and up to Hay River. There, I stayed in the roach-ridden Hay River Hotel, and I began mosquito surveys and general insect collecting (including, eventually, one member of the butterfly genus *Erebia* that showed up: *E. discoidalis*). The assistant I was assigned, Walter H. Lewis, was a budding botanist specializing in roses who conducted surveys of the flora; he later became a distinguished curator at the Missouri Botanical Garden and medical ethnobotanist at Washington University in Saint Louis, working, among other sites, among the Jivaro, fierce tribespeople who lived on the east slopes of the Andes in tropical forests of the upper Amazon. Besides making a general insect collection, my main activity was taking regular censuses of the mosquito population, using a method employed by every surveyor on the project at every site. This was done by making an S-sweep with a standard insect net through the throng of mosquitoes on your downwind side. The counts were sometimes in the hundreds, I'm sure, but I have no records of them.

It was a summer of adventures and memorable encounters. One was getting stranded in a lakeshore swamp in a fierce storm while traveling with ornithologist Wallace Good and his wife, Mary Francis. Our outboard motor had stalled, and the pull cord broke when we tried to restart it. We managed to paddle to shore and pitched our tent on a slight rise in the swamp. The next morning we were awakened by a splash-splash noise. Two big wolves trotted up, stopped in amazement about six feet from our tent, then trotted rapidly away—the best look I ever got at wolves in the wild, and a real thrill.

Another high point was meeting John Pihlainen and his permafrost survey crew. I was thus introduced to the problems of melting permafrost early: scientists today are concerned that permafrost will release so much carbon dioxide and methane as it melts that it might end up doubling the amount of carbon in the atmosphere. The consequent atmospheric heating of as much as 4 degrees Celsius or more would likely be a disaster for *Homo sapiens*.

I also visited Yellowknife on Great Slave Lake's north shore and there hooked up with a Royal Canadian Air Force (RCAF) crew who invited me, as an NIS party leader, to fly with them to Norman Wells, near the mouth of the Mackenzie River. We flew in a four-engine Lancaster bomber, the type of aircraft that dropped the highest tonnage of bombs on Germany in World War II. Our pilot was a Royal Air Force veteran with a sense of humor, which his copilot shared. When we took off early in the morning, the copilot suggested that they might drop in on some miners recovering from a drunken lakeshore party the night before. I was riding in the jump seat between them as they took the Lancaster down to a few feet over the water and zoomed above the hungover partygoers. It was a terrific rush for me as an avid airplane buff aviator; obviously it was a different experience for the hungover partygoers: a few apparently threw themselves into the lake to avoid the "crashing" bomber.

The Lancaster, with its guns and gun turrets removed, was operated by the RCAF's 408 Squadron, which was doing geographic survey work in the North. The pilots treated me to a stall-turn (a hammerhead)—pulling the nose up until the big bomber was nearly vertical, losing speed and shuddering with the approach of a stall. Then full left rudder, power back on left engines, and full power on the rights. The Lancaster rotated counterclockwise and entered a dive, the speed restoring lift (airflow over the wings producing an upward force), righting the plane, and sending it back the way it had come—a 180-degree turn. It was incredibly exciting, and it contributed to my desire eventually to become a multiengine/instrument pilot myself. Hammerheads are the recommended maneuver if you're ever foolish enough to fly into a box canyon and end up without enough room to circle back—luckily, a situation I never encountered.

I was also "lucky" enough at Hay River to have a thorough introduction to the designated targets of the NIS—biting flies (mosquitoes, blackflies, horseflies). The mosquitoes around Hay River were so abundant that we wondered where the females could possibly be getting blood meals to keep their populations going. You could drive along a road over which they were swarming and within a hundred yards half-fill a butterfly net with them. The tabanids (horseflies) were huge and aggressive, so much so that on the couple of occasions when I swam in the river to cool off, I put a head net on—a survival must at the height of the fly season. Indeed, rumor had it that in mining camps a severe, even lethal punishment was to eject a man from a building naked.

Annoyances aside, I spent the summer sampling the insect populations and logging in the data, as did the many others working for the survey in other parts of Canada. As a result, knowledge of the insect fauna of the Canadian Arctic and subarctic was greatly expanded by the publications of the NIS. And I had two of the best summers of my young life, the most wonderful being that of the following year, 1952.

My second Northern Insect Survey summer had me taking a train from The Pas, Manitoba, to Fort Churchill on the southern coast of Hudson Bay. There, I stocked up at a Hudson's Bay Company store on food and other supplies for the summer, and then at Defence Research Northern Laboratory (DRNL), I prepared to run another survey of insects, this time on Southampton Island, in what is now Nunavut, at the northern end of the bay.[1]

I flew to Coral Harbour on Southampton in an RCAF North Star, a modified DC-4 transport plane outfitted for extra speed with Rolls-Royce Merlin engines, the in-line power plants of the British Spitfires and Hurricanes of World War II fame. At the Southampton airstrip I was met by an Inuit (an Eskimo in the common term used in the 1950s) who transported my supplies and me by dogsled across a few miles of sea ice to the Coral Harbour

My equipment loaded for dogsledding across sea ice to Coral Harbour. Author photo.

settlement.[2] There I rented a small shack from the Hudson's Bay Company, then the dominant commercial institution in the Canadian Arctic.

My several months spent living among the Inuit at Coral Harbour were truly life-changing, even though their wife-sharing custom had largely been suppressed by missionaries. Learning a smattering of a non-Indo-European language, dealing with the cultural and racial attitudes of both the Hudson's Bay Company manager and the friendly Roman Catholic missionary (oblate), Father Rio, while enjoying my own interactions with the Inuit almost set me on a path to become an anthropologist.

The Hudson's Bay factor (the company establishments where pelts were collected from trappers were called factories and their managers were the factors) was Burt Swaffield. His wife and he treated me very well, often feeding me meals and including me in entertaining card games after dinner. But Burt looked down on the Inuit, calling them "huskies." I should have called him on it but didn't (pure cowardice); I limited myself to praising the diverse abilities of my growing group of Inuit friends. I didn't even enlighten him as to my family background when he announced that no Jew would ever come to the Arctic.

Tensions between the Canadian government and the Inuit were already deeply rooted by the 1950s. After 1867, the government removed more than

A semipalmated plover nesting at Coral Harbour—my first nature photography with a Bolsey camera on a tripod and a fishing line to fire it from a hiding place. Author photo.

150,000 Inuit and other indigenous children to hellhole residential schools in southern Canada. Missionaries and politicians thought it necessary to separate children from their parents and communities in order to "civilize and Christianize" them. I wasn't aware of that when I was at Coral Harbour, but I was often told of the government practice of taking people with tuberculosis, a disease introduced to the Arctic by the Europeans, "out" (south) to distant hospitals from which some never returned. The forced Inuit translocation programs, designed to establish Canadian sovereignty over the Arctic archipelago, came a little later in the 1950s. So did pervasive conditions that led by the end of the twentieth century among the Inuit to the highest suicide rate in the world, with drug use, family violence, and diets of junk food among the precipitating culprits.[3] Among those I knew in the early 1950s, by contrast, there seemed to be much domestic tranquillity—no signs of substance abuse or battered wives apparent to me despite my close contact. The only stories of violence I heard were of past dealings with disruptive individuals: "We were out seal hunting and his head accidently got in the way of a shot—*ayurnamat,*" the latter a great Inuktitut word best translated as "That's the way the cookie crumbles."[4]

I kept up my connection with the RCAF that summer as well and was invited to accompany a group of their personnel on an expedition to Coats Island, a large (two-thousand-square-mile) island uninhabited then and today, south of Southampton Island. The goal was to set up a SHORAN (SHOrt RAnge Navigation) station—part of a system that allowed precise determination of the position of the 408 Squadron's Lancasters then mapping that region of the Arctic. On the trip, I used the opportunity to name officially several prominent landmarks: Santianna Point after my friend the Inuit boat captain Santianna; Cape Netchek after the common seals we saw in abundance near there; and Shoran Bay (which I've seen misspelled on a map as Shoban Bay).[5]

On my way through Fort Churchill I had been invited by botanist Dorothy Brown to join a summer's end DRNL expedition to Duke of York Bay at the northern tip of Southampton Island. I could survey the bugs there (general insect collecting again being one of my duties, and that made a good excuse), and I accepted with pleasure. In retrospect, it turned out to be the adventure of a lifetime. On August 11 our group flew from Coral Harbour to Duke of York Bay in an RCAF Canso—Canada's version of the Consolidated PBY twin-engine amphibious patrol bomber of World War II. When we reached Duke of York, the bay was largely full of ice, with a narrow strip of clear water along its east coast and at its southern end. The pilot put the plane down smoothly; I remember my surprise at how thin the hull was: you could feel the vibrations running through it as the plane settled into the slight chop on the bay.

My field notes describe what happened next:

> We taxied into shore, winched the kite right up to the beach & started to offload. . . . We got unloaded & then discovered that the tide was dropping so fast that the Canso was stuck (the pilot had

> clearly made an error reading the tide tables). We manned the ropes & after terrific effort managed to pull a wing around so the engines could pull her off the beach. The copilot started her up but a rope caught around a crewman's foot & started to pull him into the bay. Several of us waded in and rescued him but in spite of all kinds of screaming by the pilot on the beach & much running up and down by the crewmen on the wings etc., the copilot wouldn't cut the engines & the Canso circled right back to the beach & pranged on a rock, knocking a hole into its bottom. The tide was dropping fast & as emergency repairs were made we tried to get her off, wading up to our hips in 35 degree (measured) water. . . . Finally, we realized it was absolutely hopeless so we slogged our gear up above the tide line & set up our tents. We all got dried out & then . . . sat around in one tent . . . eating dinner, drinking Father Rio's applejack & beer (of which two cases the Canso boys were writing off as "broken"). . . . Exhausted, the 7 of us turned in on our limestone beds at 0200 Tuesday, and at 0430 (high tide) the Canso got away. At 0530 the ice closed in. What a day!

That left the seven of us stranded, cold, short of food, and with polar bear sign everywhere.[6] We had only two weapons, a .30-.30 that Father Rio had lent me, and a Very (flare) pistol. We needed to guard our two tents from bear intrusions, and I took my turn with the Very for protection when others were out on tasks with the .30-.30. The idea was, if a bear poked its nose into the tent, you'd shoot the flare into the bear's face and chase it off.

My most memorable day at Duke of York was hiking thirteen miles alone (I was the only one who spoke any Inuktitut) to find a reported Inuit hunting camp. As my field notes for August 21 put it:

> It was decided that I should try to contact the Eskimos & try and bring a canoe down through the pans (big chunks of sea ice) to help move all our gear. . . . I set out alone at 0815 in my parka with 1 day's rations, my 30-30, 10 rounds of soft point, our map & tobacco for the Eskimos. The country for several miles north of our

Crewman being helped up after his leg was caught in a loop of rope being pulled by the taxiing amphibian plane. Copilot restarted engines and hit a rock. Author photo.

The flooded Canso draining, waiting to be repaired and refloated, and then to depart. Author photo.

First morning at Duke of York after the Canso got away in the night before the ice moved in. Author photo.

camp was like that of the camp area, wide gentle beach ridges. However about 6 miles north of camp the mountains started dropping into the sea & walking became more difficult, circling up the slopes became necessary. It soon began to look as if I might have to spend the night on the trail as I didn't relish travelling the rocks at night, & I started to look for sheltered spots to stop in on the way back. I saw peregrines & gyrfalcons. At 1250, some 13 miles N of camp I rounded a point & saw a settlement's silhouette on the horizon, Inuk! I jacked a shell into the chamber & let ride. I had reached the Inuk "permanent" camp, almost at Cape Welsford. I was the first white man they had seen since Oomalik (Father Rio) had visited them in May. I gave Mikkitok, my Inuit friend Tommy Bruce's son, the tobacco & a letter I had promised to deliver & met Wager Dick and Tatee, two of the more famous Eskimos on the island. The camp consisted of 3 sodded-in tents. I soon had put over the purpose of my mission & was immediately invited to

> have a caribou dinner. The boys had shot 25 caribou at Wager Bay just before the ice came in, 7 big steaks (of which I could only eat 3) were immediately done up for me. . . . I passed out my rations, took some pictures & gave the Eskimos the "gen" (genuine story) on their friends down south. It was really a big moment in my life.
>
> After lunch I decided to do an ice reccy (reconnaissance) from the top of a large mountain just to the north. Tatee, Mikketok, Tatuni & Pelikopse accompanied me on what for me was a grueling 4 mile trip. From the top saw White, Nias & small islands looming dark at our feet to the NNW. Framed in brilliant white ice it was an impressive sight. To the NW Comer Strait stretched ice-filled to the horizon. To the NE the thin dark line of Vansittart island loomed over the ice of Frozen Strait. Across the island to the ESE towards Cape Bylot could be seen the ice of the Foxe basin. . . . Since the ice was really jammed in . . . Tatee, Tatuni & I decided to head back to the camp of my colleagues, using a komatik (qamutiik) sled with 15 dogs at 1600.[7] Alternately running, wrestling the komatik over the rocks & taking short rides down slopes, we got back at 1845. We took back caribou with us for the others (I had promised canned goods in return). I was dog tired after my 30 mile walk by the time we arrived.

After a day moving our party to the mouth of the Cleveland River at the southern end of the bay, where current kept the ice away, and a day of rest, my notes continue:

> Sunday 24 August
>
> Rain, fog, cold. No kite. Theoretically our last day on rations. We have been on about 2/3 rations to stretch things. The caribou supplement helped & Barry & Cec got 3 Canada geese today to help some more. I read (James B.) Conant's "On Understanding Science" & Lecomte du Nouy's "Human Destiny" after dinner while the others played bridge. Have also read (S. L. A. Marshall's) "Island Victory." Retired 0130 Monday.

Monday 25 August

Wind has shifted from S to N. Fuel is getting low. As I write this there is a 30–45 mph wind in gust with the 36 degree f temp. It is Jesus Christ cold & getting grimmer. We have only 1 small burner on our stove going to preserve fuel. The gusts are now up to about 50 MPH. . . . Tent guy lines are snapping like threads. We just spent about 1 hour reguying & rocking & sodding the tents. The ice has been driven right back up on the shore. I doubt if we'll ever get out of this spot now. Had goose soup dinner, sang songs in the dark and retired.

Tuesday 26 August

Woke up freezing as usual. We've been taking our clothes into bed with us to keep them warm. Walked to a deserted Eskimo camp about 3 miles from our camp & collected wood for fuel. We brought in about 4 day supply & spent the afternoon digging a firepit in our tent at 1645. Lancaster passed about 8 miles to the east at about 8000 feet! It showed no signs of looking for us. 2 days short rations left. After "dinner" we were pleasantly surprised when Mikketok, Pelikopsi & Tatuni arrived with some caribou for us.

Early the next morning, I left for the Inuit camp with Mikketok and Tatuni to fetch more caribou and naphtha. We walked the whole seventeen-plus miles while ten dogs pulled the komatik. By moving fast we were there by 1300 hours, and in one and a half hours we had eaten caribou, loaded the komatik with supplies, and were headed back toward our Cleveland River camp, Tatee replacing the exhausted Mikketok for the return trip. At 1500 hours a DC-3 passed us on the trail doing an obvious search of the area. We finally hit camp at 2000 hours, having walked about twenty-six miles and ridden on the sled eight, me dreaming of finding huge piles of rations waiting for us. Evidently the RCAF aircrew didn't see or couldn't read the standard signals I had put out using remains of ration cartons that morning at the site of our old camp: they dropped neither a radio nor fuel and only enough food for a day and a half.

Thursday, 28 August, turned out to be a day of utter confusion trying to

Dogsledding over rocks to return from Inuit camp to our camp. Author photo.

reach a Norseman float plane that had disappeared in the hills and, we assumed, had landed somewhere nearby. We searched for it in several groups, wading long distances through swamps, before one of us spotted the aircraft. The pilot had been waiting for us on a small lake and promised to return for us the next day.

My field notes tell the end of the story:

> Friday 29 August
>
> Arose 0740. Struck camp, jettisoning a pile of stuff including personal gear & a Schmitt box of mine with 7 bugs in it & slogged off around 1030. I was really beat, as were Cec & Joe. Luckily Jim, Barry & Dot were comparatively fresh. Only Tatee of the Eskimos came along with his 15 dogs & komatik; at 1400 we had lunch at the foot of the hills, & then Cec, Jim & I took a load each . . . & we set off to pick a trail for the komatik. Around 1600 from the top of a hill we saw the Norseman coming. It shot us up (zoomed low overhead) & dropped behind the next ridge to land. We raced to

the lake (I got there first but had a head start). Did that kite & Pat Higgs the pilot ever look good.

As weather was closing in, it had to be a one load shot so we jettisoned everything we could, my heavy sleeping bag, tents, stoves etc, giving it all to Tatee along with rations from the kite & $70. We waded to the kite, climbed in, & piled one on top of another 3 deep behind the pilot's seat. A Norseman's emergency load is 1400 lbs & we had 1400 plus. Cautioning us not to move during takeoff, Pat gave her the gun & managed by the usual bouncing routine to stagger into the air with room to spare.[8] The flight back was miserable and Pat barely got the Norseman into a small lake near Coral Harbour. Freezing rain and fog soon closed in so tight that we got lost trying to hike to trucks that had come out to take us to the D.O.T. (Department of Transport building). I was ready to lie down & die & so were the others. We eventually found the trucks & rode to the D.O.T. to get fed, warmed, & dried.

RCAF Norseman to the rescue at a mountain lake. Author photo.

To me, it was an extraordinary and harrowing set of days lasting from August 11 to 29 but, of course, nothing compared to what Arctic explorers had endured in the past.

I also went with the Inuit that summer on my first and only episode of large animal hunting, in the form of a walrus hunt, invited along by an Inuit friend, Joe Curley. It, too, was quite an adventure, going out in a Peterhead boat (a fishing boat of roughly forty feet with an inboard engine, named after Europe's busiest fishing port, Peterhead, Scotland) with a bunch of his companions some sixty miles from Coral Harbour, hunting seals on the way, then south to Walrus Island, where we crept over slippery rocks toward where we had seen and heard walrus the previous night:

> I had Father Rio's .30-.30 Winchester model 1894 lever action carbine & 3 other Eskimos had Savage lever action 250-3000's. All of us had loaded hard points. There ahead of us were four huge Bull Walrus ("Ivik"). Joe, who was unarmed, motioned us into position & when all were set gave me the honor of the first shot. I drew a bead on the biggest specimen, a dead shot only about 5 yards away and squeezed off, killing him outright with a shot in the head right above the neck. The other three volleyed right behind me & 2 other walrus dropped mostly wounded. The fourth started for the water but I had jacked another shell into the chamber as had the Eskimos & we finished him before he got 2 feet. Typical "big time" hunting, the game didn't have a chance. The other Eskimos ran on & got 3 more. . . . A large male & a small one had dived into crevasses at the first shots, where they were stuck & later, after some teasing by the Eskimos, were finished off with 22's. . . . I think Walrus Island is a preserve which the Eskimos should not hunt, but of course I could not and would not prevent them from going. As they say (and rightly so), "Tingmik (dogs) & Inuk (people)[9] hungry, we get Ivik." . . . With the knives we re-

A carving in walrus ivory of a man in a kayak. Southampton Island, 1952. Author photo.

> turned & I photographed the goriest scene I have ever witnessed. It was much worse than the corpses stacked at the Philadelphia morgue which Dick Graves, a college roommate, and I had toured as Penn undergraduates.

I had a mixed reaction to the whole episode—I must admit to excitement in the hunt, but it was combined with sadness for the animals, especially the young walrus that got stuck. That the Inuit really needed the meat and hides was a good excuse, but maybe not good enough. I was greatly relieved more than three decades later when Anne and I sailed past Walrus Island, by then certainly a nature reserve, on my return to the Arctic. I saw that the island hosted a much bigger walrus herd than the one we had decimated. And today the Inuit are collaborating with their relatives in Russia in efforts to preserve these magnificent beasts from human-caused climate disruption, as well as overharvesting for their precious ivory.[10]

Living with the Inuit that summer was an unforgettable experience. Many among them were incredibly talented mechanically, to my considerable benefit. And most I met had a great sense of humor, and their kids were infinitely curious. Several became volunteer helpers in my insect work; among them, Ikurlik I recall was especially bright and helpful (plate 1). I've made friends with people all over the world but never with a group that actually thrived in a habitat with so few resources and such harsh conditions. I often think how mostly unnecessary it was about 175 years ago for the 129 British men of the richly equipped Sir John Franklin expedition in search of the Northwest Passage to die—if only they had been flexible enough to adopt the Inuit's survival techniques.

In addition to the thrill of being partly immersed in a new culture that summer and of having an opportunity to name officially some geographic features visible on a globe was the pleasure of some extraordinary adventures with my new companions. Being able to observe and collect *Erebia rossii*, *Colias nastes*, *Boloria polaris*, and other butterflies I'd only seen dead mounted on pins in boxes and for the first time to photograph a few species of birds whetted my scientific appetite as well. So I determined to pursue graduate school in entomology rather than anthropology. I also solidified that summer what would become a lifelong interest in the Arctic.

In fact, the next summer, that of 1953, wanting to see the high Arctic, I signed on as a student assistant (read "voluntary laborer") on the joint U.S.-Canadian resupply operation for the northernmost weather stations. I was flown with a group of other assistants to Resolute Bay on Cornwallis Island at 74° North in the Canadian Arctic archipelago. I was set to work on such tasks as learning to drive a D8 Cat bulldozer (fun), shifting fifty-gallon drums of urine so full they had a meniscus (not fun), and watching naval officers trying to clear ice from the bay with a couple of sticks of dynamite (funny).

There were no butterflies to be studied so far north, but I did get a chance that summer to see a Ross's gull—a very rare bird. Since I had started birding a little in the Arctic only the year before, taking pictures of birds nesting on the tundra when I could, I got that gull on my life list before the cardinal, much to the disgust of friends who were demon birders but had never been to the Arctic. I didn't see musk oxen (still haven't—they are on my bucket list), but I did finally get to see a wild polar bear. That was less fun.

With a colleague but without the required firearm—they all were checked out; besides, we hadn't seen a polar bear during our entire stay—I had left the Resolute base to photograph soil polygons (a honeycomb pattern in frozen soil formed by ice walls in the permafrost below the surface). We were busy taking pictures a couple of miles from Resolute base, I with my trusty Bolsey 35mm capable of getting thirty-eight pictures on a thirty-six-picture film roll, when my friend said, "Look at the hare on that slope." I saw a blob of white, rapidly expanding. "It's a polar bear," we simultaneously exclaimed, and fled in panic. Remembering my Arctic reading, I yelled, "Drop everything." Cameras, parkas, hats—all were ditched as we ran. It was the most terrified I have ever been. I was certain I was going to die. My religion is cowardice, and I'm orthodox. My feet only touched the ground a few times in those couple of miles, and I have no idea why we got away. I'd like to think that the poor-sighted bear stopped to sniff our stuff, the wind was behind us, and once we were over a beach ridge it lost us. But that's only a guess. I still have nightmares about the incident.

That was memorable, but my most memorable time on Cornwallis came when the same colleague and I decided to take an after-work walk (around about midnight, but still with bright light) to Assistance Bay, some thirteen miles east of Resolute Bay, where William Penny and John Ross had overwintered more than a century before on Penny's 1850–51 Franklin search expedition. As far as we knew, we were only the second party to visit the site in more than a century, and the cairn the Penny expedition had set up was still there (plate 3). We found interesting artifacts, including wine bottles with labels still on some of them, a testament to the Arctic rock-desert climate.

We zipped our two sleeping bags together for warmth and settled down to try to get a few hours of sleep. Unhappily for us, the standard rock-desert climate failed us, and for the first time that summer it rained rather than snowed (leading edge of climate warming?). Freezing water slowly crept into our sleeping bags, and soon we had no choice but to get up, roll the bags, and start back toward the Resolute base camp, with the rain freezing on our parkas. The small streams we had easily waded through on the way to Assistance Bay were rising, as the rain did not soak into the frozen ground. That added to the misery of the trek. At long last, we could see the Resolute base several miles away around a curved shoreline. Between us and the base, though, lay a brook that now had turned into a seemingly impassable roaring torrent. We were covered with ice and very cold; assuming we were done for, we sat down on the bank and wept. Finally, we decided it would be better to die fast trying to cross the torrent. I remembered reading somewhere about a trick that helped us. We took the .303 rifle we had been lugging with us as polar bear protection and held it between us. My colleague crossed downstream of me, bracing me with the rifle. I partially broke the force of the rushing water, almost up to our armpits, for him, and he was able to keep his footing on the rocks of the streambed. The rifle kept me from being swept away. We'd never felt anything so cold. It seemed to take hours to get across, but it was more likely forty seconds. We jogged frantically on and in a short time reached the warmth of the Resolute base.

Nearly seventy years later, in 2020 while sheltering in place during the Covid-19 pandemic, I was nearly overwhelmed by nostalgia about that incident. A wonderful, deeply researched book appeared in 2019 describing the Franklin search and centered on William Penny.[11] I was especially intrigued by descriptions of the struggles of the crews of Penny's two search ships, frozen into the ice of Assistance Bay, to visit two Royal Navy search ships frozen in near Resolute Bay, on the shores of which would be built our base camp—traveling over the same route in winter that nearly finished us at the end of summer.

My stay at Resolute ended sadly. Greatly concerned about my father's health (more later), I had stayed in touch with my family through ham radio. I spent so much time trying to make contact from the far north that I still remember the call signs: "Victor easy 8 mike baker this is W2 love xray peter, do you read me?" Reception, I was told, depended on the state of the "heaviside layer," which for years I believed was so named because ionized gas there produced a "heavy" layer reflecting medium-frequency radio waves that permitted communication far beyond the horizon. Only recently did I discover it was named for Oliver Heaviside, one of the physicists who predicted the layer's existence! Eventually I got through, found out that my dad's condition was deteriorating, and prevailed upon the RCAF to let me join a flight out. My father was in bad shape, but thanks in part to treatment with nitrogen mustards, vinblastine, and vincristine, he was released from the hospital and managed to carry on for more than a year, long enough to meet Anne in December of 1954.[12]

I had further Arctic adventures doing fieldwork in Alaska during several other summers, but these first three Arctic summers that I've described were truly formative. I'll only mention one other event that repeatedly comes to mind: in 1954 I landed in a Piper Pacer aircraft on the beach at Shishmaref on the Chukchi Sea. That beach is famous now because it no longer exists, and Shishmaref is gone as well, evacuated to a higher site because of sea level rise.

FOUR

Evolution in Kansas . . . and Chicago

Residence in Philadelphia, as well as my insect investigations in the Arctic, served me well in my entomological career ambitions: the Entomological Society of America was to meet in that city late in 1952. I would be graduating from Penn the following spring and was anxious to go to graduate school in the fall of 1953. I had been told (correctly, it turned out) that Charles Michener was the best scientist working with insects, and I was eager to talk with him at the meeting about the prospects of studying with him. Little did I realize that a single conversation with Mich would set me on a road that would take me twice to live in Kansas, once to live in Chicago, and then to Stanford—and introduce me to marriage and fatherhood.

Mich had moved from the American Museum of Natural History to become chair of the Department of Entomology at the University of Kansas, so that's where I now most wanted to go. I managed to run him down at the entomology meeting and was thrilled he remembered me. I explained that although a wild undergraduate career had resulted in lousy grades, I had done extensive entomological fieldwork in the Arctic and already published a few papers. I gave him reprints of my note on the monarch parasite and the two papers on butterfly taxonomy and distribution that I had published in peer-reviewed journals while at Penn. Would he give me a chance in graduate school?

Mich did more than that—he got me an assistantship with Robert Sokal, then a young Turk working on the evolution of DDT resistance in fruit flies. Again the luck of a 1932 birth: when I think of what graduate school applicants are put through today, I realize I'd now probably have had to follow in my father's footsteps and become a shirt salesman. Or maybe a physician. My father's best friend was Benjamin Haskell, chief of proctology at Jefferson Medical College in Philadelphia. When all the other premed seniors at Penn were sweating out med school applications, "Uncle Ben" told me that if I wanted to go to medical school, Jefferson would be glad to have me. I wasn't interested: there was no butterfly connection.

So, thanks to Mich, after my summer of 1953 spent in the high Arctic, it was off to the wilds of Lawrence, Kansas. It was culture shock. This first became clear to me when I was given a traffic ticket on my way home from the lab for speeding in a school zone—something like thirty-five miles an hour in a twenty-mile-per-hour zone. The fine was about a third of a month's income, even though I had been "speeding" past the school at 2:00 a.m. Lawrence was a religion-soaked, segregated town, with not a decent restaurant in sight, but some departments at the university, such as Mich's entomology, I knew were superb.

Robert Sokal would eventually become famous as the scientist who brought statistics into biology and as the coinventor with Mich of what became known as numerical taxonomy. In my first year Bob taught me how to raise fruit flies (*Drosophila melanogaster*) in pint milk bottles (then still in use) and small glass vials, expose them to different conditions, and then knock them out with ether and sort them by sex, after which we could set up small breeding groups and conduct further experiments. It was an incredible learning experience for me. By exposing some fly groups to DDT and others not, I could see natural selection in action, with the poison killing fewer and fewer flies of the poisoned group in each successive approximately ten-day-long generation. The ones that survived the exposure to DDT each generation became the parents of the next generation. Our lab was essentially breeding *Drosophila* with gene combinations that made them less likely to be killed by the poison. In short, I saw how raising *Drosophila* on medium (goop on which grew the fungi that the fruit fly maggots ate) containing DDT that killed many but not all of them could quickly lead to generations of fruit flies that had become resistant to DDT. When we created populations of flies by breeding the individuals each generation who had survived on DDT-containing medium, in about ten generations the flies could enjoy DDT as an aperitif. The control population, flies raised on DDT-free medium, however, still were easily killed by the pesticide.

We also managed to create a population that was extremely susceptible to DDT. For some reason we couldn't do this by breeding only flies that had died on DDT medium. How to do it? Bob told us how. We used something called sib selection. We divided the eggs from each female into two batches, kept careful track of them, and raised the maggots from one batch on DDT medium and those in the other batch on clean medium. Then we used as parents of the next generation the brothers and sisters of those who suffered the highest mortality from DDT exposure. Breeding from the brothers and sisters of DDT-susceptible flies quickly produced a population of individuals that, it almost seemed, dropped dead when just shown a bottle of DDT.

I also learned that selection could cause unexpected responses, and those in turn could prompt new hypotheses. The DDT-exposed flies bred over generations not only became resistant to the pesticide but also changed where they formed their pupae, tending to move off the goop to a spot higher on the walls of the vials. I was thinking that resistance probably evolved through developing an enzyme that metabolized DDT molecules, but perhaps the new pupal position also helped by reducing DDT exposure.

Work in Bob Sokal's lab was my introduction to evolution in action, and to evidence of the direct importance of that action. It also made me forever conscious of the problems of pesticide resistance and, by inference, of antibiotic resistance. It showed me the power of natural selection and the ways in which evolution operates, not on clock time, but on generation time: flies will evolve much more rapidly than elephants. These are lessons—staples of evolutionary understanding—too few in our society have ever learned. For example, our civilization teeters on the brink of a return to the horrid preantibiotic era thanks to the failure to appreciate how drug resistance develops combined with massive overuse of those once miracle drugs. The likely result of such overuse, widespread antibiotic resistance, was already abundantly clear to scientists and their students studying the subject in the 1950s.

KU for me wasn't all fruit flies. Shortly after I arrived, Mich invited me to the fall entomology department picnic. Of course, I accepted. Then I wondered where I would get a date. I was relaxing soon thereafter in the student union's music room when an extremely pretty young woman came in. All the local hayseeds were wheezing and gawking, but I simply asked her out for a cup of coffee. Her name was Margot Baker, the daughter, it turned out, of Phil Baker of radio game-show fame, and she agreed to go with me to the entomology picnic. I'll never forget it. I turned out to be the only man who brought a date who was not his wife. Amazingly, the only beverage available was Kool-Aid, so my date and I were stone-cold sober when the whole group gathered around a fifty-gallon drum in which paper napkins and cups and hotdog sleeves were being burned. We were led by an old man (doubtless much younger than I am now) in singing "Old MacDonald Had a Farm" (no kidding!). At around the second "moo-moo here, moo-moo there," I asked Margot, "Who is that ——?" Unluckily, Mich was standing right behind us and interjected, "He's the dean of the graduate school." I assumed then I'd have a very short graduate career; it was several months before I learned that Mich had exactly the same opinion of the dean. The incident should have taught me to keep my big mouth shut, but sadly, it didn't.

Social arrangements in Kansas did have some disadvantages for a libidinous young man from the East. At Penn women could check out of their dorms for the night but had to give the address of where they would be—the in loco parentis ethic of those dark days was still partly in place. At Kansas it was much worse: women had to be back in their housing at (if I recall correctly) 10:30 p.m. Sundays through Thursdays, 11:00 p.m. on Fridays, and 11:30 p.m. on Saturdays. Those who, evidently like the Old MacDonald dean, were horrified by the tendency of young humans to enjoy sex, also apparently believed that you couldn't do so in the daytime.

One day some months after the dean's picnic I saw another incredibly beautiful young woman in the student union. I discovered that her name was Anne Howland and that she was an undergraduate, sadly running around with a foreign student from France. But luck was on my side—she wanted to play bridge with two of my friends, and they needed a fourth. So we met. Besides being drop-dead gorgeous (to use a then-current expression), I found out quickly that she had a sharp mind and that we shared several interests. After that first bridge game broke up, we had a long discussion of the Battle of Dunkirk, and I soon discovered she had no use for religion (though coming from an Episcopalian background she had not discovered, as I had via bar mitzvah, religion's financial possibilities). I also got the welcome news that her French boyfriend was leaving at the end of the spring semester. My then girlfriend (who remains a friend almost seven decades later) and I were having some disagreements, so when the term ended I started a correspondence with Anne, who had left KU for the summer.

That summer of 1954 I was invited on a fabulous camping field trip to Mexico with Mich and some fellow grad students. The trip was intended to introduce us to the vast diversity of tropical insects and learn about them from Mich. It provided my first acquaintance with the tropical butterflies that I would work on later for more than half a century (most recently in 2013 near Zihuatanejo, on the Mexican west coast). Mich was a wonderful mentor besides being a brilliant scientist. He generally led by example, right down to taking on the nastiest chore in our camps, washing the dishes.

I remember well my first encounter with those butterflies, working my way up a river near Llera in Tamaulipas, the first spot we hit in the tropics driving south across the border from Texas. There were lots of butterflies; I especially remember several beautiful species of *Heliconius* (now called longwings) sipping nectar from flowers, and many trees featured camouflaged members of a *Hamadryas* species (perhaps more than one) sitting head-downward on their trunks. When disturbed, *Hamadryas* in flight make a crackling sound with their wings—the source of their common name, cracker butterflies. I was in paradise until, at the point where I had to turn back, a stab at a butterfly caught my net on a thorn and tore it open, ending collecting for the day. Despite the ripped net, that day gave me an experience of the tropics and a love of tropical natural history on land (which later extended into the sea) that still makes me long to do fieldwork there today. One time we were camping above the now-resort town of Xilitla, in the best campsite I've ever occupied. A cool mountain stream cascaded down into a jungle pool, perhaps twenty feet across, seemingly carved from a single rock. Floating in the pool after butterfly adventures with a couple of cold six-packs of Dos Equis on the edge, our group learned from Mich how difficult the life of a field biologist could be.

Anne and I wrote to each other all summer, and we went on our first date in September. Before Christmas, Anne Howland became Anne Ehrlich. Our correspondence and then our dates after I returned from Mexico had led me to make a quick decision: I'd take a big risk—rather than let her get away. Two weeks after we started dating, I came out and said we ought to get married. She thought I was joking at first, but eventually she was convinced I was serious. It turned out, since she then agreed, to be by far the best decision of my life. Some thought it was too quick, but interestingly, Mich didn't. He explained that he had done the same thing with Mary, who became his wife. He was still young (about thirty-six) when he told me that, but like Anne and me, Mich and Mary went on to have a long and wonderful marriage.

I did not meet Anne's parents until, I think, late October. Anne's father Winston "Windy" Howland was a reformed alcoholic and great guy, and gave us no problem. He and I both loved limericks, and while Anne and her mother were out buying Anne's trousseau (these were the olden days), we had a limerick contest that ended in a draw after more than four hours. Anne's mother, Virginia, wanted us to wait until June to get married, and I wanted to get married at 2:00 p.m. on December 18, 1954. Realizing the advantage of compromise, I agreed to wait until 4:00 p.m. on December 18.

Since then, as now, the bride's family tended to control that particular rite of passage, we agreed to be married by an Episcopal priest in her parent's living room in Des Moines, Iowa.

Effective birth control was difficult to come by in the Midwest in those days. Anne went to the student health clinic at KU just before we left for our wedding in Des Moines, hoping to get fitted for a diaphragm. Because she was only engaged and not yet married, despite a wedding date only a week away, she was refused. So we had no simple means of obtaining anything beyond what was available in drug stores for the next several weeks before and after the wedding. Meanwhile, the priest insisted on a premarital conference. Although my Jewish ancestry was no barrier, he said, he couldn't marry us unless I told him I believed in God. I told him I'd say I believed in God or even Mickey Mouse if that would get us married without trouble. He said okay, but further, he really couldn't marry us if we had agreed not to have children. I said, "Relax, she's pregnant." That worked, but for some reason really annoyed Anne, perhaps because she wasn't. So we got married, with Loy Bilderback as best man and his girlfriend (later wife) Betty in attendance along with Anne's folks and her younger sisters, Penny and Elizabeth (nicknamed Lisa, and after whom our daughter would be named), being the other family present.[1] At my request, some references to Christ were omitted from the service. We spent one night in Des Moines and then took the train east to Philadelphia for our honeymoon and for Anne to meet my family. My grandfather had just died and my father was dying of Hodgkin disease, so my folks had not been able to attend the Des Moines ceremony. My father took to Anne immediately, but then he had always been attracted to smart, beautiful women. I'm sorry he and I had such a short life together; when I was a teenager his cancer did not make him easy to live with, and I wasn't mature enough to give him space.

The laws promulgated by the religious zealots of Kansas (and of course many other states) were a source of both worry and humor. Anne and I had worried because, as noted, under the law she hadn't been able to be fitted with a diaphragm until she had a wedding certificate. So far, we had been lucky, and fortunately, condoms were then legal to buy. One day a close friend and colleague asked me to buy some condoms for him. I had intro-

I win the lottery! Anne and me—Kansas, 1955—soon after our wedding. Author photo.

duced him to a very nice young woman with whom he eventually had a long marriage. "Why don't you buy them yourself?" "I'd be too embarrassed." "Well, then, why don't you just throw a quarter (this was 1954) into one of the condom machines in the men's room of the Dynamite (the road house we all frequented)?" "Oh, that wouldn't work, those condoms are for prevention of disease only." I may be the only person still alive who actually knew someone who believed that notice, which was ubiquitous on condom dispensers—and usually the word "disease" was scratched out and "babies" substituted. Memories of the Dynamite have even found a way into my lectures. The toilet seats there had ultraviolet sterilizers, so in the 1980s when discussing ozone depletion I could point out that human beings were converting Earth into the equivalent of a Dynamite toilet seat.

Having started marriage in Kansas without a diaphragm, Anne's and my luck soon ran out, and on November 6, 1955, our daughter, Lisa, appeared in a rush of amniotic fluid. Despite my urging, Anne refused to eat the placenta as other primates do, but she was ahead of her time in determination

Anne and Lisa, 1956. Author photo.

to breastfeed despite no support from others and a lot of social pressure against it. Unfortunately, Lisa had very bad colic and after a few weeks was failing to thrive; Anne was exhausted from lack of sleep and unable to give Lisa enough milk. I had one of my life's more panicky moments and called my then-widowed mother. She immediately flew to Lawrence and helped us out. The problem was diagnosed, Lisa was put on formula, and she and her mother recovered beautifully; the only drawback was that Lisa's formula cost about half our monthly income.

That episode convinced me that there might be something to the so-called grandmother effect. Anthropologists had hypothesized that women underwent menopause rather than further childbearing as they got older, thereby increasing their evolutionary fitness (their genetic contribution to future generation) by supporting their daughters' reproduction. In contributing to their daughters' childbearing and child-rearing success, more of the grandmother's kind of genes would be passed on than, on average, would their trying themselves to reproduce when old and frail. Why frailty and death evolved in animals is one of those many basic questions for which science doesn't as yet have a fully satisfactory answer—although thoughts on the outcomes of allocating energy to reproduction versus repairing wear on aging tissues and organs may contain the seeds of an answer.

I was a lousy father in those early days, focused on finishing my doctorate, getting a job, and supporting my now huge (to me) family. I did, however, provide for them by, among other things, shooting rabbits and squirrels on the Kansas prairies with the Mossberg 12-gauge bolt-action (believe it or not!) shotgun I'd bought for $10. We shared the loot with Loy and Betty, and after I skinned the animals, Betty cooked them. There is not much meat on a squirrel, but if you bag enough of them, it amounts to something. Still, my birth-year luck persisted; the National Science Foundation invented predoctoral fellowships to support science students like me, and I got one of the first, which eased our financial worries.

Fortunately, Anne was a good mother, and Lisa grew up to be an independent and intelligent woman. She did have some psychological problems, as indicated by her eventual choice of economics for a doctorate. She took some counseling when in her twenties, and I asked her whether we had screwed her up. All the pressure we had put on her had added to her tensions, she said. I replied, "What pressures? We never pushed you on grades, school, career choices, etc." "Yes, but you and Mom always worked so hard!" In any case, she fully recovered and became a very good friend. Neither being born in Kansas nor having me as a father could ruin her.

As an undergraduate Anne was a French major with a minor in art, but soon after having Lisa she became involved in research on butterflies and environmental science. We have now done research and writing together for over sixty-five years, starting with her help in illustrating my thesis and then in dissecting butterflies and following the footsteps of Samuel Hubbard Scudder in drawing their anatomy. Butterflies led her to studies of ecology and evolution, just as they had for me. Anne continued to contribute to our collective understanding of systematic issues and the reproductive biology and ecology of butterflies, doing such things as dissecting and drawing the musculature of the prothorax (the front and smallest of the three thoracic segments, each bearing a pair of legs) of tiny lycaenids, some with less than a one-inch wingspread, with a prothorax less than two cubic millimeters in volume. Under a microscope she saw the complex of muscles and drew them, developing data for use in numerical taxonomy tests. She also counted eggs in female butterflies' ovaries and counted spermatophores (sperm packets in the female's copulatory sack), which allowed her to determine how many times a female had mated. All that gave us eventually a need to travel around the world working on aspects of butterfly anatomy and reproduction not possible with only preserved specimens. It is extremely difficult to dissect soft parts of the anatomy in pickled insects. Later, Anne would become well known for her award-winning analysis of problems of population, environment, and nuclear war, and she did invaluable work on the Ehrlich mailing list trying to keep friends and colleagues updated on our view of the state of civilization—but sex and butterflies and Anne's artistic talent started it all (plate 2).

The influence of Charles Michener and Robert Sokal on my thinking was immense; one could not ask for more challenging and thoughtful mentors. Both were dazzling intellects. Mich was, right up to his death at ninety-seven in 2016, the world's expert on bee taxonomy, evolution, and behavior, but he had also worked on butterflies. Bob, who brought statistics into biology, not only introduced me to the laboratory study of natural selection in fruit flies, but early on showed me how to do modern analyses of geographic variation in the populations of *Erebia*.

I had suggested to Mich that for my dissertation I do a "revision" of the family Satyridae—the group of butterflies that included the genus *Erebia*. Such a revision would consist of trying to determine the patterns in which the various kinds of satyrid butterfly had evolved (determine, in other words, its phylogeny, or evolutionary history) and then establish a classification that reflected the phylogeny. I was interested in seeing how the patterns displayed on the wings and in the genitalia of those butterflies might indicate how and where they had evolved. That would have been a standard taxonomic thesis for those days in an entomology department.

I had been fascinated by evolution in all its manifestations, and I had been strongly influenced by Ernst Mayr's already classic *Systematics and the Origin of Species* ever since having read it in my teens. I thought at the time that taxonomy was one route to further that understanding of evolution. The taxonomic approach seemed potentially fruitful in the study of butterflies especially, where there was much interest in subspecies, which were thought often to be species in statu nascendi—in the process of being born. In some cases that may have been correct, and I'd even named a few subspecies. To me, patterns of slight variation in *Erebia* from place to place seemed clear evidence of a gradual evolutionary process, and some seventy years later I still think that view was largely correct. Butterfly wing patterns varied from place to place in response to different selection pressures applied by different environments. When populations in varied environments evolved in isolation they could become so different from other populations that they could (or would) not mate together and would then have become different species. That's how Mayr had described the basic process of speciation.[2]

Mich, to my great pleasure, turned me on to a more ambitious project. He encouraged me to go far beyond the satyrids and do my doctoral dissertation on the morphology, higher classification, and phylogeny of all the butterflies. By "higher" he meant the evolution of the major groups of butterfly species—not that of the species themselves. If he had wanted me to study the higher classification of the birds, for example, he'd have wanted me to figure out things like whether Old World and New World vultures were closely related to one another and how closely related they were to various eagles. In taxonomic terms he'd want me to classify birds into, say, genera, subfamilies, and families. He would not want me to study differentiation in a group of sparrow species. Mich was a promoter of thinking big, and that fit right in with my too-big ego.

Following Mich's lead in searching for as many characteristics of the butterflies as I could evaluate, I ended up boiling their bodies in potassium hydroxide, which is highly caustic, and removing their scales and soft parts with fine watchmakers' forceps, eye droppers, and watercolor paint brushes. That way I was able to compare their intricate external skeletons (exoskeletons—characteristic of all arthropods, of which butterflies are one group), which had been largely ignored by most previous butterfly taxonomists. They had focused primarily on the patterns of wing veins and the shapes of male butterfly's genital structures. I dissected about 240 genera and 300 species of butterflies to sample their diversity, which includes approximately 15,000 species.

As I progressed, I was increasingly convinced that I was actually unraveling the phylogeny of the butterflies because the patterns in the exoskeleton were extremely clear. For example, a famously rare and unusual species, *Styx infernalis* from the Chanchamayo Valley of Peru, had puzzled previous taxonomists—some had thought it related to the Pieridae (whites and sulphurs), others to the Lycaenidae (blues and metalmarks).[3] *Styx* was so rare that the only specimens I knew about as a student were in the British Museum in London. Mich requested one from the museum for me to dissect; the request was granted as long as I returned the parts. I did so, and decades later in the museum I saw the wings I'd returned glued to a card and the cleaned body parts in the vial I had sent, with its cork skewered on a pin through the card. Examination of *Styx*'s anatomy immediately showed that it shared important features of its exoskeleton with the Lycaenidae, the blues and metalmarks (more recent work with molecular techniques that reveal genetic features also shows those connections).

One day in a small seminar, Bob Sokal said that those of us who thought, as I did, that we were studying phylogenies (evolutionary sequences) in our taxonomic procedures were not actually doing that at all. We were just grouping animals together according to their overall similarities, not actually establishing an evolutionary sequence. "I could do basically the same job with correlation coefficients," Bob claimed, referring to statistical measures of the strength of the relation between two variables. Mich and three students—Earl Cross, James Chillcott (a Canadian friend from the Arctic summer of 1952 who had also decided on KU for graduate studies), and I—strongly disagreed, and a couple of weeks of debate ensued. Finally Mich and Bob decided to put Bob's idea to a test.

Mich had a student measure or otherwise numerically evaluate 122 characteristics (shape of parts, patterns of wing veins, and so on) of 97 bee species and gave the numbers to Bob, who didn't know a bee from a beetle. Bob calculated the 4,656 correlation coefficients between the 97 sets of numbers representing each possible pair of species and worked out a mathematical scheme for translating that incomprehensible mess of numbers (a 97 × 97 matrix) into a treelike diagram in which the species with high similarity were close together and those with low similarity were far apart.[4] It was a phylogenetic tree in whose construction, as Bob had claimed, only degree of similarity was considered. When Bob returned with his bee "phylogeny," Mich, the world expert on bee taxonomy, agreed that it was better than his own first attempt at constructing one. Bob, utterly ignorant of bees and having been given only numbers, had accurately placed a couple of parasitic bees that Mich thought he had originally misplaced. Thus numerical taxonomy was born, and I was shown that one of my deeply held scientific beliefs—that I was studying phylogeny directly—was dead wrong.[5]

I was not making assumptions about what characteristics were most important in butterfly evolution (say, wing venation) and basing my ideas on which species had descended recently from common ancestors on the basis of wing venation, as was common taxonomic practice in those days. Instead, thanks to Mich's guidance, I had been comparing every aspect of the butterfly's physical structures that I could conveniently compare. My mistake, and that of other taxonomists including Mich, was superobvious in retrospect—we were always working with similarities calculated by that most marvelous of computers, the human brain. But we framed our conclusions as if we'd been working directly with how those similarities came about. It was one of the greatest lessons I've ever been taught. I have never "believed" like that again.

I had witnessed personally a scientific "paradigm" dynamited. What mobs of taxonomists thought they were doing wasn't what they were doing at all.

Sokal had shown us that we were all wrong, and all of our group accepted that. Fortunately for me, with Mich's guidance I had already done the data collecting for my thesis so that, although I couldn't then have quantified the work, I was already headed in the right direction by comparing many, many characteristics and actually grouping butterflies on the basis of their overall similarities.

Many old-time taxonomists couldn't accept the Sokal-Michener tests. So, not unexpectedly, the invention of numerical taxonomy led immediately to the numerical taxonomy wars in which the vast majority of taxonomists claimed that using statistics to group organisms by their similarity couldn't work (they never were explicit about what "working" meant—and too many taxonomists don't think about the meanings and uses of classifications to this very day). Science is classically a conservative enterprise; scientists wisely don't usually jump immediately on board new-idea bandwagons—as, for instance, long battles over evolution, childbed fever, phlogiston, plate tectonics, and the ether wind have demonstrated. In this case, I had the fervor of a convert to numerical taxonomy, and I pitched in. After all, before the advent of numerical taxonomy, taxonomic work was generally judged by consensus on the quality of a taxonomist's research, meaning largely whether other taxonomists looking at the same groups thought the phylogenetic relationships proposed seemed "right" (my trouble in wording this gives some idea of how shaky the grounds were). With numerical taxonomy, work could now be judged on the basis of the evidence and its analysis—for the first time taxonomic work was becoming *repeatable.*

As a convert, I naturally enjoyed engaging in those wars. At a small meeting at the Missouri Botanical Garden, after I gave a talk on numerical taxonomy, a distinguished botanist asked me in public if I thought computers would replace taxonomists. Unable to control myself, I replied that I thought most taxonomists could be replaced by abacuses. My reply did not make me a hero of many colleagues. I just had a hard time not entering into debates. In 1956, to take another example, I attended my first big scientific conference, the Tenth International Congress of Entomology in Montreal. I gave a paper on some of the work I'd finished in the Arctic in the summer of 1952 with my beloved *Erebia*, but my most vivid memory was of a short debate I had with Bill Brown in front of a huge audience.[6] Bill had recently published a now-classic paper with E. O. Wilson attacking the usefulness of the subspecies as a taxonomic category, and I differed with him on some points.[7] In retrospect, Bill and Ed were right. I later realized that describing and naming subspecies is scientifically largely a waste of time. The 1953 paper by Wilson and Brown, followed by one of Nick Gillham's in 1965, convinced me of that.[8] How the populations of a species were divided into subspecies depended on what characteristics were analyzed and what weight they were given. Naming subspecies was, however, great fun and eventually could have conservation significance because environmental rulings may specify particular subspecies for conservation. Important suites of populations can thus sometimes be protected from destruction by naming them as a subspecies.

When moving from numerical taxonomy results to attempting to describe accurately patterns of past evolution, it is an easy, and probably usually valid, assumption that the more statistically similar several organisms were, the more likely they had diverged from one another more recently than did statistically more dissimilar creatures. Taxonomists have become deeply involved since the numerical taxonomy wars in trying to find ways to better estimate phylogenetic patterns and figure out the speed by which evolution is causing two groups of populations to differentiate. Indeed, an entire school—cladistics—has developed that struggles with constructing such evolutionary trees. I continue to wonder why. Similarities form a nice basis for classification and prediction of such features as behaviors, potential to transmit disease, possibility of becoming a dangerous agricultural pest, and so on much better than hypothesized evolutionary relationships. Birds and crocodilians are thought by some to have diverged from each other relatively recently in evolutionary time. Thus a cladist might want to group them into the same class rather than put them into two classes, Aves and Reptilia. But for purposes of communication that might not work so well. If your fellow cladist at a field site said a "birdcroc" was approaching, you would not know whether it was going to sing you a song or stuff your body under a muddy bank to devour you later.

There are some interesting technical evolutionary questions that could be answered by detailed studies of well-known groups (like birds, butterflies, and *Drosophila*), but even doing numerical taxonomy studies of all of biodiversity would seem to me an utter waste of time now. Anyone concerned with the flourishing of biodiversity, including *Homo sapiens*, needs to be taking action to halt its disappearance, not struggling with the hopeless task of finishing its formal description when it is perpetually evolving.

At the time numerical taxonomy was invented there was an ongoing debate on how to define "species." It did not influence my dissertation work on butterfly "higher" classification, but it played strongly into my fascination with the evolutionary structure of nature. In retrospect, with the knowledge of evolution then available, it was evident that species were simply bunches of terminal twigs of arbitrary length on an ever-differentiating tree of life—bunches of twigs distinct enough for a taxonomist to think of them as different kinds. The length of the twigs is determined by how strongly selection had been working to differentiate a population from others, and for how long. For instance, originally most taxonomists considered European brown bears (*Ursus arctos*) to be a different species from North American grizzly bears (*U. horribilis*), but members of the same genus, *Ursus*. Famously, in 1918, C. Hart Merriam divided North American brown and grizzly bears into eighty-two species (in two genera). In his scheme nearly every bear was a distinct species—not a very useful scheme for thinking about their evolution, ecology, or behavior. Now the tendency is to consider most North American grizzlies to be a brown bear subspecies *U. arctos horribilis*, except for a genetically somewhat distinct population on islands off of Alaska, *U. arctos middendorfi*. Of course the latter, already a longer twig, may someday be elevated to species rank, because if there's one thing taxonomists love (I've had that disease), it's changing the names of animals and plants (heaven help us if they get going on the trillions of bacteria).

Myriad examples from coyotes to fritillary butterflies to clouded leopards and orangutans show that how to decide which populations of a gradually differentiating diversity of life rate being denoted "subspecies" or "species" resides mostly in the brains of taxonomists. This has become particularly evident in recent years as molecular-based phylogenies of recent adaptive radiations (relatively rapid diversifications of the descendants of one group of organisms in response to favorable environmental changes) show a continuous degree of differentiation of populations, just as one would expect. They suggest that the whole "what is a species?" literature is the intellectual equivalent of geologists arguing forever about how to define a "mountain." Are Lhotse and Nuptse different mountains or "submountains" of Everest? Is a mountain in England the same sort of entity as one in Nepal? The species question has persisted as an emotional debate to this day, fifty years or more after the issue was basically settled in papers by me (1961) and by Bob Sokal and Ted Crovello (1970).[9] It's remarkable how much human brains like to fractionate continua into categories, presumably to make communication about them easier. The colors we extract from the spectrum are a classic example. Unfortunate examples of fractionations of continua that instead often plague humanity include: black–white, conservative–liberal, rich–poor, pretty–ugly, friend–enemy, true–false, and on and on. Obviously there are often distinctions to be made, but categorization can miss important gradations. Convenience in communication is often gained by the fractionation, but the resulting distortion of reality can carry a high price.

My 1961 paper "Has the Biological Species Concept Outlived Its Usefulness?" attacked the idea that populations that cannot share genes (fruitfully mate) should necessarily be defined as separate species.[10] And the converse: Must populations that can exchange genes always be classified as belonging to the same species? Unfortunately there are nearly infinite ways to judge the "share genes" criterion. Can brown bears from Poland fruitfully mate with Canadian grizzlies? Polar bears can and have exchanged genes with grizzlies, yet polar bears are sometimes even put in a different genus (*Thalarctos*). Recent genetic evidence shows complex evolutionary relationships between brown and polar bears and underlines the fruitlessness of arguing in favor of rigid species definitions. Even those who want potential mating success as the defining criterion of species actually tend to fall back on "kind," considering brown and polar bears as separate species in practice.

Amusingly, I initially sent that heterodox 1961 manuscript to the journal *Systematic Zoology*, then edited by Libbie Hyman, a great expert on the taxonomy of marine invertebrates. Submitting my paper there was treated as a microanalogue to nailing it to her door as it was once said Martin Luther nailed his Ninety-Five Theses to the Castle Church door in Wittenberg. She rejected the paper, claiming that reviewers were uninterested in it and that I should consult Charles Michener to find out what was wrong with it. Unhappily for her, Mich had read the paper and was the one who suggested that I submit it to *Systematic Zoology*. Mich, who was deeply respected and thus, in science, powerful, got on the phone with her. With ease he discovered that Hyman hadn't even sent the paper out for review; Mich applied some peer pressure and convinced her to have it properly reviewed, and the paper as a result was eventually accepted by *Systematic Zoology*. Hint: there are politics in science.[11]

Engagement in controversies over numerical taxonomy increased my general interest in how nature is structured. It led me when I left Kansas to start trying to use what I knew about butterflies to answer some of the questions raised as numerical taxonomy reworked the standard taxonomic paradigm. One goal was to test Sokal's nexus hypothesis: that the genome was so thoroughly integrated that any large set of characteristics, when analyzed, would produce essentially the same set of similarity relationships. If one taxonomist could only analyze the characteristics of the butterfly's exoskeleton and another only the characteristics of the musculature, for example, they would come up with essentially the same trees of relationships. Measure enough features on any major part of an organism, do a numerical taxonomy analysis, so the thinking went, and the same taxonomic relationships (similarities) would be revealed. When I compared butterfly similarities based on, say, internal versus external or wing versus body characters, that was pretty much what I found.

The most important question I think I've raised about such taxonomic analysis is what should be the limits of such research? There are billions of different kinds of organisms (possibly more if one considers viruses organisms), and only a tiny fraction of those larger than viruses or bacteria have even been analyzed to the level of butterflies—that is, with most kinds illustrated, described, given Latin names, and arranged in genera, subfamilies, families, and so forth. As I've indicated, some people seem to think that the goal of taxonomy is to finish the job, as it were, but I suggested, originally in 1964, that a careful *sampling* of diversity (as I did when working on my dissertation) is the way to go to answer questions such as "How common are adaptive radiations?"[12] After all, as I've mentioned, it has long been clear that most of present biodiversity will likely be extinct before the job of exhaustive taxonomic compilation can be completed—and much of remaining biodiversity would have evolved into something else before such a Herculean task came remotely close to being finished.

Graduate school, second only to the Arctic and Anne, shaped my professional life. Both Mich and Bob taught me many lessons that have stood me in good stead throughout my career. When I had just arrived at KU, I attended a seminar given by a graduate student nicknamed Bobo. Graduate seminars in the Department of Entomology were pretty cutthroat at the time, and I was having trouble following Bobo's discussion of the translocation (movement from cell to cell) of tobacco mosaic virus. "I don't see how you get from A to B," I said. "That, Ehrlich, is because you're both ignorant and stupid," was his response. From behind me came Mich's soft voice: "I don't get it either." I never learned whether Mich did or not "get it," but later, with my graduate students, I always emphasized that, when they went off to professorships, they remember that smart people always ask questions if they don't understand and one should never ridicule a student who shows doubt or asks a question.

The perils graduate students may face from irresponsible faculty members is illustrated by another Mich story. Wallace LaBerge, a student of Mich's who was ahead of me, was a gentle soul whose dissertation was a taxonomic revision of a big bee genus, *Melissodes*. The chair of the zoology department, E. Raymond Hall, was on his doctoral committee, and Wally followed the standard procedure of giving Hall a typewritten copy of his dissertation, photographic copies of the many distribution maps he had drawn (a black dot on an outline map of North America for each location where a *Melissodes* of each species was collected), and four signature pages (to be bound with four copies of the thesis to be deposited with the university). Nevertheless, Hall summoned Wally and told him his dissertation was not satisfactory. "I see you've used the word 'particularly' where it doesn't refer to 'particles'—I don't approve of that. And your maps don't have latitude and longitude on them, and where the dots overlap you haven't drawn white lines around them." I won't comment on "particularly," but the outline maps showed all the states and provinces, and it was standard practice *not* to include white circles around the overlapping dots representing close geographic locations at which a species had been recorded. Mich was enraged by Hall's objections but helpless; he told Wally that the entomology department would pay for the (expensive) retyping of a single official copy of his thesis and for the (expensive) rephotographing of an official set of maps (no Xerox then). All Wally's fellow graduate students were very sympathetic with his plight and the several months he had to waste inking in latitudes and longitudes and drawing white circles around black dots. He then took the official copy to Hall and got all four signature pages signed.

On the day of Wally's thesis defense, which at KU was a closed meeting with his committee, Mich walked over to the administration building to pick up the official version of the thesis to have at the defense. Another member of the faculty, Robert Beer, showed up characteristically a little late, picked up an unofficial copy in the department office, joined the group, sat next to Hall, and plunked down the thesis between them. All through the examination Hall was flipping through the unofficial copy of the thesis. Mich finally asked, "Are there any more questions?" Hall said, "I see the word 'particularly' where it doesn't refer to 'particles,' and the maps don't have latitude and longitude on them, and where the dots overlap there are no white lines around them." Mich explained that all that had been changed in the official copy, and changing the unofficial copies would have been too expensive. "But," announced Hall, "my signature is on this copy." Mich simply said, "*We'll cut it out!*"

When this was reported, all of us who knew Mich realized it was his equivalent of lunging across the table and ripping Hall's heart out. The next day Mich sent around a notice saying Professor Hall could no longer serve on entomology department committees. Years later when visiting KU, I lifted

Wally's dissertation off the shelf and was reminded of the incident by seeing part of the signature page missing.[13]

I was lucky enough in 1957, just after receiving my PhD degree, to get a postdoctoral fellowship with Joe Camin, a wonderful scientist. The job would be working on the genetics of vector ability (capability to transmit disease) in mites that parasitized snakes, my office would be at the Chicago Academy of Sciences, and I would get one day a week to do my own research. Anne and I were delighted to be saying good-bye to the second floor of a drafty ancient firetrap of a house in Lawrence and moving with Lisa, then eighteen months old, to Chicago. I went to Chicago first to find a place to live, and Joe and his equally wonderful wife, Em, invited me to stay with them to avoid the cost of a hotel.

Joe was a returning World War II veteran who had been stationed in Monterey, California, and thereafter hoped eventually to move back there (but never managed it). They had bought a "crack-in-the-picture-window" tract house and had been cheated, like many veterans, at the hands of real estate developers.[14] No surface in the home had been painted that wasn't visible to someone of average height. When Em had just finished putting their dishes in the kitchen cabinets and was still on the stepladder, the cabinets separated from the wall and came crashing down. She was fortunate not to be injured or even killed. The cabinets had been attached to the wallboard with tiny screws, just adequate to hold them when they were empty. But the house was cozy, and Joe and Em and I hit it off immediately. By the third morning I felt comfortable telling Em, as she again fried up ham and eggs for me, that I didn't like ham and eggs. "Jesus Christ," she said, "we hate them and have just been eating them to keep you company!" Live and learn—ever since then I've tried to be polite but honest whenever I eat at a friend's house.

Like most scientists, I was interested in doing work that would help humanity understand both itself and the universe in which it lived. It didn't look as if butterfly taxonomy or even numerical taxonomy was a really good route to that goal. Joe gave me my first chance to move in what seemed a more relevant direction. Understanding how the ability to transmit disease evolved (in our case the disease was a malaria-like parasite of reptiles and amphibians called haemogregarines) seemed obviously more relevant than patterns of butterfly relationships. But Joe accidentally also gave me a chance to see evolution in action in the field, as Bob Sokal had in the lab with vials of fruit flies.

We began with a field trip to the Lake Erie islands, where Joe knew we could easily gather the snakes on which to raise the mites necessary for our genetic studies. The common water snake *Natrix sipedon* (now called *Nerodia sipedon*) was abundant along the islands' shores, often sheltering under flat limestone rocks on the islands' peripheries. We had a great time, staying (with the owner's permission) on Middle Island in a spacious, comfortable home with a series of tiny bedrooms above a largely open downstairs. It was just over the Canadian border, and during Prohibition it had been a fancy brothel and bar. Those days were over, but it was a good place to stay. We collected many specimens, often rolling over a rock to find two or three four-foot-long snakes under it. We would grab them, and they would grab us. The bites were painful and contained a mild anticoagulant venom: when we drove back to Chicago a few days later with the snakes in bags, blood was still oozing down our arms.

It was the designation of a subspecies among snakes that opened the door to one of the early demonstrations of evolution in action. The island *Natrix* populations had been described as a subspecies because the adult snakes tended to have less prominent banding than adults from other populations. Joe had noted in an earlier (1954) paper that juvenile water snakes on the islands were more likely to be prominently banded than the adults, suggesting that less-banded juveniles might have a survival-enhancing camouflage on uniformly colored island shores and thus be more likely to survive into adulthood. In contrast, more prominently banded individuals might be favored in the well-vegetated swamps that housed most *Natrix* populations. The banding made them less conspicuous among the stems of the plants.

I had been following the evolutionary literature closely and was well aware of the attention being paid to H. B. D. Kettlewell's work in the 1950s on what was known as industrial melanism, then widely recognized as an example of natural selection operating in nature. In brief, a dark (melanic) form of the peppered moth, *Biston betularia*, had taken over populations in Britain's industrial Midlands as tree trunks there became covered in soot. Kettlewell's pictures showing the prominence of normal (nonmelanic) peppered moths sitting on industrially blackened trees and, by contrast, melanic moths visually very obvious seated on lichen-covered tree trunks in unpolluted areas were the opening slides of many lectures on evolution—regardless of detailed topic. A Kettlewell movie of birds eating nonmelanic peppered moths on sooty trunks and missing the melanic ones there, and vice versa on lichen-covered trunks, started circulating; I later used it for years in the evolution course I taught.

So when Joe and I isolated pregnant female snakes in the lab and they produced litters of young that were almost all heavily banded, it dawned on me we might have another visually powerful story of natural selection in the field. We decided to try to see if we could show that the relative lack of banding actually did serve as camouflage in shoreline conditions. Joe was a friend of Marlin Perkins, then famous as host of a television show called *Zoo Parade* and the director of the Lincoln Park Zoo, right next to our small institute. We asked Marlin if he could lend us a cage and a captive seagull; always helpful, he was glad to. We thought that seagulls were probably a main predator on baby island water snakes. Our plan was simple and, by today's standards, I think unethical. We would make two fake limestone rocks with plaster and paint, put both more and less prominently banded young snakes on them, release a hungry seagull, and see which it discovered and ate. All done, with a mix of live young snakes Scotch-taped harmlessly to fake gray stones, we released our hungry seagull, nicknamed Herman. The seagull marched quickly to the targets, stepped on a "camouflaged" snake and grabbed an "obvious" banded one. Perfect result. Unhappily, the next test went in a different direction, and in the end Herman outsmarted us at every turn. The only conclusion we could safely draw from our experiment was that seagulls (or at least *our* seagull) liked to eat young water snakes.

Getting a good water snake–evolution paper put together involved doing some tricky statistics, but we were successful, and our basic *Natrix* story, that selection was maintaining the island population less banded, was published, without Herman's contribution, in *Evolution*.[15] Follow-up studies by others have suggested the story is likely more complex than we had it, but our version was basically correct. Along the way a big lesson was taught to me in scientific politics.

Joe, a top expert in the taxonomy of mites and with a strong interest in medical issues, had the essence of the banding natural selection story in his 1954 paper I referred to above. But he was handicapped by being unfamiliar with much of the evolutionary literature, by having published his paper in an impossibly obscure journal (*Natural History Miscellanea* of the Chicago Academy of Sciences), and by not making the key points prominent in either the title or the body of his paper.[16] The basic lesson, which I have ritually passed on to my graduate students, is that proper packaging of results and place of publication are essential to a good scientific career. When graduate students came to me and suggested dissertation projects, I would ask, "If this works out well, what's the title of the paper you'll submit to *Science* describing your major results?" (*Science* and *Nature* are generally considered the top journals in which to publish papers you think are important). A subsidiary to that lesson is an easy one for good scientists: read as much and as widely in the literature as possible.

A second lesson I learned with Joe is how brilliant snake mites (*Ophionyssus natricis*) were. The little bastards, key to the original research we had planned on disease vectors, thwarted me again and again. Trying to find a way to rear them in vitro ("in glass," that is, in lab culture rather than on the snakes) was extremely difficult. It was easy to get heparinized blood (blood treated with a thinner so it wouldn't clot) to feed them but impossible to get them to feed and survive. We tried dozens of kinds of membranes—mites on one side, anticoagulated blood on the other. We even tried descaled butterfly wings. The problem was that the mites normally jam themselves under a snakeskin scale to feed, and this contact on their backs stimulates the feeding behavior. Unhappily, anything we put on the membrane for the mite to crawl under caused the membrane to bleed through, drowning the mite. Designing the system was my chore. I failed.

Another task for me as a postdoc was to determine the patterns of egg-laying over time among the female mites. I designed an ingenious apparatus, so ingenious that Joe and I signed up to show it at a scientific meeting. Female mites were glued by their backs to stubs poised above a sticky tape moving at a fixed speed. The eggs would drop to the tape while I slept, drank, worked on butterfly morphology, or whatever. When I returned after having a female on the apparatus overnight, I found that the female had laid a bunch of eggs. None were on the tape; all were stuck on the female's legs. Failure again: the demonstration, already listed on the scientific program, was as a result given "by title only."

Next was the problem of determining what temperature the mites preferred. I got a long glass tube with several right-angle branches plugged with rubber stoppers. They were for introducing the mites into the apparatus, with one end on an electric heater and the other in an ice bath. An electric thermometer would measure the temperature at which the mites settled. Alas, they settled in the right-angle tubes, pressing their bodies into the gap between stopper and glass, a snake-scale sort of situation. Outwitted again. Then I came up with a truly inventive solution. I had a yard-diameter steel disk with a raised moat welded to its outside rim put on legs. Then I put an electric heater under the center and filled the moat with ice and water. In that setup, mites put on the plate would be only constrained by too hot and too cold. The little demons could settle down wherever they felt most comfortable. Guess what? They moved around until they either fried or froze. Joe should have fired me—he got a raw deal when he took me on as a postdoc.

In my work in Joe Camin's lab, a third lesson I learned—more than once—had to do with human behavior. Its subject was habituation (diminishing response to a repeated stimulus), in this case to danger, specifically to working around poisonous snakes and the carelessness that can result. Joe's lab contained a snake menagerie as livestock for snake mite experiments. One day, despite numerous warnings, I found our nice young lab assistant sticking a fresh water bowl in the cage of a cottonmouth, with the fast-striking and potentially fatal snake (*Agkistrodon piscivorus*) coiled inches from her hand. Joe's solution in this instance was to buy some little cheap key locks for all cages with venomous critters to serve as a reminder.

A sad and dramatic example of the potential perils of habituation also occurred while I was in Joe's lab. We received an urgent call in September 1957 from Chicago's Field Museum of Natural History asking for help. The famous herpetologist Karl Schmidt had been bitten by a juvenile boomslang (*Dispholidus typus*), a rear-fanged African tree snake. Museum herpetologist Robert Inger had handed the snake to Schmidt. Inger and Schmidt had each handled thousands of poisonous snakes, but this time carelessness intervened and Schmidt was bitten on the skin between two fingers. Schmidt wanted to determine how much distress would be caused by the young snake's bite and began to take notes on his reaction. He refused medical help because he didn't want to spoil his experiment. The call came in when Schmidt suddenly went downhill: the museum was seeking information from us on the characteristics of the venom. A quick literature search turned up nothing then—only later was it learned that boomslang venom is very potent but slow acting—and almost immediately the museum called back and told us that Schmidt had died. Habituation is an important human reaction that helps us to interact successfully with the world, but in many situations it can have both personal and societal nasty consequences. Habituation to respiratory diseases like common colds and flus, for example, seems to have contributed in the spring and summer of 2021 to an often blasé attitude to being vaccinated against the dangers of the SARS-CoV-2 virus. This put many people unnecessarily in danger of sickness and death.

While I was a postdoc with Joe Camin, Anne and I were flat broke, first at the Chicago Academy of Sciences and then, starting in 1958, back at Kansas, when Joe joined the faculty there as a full professor. So it wasn't just my infatuation with Lepidoptera that led me to write and Anne to illustrate our first book, *How to Know the Butterflies* (1961)—it was very tight budgets. Both of us had made the major mistake of not acquiring a rich spouse, and we looked to the possibility of royalties to keep daughter Lisa fed. Since there was no scientifically modern, inexpensive guide to North American butterflies, and since Anne was a talented artist, we decided to give creating one a try. Anne met the challenge by doing beautiful pen-and-ink drawings

HOW TO KNOW THE BUTTERFLIES

of Fig. 18, most of the major systems can be recognized. The silvery tracheae (respiratory tubes) can be readily located at the spiracles and traced. The delicate loop of the heart through the longitudinal wing muscles can be seen by carefully picking away the overlying muscle fibers.

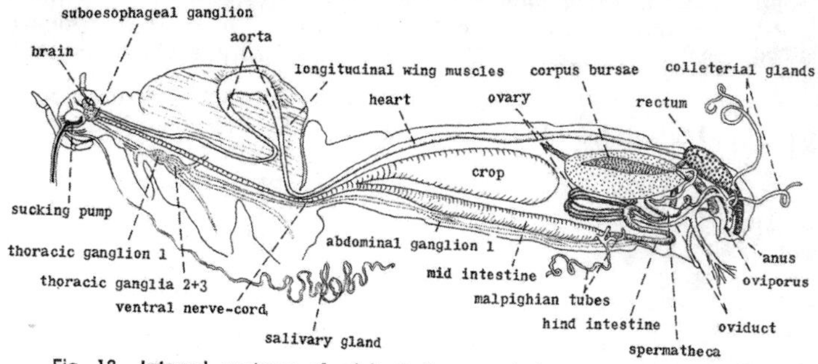

Fig. 18. Internal anatomy of adult ♀ *Danaus plexippus*, tracheae, most of malpighian tubes, and left ovary removed (modified from Scudder).

In general, dissections should be done under a binocular dissecting microscope. Use a shallow dish with a paraffin bottom. Various parts can then be held out of the way with insect pins.

The comparative visceral morphology of the butterflies is largely *terra incognita*—new discoveries await you at every turn.

STUDYING BUTTERFLIES SCIENTIFICALLY

Collectors often ask "can I make scientific contributions by studying butterflies?" The answer is emphatically "yes." The relatively untrained worker can contribute in many ways:

COLLECTING. He can collect long series of carefully labelled specimens and make them available to scientists through loans and by depositing duplicates in major museums. Material properly preserved in fluid is especially valuable.

REARING. He can add to our knowledge of butterfly life cycles and genetics. Whenever a species is raised, specimens of the eggs, all larval stages, and pupae should be carefully preserved. If the parents are known, they should be clearly cross-labelled with the offspring. Any parasites attacking the butterfly should also be saved (mount flies and larger wasps on insect pins, place smaller wasps in 80% alcohol). Through the Lepidopterists' Society you can learn where to send these parasites to have them identified. If you are not sure of the identity of the larval food plant, be sure to press some specimens (leaves, flowers and fruits if possible—if too large, take notes on size, bark color and consistency, etc.) so that they can be identi-

22

How to Know the Butterflies (1961) was unique among butterfly guides in illustrating aspects of the morphology with which Anne worked extensively, doing dissections and illustrating the findings for our peer-reviewed taxonomic papers. Author photo.

HOW TO KNOW THE BUTTERFLIES

1b VHW with postmedian series of spots or postmedian band prominently colored some shade of red or orange-brown, or at least a dot of red or orange-brown in each spot........................2

2a D with a wide, prominent orange-brown postmedian band, median spot band white or pale yellowish and marginal and submarginal bands reduced in size (almost obsolete on HW of some specimens). Fig. 238............................*Euphydryas gillettii* Barnes.

Range: Yellowstone National Park area north through Montana to Glacier National Park. Food plant: unknown. One brood (vii-viii).

Fig. 238. *Euphydryas gillettii* ♂ D. Soldier County, Montana.

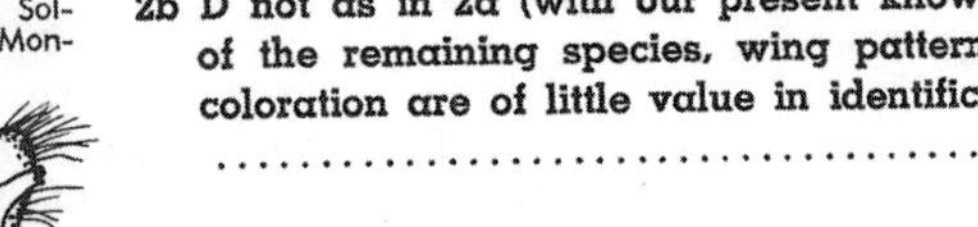

2b D not as in 2a (with our present knowledge of the remaining species, wing pattern and coloration are of little value in identification) 3

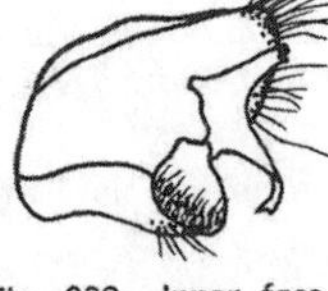

Fig. 239. Inner face of valva of *Euphydryas editha*.

3a Male genitalia: clasp of valva with two prongs directed at a wide angle (more than 90°) from each other; upper prong heavily armed with tiny spines (Fig 239); food plants predominantly Plantaginaceae. Fig. 240...........................*Euphydryas editha* Boisduval.

Range: Baja California to British Columbia and Montana; not found in Arizona, New Mexico or Colorado. Food plants: Plantaginaceae. One brood, ii-viii, depending on locality.

Fig. 240. *Euphydryas editha* ♂ V. Lake Hodges, California.

3b Male genitalia: clasp of valva with two prongs at right angles to each other, or upper prong curved downward and often running roughly parallel to lower prong; food plants predominantly Scrophulariaceae....4

128

Page 128 from *How to Know the Butterflies*, showing the unique use of keys and morphology to identify different species, and, above all, Anne's fine pen-and-ink drawing, one in this case being of *Euphydryas editha*, a major target of my lifetime research. Author photo.

HOW TO KNOW THE BUTTERFLIES

2a VHW with two large submarginal eye spots, each as broad or broader than the cell in which it is centered. Fig. 297. . . . . *Vanessa virginiensis* Drury. The Painted Beauty.

Range: transcontinental in southern Canada and the United States, south to Central America. Food plants: *Gnaphalium* (cudweed), *Antennaria* (everlasting), *Artemisia* (sage) and other composites.

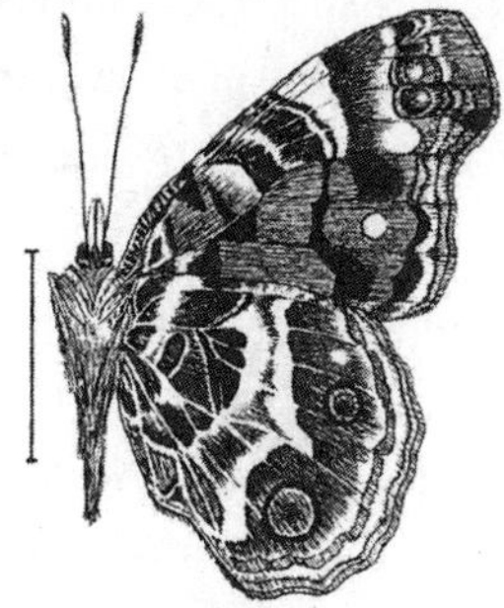

Fig. 297. *Vanessa virginiensis* ♂ V. Lawrence, Kansas.

2b VHW with 3 or 4 submarginal eye spots, none as broad as the cell in which it lies. 3

3a DFW with subapical bar white. Fig. 298. . . . . *Vanessa cardui* Linnaeus. Cosmopolite, Painted Lady, Thistle Butterfly.

Range: cosmopolitan in our area except for the arctic. This is the most widespread of butterflies, found in virtually every corner of the world except the arctic, antarctic, parts of South America and most of southeast Asia and the East Indies. In Australia and New Zealand it is replaced by a closely related species, *Vanessa kershawi* McCoy. Food plants: numerous composites, rarely other plants (Malvaceae). This species often migrates.

Fig. 298. *Vanessa cardui* ♀ V. Richfield, Kansas.

More of Anne's butterfly drawings for *How to Know the Butterflies*. Depicted here: the most widespread butterfly in the world, *Vanessa cardui*, the painted lady or cosmopolite. The scale lines drawn next to each specimen represent one-half inch. Author photo.

for the book; most of the credit for its success was hers. But I think it remains the only field guide to butterflies that includes keys (systematic steps) to aid in identifying specimens and some detail on their anatomy and evolution.

Publication royalties eventually eased our financial plight a little, Lisa did not starve, and the effort encouraged us to develop other book-writing projects.

The book also led to one of the most pleasing and memorable incidents in my career, because to write the keys I had to learn the most prominent identifying marks of all North American (north of Mexico) butterflies. Noel McFarland, then a young undergraduate moth specialist at KU, brought me a beautiful specimen of a hairstreak butterfly from the Sandia Mountains of New Mexico. Although I was just then writing the keys, I couldn't even determine the genus to which the specimen belonged! In a quick field trip to the Sandia Mountains with some butterfly-collector friends, we were able to find a population by following Noel's directions. By pure luck I was also able to work out the butterfly's entire life history. It was a good example of the phenomenon often termed "search image," referring to the ease of seeing a certain object one is looking for after the first example is perceived. In line with the relationships I had guessed about the butterfly, I had assumed that its caterpillars would feed on a coniferous tree, just as many of its relatives do. All at once while I was stalking an adult hairstreak sipping nectar from the commonest flowering plant in the area, I realized that there was a camouflaged sluglike lycaenid caterpillar on the plant—and once I'd seen one, I realized there were dozens there. The butterfly's caterpillars were feeding on the flowering stalks of a yuccalike plant called beargrass (*Nolina microcarpa*).[17] With the collaboration of the hairstreak specialist and cofounder of the Lepidopterists' Society, Harry Clench at the Carnegie Museum in Pittsburgh, I named it *Sandia mcfarlandi*. It was the most distinctive new butterfly species found in North America in the twentieth century—deserving of a new generic or subgeneric name (depending on your taxonomic taste!). Discovering a previously unrecognized butterfly of such distinctness was a great thrill for a butterfly collector like me, and I've learned that in 2004 it became the official state butterfly of New Mexico (Sandia hairstreak). That was a suitable honor for Noel, who recently died after a fine life and career illuminating moth life histories and food-plant choices in Australia and the American Southwest.

In the first years we spent in Lawrence, the restaurants and public swimming pool were segregated, as they were in so many places in the United States in the 1950s. Racism pervaded the attitudes of many at the university, including the chair of the zoology department, E. Raymond Hall, whom you met above. Hall wrote a nonsensical tract claiming that the five subspecies of human beings he imagined existed were so different from one another that they should not be permitted to live together.[18] My liberal parents were vigilant in wiping out whatever racist views I picked up as a young child in what I later came to recognize as a deeply racist country. I knew that if I used a common swear word in front of, for example, my grandmother, I'd get a lecture on how there was nothing intrinsically wrong with the word, but it would be offensive to some people and I should be careful when and where I used it. If I used a racial slur for a person of color, I knew I would get the verbal equivalent of having my mouth washed out with soap. Furthermore, recent research I had read, including the Wilson and Brown paper on "The Subspecies Concept and Its Taxonomic Application," had convinced me that racial classification of people was ridiculous scientifically (classifying by different characteristics produced different "races" simply as an artifact of the choice of characteristics) as well as evil socially. Once I had taken a date to Topeka, the nearby capital of Kansas, and we had supper in a diner. Hung by the cash register was a prominent sign, "Negroes and Mexicans Served in Bags Only." I asked my date what would happen if I went up and asked for "two Negroes and three Mexicans in a bag." She said I'd probably end up dead. In some circumstances I did learn to keep my mouth shut.

My abhorrence at racism shifted to action in the mid-1950s when a distinguished Jamaican visitor from the World Health Organization arrived enraged one Monday morning in the parasitology lab of my friend Ralph Barr, with whom I studied the distribution of mosquitoes for the U.S. Air Force in

Alaska the summer of 1956. The visitor had arrived Friday afternoon and been admitted to the local hotel, but no restaurant would serve him. No one told him that the student union on campus was not segregated, so he fed himself for the weekend with candy bars from vending machines. In protest of the restaurants' discriminatory practices, Ralph and I organized mixed groups of African American and white students to patronize Lawrence restaurants at lunchtime. We would not get served, but other patrons wouldn't either. We called them "profitless lunch days."

About that time the movie theaters in Lawrence had been desegregated. The university in 1955 had recruited Wilt "the Stilt" Chamberlain to play basketball for it beginning in 1956. Wilt was a giant (seven foot one)—I first met him in a bar, and he is the only person, when he rose off the bar stool, who ever made me feel like a dwarf. The university had found his father a job, but Wilt's other requirement was that he not have to sit in the balcony of the segregated movie theaters. Frank Murphy, the KU chancellor, called a meeting of Lawrence's theater proprietors and asked them to desegregate. One of the theater owners was the reputedly racist Phog Allen, *the basketball coach!* Despite his prejudice, Phog was dying to have Wilt play for him. Nonetheless, he and the others all refused to desegregate. They'd lose all their white customers, they claimed. Murphy then responded, "To get Wilt, I guess I'll just have to show first-run movies free on campus every Friday and Saturday night." Instant desegregation.

We regularly visited restaurant owners before a sit-in and asked them to desegregate. One of our lines was, "What would you do if Wilt [by then a local hero] came in?" The standard response was, "Oh my God, I don't know what I would do. That would be terrible." I'll always remember one restaurant owner with at least the virtue of consistency who simply said he'd throw him out (adding a racial slur). But eventually, after death threats against our mixed-race group but no actual violence, the restaurants followed the theaters and agreed to serve nonwhites.[19] There is no question that Wilt deserves part of the credit. The episode solidified my interest in social justice, which continues to be a motivating force in my life today.

Graduate school in Kansas together with my postdoc experience with Joe was a major turning point in my life. I saw natural selection in both the lab and the field. I took great joy in adding Anne to my life and gained a daughter, enjoyed the mentorship of three outstanding scientists at a time when two of them were destroying a paradigm and starting to develop a new one, got to know more thoroughly the trials of experimental research, and saw the face of American racism up close. Another momentous turn in my professional life lay immediately ahead.

FIVE

Joining the Only Junior University

Besides being such fun to observe, butterflies—with a little help from Joe Camin and our paper on water snakes,[1] my work on numerical taxonomy, and as I discovered later, strong support from Charles Michener and Robert Sokal—got me an invitation in the fall of 1958 to interview in the Department of Biological Sciences at Stanford University. The interview was for a faculty position replacing entomologist Gordon Floyd Ferris, a specialist in lice and scale insects. After an initial setback, luck would soon intervene in a curious way.

Joe came back from the Entomological Society of America meeting that fall with the bad news for me that Bill Brown was being hired to replace Ferris. I was tempted then to beg off on the upcoming interview, but I'd never been to California and had always wanted to visit the entomology department at Berkeley, where I knew two leading entomologists. So in January 1959 I flew out to San Francisco, where I was met at the airport by Victor Twitty, a distinguished embryologist who was then chair of Stanford's Department of Biological Sciences. He took me, late in the evening, to a dormitory apartment reserved for visitors. Unhappily, it was already occupied by a visiting priest who, to Victor's great embarrassment, offered to share the bed with me. Vic got me a hotel room.

The next day I gave my seminar, which had two parts, one on the higher classification of the butterflies and one on natural selection in water snakes. I explained that I wasn't going to be a taxonomist. I was going to undertake some theoretical investigations in taxonomy, but I was interested in using insects as a tool for looking at evolution and ecology, and I wanted to use field studies (in nature, not the lab) to answer questions I considered important. They included the causes of changes in population size and the relationship of those changes to genetic variability and natural selection. I wasn't interested in continuing the work Ferris had been doing in developing the taxonomy of scale insects and lice, I said. I was perfectly relaxed and frank about it, because I knew Bill Brown had been given the job. When I knocked over a box of butterfly specimens during the talk, I took it in stride. When Arthur Giese, a world expert on electrophysiology and a gracious host, offered me a tray of martinis at the postseminar gathering I took two, saying I needed them (I later learned this had quite shocked the very nice Professor Giese).

The next day I was taken to lunch at Rossotti's outdoor hamburger joint (now Rossotti's Alpine Inn) in Portola Valley. It was January, yet acorn woodpeckers were flying about and ground squirrels frolicking in seventy-plus-degree temperature. Having left dismal Kansas in a hideous blizzard, it looked like paradise to me. After lunch I was shuttled from faculty member to faculty member for interviews. They all seemed very old (most were in their fifties). Finally I got to Charles Yanofsky, then an associate professor and just seven years older than me, a war veteran who had been badly frost-bitten fourteen years previously in the Battle of the Bulge, and a recent hire (1958). He was the first one who seemed like a possible sympathizer. We chatted for a few minutes, and then I decided to stop the farce. Look, I said in effect, I know the job has been given to Bill Brown at Harvard, so why don't I stop wasting your time and I'll go up to Berkeley to meet some friends?

Charley reassured me that no one had yet been appointed; there were still more applicants to give seminars, and the faculty would then meet to discuss them and come to a decision. I could hardly believe this good news. At that moment the phone rang. When Charley hung up he said Professor Twitty would like to see me in his office.

When I got to Victor's office, he didn't waste time—he just offered me the job. I was flabbergasted, but considering the alternatives—a "chicken-plucking" (poultry science) job at Clemson, a position at a military-oriented school in the Deep South, or a job as a butterfly taxonomist at the Smithsonian—I almost asked Twitty how much I'd have to pay Stanford. It turned out they weren't going to hire somebody with strictly taxonomic interests, so my frankness had worked well. Charley and I became good friends, ruined our knees playing handball together, and frequently laughed remembering as two young punks how we'd both been totally deluded about Stanford's hiring procedures in 1959. So that's how I became a faculty member at Leland Stanford Junior University, named after Senator Leland Stanford's son, who died tragically young.

I later found out that E. O. Wilson had been offered the job before me but had, to my eternal gratitude, turned it down to stay at Harvard. Ed did very well indeed, and we became friends and comrades in the battles to save biodiversity, but that did not stop me from kidding him about the sometimes stultifying intellectual environment of that school in Massachusetts, and I always felt a little sorry for him wading through the slush while I lived where I could walk to work in decent weather almost every day. Before climate disruption, droughts, and fire started taking hold, Palo Alto truly was the land of milk and honey.

My 1932 luck persisted, and its next manifestation was dramatic. Although I had been hired at Stanford, I was still completing my postdoc at KU, so I didn't plan to leave for California until late summer. One day I received a phone call from David Keck, a leading plant ecologist whom I knew slightly, congratulating me on the Stanford job. Dave had done classic work on the ecology and genetics of *Achillea lanulosa* (yarrow), while based at the Carnegie Institution on the Stanford campus. Along with Jens Clausen and Bill Hiesey, he had shown, by transplant experiments, how the yarrow evolved local forms genetically and phenotypically to adapt to altitudes ranging from those of the High Sierra to that of sea level. Some seventy-five years later these and related studies remain among the most cited work in plant evolutionary ecology.

Dave said he was in Washington, D.C., at the National Science Foundation (NSF) and had just started a systematics (taxonomy) program. He would be coming through Lawrence the following week and offered to come by to help me write my first grant proposal. When he stopped by the next week, together we prepared a proposal to explore some key issues in numerical taxonomy, which I then submitted to Dave. Curiously enough, he gave me every nickel I asked for. I am cruel enough to tell this story to junior scientist colleagues today, who often must close down their labs for months to prepare detailed NSF proposals that have a 10 percent chance of being funded at all and, when successful, almost always entail less money than is really needed. Dave (and the NSF in those days) was forward-looking, and my being a Young Turk gave me a definite advantage. But a decade or so later Robert MacArthur, a great pioneer of theoretical ecology, and I spent a long evening discussing the extent to which, overall, the NSF was a good thing for science. It did steer much of science in a direction bureaucrats wanted, but that wasn't always the best way to address societal aims or promote the advance of scientific knowledge. To a degree, though, the NSF somewhat balanced the flood of money going into medically oriented science to cure disease (while funds for often-more-important *prevention* were and remain relatively scarce) by encouraging a wide range of pure science that made the world more understandable (and prevention easier). We concluded that there were no obviously easy ways to support science in a culture built around money.

Leaving boiling Kansas late that summer of 1959 for the paradise of Palo Alto was, after marrying Anne, the luckiest move of my life. Besides the splendid physical climate, California's intellectual climate was extremely stimulating. At Stanford butterflies also introduced me early to two people, neither of them biologists, who became wonderful friends. John Montgomery, who was an attorney, and his young court-reporter wife, Nancy, nursing her second child, showed up in my office one day in late 1959. A member of the Lepidopterists' Society and a demon butterfly collector, John had heard that a butterfly specialist had joined the Stanford faculty. Rarely has a strong and lasting friendship formed so fast. Tragically, John, concerned about a heart problem, took his own life in 1974 on his fortieth birthday. Anne and I have remained close to Nancy and their daughter, Jen, who became a county supervisor and then headed California governor Gavin Newsom's Forest Management Task Force.

Besides John and Nancy, at Stanford I started working with botanical evolutionist Richard (Dick) Holm, then an associate professor, who shared my religious convictions (none) and my concerns about the nature of science (deep). Dick became one of our closest friends from our arrival in 1959 to his death in 1987. In addition to having the office next to mine, he was a frequent guest at our house, became our housemate later on working trips to Hawaii, and joined us for some wonderful travels. Besides coauthoring *The Process of Evolution* (mentioned in chapter 2), Dick and I started editing for its publisher, McGraw Hill, in the early 1970s. For them we also created Biocore, an innovative set of paperbacks covering basic biology at the college level. Phil Hanawalt, a longtime Stanford colleague who wrote the Biocore unit *Cell Growth and Proliferation*, and I recently were reminiscing about the McGraw Hill editor Jim Young who supported and promoted this pioneering effort—the first Black professional with whom either of us had worked.

My experiences with the birth of numerical taxonomy and discovery of a distinct new butterfly had led me to consider questions still debated among philosophers and scientists—the most basic of which was: Are scientists uncovering an objective natural reality, or is "reality" a mental construction generated by human nervous systems and cultures interacting with a biophysical entity, albeit built out of our careful observations and experimental evidence drawn from that entity? Taxonomy, so directly concerned with detecting patterns and constructing categories, was an ideal area of science for stimulating one to examine such still mind-boggling questions about the nature of the world and our perceptions of it. Dick happily shared my interest in how we know what we know and how sure we can be about it—epistemology—still to me a fascinating but frustratingly opaque area. Dick also joined me in a project pushed by the then-well-known anthropologist Ashley Montagu: a chapter for one of his books on race and racism. That chapter even today I think stands up well as a basic scientific explanation of the deep unreality of standard ideas about "racial" divisions of humanity.[2] We also learned about an interesting side of Ashley, who told us he lived by his wits. True enough, he invited Anne, Dick, and me to dinner and an evening in San Francisco and somehow was absent whenever a check appeared.

Dick and I, much influenced then by the operationalism (knowledge based on nature, not metaphysics, with scientific concepts defined in terms of operations used to determine them) of the American physicist and Nobel Prize winner Percy Bridgman, saw the move toward numerical taxonomy as a move toward a more "scientific" taxonomy. In a paper Dick and I published in 1962 in *Science* entitled "Patterns and Populations," we advocated for the creation of a unified discipline of population biology and stuck our scientific necks out by advocating a more operationalist approach to population biology.[3] We wanted the parts of the classic disciplines of zoology and botany (often represented in separate departments, as was entomology) that dealt with population issues—population dynamics, population genetics, evolution, ecology, much of behavior, and the like—combined to form a new discipline. How, for example, could one understand butterfly evolution without understanding how butterflies interacted with the plants on which they fed? Could scientists understand that interaction if they didn't consider how plant and butterfly populations changed in size relative to one another and how this influenced their genetics?

Our paper fit right in with the views of many of our younger colleagues, such as neurobiologist Donald Kennedy at Stanford. But it generated a lot of controversy and led Dick and me into a public confrontation with two distinguished Berkeley professors, botanist Ledyard Stebbins and zoologist Frank Pitelka, in front of some three hundred faculty and students. Ledyard and Frank both later became friends of mine, even though at the time, I must objectively admit, we effectively demolished their arguments.[4] The paper was our first attack on the classical structure of university departments that was slowing scientific advance in critical areas. Ledyard and Frank were both solidly established within departments whose structure contained the elements most useful for their support and advancement. We mostly converted them, among other biologists, to our views—many universities began to reorganize away from the compartmentalized approach of zoology, entomology, or botany. But Stanford and most other colleges and universities have failed to alter that institutionwide departmental structure, which is a major reason for the relative inability of universities today to help civilization deal with existential threats. There are now more interdisciplinary programs, but sadly the problem lies fundamentally in the disciplines themselves, exemplified by conventional economics and political science departments that approach their subjects with little or no regard for underlying crucial environmental issues. Economics departments invariably fail to recognize, as Herman Daly put it, that "the economy is a wholly owned subsidiary of the environment, not the reverse."[5]

Dick, my fellow associate professor and friend Don Kennedy, and I (Don and I were promoted to that rank with tenure in 1962) oversaw a revision of our department's teaching program following Dick's and my *Science* paper and egged on by Charley Yanofsky, initiating a levels of organization approach. We divided the life sciences into molecular, cellular, organismal, and population biology. Largely, I think, because of the stunning advances in molecular biology, most major universities subsequently followed Stanford's lead. But today a total reorganization of higher education seems necessary if college-educated people are to have the basic knowledge needed to deal with the world of the mid-twenty-first century.

Moving to Stanford also introduced me to my third great love, wine. Shortly after I arrived on campus I was invited to a cocktail party at Victor Twitty's new house. Only faculty were invited (no spouses and at that time, sadly, all faculty were male). I drank four or five martinis, and then the whole gang went out to a wine-soaked dinner with engineering professor Frederick Terman, then the university's provost. Fred was the son of Lewis Terman, who had invented the Stanford-Binet IQ test, and Fred himself was a brilliant electrical engineer. In large part by persuading his students William Hewlett and David Packard to remain in the Bay Area rather than move their start-up to Boston, Fred became known as the "father of Silicon Valley." He developed Stanford's industrial park and worked hard to attract electronics scientists and firms to leave the East and migrate to the wonderful climate of the Bay Area. He was a major player in post–World War II discussions of the role of universities in society and increasing industry and government research support for universities—especially in the form of military contracts. At the dinner, Fred announced that two Stanford engineers had been elected to the National Academy of Engineering, and smashed as I was, I asked him what railroads they had driven for. Fortunately, Fred was pretty far gone himself and didn't take offense. After dinner more martinis were offered. I don't recall how I got home, but I do recall waking Anne by falling off the toilet. That night convinced me to shift from cocktails to wine.

The shift to wine enthusiast was accelerated several years later when a friend interested in ethnic art took Anne and me to a wine crushing at the home of winemaker George Burtness and his schoolteacher wife, Yvonne. We hit it off immediately with our hosts and were soon blind-sampling wine at each other's homes every week or so—and have remained friends and winos for over half a century now. We got in the habit of concealing the labels on bottles by pulling old socks over them—a great way of solving the odd sock dilemma. One night George and I fooled each other by each bringing a hidden bottle of Egri Bikavér. It was a Hungarian wine of little distinction; the two bottles (same vintage) were quite different—typical of the communist years—and we were both fooled.

We once hosted David Perlman, the prominent environmental reporter for the *San Francisco Chronicle*, and his wife, Anne, for one of our Burtness-Ehrlich wine dinners. Anne Perlman gained eternal fame in our group by downing a series of predinner martinis and then correctly calling all the wines. Dave told columnist Art Hoppe about the socks, and we made his column: "A naïve domestic argyle, but we were amazed at its presumption."

In the early days our ability to indulge in decent wines was severely limited. Our move to the relatively expensive Bay Area had brought further financial stress to Anne and me. I was egotistical and naive enough to assume that after I had been there a year with a low salary, the university's administrators would see what I could do, and they would give me a bigger salary. I didn't want us to be rich, I just wanted enough for us to be able to live decently. When I complained about my poor salary, Vic Twitty quipped that I had gone into the wrong field. Stanford would likely never pay me a decent wage, he said; I must find, like many others on the faculty, a way to supplement my income.

The inadequate salary led us further into the book-writing business, which eventually became a lifelong habit. Butterflies started it, with the publication of *How to Know the Butterflies* that Anne illustrated and I wrote, but the first real moneymaker was different. It originated in a roundabout way. One day, a year or two after I arrived at Stanford, a psychologist named Allen Calvin, who then ran a company known as Behavioral Research Laboratories, asked Don Kennedy if he'd like to write a "programmed" high school biology text (a book that presented material in small steps designed for self-instruction). Don declined but suggested that Allen talk to me. I then consulted Dick Holm, and together we met with Allen, who offered us an attractive deal. We would dictate a given amount of the book each week, and he would have it transcribed and edit it. For this work he would pay us \$100 a week. For someone strapped for money and making \$6,000 a year, it was a great deal for what took me roughly two hours a week dictating and a few minutes each week meeting with Allen.

Dick and I had some wonderful experiences working on the book with Allen. One day, Allen told us the vocabulary we were including was likely too hard for many high school students. His example was the word "parallel." We said he was crazy, everybody knows what the word means. Allen invited his assistant to come in and asked what she understood the word "parallel" to mean. With appropriate gestures, his assistant said it meant going up and down. Allen thus taught me an important lesson in communicating with the general public. More enlightening was the moment when the transcriber returned to me some dictation in which I had developed a great principle of biology: "Most frogs are not turtles." True enough, as I had seen from many examples, but what I had dictated was, "Most frogs are nocturnal." We eventually finished the several-volume book, with substantial help from an old KU friend, physiologist Ken Armitage. The multivolume book was ahead of its time and never went anywhere—but I learned a lot writing it, and the money really helped.

Over time I've often described *Homo sapiens* as a "small-group animal" struggling to live in groups of millions or even billions. Maybe that's because I'm the personification of that in my professional and private life, always most comfortable with a gang of people close enough to me that I can say whatever I'm thinking without giving offense. My three botanist colleagues at Stanford—Dick Holm, John Thomas, and Peter Raven—were such a "gang." They not only broadened my taxonomic horizons but also provided a great social payoff by becoming close friends. My botanist buddies had knowledge in vast areas of which I was ignorant and shared all of my prejudices. In the early 1960s, the four of us, along with Benjamin Dane, an animal behaviorist who did classic work on the sex life of goldeneye ducks and mountain goats, had formed a Saturday lunch group where we discussed everything from evolution to the Vietnam War.

In 1966 we shifted restaurants because our bills were getting too high—creeping upward of $2.00. The new locale, the London House, was a family favorite for years and we became good friends with the proprietress, Sheila Shadwell, and her daughters. Sheila loaned Anne and me her apartment in London once.

Ben dropped out in 1966 after he failed to get tenure—a loss for Stanford—and moved to Tufts University, where he became a scientific leader and eventually department chair of biology. Peter stayed in the lunch group until 1971, when he moved on to become director (and later president and director) of the Missouri Botanical Garden.[6] Dick, John Thomas, and I kept the Saturday lunches going until Dick died in 1987 after a long battle with alcoholism. John Thomas and I carried on our Saturday lunches after Dick's death, joined by our wives, until John succumbed to Alzheimer's disease about ten years later.[7]

Not long after I started at Stanford I was able to recruit some remarkable graduate students to study with me, some of whom became lifelong friends and colleagues. In the beginning, however, I still had to address the needs of PhD candidates who had been students of my predecessor, Gordon Floyd Ferris, and who had taxonomic doctoral dissertations to complete. The best of them was a bright, friendly young Jesuit priest named Thomas Acker. I had announced that any of Ferris's students who finished promptly (I think within two years) I would judge on what I perceived to be Ferris's standards (I had different ideas on what I wanted my new students to study—more evolution and ecology than taxonomy). Tom promptly completed a competent dissertation.

Tom and I have stayed in touch for more than half a century; he became president of a couple of Jesuit universities and was a friend of the powerful late West Virginia Senator Robert Byrd. At one university, he founded a Zero Population Growth (ZPG) chapter, and he still soldiers on in his nineties, running a school and a congregation and generally doing good in the world. We share admiration for Pope Francis.

My experiences with graduate students when I first got to Stanford were an eye-opener. I had thought I was moving into the big time, but training had been much more rigorous at Kansas. Early in my Stanford career I was asked to sit in on the final oral exam of a student whose dissertation was in plant ecology; he had studied the positions of lodgepole pines on a slope, and his conclusion was that they were randomly distributed.

When it came time for me to question him, I asked how he knew the trees were randomly distributed, expecting to hear a standard sort of answer, one centered around their positions fitting a Poisson distribution (subject to statistical test). His reply: "I just looked at them." I happened to have a pocketful of change, so I strewed it out on the table and asked, "Are those randomly distributed?" "I dunno," was the response.

At that point, I switched to exploring whether the candidate had the necessary basic knowledge in his (rarely "her" in those days) chosen specialty. I asked if he knew of experiments that demonstrated that plants of a species that grew up the slopes of the Sierras and were shorter at higher altitudes were partially genetically dwarfed. He did not. The experiments, certainly the most important and famous in plant ecology at the time, had been done by the team of Jens Clausen, Dave Keck (the NSF innovator mentioned above), and Bill Hiesey at the Carnegie Institution on campus.[8] Clausen and Hiesey were professors by courtesy in our department. So I asked the candidate if he knew who Jens Clausen was. No. "How about Dave Keck?" No. I didn't ask him if he knew who Bill Hiesey was, because Bill was on his committee and sitting right next to him. In the private discussion of the performance that followed, Bill, one of the nicest guys in the world, said, "He was a little short on fundamentals"—and voted against him. It was the only time in fifty-six years on the Stanford faculty that I saw a student flunk a final oral, although in the early days several others deserved to. Or rather, their major professors did—there's no point in letting a young researcher be unprepared for that ritual—preventing such disasters is what private mentoring, group meetings, and practice seminars are for.

My own first graduate students seeking PhDs, Michael Soulé and Harry Recher, who I met initially in 1959, were another matter entirely compared to some of those I first encountered. I couldn't have picked better or more different students. Michael, following up on his quip after Ernst Mayr's seminar, did pioneering work on such topics as the evolution of asymmetry in island lizards and mesopredator "release." The latter occurs if the population of a top predator like the coyote is decimated and leads to proliferation of their mesopredator prey, such as domestic cats, which in turn can lead to extinction of a population of one of *their* prey, such as a songbird.

Michael became famous as the father of the field of conservation biology, the study of the causes, consequences, and prevention of extinctions and the diminishing of biodiversity in general. Our daughter, Lisa, who had adored him since she was four years old, was briefly put out when he failed to wait for her to grow up and instead married an extremely bright, activist woman named Jan. Michael and Jan, a medical doctor, had two sons and adopted an initially deeply disturbed Cambodian orphan girl, a victim of the Vietnam War. In the late 1970s, Michael was so fed up with academia he gave up his tenure at University of California, San Diego, and he and Jan moved into the Zen Center of Los Angeles, of which he later became director. He continued to be active in conservation biology until his death. I always admired him for his deep concern about the state of the world and about our responsibilities in it and sympathized with his intellectual and ethical struggles concerning the world and his own life.

Harry, my other "first graduate student," was an entirely different story. He was always his own man, very smart, very productive, and very sure of himself, with no obvious intellectual or ethical struggles. With my encouragement, Charles Birch hired him as a faculty member at the University of Sydney in Australia. He soon had disagreements with Charles, left the university, and held a series of positions in which he became a major force in environmental research and activism in Australia. Neither Harry nor anyone he was communicating with ever had any doubt about where he stood on an issue. Fortunately, his wife, Judy, married to him almost as long as Anne has been married to me, is (as Anne is with me) often able to keep him under control. When we last lunched with Harry, in November 2019, he was as disgusted as ever by the ignorance of the many politicians and others who were, through their actions, turning the world, as Harry put it, "into an uninhabitable hot garbage dump."

Both Michael and Harry, as they approached their dotage, continued to do what they could to save the world as scientist-advocates. Michael lost a long battle with heart disease in early 2020; Harry soldiers on, but sadly Judy died after a long and brave battle with Parkinson's as I was editing this. I couldn't be more proud of both of them. Looking back on my own life, one of the luckiest things that ever happened to me was to spend more than a half century as a friend of these two extraordinary (and very different) colleagues—and a sequence of later graduate students of similar quality.

My original appointment at Stanford was not just as an assistant professor but also as curator of the entomological collections. As one might imagine, those specimen collections related to Ferris's expertise in the taxonomy of scale insects and lice, preserved on microscope slides, were in good shape. Scientists, I guess, are not supposed to have a sense of humor, although in my experience it's almost a defining characteristic of good ones. The louse collection led to one amusing incident soon after I became curator. A young woman taxonomist visiting to study the collection came to me and said she had discovered a new species of louse in the collection. "Can I borrow the specimen so I can describe and name it?" "Sure," I said, "if you promise to name it after me and say you did so in the publication because that was my condition for lending you the specimen, demonstrating I was a real louse." She thought the idea was hilarious and proceeded to prepare a manuscript. But the entomological journal to which she submitted the paper refused to publish it containing that statement!

If the louse collection was in reasonably good shape, that could not be said of Stanford's general insect collections, which had largely been eaten by dermestid (carpet) beetles—a classic pest in museum collections. Some potentially valuable specimens, especially a few from the Galápagos Islands, had been destroyed. At Stanford there was no tradition of, or funding for, maintaining collections. There was also little support for them in a department that was entering into the era of population and molecular biology, in an institution that was then trying to move into the front lines of global universities. In light of the sizable extant insect collections already in the Bay Area at the University of California, Berkeley, and the California Academy of Sciences, Dick Holm and I came to the conclusion that Stanford's collections should be given to the Cal Academy and the biological wing of Stanford's museum abandoned. Peter Raven, who joined us on the faculty in the early 1960s, agreed, and the remnants of the museum's insect collection were moved and my work as curator came to an end.

The director of the museum in those days was a gentle plant geographer named Ira Wiggins. His wife, Dorothy, was a strict teetotaler and expected Ira to be also, so he had to take his occasional drink on the sly. When Peter first arrived, Ira invited him and his wife, Sally, to dinner. Dick and I warned him that it would be a dry dinner, that all he would be served was iced water and mints, and that he and Sally should have a few stiff drinks before they went. Peter laughed and accused us of kidding him. The next morning Dick and I were drinking coffee at the table outside of Peter's office when Peter came in. He stalked past us and as he entered his office a small object arced through the air and landed in the middle of the round table—the same one at which Peter and I later developed the idea of coevolution. A mint.

On our first trip to Europe in the summer of 1960, Anne and I visited the British Museum, which then held the world's largest butterfly collection. I've always remembered the "keeper" of that collection bragging to me that for a couple hundred years the museum had been buying collections, "keeping the aberrations and throwing out the junk." It was a striking example of unscientific sampling procedures—one reason why museum collections are nearly useless for answering many evolutionary questions. For example, in the famous peppered moth case of industrial melanism, early in the be-sooting of the English countryside melanic moths were rare "aberrations." Later, it was the peppered individuals that became rare "aberrations." That meant that it was impossible to get accurate estimates of shifts in the frequencies of the two types from the British Museum's peppered moth collection.

Scientists are not always brilliant seekers of truth in their personal relationships either. By pure chance, an older fellow Stanford curator who didn't like the changes Dick, Peter, and I were advocating was in London at the same time we were. As Anne and I left the museum one day we ran into him on the street. We offered to buy him a drink, but he refused. Later we learned that he had written a letter to the provost claiming that we had been on a drunken binge in London (if only it had been true—we were practically penniless at the time). Fortunately, our colleague's personal reputation was such that the letter only helped a poor assistant professor gain credence with the administration!

Stanford has been nearly perfect for my career; in at least some small ways I was able to return the favor. I am especially proud of my involvement in the creation of Stanford's Human Biology Program. As interest in the environment and concerns about its degradation escalated in the late 1960s, Gordon Harrison, a friend who worked at the Ford Foundation, came to

Stanford to talk with psychiatrist David Hamburg and me about ways the foundation could help deal with environmental issues. I had known Gordon because of our mutual interest in mosquitoes, malaria, and military history. Ford, he said, was interested in putting substantial sums of money—millions of dollars—into research on environmental problems. I told him that the money was likely to be largely wasted. In those days, relatively few scientists had the broad outlook required to ask the right questions and to know how to seek the answers. What was most needed then instead was the rapid training of a new cadre of environmental scientists. Dave told him the same thing. Gordon wanted to know if we would be willing to start a new undergraduate curriculum at Stanford, and to that we gave an enthusiastic "yes." Dave, much more accomplished at university politics than I was, took over the negotiations, and Stanford's famous Human Biology Program was born. Its curriculum basically combined the physics, chemistry, and ecological context of *Homo sapiens* with its evolutionary history and behavior. It was one of the all-too-few major interdisciplinary programs in American universities at the time and among the very first with an environmental theme.

In the process of establishing such a comprehensive program, I learned some valuable lessons in academic politics. Dave and I had had trouble interesting other faculty in the initial development of the Human Biology Program, but we did manage to recruit some powerful friends, especially Don Kennedy, Joshua Lederberg (who had received the Nobel Prize for discovering sex in bacteria), and sociologist Sanford Dornbusch. Once the money appeared, however, interested people came out of the woodwork. One day, Don, Josh, Dave, Sandy and I, and probably a few others were meeting to discuss who should head Human Biology. None of us wanted to, and Josh suggested one of his colleagues "who seems at loose ends these days."

We asked him, a nice guy, to do it, and he agreed. Over the next year or so we found out why he had been at loose ends—despite other fine qualities, he was a champion of administrative incompetence. I learned then that if you want someone to do an important job, find a person who is already busy. The program survived and thrived, nonetheless, and I taught in it longer than I wanted to (almost a decade longer because Don took it over and leaned on me as a friend). Its major flaw was that we were never able to require calculus for its completion, but it became one of Stanford's top majors, and it broke with the tradition (still in place in most Stanford departments and in other major universities) that you could get a bachelor's degree but still not have a clue where humanity came from or, more important, where it was likely going.

Gordon Harrison was extra nice to me; with his support, Ford provided not just the founding funds for Stanford's Human Biology Program but also funds for me to start, in 1971, a graduate training program in population biology. That money funded our early work in tropical conservation biology and eventually, in 1984, morphed into start-up funding for the Center for Conservation Biology (CCB), the only such center the Department of Biological Sciences at Stanford had ever allowed to be formed. As its website stated, "The CCB conducts interdisciplinary research to build a sound basis for the conservation, management, and restoration of biodiversity and ecosystem services, to evaluate factors that are leading to declining environmental security and increasing inequity, and to find practical solutions to that predicament." Why did we feel a separate center was needed? The answer was twofold. One was to call attention to the many biological and policy issues that were then (and to a large degree still are) intertwined and neglected in universities. The other was to make easier, we hoped, what is academic scientists' most difficult chore—begging and groveling to get financial support for their work.

The Department of Biological Sciences when I joined it was almost totally devoid of female faculty. The sole exception was Isabella (Izzie) Abbott, a world expert on marine algae, who had a half-time slot in the department's Hopkins Marine Station down the coast in Monterey, where her husband, Donald Abbott, was a professor. With the appointments of Charley Yanofsky, Cliff Grobstein, Don Kennedy, Peter Raven, and me, all between 1959 and 1962, the pressure to appoint a woman increased—but not so much that anything substantial was done for some years. Finally, in the 1970s, the department attempted to hire Virginia Walbot, a fine maize geneticist who had been a Stanford undergraduate and gone on to get her PhD and teach at Washington University in Saint Louis. Our departmental chair at the time announced in a meeting of tenured faculty that he would make Ginny an offer, but he would tell her that she'd have to give up her work in a women's cell biology group if she wanted to get tenure. I moved that "the chair be instructed not to say one word to the candidate about her extra-curricular activities. She is an adult scientist well aware of what is required to get tenure." Don Kennedy seconded my motion, and the department voted it unanimously.

Ginny turned us down. I suspected that the chair had somehow passed on the forbidden message and she had (understandably) taken offense. In 1980 the department approached Ginny again and in 1981 succeeded in hiring her. A couple of decades later I happened to be sitting next to her at a faculty meeting, and the whole incident returned to my bored brain. When I asked Ginny if the chair had hinted at her women's group activities, she nearly fell out of her chair laughing. "Hinted at—he wrote me a page-and-a-half letter about it. I took it to the president of my university, and he said I probably had a basis for legal action but that pursuing it was unlikely to advance my career." In defense of the chair, I don't think he was against having a female faculty member but was concerned that he might be involved in denying tenure to our first female appointment. He needn't have worried: Ginny has had a great career. Our department has since hired a series of brilliant female scientists, and I'm proud to say my discipline of ecology may now globally be moving toward having more female leaders than male.

Lack of women faculty members was not the only inequity in Stanford's staff structure. There always was, and still is, a great shortage of faculty members of color. And even white males were hardly treated with equity. During the Vietnam "troubles" in the late 1960s, students broke into Encina Hall, Stanford's administrative center, and released information on faculty salaries. It turned out that there were people in the English department who had never even written a book but were paid more than people in biology. Salaries in biology at Stanford had always been very low.

Salary aside, of course, it was my privilege and pleasure to serve on the faculty of such an extraordinary department at one of the world's best universities. Sure, like any large institution Stanford was run in ways that conformed to the interests of the national elite power structure. It had—and has—many flaws and its own ration of idiots working for it. Stanford even briefly had one terrible president. He was a poor lost soul who, among other things, during the Vietnam War wanted to invite the rich and high-born to a vast pageant of an inaugural ceremony (for himself). In contrast, the other five presidents I served under were all smart, hard-working, dedicated men. There were no women, and the only woman high in the administration before my retirement was, sadly, Condoleezza Rice, who was provost in the 1990s and performed as one would have expected if we had known about her subsequent career as national security adviser and secretary of state under President George W. Bush. She missed the warning signs before the 9/11 attack and then promoted what many consider war crimes in helping the administration to launch an illegal and disastrous war as well as defending the torture of war prisoners.[9]

By 1959, when I joined the faculty, the days when Stanford, like many universities, was openly anti-Semitic were gone, but not long gone. Shortly after I arrived in 1959, President Wallace Sterling and Provost Fred Terman announced that there were no longer going to be any *student* quotas for Blacks, Jews, and so on. Nevertheless, a few years later it was discovered that the old quotas were still being enforced. The top-down decision by itself hadn't been enough. The admissions office personnel down in the basement of Encina Hall were still throwing the applications from those they considered undesirables into the reject piles. Casting daylight on it finally ended the practice.

At least Stanford hired me although, for example, its political science department was then said still to be a hotbed of anti-Semitism. When Don Kennedy was first approached in 1959 by Vic Twitty for an assistant professorship, he turned Stanford down. When then asked to recommend someone else, Don told me that he suggested Tim Goldsmith, but Vic replied that with Josh Lederberg, Cliff Grobstein, Charley Yanofsky, and Paul Ehrlich, they had already hired too many Jews. (Northwestern had once turned me down for a job on a similar basis, I later learned from a friend and colleague, Bob Hull.)[10] Ironically, when Tim Goldsmith subsequently joined the Yale faculty in 1961 it was known as one of the most anti-Semitic universities but has since been very active in correcting that and dealing with current anti-Semitism.[11]

As indicated earlier, I say I'm Jewish only for purposes of persecution, but the possibility of anti-Semitic encounters, and the huge mistake I believed the world made in establishing Israel rather than (partly thanks to anti-Semitism in the U.S. State Department) admitting World War II's Jewish refugees to the United States, have usually been drifting around in the back of my mind.[12] I frequently remember Bob Sokal, who had fled Austria in the 1930s, telling me: "The one thing we learned was, if someone came to your house and said he was going to return the next day and kill you, when he came back you should immediately shoot him." Bob was a most peaceful man, but the lesson of Sobibor clearly was learned. Unfortunately, Israel now behaves much like other Middle Eastern states run by semidictators, especially those empowered by support from Washington (or Moscow). I wish the Israeli government had led the world with higher standards of humanity, but it hasn't. If only it treated its Arab citizens especially well, and done that from the start.

Anne and I have a mob of atheist Jewish friends and colleagues who feel an attachment to Israel, an attachment that I understand but don't much share. In 2003 one of those friends, colleague and ex-postdoctoral student Marcus Feldman, was approached by a New York–based Israeli-American businessman, Mati Kochavi, who asked if Marc would be interested in exploring potential Stanford involvement in research collaborations between young Israeli and Jordanian scientists. Mati had been inspired by conversations with residents of the Central Arava, the Israeli desert region on the border with Jordan, who thought that better Israel-Jordan relations might begin with some collaborations on the ecology and possibly agricultural technology in that region. The two countries—on either side of the Rift Valley, penetrated by the Jordan River—had similar environmental conditions but dramatically different levels of agricultural and technical development.

Mati called the nascent project Bridging the Rift. Marc got in touch with Professor Hanan Malkawi of the Yarmouk University in Jordan, as well as with Israeli ecologists and microbiologists from Tel Aviv University, the Hebrew University of Jerusalem, and the Technion–Israel Institute of Technology in Haifa. Initial gatherings at Stanford of scholars from both countries and potential Stanford colleagues, including Dmitri Petrov, Gretchen Daily, and me, were organized by Marc and attended by Stanford's president, then Don Kennedy.

Several young Jordanian biologists were invited to Stanford over the next four years together with young Israeli biologists, with the idea that on their return to the Middle East, they would be able to collaborate on field research, especially in the desert regions close to the Jordan River in both Israel and Jordan. The project gained support from leaders in both countries to the extent that an actual building was planned for the Israeli desert as the future home of the collaborative project. Along with professors from many countries on March 9, 2004, I attended the cornerstone ceremony for the building, as did leaders from both Jordan and Israel, including Benjamin Netanyahu. I was also a member of a delegation from the project that then met with Israeli prime minister Ariel Sharon in Jerusalem and a few hours later with King Abdullah in Amman, both of whom expressed support for our efforts.

My main memories of the ceremony itself were my general boredom with the remarks given and an especially awful speech by Netanyahu, basically bragging that Israel would pave over the Negev desert and build a city there. I wandered out in the desert looking for birds and on my return was greeted by two Israeli security agents with Uzis, concerned I might be a terrorist.

Research projects were begun, including an exploratory research cruise on the Dead Sea, with microbiologists from both countries participating in a search for potential life in that extreme environment. The collaborative science project seemed to be progressing well, and in 2010 Mati and Marc, at the suggestion of marine biologists from Stanford and Israel, encouraged a program of further collaboration between an Israeli institute and a Jordanian institute located a couple of miles apart, both working on the oceanography and marine ecology of the Red Sea.

Mati offered to fund construction of a proper marine research facility at the Aqaba site to replace the inadequate Jordanian facility there. The proposal involved preparing a memorandum of understanding (MOU) between the Jordanian and Israeli universities and Stanford to develop joint research in the Red Sea. Within the Jordanian academic establishment, there appeared not long after this to have been some kind of upheaval, and the Jordanian side refused to sign the MOU with Israelis as collaborators. After what seemed like a very hopeful five years, this sounded the death knell for Bridging the Rift. Perhaps sometime in the future the project, or one like it, will be resurrected to continue what appeared to be such a promising peace-enhancing period of joint Jordanian-Israeli-Stanford cooperation in an area fraught with conflict.[13]

Though this project wasn't particularly controversial at Stanford, it illustrated how broadly we could act as Stanford employees. As a faculty member I found I could teach, say, or investigate anything I wanted with no, zero, concern about what the administration thought.

I was reminded in 2011 of what a great place Stanford has been to be a faculty member, despite its faults. It happened soon after my colleague, frequent collaborator, and dear friend Stephen Schneider died. For years Steve was a leading researcher in climate science, but more important, he was a great pioneer in bringing evidence of the threat of climate disruption to the general public in ways that could be easily understood. He was also a fantastic mentor of students and young scientists, and he formed strong bonds with many of us in other disciplines. His numerous contributions made me proud of the role I had played in recruiting him to Stanford and convincing the Department of Biological Sciences to take him on even though he wasn't a biologist by training.

Steve was great to have on your side in any fight, and eventually he fought a nearly ten-year-long battle against lymphoma, as detailed in his fine book *The Patient from Hell*. He didn't allow a bone marrow transplant or other tough procedures to keep him from vigorously pursuing his crusade to bring sound climate science to the public arena. Nor did it keep him from bird-watching expeditions with Anne and me, his avian biologist wife, Terry Root, and conservation biologist Tom Lovejoy. Steve died of the consequences of his disease in an airliner on final approach to Heathrow, on the way home from a meeting of climate scientists in Sweden.

Now to the event I referred to above: After Steve's death, the insurance company Stanford used wanted to interview me as the then-chair of the eco-evo group, of which Steve was a member, to help them determine if Steve was legitimately on university business at the time of death and therefore covered by the company.

At the end of the interview the insurance investigator asked me to clarify what Professor Schneider's duties were. After some back and forth, I finally explained, "You know, I have been at Stanford for more than fifty years. When I first came as a beginning assistant professor, Victor Twitty, the chairman of the department, asked if I could teach a course in evolution and a course in entomology, and I said, 'Yes.'" And then I said to the investigator, "That is the total, *total* conversation I've ever had with any administrator at Stanford about what my duties were. Since Schneider came here not as an assistant professor but as a distinguished full professor, I doubt if he had *that* much conversation about his duties." The insurance investigator's parting request was to direct her to *another* administrator who might be able to tell her more about Steve's duties.

That encounter underlined an important dimension of what I loved about the university. Stanford left you alone—if you were a recognized productive scholar (most important) and at least a mediocre teacher, you could do what you damn well pleased, although there of course was peer pressure to do your share of chores, such as serving as chair of the eco-evo group.

I can only recall one time when my performance at Stanford was questioned by the university. It occurred probably thirty years ago but is very contemporary in context. It was before Stanford had formal procedures for dealing with sexual harassment; instead, teams of lawyers visited departments to discuss the issue. At the biology department's meeting, my evolutionist colleague Deborah Gordon and I discovered we'd both supposedly been sexually harassing students. It was the early days of DNA analysis, and when we were teaching behavior, we both reported on then-recent work showing that when the fertile eggs from "monogamous" birds' nests were analyzed, it was not unusual to find that different eggs had been fertilized by different males. We'd point out that similar results often came from DNA tests of human babies in the same family. We were informed that telling classes of that possibility could be interpreted as sexual harassment and that we should desist. "You're kidding," we responded, "No one would call that sexual harassment." Listen, the lawyers said, in the back of your class could be a kid from a holy roller church who is shocked and lodges a legal complaint. The judge turns out to be an ancient conservative Catholic, and the jury is made up of outpatients from Agnews (the then local mental institution). You'll be convicted. So far Deborah and I have avoided prison.

Stanford also had some great advantages compared to some other first-rate institutions when it came to administrative issues and the time one was forced to devote to them. When John Holdren was a professor in the energy and resources group at Berkeley, we compared notes. He said he spent about half his time on administrative tasks. If, for example, he wanted to teach a new course he had to work it, seriatim, through two committees of academic apparatchiks. It took months, and to stop teaching the course he'd need to back it out through the same two committees. In John and Berkeley's defense, however, it should be noted that he was running a pioneer multidisciplinary program beholden to many departments. In contrast, when I decided to teach a course in human evolution and the environment, no endless committee meetings and approvals were necessary. I simply called the department secretary and asked, "What's the lowest number of a biology course in the catalog?" There was no Biology 1, I was told. "Okay, there is now—please put this in." And I dictated the course information. If I had wanted to stop teaching it, I would have had to call and say, "Please take Biology 1 out of the catalog."

Personally, I never felt constrained in what I could do or say while on the faculty there, despite the advice of attorneys. Even after calling Richard Nixon a war criminal on national television, I never heard a peep from any colleague or the Stanford administration expressing concern over what I was saying. Indeed, the administration was always respectful and supportive.

Stanford's tolerance of me was well demonstrated in the 1980s in the aftermath of a talk I gave at the University of California, Davis, a branch of the University of California system with a large agriculture division and, not incidentally, notoriously influenced by pesticide peddlers. I talked extensively about the misuse of pesticides (they do have their place in some situations) and compared some of the agribusiness representatives to drug dealers. Because of the evolution of resistance to these chemicals and the elevation of some nonpests to pest status through the overuse of pesticides, the dealers could always advise using more pesticides if the pests persisted and, in so doing, lure unwitting farmers onto a pesticide treadmill. My talk pleased neither the industry nor the hacks they paid. Stanford's president's office was subjected to an organized storm of letters demanding my firing. The campaign was nasty, but nowhere near as nasty and sophisticated as the one the industry later launched against Tyrone Hayes at UC Berkeley for revealing the dangers of the herbicide atrazine.[14] In my case, my close friend Don Kennedy was president of Stanford when the industry tried to get me fired. The industry representatives didn't even bother to learn that much of what I had said was lifted from a report on pesticides Don had written for the U.S. government when he had been head of the Food and Drug Administration. As university president Don fortunately had a great talent for gently and politely telling such individuals to back off.

Tyrone Hayes is a superstar, a leader in revealing the threat of endocrine-disrupting toxic chemicals, a brilliant lecturer, and an outstanding mentor of students. He also is African American. A group of us wanted to lure him away from UC Berkeley to our department and possibly snare his outstanding public health scientist wife, Kathy Kim, from UC Davis. What we got was a lesson in subtle institutional racism of the "he hasn't published enough in *Science* magazine lately" sort—coming from scientists whose research was trivial by comparison, who couldn't begin to lecture or mentor at Tyrone's level. Scientists with a Jewish background may have invaded population biology, but I've only known personally two Black environmental scientist colleagues besides Tyrone, Gregory Florant and Daniel Pauly, both leaders in their respective fields. There are a few others, such as Steward Pickett, that I know about, and I hope that's changing in the younger ranks as it has with women. Environmental science can ill afford not to recruit neglected talent regardless of skin pigmentation or gender.

My freedom of speech was not at the time of the pesticide talk, indeed ever, restricted by the Stanford administration, but earlier the administration had faced another issue of speech and behavior that it treated more seriously. During the Vietnam War, the most prominent protestor on campus was an associate professor in the English department, H. Bruce Franklin. We were both against the war, but Bruce's communistic beliefs also made him an enemy of me. Because I thought (as I still do) that there were too many people in the world, he kept calling me a fascist. As an enemy of all ideologies—communism, fascism, capitalism, and other religionlike paradigms that are not largely evidence-based—I was used to that sort of attack.

The university launched a pseudo-legal effort to fire Bruce for his putatively disruptive activities, accusing him of preventing a speaker from speaking and inciting antiwar actions. It was a tough issue then with great difficulties in determining what his actions had been. It would likely be even tougher now. My only direct involvement came when Dick Lyman and Don Kennedy, both involved with the "prosecution," asked if I could raise a Franklin defense fund. As they pointed out, Stanford had a bunch of high-powered attorneys, and didn't Bruce deserve good representation? I agreed, and then had a most interesting experience. I called several of my faculty friends and acquaintances, starting with some of the most liberal ones. They all refused; they didn't agree with the defense they thought Bruce would mount. Then I called a very conservative engineer, who readily agreed to contribute; under our system, Bruce deserved a strong defense, he said. Bruce was eventually "convicted" and ejected from his tenured position. Even in retrospect I'm not sure what was right, although I think one often has to defend on principle the behavior of those you disagree with. Regardless, Bruce wasn't destroyed—he went on to have a distinguished career elsewhere, and if he was wrong on population he was certainly right on the Vietnam War, in my view.

How did Stanford tolerate me no matter how outrageous I was? Unlike Bruce, I couldn't be accused of breaking any university rules. Besides, I think it was related to how the university became exceptionally good. Despite a history of struggling to join the first rank of universities, Stanford was still pretty much of a finishing school when Wally Sterling took over the presidency in 1949 and in two decades put Stanford well on the road to becoming one of the best universities in the world.[15] That process was still under way when I joined in 1959, as my experiences with graduate training so clearly indicated. In 1955 Sterling had appointed Fred Terman as provost, and the two of them decided to fix the university up with (to use, I think, Terman's phrase) "steeples of excellence." The basic idea was to bring in the best scholars they could find in carefully selected areas, especially ones that would attract support from industry, and not put equal emphasis on all classic disciplines (you can't do everything at once). They planned to turn the scholars loose, binding them as little as possible to departmental needs, teaching, and university politics. Even if they had an impulse to do so, I think they would have shied away from censuring a young science professor in a rising field for speaking his mind, especially one with access to the media.

Stanford kept Vic's promise never to pay a decent wage, but otherwise it has been wonderful being on the faculty of one of the world's best universities and especially good for a conservation biologist with broad interests who liked teaching smart undergraduates and helping some get involved in research. One of the clear, more specific research advantages of being at Stanford for me was the availability of brilliant colleagues such as Dick Holm, who was joined by two more top-rate botanists, Peter Raven and John Thomas. That allowed me to leave largely to others the fine points of those dull-green leafy animals that never run away from you. I could work on plant-animal interactions without learning to discern "extrorse dehiscence."

SIX

Coevolving with Botanists and Butterflies

One day in 1963, while Peter Raven and I were having coffee at the round table in the Stanford Herbarium of mint fame, I happened to remark that I couldn't understand why *Euphydryas editha* larvae (caterpillars) fed on plants of two different families, Plantaginaceae (plantain family) and Scrophulariaceae (snapdragons and their relatives). He replied that plantagos were "just wind-pollinated scrophs" (meaning that the two families are close relatives). Peter and I then embarked on a series of discussions over some weeks about butterfly diets—just what did their caterpillars eat, and why?

A start on that question was easy, because enthusiasts had studied butterfly life histories so energetically that they had made butterflies the only large group of herbivores in which the diets of a substantial proportion of the species were known. And having worked hard on butterfly taxonomy and written a field guide to North American butterflies that included their food plants, I knew much of the data and had a good idea where to find the rest. Peter was similarly familiar with the diversity of plants and their characteristics. Much of the work determining the food plants that caterpillars preferred had been achieved by amateur naturalists wanting to get perfect specimens, freshly emerged from the pupae, for their collections—instances of the butterfly-beauty connection that initially attracted me and so many others to those insects. When investigators determined what the caterpil-

Peter Raven and me on my seventy-fifth birthday, standing on the round table where we first developed the coevolution concept, now preserved at Jasper Ridge. Photo by Gerardo Ceballos.

lars of a given species ate, they usually posted a note about it for publication in a journal (as I had when I discovered that the Sandia hairstreak fed on beargrass).

It was long known that some groups of butterflies tended to feed on certain groups of plants and this was sometimes reflected in their common names: cabbage butterflies, for example, and Aristolochia swallowtails. Cabbage butterflies, members of the subfamily Pierinae (of the Pieridae), often fed on plants of the family Cruciferae (cabbages and their relatives—now called Brassicaceae) or the closely related capers (Capparidaceae). That led Peter and me to search the literature to discover what common characteristics bound together the groups of plants upon which certain groups of butterfly caterpillars dined.

The case of the cabbage butterflies was typical. The plants they fed on contained mustard oils; their caterpillars would eat another plant, or even filter paper, should it be smeared with mustard oils. In contrast, the mustard oils served the plants as chemical defenses against caterpillars of other species and other herbivores (concentrated mustard oils can be bad for your own heart). These defenses and other chemical compounds plants manufactured—often called secondary metabolic substances—certainly were not simply excretory products, as some claimed. Organisms don't make energetically expensive products to dispose of wastes and then metaphorically "stick them in their ear," rather than excreting them.

We concluded that butterflies and plants were in a kind of war with each other across evolutionary time: plants evolving chemical defenses against butterflies and other herbivores, and species among the latter (such as cabbage butterflies with mustard oils) finding evolutionary ways to get around those poisonous barriers. The defensive chemicals turn out to be very diverse, including chemicals that load leaves with needlelike crystals or others that dose herbivores with cyanide. People use many plant defensive compounds as drugs, both medicinal (digitalis) and recreational (opium), or for their gustatory or mood-changing qualities (spices, caffeine). Peter and I saw that ecologically intimate organisms—herbivores and plants, predators and their prey, parasites and their hosts, and so on—were often acting as selection agents on each other, reciprocally influencing each other's evolution—that is, coevolving. We published our analysis in late 1964 in what proved to be each of ours (I think!) most-cited paper, "Butterflies and Plants: A Study in Coevolution," which founded the field of coevolution.[1]

It turns out that most parts of the coevolutionary story had been told before we published that paper. Some scientists, for example, had discovered the defensive function of some plant "secondary" compounds, and my hero Charles Darwin came close to telling the whole story in *On the Origin of*

Species. Why was it, then, that our paper led to an explosion of new research and the establishment of what amounted to a new field? Perhaps we crystallized the conception of a general process (and named it) that others typically had noted only in particular manifestations. I think there are two other answers. One is that many ecologists and evolutionists immediately saw its relevance to their own work (as, in fact, Peter and I did). Second and perhaps more important, we published the story backed by a lot of data. Having an idea in science is good, but having lots of examples to support it is better. The classic case is Alfred Russel Wallace, who had the basic idea of evolution by natural selection simultaneously with Darwin. But Darwin published his idea in an example-rich book, so we have Darwinism and not Wallacism.

The coevolution work underlined one of the great advantages of working with botanists, as I had learned earlier with Dick Holm. It also highlighted arguably one of the epic contributions of citizen science: amateurs had collected and published much of the data on caterpillars' food plants.

A few years after publication of the coevolution paper, a piece of good luck at one of my research sites led to powerful support for our coevolution theory. Besides the excretory products nonsense, some scientists also claimed that the "world is green" and that insect damage to plants is generally trivial. One summer's day in 1968 at Rocky Mountain Biological Lab, I noticed small lycaenids (blue butterflies), *Glaucopsyche lygdamus*, laying eggs on the flowers of a population of lupines. I recruited a botanist colleague, Dennis Breedlove, and we started an experiment. We marked one hundred flowering stalks of the lupines and then removed the lycaenid eggs from every other stalk. Then we recorded the seed set of each stalk. We found that the little butterfly had a big impact on the plants, contrary to what one might think with an "insects don't hurt plants" point of view, destroying a substantial percentage of their reproductive potential. It also indicated a strong coevolutionary selection pressure, likely favoring the plants that flowered early, before the butterflies emerged. We observed one year at RMBL a very late snowstorm that killed all of that year's lupine flowers and decimated the *G. lygdamus* population. Damage from late frosts appeared to be a small price for the lupines, which would survive to flower again the following year, to pay to be relatively free of its tiny but effective predator's destruction of its reproductive output. It was, besides, not only support for coevolution (indicating the great selection pressure a tiny insect could put on a big plant) but also the first of many instances where our research showed the great importance of climate and weather in the fates of natural populations.[2]

Our work on butterflies and their food plants was just the start. Other scientists, such as Michael Singer, Stuart Weiss, and Deane Bowers, continued to examine the relationships of checkerspots and their food plants. As Peter and I had pointed out, coevolutionary processes had broad implications, and our paper launched a flood of research beyond checkerspots that continues to this day.[3] By 2021 the coevolution paper had been cited more than five thousand times in the scientific literature. In February 2015, fifty years after the initial publication of our paper, I listened to a seminar presentation by a brilliant young scientist, Cassie Stoddard, who had been dissecting the coevolutionary races between avian brood parasites and their hosts, right down to the molecular level, using techniques developed well after the Ehrlich-Raven paper. The work on that fascinating system has recently been summarized in a wonderful book, *Cuckoo: Cheating by Nature*, by one of the top scientists in the field, Nicholas Davies.[4] It described, among other things I had not known, how a population decline of cuckoos at Davies's research site at Wicken Fen, near Cambridge, England, had changed the behavior of its favorite host bird, the reed warbler. In 1985, 24 percent of reed warbler nests had been parasitized by cuckoos, in 2012 just 1 percent. As there were fewer cuckoos to lay eggs in the reed warbler nests, the defensive reactions of the warblers declined in response. There was less mobbing of cuckoo females, and the warblers became less adept at identifying and discarding cuckoo eggs. The warblers' behavior changed because they did not need to spend as much energy in defending their young—coevolution in action!

A piece was recently added to one of my favorite coevolutionary stories. It has long been known that bats use sonar—echolocation, detection by the return of sounds the bats generate—to paint a picture of their environment. That picture allows them to detect and devour moths and other flying insects at night. In response, some moths have evolved a pair of simple ears at the base of their abdomens that hear the pinging produced by predatory bats, allowing the target moths to take evasive action. There are tiny parasitic mites that live in the moth's ears, climbing on board when a moth visits a flower to obtain nectar. Mites that invade the moth subsequently always follow the path of the first invader and go to the same ear, so that only one ear is damaged, and the moths can still hear the bats' sonar with the uninhabited ear. Otherwise the moth would be deaf and vulnerable to bat predation. Mites don't do well in bat digestive tracts; selection would quickly weed out mites lacking genes that made them tend to follow their predecessors' tracks. What about moth species that have not evolved ears and are deaf? How do they defend themselves? That's the recent news: they have evolved fur on their bodies that serves as a type of stealth coating, an acoustic camouflage to hide them from hungry bats.[5]

In September 2016 an Indian ecologist, Hari Sridhar, interviewed me about Peter's and my paper in which we introduced the term "coevolution." He asked if butterfly-plant coevolution was my favorite paper. I said yes, for a number of reasons. First, we wrote it without looking at an organism living or dead. We only studied the literature, falsifying the old saying that "one should study nature, not books." Second, it turned out to be a professional success, garnering all those citations and being long ago christened a "citation classic." But most of all, as obvious as the results were in retrospect, it created a new subdiscipline of evolutionary ecology by offering an explanation for a vast diversity of natural phenomena—exactly what I believe is a main role of science.

The founding location of my professional engagement with living butterflies, indeed of my professional career as a population biologist, was the Jasper Ridge Biological Reserve, a twelve-hundred-acre area on the Stanford campus protected for use in research. It not only hosted my research on the ecology and evolution of checkerspots but also fathered Peter Raven's and my work on coevolution and provided me with my first big lessons in conservation biology. Research at Jasper Ridge occupied a lot of my time, especially during the first ten years I was at Stanford. Its location allowed me to do fieldwork every March and April, actually for much of the school year when I was teaching, just ten minutes from my door. That turned out to be super convenient, because I soon established a field site in the Colorado Rockies near where I had captured my first *Parnassius* in 1947. There, at the previously mentioned Rocky Mountain Biological Lab, I could have a second butterfly field season with my students June through August during Stanford's summer break.

I first heard of Jasper Ridge soon after I arrived at the university. I was on my way to a meeting of the West Coast Lepidopterists' Society in Santa Barbara in the early fall of 1959, driving there with a butterfly collector, Elton Sette, professionally a fisheries biologist who was stationed at Stanford. I told him I was looking for a butterfly population to use as a study system for answering questions about ecology and evolution. Elton told me that there was a population of the Bay checkerspot, *Euphydryas editha bayensis*, on Jasper Ridge, an undeveloped but not at that time reserved part of Stanford's large campus—originally Senator Leland Stanford's "farm." So, fortuitously, I was to be reunited with the butterfly to which Bill Hammer had kindly introduced me more than a decade earlier (plate 4). I visited the ridge-top site Elton described as soon as we got back, mapped it, and divided it into study areas where I expected butterflies to appear the next spring.

Then on a beautiful sunny morning, March 31, 1960, at 10:00 a.m., I caught my first *E. editha*, a freshly emerged male in area G, and marked it #1 with a Magic Marker (the ancestor of all felt-tipped pens; Charley Yanofsky had suggested I try them after he discovered their usefulness in marking his test tubes). I wrote down the data on #1 on a special mimeographed data sheet (no photocopying then) on a clipboard (plate 5). One of the great aspects of butterflies is the ease of marking them. On smaller species, those of checkerspot size or smaller where the markers were too crude to write actual numbers, we gave them numbers using a 1–2–4–7 system (plate 6). That involved putting Magic Marker smears at certain positions on the edges of the underside of the wings. For instance, left forewing forward edge (actually

Checkerspot Area H on Jasper Ridge with a wildflower display on serpentine soil, spring 1960. Author photo.

forward corner) was 1, trailing edge 2. Same on left hindwing for 4 and 7. To mark a butterfly number 9 you put smears in the 2 and 7 positions. With eight places on the edges of the wings we could mark up to 99—spots of marker ink on places 20 & 70 and 2 & 7. With spots on the bases of the four wings we could go to 999 (200–700, 20–70, and 2–7). With larger species and the development of finer markers, we eventually could just write a number on the wings. I probably hold the world's record for marking and releasing butterflies—maybe some hundred thousand of many species.

I marked another male and a female on that long-ago morning and recaptured #1 at 11:10 a.m. about twenty-five feet from where it had been released. I still have that data sheet. The mark-release-recapture program I began that day not only gave me information on how the butterflies moved around but also let me estimate their population size. The details can be complex, since individuals always can be entering the population (hatching from pupae, immigrating) or leaving it (death, emigration), but in principle the program is straightforward. Say you mark one hundred butterflies and release them

On Jasper Ridge in my first field season, 1960, catching *Euphydryas editha* with an assistant. Author photo.

back into the population. You wait a day to give them room to move around, and then capture another hundred. If ten of them turn out to be marked, your rough estimate of the population size is one thousand (since 10 percent had been marked when you marked one hundred).

Thanks in part to climate disruption, some *E. editha* populations we've studied are now extinct, but the butterfly and its relatives still exist in scattered colonies over North America, still a subject of study by some of my former students, by others, and occasionally by me. With my former student Dennis Murphy, led by his Stanford freshman son Matt, and my Stanford

Tagging butterfly number 30 (wing apex = #10, near trailing edge = #20, #10 + #20 = #30) with a marker. Author photo.

colleague and friend Rodolfo Dirzo, we are now revisiting many former *E. editha* colonies in California to see how many have persisted in this era of global change.

From quite early on, the Stanford administration was well aware of my commitment to the Jasper Ridge site and its Bay checkerspot populations. Once around 1980, when lunching with Stanford's then provost (and old friend) Bill Miller, I asked why he was keeping my salary insultingly low. He replied that was easy: Stanford knew I would never leave Jasper Ridge. Butterflies got me to the land of milk and honey, but it was a butterfly-triggered mistake, doing long-term research on a campus site, that long prevented me from getting a better salary by the usual academic route—threatening to accept a job offer at another university.

Initially, it took a lot of work on my part and Dick Holm's and a big ration of treachery and deceit to get Stanford to put aside Jasper Ridge as a reserve. We convinced the university to use the importance of Jasper Ridge's inviolability as an excuse for . . . I can't even remember the details now . . . why a dam should not be built by the municipality of Palo Alto where it would have interfered with putting in a linear accelerator (now the SLAC National Accelerator Laboratory) for research in nuclear physics. The argument the university made was that Jasper Ridge would be harmed by the dam, but then, shortly thereafter, they decided that they would develop Jasper Ridge for housing because, of course, it would be worth a fortune. Dick and I said, "You do that and we will go to the press and say that Stanford doesn't give a damn about the people of Palo Alto, that they really were lying when they said they opposed the dam to protect Jasper Ridge."

Alf Brandin, vice-president for business affairs, had consistently battled the Department of Biological Sciences for control of Jasper Ridge. Vic Twitty as department head tried to help Dick and me, but although a fine scientist, Vic had a sad habit of caving in before administrators. At one meeting Vic asked Alf if we could have Jasper Ridge for a couple more years before Alf developed it. Brandin had no academic interest, as meetings with him clearly demonstrated, although he was apparently a good businessman when it came to raising money for Stanford. But Dick's and my threat to reveal the university's perfidy turned the tide, and Jasper Ridge was on its way to total protection.

The route to preservation was not without further trials and amusements, however. Early on, for example, Dick and I found some money to hire private guards to try to keep local people from invading the Ridge. One neighbor, for example, had bulldozed a horse trail for his own use through Ridge chaparral, and hikers, horseback riders, and campers used the Ridge as a public facility. It turned out the guards did more damage driving after intruders than the intruders did, but before we terminated the program, they did give us one classic report:

"Doctors, we threw a couple off the Ridge today."

"Oh."

"They said they was sun bathing."

"Really?"

"But she wasn't getting no sun."

Much later, in the mid-1980s, and less amusing, one of the reserve's neighbors cut down trees on the Ridge to improve his view. By then Stanford's administration took the Ridge very seriously, filed a lawsuit against him, and hired a brilliant San Francisco attorney, Lynn Pasahow, to represent the university. Lynn asked me to testify. If the opposing attorney was smart, Lynn told me, he'd just ask me if I had any direct knowledge of the fate of the trees; I'd have to say "no," and that would be the end of my testimony. Instead, I was allowed to testify on the scientific value of the Ridge for an hour. The defense's claim was that unknown "vandals" had cut down the trees. The judge, who was from Sacramento, helping out the overcrowded Bay Area courts, went to the crime scene (trees neatly cut down in the sight line of the neighbor's picture windows). He remarked in court that at Stanford we must have a better class of vandals than there were in Sacramento. Eventually, after much maneuvering, in 1987 Stanford won. The neighbor paid Stanford $70,000, and there were no more incidents.

Jasper Ridge is now recognized as probably the best on-campus field site in the world. Certainly, it's the best at a major university with first-rate research in ecology and evolution. In 2018 more than seventy-five researchers were involved in sixty projects using the Ridge as an outdoor laboratory. On top of that, the Ridge has an extensive outreach program and is a force for conservation. All these developments make me personally very happy, as does the fact that a power couple, Faculty Director Elizabeth Hadly and Executive Director Anthony Barnosky, are friends and colleagues who share Anne's and my concerns over the human predicament. The same can be said for the reserve's brilliant staff scientist, Nona Chiariello, who has long shared my dedication to the Ridge, organizing the diverse projects so they don't interfere with each other, and pursuing her own research on global change biology.

Much of my enjoyable time in the field with *Euphydryas* and with coevolution when not at Jasper Ridge occurred, as I've indicated, at the Rocky

Mountain Biological Lab in Colorado. The lab owned a beautiful piece of valley at about 9,500 feet in the West Elk Mountains of Gunnison County. It had no formal connection to Stanford, but it became part of the rhythm of my Stanford years, a time shared with many Stanford graduate students. It is located in the wettest part of Colorado and provided access to habitats from 7,000 to 13,000 feet elevation. The lab is a butterfly paradise to which I was originally introduced in 1960 by the Lepidopterists' Society cofounder Charles Remington. Charlie invited evolutionist Richard Lewontin and me to teach a course in biometry (biological statistics) there in 1960. With only two exceptions I did research at RMBL every subsequent summer through 2017, when Anne's and my aging bodies made work above 8,000 feet impractical.

The lab was so clearly a wonderful place for the research I wanted to do that we immediately (in 1960) took out a lease on a cabin site the first summer we spent there. It was a quite reasonable two-way deal: for a token fee you got a twenty-year lease, renewable once, you could build your own cabin, and after forty years the cabin vested to the lab. We built the first section of our cabin and started our summer fieldwork on butterflies in 1961. Our site was gorgeous: the lab was at 9,500 feet, and our cabin was at 9,600 feet facing the sheer wall of over-12,000-foot Mount Gothic.

John Johnson, a forward-looking biologist at Western State College in Gunnison, some thirty miles south of the RMBL site, founded the lab in 1928. Johnson bought for pennies the ghost town of Gothic, deserted after a silver boom, which became RMBL's locale. When Anne and I got there Robert Enders, a faculty member from Swarthmore College, was the lab's director. He along with a number of others were interested in keeping the lab as a sort of primitive Quaker work camp. But a growing group of scientists including Remington, William Baker (then chair of biology at the University of Chicago), Eddie Novitski (distinguished *Drosophila* geneticist from the University of Oregon), and Bob Wagner (a founder of molecular genetics from the University of Texas) were pushing for the basic lab facilities (clean running water, labs with temperature controls) that would support more modern science. They wanted the lab to teach courses that did not just focus on local flora and fauna.

In the early 1960s these divergent interests generated the so-called Gothic wars, which nearly destroyed the lab as the "geneticists" (full disclosure, I was one of them) pushed for basic lab facilities and, on the other side, the "hunters and trappers," who felt they were being shoved out, resisted strongly. Things got nasty. The geneticists got a grant from the National Science Foundation to build a modern laboratory, but Enders arrived early that summer and built three utterly inadequate shell buildings with no space that could be temperature controlled.

Fortunately a few years later, Chris Johnson, son of the lab's founder, was elected director by the old timers, but he wisely worked with both groups, treating all fairly. Chris made it possible for me to continue my work even though my sentiments were strongly on the modernization side. He's gone, but I remain in his debt. In recent years, a number of younger scientists have become RMBL members and are carrying out modern ecological studies involving fieldwork, lab work, and theory. Tensions persist, however, especially over how to deal with the increasingly rampant and schlocky development of the surrounding area as it has become a major center of tourism (skiing, hiking, mountain biking, and so on), which could have substantial impacts on research projects.

Some of my most memorable moments at RMBL came when Don Kennedy and his wife, Jeanne, visited us, starting in 1964. Our cabin was still tiny then (about four hundred square feet), and Anne and I slept in the loft, while Don and Jeanne slept on the floor below. In the morning Don, a fine naturalist, called up, "There's a weasel in the woodpile." Anne and I scrambled down the ladder and saw the beautiful little creature as it disappeared into the pile. "You can hear its mating call," I said. Don: "What? I don't hear anything." Paul: "Listen, it's a pop-pop-pop." "Don: I can't make it out." Paul: "There it is again, pop-pop-pop." Pause. Anne starts humming a familiar tune. Don: "Oh shit, pop goes the weasel!" Typical bad Ehrlich "humor," but the only time I ever "got" my friend. Writing this brings to mind a serious problem that I've done much too little to rectify. I wrote about "getting" my brilliant friend Don Kennedy. But I should have said "getting" my brilliant friends, Don and Jeanne. Jeanne is one of those women, common in my generation, who gave up a possible career (for Jeanne, in mathematics or in another profession) to dedicate her life for decades to enhancing her husband's career. Only after Don and Jeanne divorced, when she launched a career of her own, did she get at least some of the credit she deserved, eventually transforming patient relations at the Stanford University hospital. Indeed, as anyone who knew the couple well could testify, Jeanne had much better judgment in many areas than Don did (fortunately for me, I have one of those wives myself).

The lab led to many wonderful friendships. One day in the late 1970s or early 1980s, a handsome woman with a little girl knocked on our cabin door—Wren Wirth, wife of Colorado Democratic congressman Tim Wirth, and daughter Kelsey. They had a small summer home in Crested Butte. The Wirths, like the Ehrlichs, were deeply concerned about environmental deterioration. It was a natural match-up that has lasted to this day. Tim served in the House from 1975 to 1987 and was elected to the Senate in 1986, where he served a single term before quitting in disgust over changes in how the Senate operated. Tim was a pioneer in pushing environmental quality in both Colorado and the nation, working extensively with his grammar-school friend, Republican congressman and then senator Jack Heinz (the Heinzes of the "57 Varieties"). It was the now-bygone era in which Tim (Democrat) and Jack (Republican) were friends who collaborated for the public good.

All of our mountain fun was not the wonderful hiking. I found another passion thanks to ecological economist Dick Norgaard. He was a demon swift-water rafter, and under his tutelage I learned the excitement of paddling rubber rafts or kayaks through rapids. I also learned to respect the strength of seemingly innocuous currents, starting with the experience (which Dick insisted upon as part of my training) of swimming a rapid. I even celebrated my sixtieth birthday kayaking a mountain torrent.

Indeed, the peak of the Wirth-Ehrlich social life so far was perhaps a river journey down the Colorado through the Grand Canyon in which Tom Lovejoy and I floated what must have been the best-stocked wine raft ever to make the trip. The highlights of the trip for me were running some of the famous rapids in a paddle raft and wine-drinking around campfires. One night topped them all. One of the guides was a doctor (Rebbie—last name forgotten) who the rest of the year provided reproductive services to poor women in Los Angeles. Around the campfire, she told the group that many of the women said they couldn't use condoms because their boyfriend's penises were too big. Rebbie said she always replied by asking if the boyfriend's penis was larger than her head. Then, when the women said no, she demonstrated for us what she did. There in the Grand Canyon by the firelight, she whipped out a condom and pulled it down entirely over her head. I doubt if any of our gang will ever forget it. And I've never forgotten the rafting experience—as I wrote about the canyon's most challenging rapid in *Human Natures*, I'm "forever above Lava."

Wren and I get along particularly well, since both Tim and Anne tend to be optimists, and Wren and I aren't. Tim and Wren's son Chris was a student of Anne's and has made a career creating high-art three-dimensional jigsaw puzzles. Their daughter Kelsey grew up to be a friend as well, the "little girl" of that fateful day so long ago. Kelsey went to Stanford business school and afterward cofounded Invisalign, a novel tool for straightening adult teeth. Our faith in Kelsey was such that we invested in the start-up—one smart move that, combined with the dumb luck of buying a house we couldn't afford on Stanford campus in 1962, allowed us to finish our lives in a comfortable retirement complex. Kelsey has gone on to organize Mothers Out Front, a group dedicated to reducing human disruption of the climate.[6]

Some of our group's most fun nonbutterfly research at RMBL involved the fascinating woodpecker relatives, the sapsuckers. Red-naped sapsuckers (*Sphyrapicus nuchalis*) were common around the lab, living in tree holes they excavated (especially in aspens), pecking "wells" in the bark of trees and shrubs (mostly willows in the sapsucker breeding season), which oozed sugary sap. They raised their families in the holes, with the chattering of the hungry young being frequent background music in the woods. Around 1990 my then–graduate student Gretchen Daily and I decided to take a closer look at their interactions with other organisms, and we recruited a promising Stanford undergraduate named Nick Haddad to help us. We netted sapsuckers (thereby discovering that they are specialists in driving beaks and claws into tender parts of hands) so we could put identifying bands on them, marched through dew-soaked meadows from aspen grove to aspen grove surveying nest holes and wells, drilled cores in aspen trees to see how tough they were, and drank in the evenings.

What we discovered was a surprisingly subtle web of interactions, more the sort of phenomenon we would have expected in the tropics than in a relatively simple subalpine ecosystem (that is, the organisms of an area just below tree line and their nonliving environment). First of all, the sapsuckers' home construction made it possible for two species of swallows to be part of the same ecosystem. The swallows depended on abandoned sapsucker holes for their own nest sites, being unable to drill their own holes. But they also depended on a heartwood fungus that invaded many of the aspens, making the trunks soft enough for the sapsuckers to drill their nest cavities, which they did each season. The sapsuckers added calories to their diets by sucking the sap that oozed into their wells, often actually dipping captured insects into the sugary juice before delivering them to their nestlings.

Other animals had no compunction about robbing sap from the sapsuckers' wells—thus those industrious birds provided a free dietary supplement to hummingbirds, warblers, chipmunks, and others. We announced that we had discovered a keystone species complex (a group of species, members of which have disproportionate influence on an entire ecosystem, which would change greatly if a keystone were removed).[7] The complex depended on four keystone elements—sapsuckers, aspens, willows, and the fungus—without all of them, the ecosystem would greatly change.

My most recent research at RMBL was helping my Stanford colleague Carol Boggs and her gang on a project that my student Cheri Holdren and I had started at RMBL in 1977. Carol, a fine scientist, ran my Center for Conservation Biology at Stanford for years, did much basic work on the *Euphydryas* project, and then did a magnificent job as director of Stanford's Human Biology Program. She is now a distinguished professor and director of the University of South Carolina's School of the Earth, Ocean & Environment. She is wedded to my second longest-suffering butterfly friend (after Mich), Ward Watt. A pioneer molecular geneticist, Ward has used *Colias* butterflies at RMBL as an experimental system for many decades.

We met at a Lepidopterists' Society meeting in Washington in 1957 when I was a postdoc and he was in high school; subsequently he was a faculty colleague in Stanford's biology department for many years.

When Cheri Holdren was earning her doctorate with me in the late 1970s, we were trying to solve a biogeographic butterfly mystery. *Euphydryas gillettii*, a checkerspot species, lived only in locations in the Rockies north of Wyoming's Red Desert gap in the mountain range. Would what appeared to be good *E. gillettii* habitat in Colorado actually amount to an empty niche (fully suitable but unoccupied habitat)? Had *E. gillettii*, a species with its closest relatives in Eurasia, invaded North America but been unable to cross the desert gap to reach the RMBL area, or was our apparently hospitable Colorado habitat actually somehow unsuitable? With permission from RMBL, Cheri and I had transplanted dozens of *E. gillettii* larvae from populations in Wyoming to locations with the proper larval food plant and abundant nectar sources near RMBL. To summarize a long story, the species has survived so far in its transplanted environment, but thirty-nine years later it was still not clear, despite the careful work of Carol's group, whether the transplant populations would become permanently established. The RMBL transplant populations have fluctuated greatly in size and have spread somewhat geographically.[8] My hunch is that, barring dramatic changes from climate disruption, the species will persist in its Colorado environment. The largest population that established itself by spreading from the original transplant site went undetected by us for a substantial time until our now Australian colleague Chris Turnbull, visiting RMBL for the first time in several years, discovered it. The edge of the new population was just a couple hundred yards beyond where my standard searches (which extended a couple of miles) ended. Butterflies, like mites, can often outsmart you.

Our butterfly work was by no means the only or the main research that has taken place at RMBL over the decades. Bobbi Peckarsky, for example, has spent a lifetime there uncovering how stream ecosystems work; Dave Inouye has been documenting the shift in flowering times and a decline in insect biomass in response to climate disruption for another lifetime; billy barr, the lab's financial officer and high-altitude cricket champion, has become famous for documenting snowpack shifts in response to climate disruption; and environmental scientists and evolutionists Ken Armitage and Dan Blumstein have spent years unraveling marmot behavior and its significance for human behavior.

John Harte has done some of the most significant contemporary research on the impacts of climate change, having set up a wonderful experiment at RMBL in 1990. He used electric heaters to warm experimental plots in a Gothic meadow as a way of mimicking global heating. When decades ago he described his plan to me, I said he was crazy—it would never work. I was crazy: it worked brilliantly, and it proved to be among the most significant science ever done at RMBL. His "control" plots (those not artificially warmed) followed closely the trajectories of his experimental plots (change in vegetation, loss of much carbon from the soil) as the whole planet has warmed.

RMBL remains an excellent place for scientists to take the pulse of the biosphere at high altitudes, and a gang of younger colleagues is still at it. I'm just very sorry Anne and I can no longer analyze our eco-EKGs with them.

It was my fascination with butterflies that in no small part led me to develop an enduring concern about human population and the environment—and led me into a career as a part-time politician of sorts. As a teenager, remember, I found it very difficult to raise butterflies in northern New Jersey because so much DDT had been sprayed for mosquito control. On top of that, I found my favorite collecting sites disappearing under new housing developments. To collect butterflies, I visited my aunt and uncle, who lived in Bethesda, Maryland, and well remember catching a single Baltimore checkerspot (*Euphydryas phaeton*) in the damp field across from their house. In 1947 there was but a single house in sight from theirs; a half century later Lisa lived in Bethesda and it was solid houses, and the checkerspots (and most other butterflies) were long gone. In addition, as I've described, overpopulation and overdevelopment, especially as articulated by William Vogt and Fairfield Osborne, were common topics of discussion with my roommates when I was an undergraduate at Penn, and that helped me to think about what I was seeing in a larger context.

The consequences of habitat destruction have followed me throughout my career. Almost everywhere I have worked with butterflies—New Jersey, Maryland, the San Francisco Bay Area, the Sierra Nevada, Colorado, New Mexico, Canada, Mexico, Australia, New Guinea, Malaysia, India, Tanzania, Zimbabwe, Panama, Brazil, Spain, Morocco, Costa Rica—I've seen natural areas in retreat before an expanding human enterprise. The increasingly depauperate lepidopteran fauna of the eastern United States (loss of a third of the butterflies in the past twenty years in a carefully monitored site in Ohio, for example) and in the Bay Area always makes me wish they could be restored to their previous glory. The famous lepidopterist William Henry Edwards wrote of seeing "countless" zebra swallowtails (*Graphium marcellus*) in West Virginia in the 1860s. I still remember with a thrill catching the only one I have ever seen, along the C&O Canal near Washington, D.C., some eighty years later—and many decades and countless housing developments before the present.

My friend and former student Dennis Murphy seems to suffer from a special curse with me. In Colorado, Nevada, and Morocco we've gone together to sample reported checkerspot populations but found on arrival bare ground rich in sheep or goat droppings, and no sign of butterflies or their food plants. But worst of all, as Dennis and I, along with Carol Boggs, Jessica Hellmann, John McLaughlin, Ray White, and others of my group slowly realized, the twelve-hundred-acre reserve of Jasper Ridge was no longer adequate to support even one population of a small herbivorous insect. Watching *E. editha*, the butterfly I had studied for decades, go extinct at that location, partly in response to climate change that had made its small habitat there useless or marginal, was deeply dispiriting. In 1997 our group handled seven Bay checkerspots on Jasper Ridge. Then they were gone.

Butterflies brought me enormous joy and incredible opportunities to see the world. But, in letting me see, as Aldo Leopold called it, that "world of wounds," butterflies have also produced in me a deep sadness—and a drive to reverse the ongoing destruction of the living world before it's too late.[9]

Still, butterflies gave me my biggest scientific thrill, the "discovery" of coevolution. Butterflies' most profound gift, though, I found anew every spring on Jasper Ridge with *E. editha* and then every summer in the form of the *Erebia, Oeneis, Colias, Glaucopsyche, Papilio, Chlosyne,* and other marvels of the Copper Creek valley above RMBL. I wouldn't trade those, and the other "gifts" traceable to butterflies such as Anne, and the students and dear friends who have shared butterflies with me, for anything. And even in the sad domain of conservation, in the constant failure to make more headway, being able to work with an incredible group of colleagues and good friends to save what we can of the natural world has kept my butterfly-generated luck intact. I wish the butterflies luck, too—I'm still reasonably sure *Pieris rapae* will outlast *Homo sapiens.*

SEVEN

Australia and a Trip around the World

It was World War II that first inspired me to become a pilot. In the early 1940s I was hoping the war (which I followed in detail with many colored pins stuck in maps) would last until I became a fighter pilot. That my red-green color-blindness would prevent this didn't dawn on me. I remember being thrilled at a museum in New York to see the remains of a Spitfire with bullet holes in its wings and to view gun-camera footage of Nazi bombers being shot down over Britain.

I didn't actually fly in an airplane until shortly after the war, when my parents took me in a DC-3 to Washington, D.C., from Newark airport. I was sad that it didn't rain during the flight—a friend of my parents had told me that when she flew, the plane had been going so fast that the drops rolled backward on the window. My summer adventures in the North, including the stall-turn in the Lancaster and being allowed to manipulate a Piper Pacer's controls on the flight to Shishmaref, all reinforced my determination to become a pilot one day. Just before I got my PhD I paid a few dollars at the Lawrence airport for two lessons in a Cessna 172, but going all the way to a license at the time was far out of reach financially.

Then my fortunes began to change, both in means and in a rationale. The means came with the extra money Dick Holm and I earned by writing the high school textbook, which made it possible for Anne and me to afford flying lessons. The rationale came with an opportunity to work with Charles Birch in Sydney, Australia. He had been one of my great heroes in the 1950s and with Charles Elton in England and H. G. "Andy" Andrewartha in Adelaide, he was one of the world's three foremost ecologists. My graduate school friend Howell Daly had given me the great book by Andrewartha and Birch, *The Distribution and Abundance of Animals*, and ever since I had wanted to work with Charles. I met him at the 1963 International Congress of Zoology in Washington, D.C., and persuaded him to let me spend a sabbatical year, 1965–66, with him at the University of Sydney. Charles and I had common interests in the theory of ecology, especially in the dynamics of populations (how and why they grew and shrank). I also was anxious to add Australia's interesting butterfly fauna to the work I was conducting on the theory of numerical taxonomy.

It was an ideal time for butterflies to lead me further afield. I had been promoted to associate professor with tenure in 1962, and the National Science Foundation had awarded me a postdoctoral fellowship to pay my expenses while in Australia. With that country's still-primitive road and rail system at the time, a light aircraft seemed an ideal tool for extensive fieldwork.

With means and rationalization secured, I started my lessons at Palo Alto airport in a Piper Pacer but quickly switched to a Cherokee 150, which Piper was just introducing. I had no natural talent for flying, and a reasonable ration of fear, reinforced in an early training flight by a near miss with two Douglas Skyraider attack aircraft climbing rapidly out of nearby Moffett Field. They came across our nose perhaps a hundred yards away, more than close enough for *any* pilot. But real terror almost gripped me later on my first solo flight away from the airport. It dawned on me, as I soared several thousand feet above Crystal Springs reservoir just south of San Francisco, that my life depended on some thin aluminum mated to a little reciprocating engine, all under control of the world's most incompetent pilot. I couldn't imagine that a few years later flying on instruments in forest-fire smoke across southern Canada on an *Erebia*-collecting trip, I would be so bored that I had to fight to stay awake. In any case, I overcame my terror and passed the test in 1964 to get my "airplane, single-engine, land" license, before Anne and I departed for Australia.

I was lucky in my training to be able to do some of it in Gunnison, Colorado, near RMBL, where the airstrip was at an elevation of over seven thousand feet, giving me practice at high-altitude operations. That would come in handy considerably later when I operated for years out of Gunnison in our Skymaster, a twin-engine aircraft whose single-engine ceiling was lower than the field altitude. Fortunately, one of my instructors did some crop dusting and had taught me about low-altitude maneuvering, too. It was Charley Alcock, my original instructor, though, who gave me the best standard advice for pilots: There are old pilots and bold pilots but no old, bold pilots.

In June 1965, Anne, Lisa (age nine), and I were off to Australia ("Oz") on the luxurious Matson Lines SS *Mariposa*—off on our greatest family adventure. In retrospect it was a fine choice of transport because, of course, "mariposa" is Spanish for "butterfly." It was a thrill to pass under the Golden Gate Bridge, and after an overnight stop with old KU friends in Los Angeles, we sailed for the South Seas and, eventually, a trip around the world. It would be a life-changing adventure more transformative than any other except perhaps my time with the Inuit in the Arctic. It would not only be an introduction to the flora and fauna of the globe but also an opportunity to experience an array of human societies in the flesh and gain an emotional appreciation of global inequities.

Despite being crammed together in a tiny inside cabin in the *Mariposa*, we began to get VIP treatment. It turned out Matson Lines thought I was the son of the famous San Francisco attorney Jake Ehrlich. Besides a special tour of the bridge, this had the great advantage of our getting to know Hal Wagner, the purser. He became a long-term friend, and greatly changed our lives.

Our first stop, on June 6, was at Bora Bora in the Society Islands of French Polynesia. We were stunned with the beauty of the place, and it was there that I first saw a gorgeous reef fish (a blue *Chromis*) from the beach through a dive mask. According to the letter I wrote to family and friends, "Anne said she had never seen me so manic as when I returned." Just one dive and I was hooked on underwater investigations. The next day we landed on Tahiti and took a launch to Mooréa, which I thought even more beautiful than Bora

Lisa and me before the captain's dinner on the Matson liner *Mariposa*. Anne made Lisa's outfit. Author photo.

Bora. There, the purser and I went off to do some serious snorkeling together, my first over a coral reef.

The mesmerizing spectacular beauty and diversity of the reef fish greatly reinforced my views as a preservationist—as well as a conservationist. The difference between these points of view in the United States traces back primarily to John Muir, a preservationist who founded the Sierra Club and gloried in nature for its own sake and for wilderness as a tonic, and Gifford Pinchot, who wanted to exploit nature carefully and sustainably for the benefit of humanity. This division persists today, with some thinking the battle

Anne and Lisa the same evening. Anne made her own outfit, too. Author photo.

is to save biodiversity for human benefit (preserve ecosystem services), others to save it for its own sake. A senseless dichotomy, since both reasons are valid to many, and the goals of both groups are similar.[1] And certainly everyone possible is needed to try to counter the forces that are destroying biodiversity, one of the most critical challenges facing humanity.[2] The debate became even more complex recently when it was revealed that Muir, like most of his white colleagues in the late nineteenth century, was a racist.[3]

For dinner on Mooréa we had our first *tamara'a*—roast suckling pig feast. The next day we hired a car and driver and took a trip around Tahiti, visiting all the tourist spots, such as Paul Gauguin's home and Point Venus, where James Cook observed the transit of Venus (the very rare and then scientifically important event of that planet passing across the face of the sun) in 1769, and, as I wrote at the time of our visit, "heard many hilarious tales of Marlon Brando's sex life (they say he was ambidextrous)." After enjoying the daytime beauties of Tahiti, Anne and I worked the bars at night, not quitting until 1:00 a.m., when the bar door closed behind us, and our cab load, smashed to the gills, had arrived back at our ship singing "La Marseillaise." This grim life of the field biologist continued with an offshore visit to beautiful Rarotonga in the Cook Islands (where Anne picked up two "gorgeous" seventeen-year-old boys who came aboard; they were "distressed to discover me, and worse yet, Lisa"). Rarotonga was followed by several interesting days in New Zealand. There, I visited the famous glowworm caves and listened to a botched description of the phenomenon, the luminescent fungus gnats (flies) that make a nice display on the cave walls being described as "beetles." We also found an island nation, as far as I could tell then, without decent food or drink.

Australia in 1965 also turned out to be a culinary desert. What a difference time makes, though—both New Zealand and Australia now boast excellent restaurants (on the whole we'd rather eat in Sydney than in Paris) and great wines. Our favorite whites now are Marlborough sauvignon blancs from New Zealand, and if we could afford them, there's no red we'd rather drink than Aussie Grange (well, we might make an exception for '45 Mouton, a '61 Petrus, or a '62 La Tache).

Charles Birch met us at the dock in Sydney, helped us buy a used car (a GM Holden, Australia's last production car), and located a fine apartment to rent near his, on Darling Point in Sydney Harbour. He quickly introduced me to the groups at Sydney University (where I was to be based) and at the Australian Museum, where Frank Talbot, whom I had previously met at Stanford, was curator of fishes, and his wife, Sue, was a marine biologist. Everyone was very welcoming, throwing parties, and introducing us to Aussie wines (Don McMichael, curator of mollusks at the museum, was a member of the Australian Wine Consumers' Union; he and his wife, Helen, became yet another couple of long-term friends). Frank was a demon sailor, and we have, over the years, enjoyed many a yachting excursion on Sydney Harbour with the Talbots.

Early in our stay I developed a weird but nasty allergy. At seemingly random times my upper lip would swell and large, watery blisters would appear on my back. I knew I wasn't allergic to Anne and had not acquired any Aussie girlfriends, so the source of the problem was a great mystery. Virtually everything I had contact with—from soaps, furniture, detergents, and Australian butterflies to Australian fruits, smoked fish roes, and local newspaper—was new to my immune system. Anne and I tried eliminating contacts with various of these items, but the attacks, though distressing, were not frequent enough to make that an effective method of isolating the cause. Then one day when I settled down to do a dissection, the allergy and the answer came upon me simultaneously.

Before our Australian trip I knew we would be traveling with a fine dissecting microscope—essential for the research we would do. I had bought a special cushioned case, designed for cameras, in which to pack the scope. Using a razor blade I had carefully cut the plastic foam inserts of the case to fit the scope. The outgassing of solvent from the cut foam caused me a bad coughing, gasping, nausea fit. It had cleared up in a few minutes, but apparently that episode had sensitized me to the solvent: every time I extracted the scope from the case and used it, the allergy soon returned. Anne was unaffected and took over the packing and unpacking of the scope, which served us well around the world.

It was my great good fortune, in Australia and beyond, that Charles and I had similar heterodox views on ecology and evolution, and we hit it off not just personally but also scientifically. Charles was quiet and unassuming, but he had a great and devilish sense of humor. One instance of that was persuading the distinguished evolutionary cytologist Michael J. D. White to invite me to give a seminar at the University of Melbourne. White was born in London, but curiously had an accent that resembled Dobzhansky's Russian one. Once when he asked a question after a Dobzhansky seminar, the audience cracked up thinking he was imitating Doby.

I gave my seminar, which was basically an attack on what I considered (and still consider) silly ideas about "species concepts." When I was finished, White, who was chair, started what I thought was the Q&A session with comments on the errors I had made. Little did I know that it was his custom to instruct his group about what they should think of any seminar, so I naturally pointed out that he was completely wrong. This led to a general intellectual brawl, in which one of White's colleagues, Murray Littlejohn, who would later have a distinguished career studying frog vocalizations, argued hard with me that frog populations having different calls showed that they were "good species" (that is, fitting Ernst Mayr's concept of different species). I responded by saying something like, "Just because one frog says 'breckix, breckix' and another 'ribbbit, ribbbit' doesn't tell you whether or not they will mate and produce viable offspring." A month or so later Charles, having known perfectly well what likely would have happened, ran into White and asked him how my seminar went. White responded in his Dobzhanskian accent: "Vary interesting, vary prowakitive. Vary insoolting. Vy, he efen imitated frog calls."

Hal Wagner's introduction of me to reef fishes led to what became one of the most delightful periods of our lives and in a way reconnected me with the guppies of my childhood. While we were in Sydney that year, we made a trip to Heron Island, where Anne and I enjoyed a lot of snorkeling and started to learn the different reef fishes and their ecology. I could hardly believe the beauty and diversity of the reefs, especially the varied forms of the corals and the multitudes of gorgeous fishes. It was like the rain forests to which I had been introduced in Mexico, but with all the animals to be enjoyed in plain view and in great abundance.

One of the major mysteries of the time was the evolutionary origins of poster colors—the spectacular color patterns—of reef fishes. The famous behaviorist Konrad Lorenz had hypothesized that the colors were territorial signals, one fish telling another member of the same species that a chunk of reef was its exclusive domain. But even with little reef experience, I didn't believe it. Among the most gloriously colored reef fishes are the butterfly fishes (Chaetodontidae), and I had repeatedly seen them schooling—not a typical behavior for a territorial animal (plate 15). Frank Talbot confirmed this observation, and after I returned to Stanford we brainstormed by mail about how to test territorial behavior under water. That led to great adventures together in the 1970s.

I had started a project to test territorial behavior in starlings on Jasper Ridge, using the classic technique of putting out a stuffed starling in various places and seeing who would fly out to attack it. My early results suggested the starlings were territorial, but I lacked the time and assistance to do a proper study. But stuffed butterfly fishes didn't seem like a great idea. Then Frank, who had just taken over as director of the Australian Museum, showed his genius: he suggested that the museum's exhibit department make us some models. And we soon had in our hands a set of beautiful simulated butterfly fishes, carved from wood, exquisitely painted, and waterproofed with transparent plastic (plate 14).

We ended up presenting the models on Lucite wands to real live butterfly fishes at Lizard Island on the Great Barrier Reef. Most species schooled with the models, we found. By doing a lot of dusk and dawn diving (just when the sharks came up over the reefs), we found that real territorial tiffs occurred between individuals over favorite nighttime shelters in crevasses in the reefs. So much for Lorenz's hypothesis that poster colors were primarily territorial signals. We concluded, instead, that they primarily functioned in other behaviors such as pair bonding and predator avoidance. The colors made it easy to recognize members of their own species, and their thin, flat bodies made them seem to disappear when they turned to flee and their brightly painted sides were no longer visible to an attacker.

Frank's and my next Pacific project at Lizard was a study of the community ecology of butterfly fishes. We assembled the usual gang and recruited my very smart Stanford colleague Jon Roughgarden (who later became Joan Roughgarden) for the research, and the great advantage of working with reef fishes came home to me again. Jon did not know the fishes at all, but during our flight to Australia and on a couple of snorkels, I was able to teach him to identify twenty or so of the distinctively colored species of chaetodontids that he would see close up, swimming slowly as they feed over the reef on small animals and algae. (In contrast, it might take months to train a colleague working with me inside a tropical forest to identify twenty tanager species—with the birds flitting through the vegetation and only rarely moving slowly in view.)

We censused the fishes at a series of sites from the outer barrier where the reefs ended in the Coral Sea, all the way in to the shallows off the Queensland beaches. In the latter sites, we scuba dived with all exposed skin covered with plastic bags to protect against the stings of box jellies—the sometimes lethal relatives of man o' war jellyfish that are common in those waters. Our work strongly suggested that marine vertebrate communities were structured in ways very similar to terrestrial communities. For example, coexisting reef fish species often obviously occupy different niches, as do coexisting species in terrestrial communities—just as lions and cheetahs use different techniques (sudden ambush versus long pursuit) for hunting some of the same prey animals.

In order to dissuade sharks, those of our gang who were scuba diving wore black wet suits we had painted with wide white stripes. That was based on a then-famous "experiment" in which a researcher donned such a suit, put a raincoat over it, entered an area where he had attracted sharks with meat chunks, and then opened the raincoat. When he "exposed himself" to the sharks, they reportedly fled. The utterly unsupported thesis was that by doing this we were mimicking poisonous sea snakes that supposedly freaked out the sharks. We had no real trouble with sharks; I was threatened once or twice by reef sharks (about six feet long) with pectoral fins down, arched-back, head-thrashing territorial displays, but I always just moved away, and that usually ended the interaction. Four or five of them once backed a colleague, Barry Russell, and me up against a reef wall, but maybe they were just curious. We had bang sticks—shotgun shells in gun barrels on the ends of poles (jamming one hard into a shark would detonate the shell and kill the shark)—but I had serious doubts of my ability to use one well if attacked;

reef sharks are damned fast and agile. I once saw Anne circled by reef sharks several times when she was taking data on chaetodontids while snorkeling, but she never noticed them, and she never worried, because, she quipped, she knew the dangerous sharks were *man*-eaters.

One of the most memorable underwater bits of research Anne and I later did together was an investigation of dominance hierarchies in schooling reef fish. We chose to do it on gorgeous Bora Bora, where, with Hal Wagner, I had first seen a reef fish in the wild, and where the Hotel Bora Bora featured cabins on stilts over the reef, complete with lights trained on the reef and a transparent plastic plate in the floor so you could watch the fish at night from your bed. There was a porch, and below that, a sea-level platform with a freshwater shower to which a boat would deliver fresh scuba tanks each day and take away the empties. Throw in a good restaurant nearby, and doing fieldwork there was pure hell, every minute of it.

The classic method of determining whether nonhuman animals had dominance hierarchies was to show them themselves in a mirror. The animal interprets this image as a stranger, and if it is in a dominance hierarchy, it will take steps to determine the rank of the stranger—usually by attacking it. We thus brought with us to Bora Bora a couple of big plastic mirrors and propped them up under our cabin so they would be encountered by a variety of fishes. It was often quite amusing to see a wrasse (labrid) viciously pecking at its image while moving up the mirror. When it reached the top of the mirror, its "enemy" would magically disappear, much to its obvious consternation. The advantage of this method over using models was that it could present a precise replica image to a visually oriented animal; the disadvantage was that we could not control which individuals were exposed to their own image.

Our experiments showed that many of the local reef fishes clearly had dominance hierarchies. When individuals saw themselves in the mirror, they would often attack the image as a stranger; when not at the mirror they swam peacefully with other members of their own species (with whom they had presumably established relative ranks). Perhaps our most interesting discovery was that surgeon fishes did not peck at their images but rather swiped at them with their tails. The bony spines at the base of those tails (which give

Surgeon fish (*Ctenochaetus*) at Bora Bora demonstrating the existence of a dominance hierarchy. It is attacking its image in a mirror, mistaking it for an individual it hadn't previously encountered, in an attempt to assume dominance. Author photo.

the fishes their name) were thought to be defenses against being eaten. Perhaps so, but in our case they were used as offensive weapons against members of their own species. The resulting paper, like our other reef fish publications, had a stunningly high (research) fun-to-page ratio.

A great part of our 1965–66 Australian sabbatical adventure turned out to involve flying to various otherwise remote locales. Soon after getting to Sydney, I joined the Royal Aero Club of New South Wales, which checked me out for flying under rules much more strict than those in the States.[4] Once certified, I was able to rent a Cessna 172, call sign VH-DIR, from the club. My initial foray with it was to Canberra to consult with Ian Common, the leading butterfly expert in Oz.

Anne and I were working over the course of the sabbatical on the internal anatomy of various species of butterflies, especially on determining whether females had mated and, if so, how many times and how many mature eggs they carried. We were also dissecting other internal anatomy to test the numerical taxonomy nexus hypothesis (remember, that the basic similarities between kinds of butterflies would be revealed in any large selection of characteristics one chose to analyze). Both studies required us to get fresh individuals for Anne and me to dissect. Anne had by this time moved on from creating gorgeous illustrations to collaborating with me on studies of the microscopic anatomy of the butterflies to studying their mating habits. Getting a broad taxonomic sample of living butterflies involved a lot of travel to where interesting species could be found. For instance, we flew VH-DIR north to Gladstone in Queensland to find the big greasy (*Cressida cressida*) to dissect. It is the only swallowtail butterfly whose males apply an impressive structure to the female's genital opening after transferring a packet of sperm to her. The idea is to protect the male's genetic investment by blocking out sperm from a subsequent male (remember, natural selection works by some individuals outreproducing others). *Cressida cressida* is restricted to northern coastal Australia and New Guinea, and VH-DIR conveniently took us to a recommended area to find and dissect it. Which we did.

As my student Pat Labine had shown in the early 1960s, it turns out that male checkerspots also plug the female genital opening after copulation—but not with a spectacular external structure.[5] In some clever experiments, she showed that if she removed the plug, revirginizing a female, the sperm from a second copulation were nearly always the ones that fertilized the eggs. Human males have also evolved ways to enhance or protect their genetic "investment." Their penises are shaped to excavate sperm from previous copulations during intercourse, and the last part of the ejaculate tends to be spermicidal, producing a nasty environment for the next partner's sperm.

I started doing fieldwork in more distant sites as well on the Oz sabbatical. The first of those trips, to New Guinea (which included the Solomon Islands), was my first tropical forest fieldwork expedition since the Mexico trip with Mich, and our first en famille. We flew commercial to Port Moresby in early November and were met by Joe Szent-Ivany, a local entomologist who specialized in setting up New Guinea field trips for other entomologists. Lisa (then ten) and I did the collecting, and poor Anne spent most of her days over a microscope doing dissections—an activity in which I joined her whenever I returned from the field.

One especially memorable part of the New Guinea trip was a visit to the Wau field station in the highlands. Getting there included a spectacular landing in a DC-3 on a short uphill strip and then travel by a road that traversed a considerable altitudinal gradient and gave access to a great diversity of butterfly species. The Wau field station itself featured a ten-by-twenty-five-foot front porch overlooking the lowlands. On the porch were sheet-covered walls and ceiling and a mercury vapor lamp. On a good night I calculated that there were more than twenty thousand moths on the porch, and probably more than a hundred species (plate 7). It was fantastic—almost enough to make me switch from butterflies to moths. I sent a sample of about three thousand moths to the American Museum of Natural History. Just trying to explain their resting patterns on the sheet could occupy many PhD dissertations, if they could be explained at all.

We could still see (and hear) signs of the pre–World War I German occupation of New Guinea while we were there. Shillings were still called "marks" by the locals, house was "haus," and you told the dog to "raus." The station staff always addressed me as "Mastah." While at Wau, I came to the rescue of our helper, Beenak. He had been told by a missionary that he couldn't attend church without a necktie. He needed a lift into town to spend eighteen shillings (two weeks' wages) for one, otherwise he would be condemned to hell. I bought Beenak the necktie.

New Guineans had had relatively little contact with the developed world until World War II, when they were suddenly introduced by the Japanese, Australians, and Americans to unprecedented levels of cruelty and material abundance. Some New Guineans were extremely helpful to the Aussies fighting to stop the Japanese force aiming to attack Port Moresby. The Imperial Army was attempting to cross the island's Owen Stanley mountain spine from north to south via the steep, muddy, mosquito-infested Kokoda Trail—a hideous World War II campaign now little known outside of Australia and Japan. The abundance of weapons, vehicles, food, and other materials that flowed in with the troops led other locals, logically enough, to believe that there was a magical source of that cargo that was attracted to the airfields and the harbors the foreigners had constructed. Some locals then formed what became known as cargo cults, constructing mock airfields and conducting imitation military drills to try to attract cargo to themselves. It's an idea similar to that of perpetual growth, still found among peoples addicted to magical thinking in university economics departments.

In 1965–66 many of the expatriates we met speculated on what would happen if the Aussies pulled out of New Guinea, which many wanted to do because of the administrative and financial drag on their own government. One common comment was that "hundreds of tribes, all speaking different languages, would return to slaughtering each other." It was true that intergroup warfare had been common in New Guinea before colonial occupation, just as it had been in Europe between dynasties and religious cults for centuries through World War II, but much, perhaps most of it, in New Guinea was ritualized, with light casualties. A few dozen killed was nothing compared to the millions slaughtered in, say, the Hundred Years' or Thirty Years' Wars and, of course, the World Wars. Fortunately, there was none of the predicted massive warfare after 1975, when New Guinea gained independence, but low-level intertribal violence was still common. On a Stanford alumni trip to New Guinea in the 1990s, for example, our tourist bus had to be guarded when it went through one tribe's territory. New Guineans, like other people, are great politicians. Unhappily they, like us, often have corrupt leaders; and relative ignorance of the modern world does not help those leaders when negotiating deals with, say, Japanese or Chinese timber companies (just as ignorance of the modern world fueled the Trump administration's withdrawal from the Paris Climate Accords). Much of New Guinea is being deforested, and the remaining forests are threatened by climate disruption as a result. Ritual warfare persists in some remote highland areas, sadly now made much more lethal by a gradual influx of AK-47s. Ritual warfare now endemic in U.S. foreign policy of course dwarfs in lethality that of New Guinea.

When I went butterfly collecting in the lowland area around Lae, site of fierce battles between Allied troops and the Japanese army, I found lots of abandoned artifacts, including two magazines of rusted cartridges that I assumed came from a Japanese Nambu light machine gun. There, besides collecting, I took a day off and, through my NSW Aero Club contacts, got to do aerobatics with an instructor, a Trans Australia Airlines (TAA) captain, in a Victa Airtourer 115, an unusual light aircraft with coordinated ailerons and flaps (called flapperons).

We were then off from Lae to Mount Hagen in search of more butterfly species in the highlands. Thanks to my new TAA connection, I was invited to the DC-3's cockpit and was given a wonderful tour of old Japanese airstrips and opportunities to take photos of some villages. Mount Hagen itself was pretty much of a bust as a butterfly collecting area, though. When I was a kid, I used to pore over *National Geographic* maps imagining butterfly-rich areas on the islands of the southwest Pacific. But in truth, accessible areas were often depauperate, with seas of kunai grass (a notorious invader of disturbed areas) surrounding villages. It was only through the courtesy of the district officers Joe Szent-Ivany had contacted for us that we usually got to the small patches of remnant native vegetation that would yield samples of the butterflies we needed for dissection. Nature again was shrinking in the face of human expansion; throughout a year of global collecting we repeatedly had to search for remaining patches of unmutilated terrain.

We then proceeded in a DC-3 to Madang on the north coast through bad weather, but I was invited once again on the flight deck. The aircraft had been the command plane in the western desert of the famous World War II British general Bernard Montgomery, reengined many times, and it was thrilling to steer it around the sky. We went on to Wewak the next day, November 26, 1965, from whence we had a chartered flight to Maprik. Then a remote settlement on the Sepik River about two hundred miles from the sea, Maprik was famous for Sepik art, often displayed in, or on, Haus Tamburans (spirit houses). We had some good butterfly collecting excursions there in spite of lousy weather. I was lucky enough to see for the first time a tree kangaroo in the field, and Anne, according to my letters, "went blind dissecting." One day Anne, Lisa, and I drove to the middle branch of the Sepik, rented a dugout about thirty-five feet long with an outboard, and the three of us took off for a day's excursion down the surprisingly wide river with a local agricultural officer and crew. We passed many small settlements, and the presence of Anne and Lisa caused quite a stir, since white women and children were rarely seen in the area.

Before returning to Maprik, we saw in the village of Korogo a spectacular Haus Tamburan, about fifty feet high with a beautifully decorated facade. Haus Tamburans are the sites of long series of initiations of a tribe's male members. When in use, they are crammed with the painted ancestor carvings for which the Sepik area is famed. Women are not usually allowed inside, but since this one was not in ceremonial use, I got Anne and Lisa in.

We also saw the tightly woven reed mats slept in by the locals to protect themselves from the area's famous mosquito plague. How they escaped suffocation inside the mats we couldn't figure.

We wanted to buy some local art at Maprik—since the art of the Middle Sepik was world famous. Anne and I had already decided that rather than stocks and bonds, we'd do our long-term saving by investing in art. The council house didn't have anything for sale then, so we decided to gamble and left $100 (a fortune for us at the time) with the local missionary and asked him to buy and send us something nice when it was available. We figured people there needed the money more than we did regardless, and we basically forgot about the arrangement. But several years later when we were doing fieldwork in the Caribbean, John Montgomery, our attorney friend in Palo Alto, took delivery for us of two four-by-four-by-eight-foot cases full of Sepik art. They had been put on a tramp steamer and traveled for years to reach San Francisco. Our friends all benefited, and we've been living with several especially nice pieces ever since. The New Guinea artists had been super generous.

My letter home from Maprik contained the following New Guinea "bits of local color" in an area of sad contact between cultures:

> The chirping of gekkos in your room as they devour the bugs. Mt. Hagen men with leaf jock straps and birds-of-paradise feathers stuck in their hair. Natives in the bush around Maprik trying to sell you spears. Native kids trailing you around offering to help "kissim bimbi" (collect butterflies) for money or cigarettes. Natives disfigured with grilli (a fungus disease of the skin). The stink of feces (almost everywhere). Polluted streams. Cicadas 10 times as loud as I've ever heard them. Confused roosters that start crowing at 2:00 AM. The drunk down the hall barfing at 3:00 AM. Native drums and howling at 4:00 AM. Ants, roaches, and spiders crawling around at 6:00 AM. The alarm going off at 6:30 AM. No drinkable water—must subsist on beer and soft drinks ("lolly water"). Big elapid snakes in the bush that come for you instead of retreating like a good snake should. In some ways I prefer Palo Alto.

Our next stop after New Guinea was Rabaul, New Britain, where, after a miserable night in an awful hotel we were taken in by a wonderful couple who put us up at their home for a few days while we continued our butterfly research. Our final stop on the research tour was Honiara, on the island of Guadalcanal, where butterflies again brought Anne and me together with our longtime interest in World War II. It was weird to collect birdwing butterflies along the Tenaru River, the site of a famously bloody battle between the U.S. Marines and Imperial Japanese infantry in August of 1942. I captured one gloriously beautiful specimen just a few yards from a presumably still-live five-inch naval shell lying in a pigpen near the river.

Back in Australia, thanks to the kindness of Charles Birch, I met John Le Gay Brereton, a parrot evolutionist, ecologist, and animal behaviorist, and we became friends and flying companions. John was an ex–Royal Australian Air Force fighter pilot known as "Cocky" Brereton, who had flown P-40E Kittyhawks in New Guinea in 1942.[6] He was an infinitely more experienced and skilled pilot than I was, having flown close air support in the desperate battles for Milne Bay. We visited together some of his outback parrot suppliers, and I vividly recall the lunch to which we were invited at a sheep station in western New South Wales. The friendly couple served us what I described as "paved" mutton chops, one of which has been in my stomach for five decades, unable to get through my pyloric valve. Unhappily, the place was bone dry, and I got no butterflies.

I wanted to see more of the Australian fauna, butterflies and otherwise, and Anne and I were becoming increasingly interested in Aboriginal art. In those days few people were, and we could buy bark paintings from the Church Missionary Society for $5 to $10. Anglican missionaries were trying to convince Aborigine artists to bowdlerize their paintings, but we were early enough to get a fine thunder-god bark painting where the god still had his balls.

John Brereton, Charles Birch, and I planned a trip to Aboriginal villages in northern Queensland. Anne could not go because she had to stay with

Lisa (sexism in retrospect). John was part owner of an air taxi company that included in its fleet a Piper Comanche, a fast, light aircraft with retractable landing gear that I was anxious to fly. Charles had a key contact: he was acquainted with the bishop of Carpenteria, whose permission in those days was required to visit the Aboriginal villages. Australia had a long tradition of copying the worst aspects of Britain, as in their early cuisine, a dismal banking system, and an established religion (the Church of England) to whose "care" the Aborigines that had survived the British invasion of their homeland had been consigned.

Charles extracted a letter of permission from the bishop, and we flew to Cairns on the first day, John letting me take the controls to get accustomed to the Comanche. Before we landed we got out the pilot's manual, actually a typewritten copy of the real thing, to check the approach speed for the short-field landings we expected to need at the strips near the Aboriginal villages. I happened to look at Charles in the back seat. He was white as a sheet—he thought his pilots were reading up on how to land the airplane!

I went into the Cairns landing, practicing short-field technique on its long runway, keeping the airspeed precisely on mark. But very near touchdown the Comanche did a slight judder, indicating the approach to a stall. Before I could react John's hand was over mine, jamming the throttle forward. The plane recovered nicely, and we later discovered that the manual had been miscopied, with the short-field approach speed reduced by ten knots, essentially removing the safety margin. It pays to have a pro as your copilot.

Visiting Mitchell River and Edward River was interesting but depressing, the Anglican Church having tried to change the Aborigines' nomadic ways by pushing them into sheet-metal versions of Cape Cod cottages. We were told they mostly slept outside—their ancient custom. We then flew on to Karumba, where we spent the night on our way to visit the Aborigines of Mornington Island.

On Mornington Island, there had been no tradition of bark painting, but we met Goobalathaldin, an ingenious Aborigine artist who had heard about the practice years earlier and had gotten some books illustrating bark paintings from Sydney. When Goobalathaldin was about eight, he was taken into the Mornington Island Presbyterian Mission and renamed Dick. The missionary found out that Dick's father's name was Kiwarbija, meaning Rough Sea, and thus Goobalathaldin became Dick Roughsey to the English-speaking world. We were lucky enough to add an acrylic as well as a bark painting he had done of the same scene to our collection. Subsequently, Dick became famous through his art, writing, and organizing of performances for introducing Aussies to the culture of one of the longest sustained societies in the world. He was the first Aborigine to write an autobiography, and his wife wrote one, too. He died on Mornington Island in 1985 at the age of sixty-five.[7]

I continued flying in Australia when I could the rest of that sabbatical year and even learned some aerobatics in a de Havilland Chipmunk, an old RAF trainer the aero club owned. Besides the feeling of freedom, the liberty to go where you wanted and view what you wanted, and the tremendous advantage of getting quickly to obscure field sites and photographing them from the air, it was largely the challenge of flying itself that appealed to me. Science and blabbing came easily, but I was no natural pilot. I studied and practiced religiously and always read the accident reports in the aviation magazines. In science, it was normally years between starting a project and getting the reviews of your publication that would indicate whether it had been a success. In aviation you planned a flight in the morning, and by the end of the day it was unambiguous whether it had been a success. Few things in life were as thrilling to me as, after flying in clouds for a couple of hours, breaking out on an instrument approach and seeing the sequenced flashing lights of the so-called rabbit and the big white number on the approach end of a rainy runway just ahead.

Our year in Australia was wonderfully productive scientifically, especially since, in addition to the butterfly research, Charles Birch and I had close interactions and coauthored several papers on a theoretical issue in population dynamics. Along with Charles, I made one of my best secondhand contributions to population biology. Charles and I met several times with Robert

May, then starting a career as a theoretical physicist but also interested in evolution and ecology. We explained to Bob that the latter area was (and is) much more exciting and important; he seems to have believed us and became one of the world's leading theorists in our field. Bob ended up in Britain, became Lord Robert, president of the Royal Society, and chief science adviser to the government. "Lord Bob" likely was my best contribution to theory!

In the summer of 1966, on the way back from Oz, Anne, Lisa, and I collected and dissected through Malaysia, Cambodia, Thailand, India, Kashmir, and East Africa. In Malaysia, by pure chance, we ended up staying in a hotel in the Cameron Highlands owned by a Chinese millionaire who was deeply interested in butterflies. Anne and I showed him how to dissect and identify them. In return, he asked a group of his indigenous Malay employees to climb tall trees and net the nearly-impossible-to-get-from-the-ground females of *Trogonoptera brookiana*, the beautiful Rajah Brooke's birdwing, for us to dissect (plate 10). He later helped us to obtain some traditional sculptures from those same Malaysian aborigines, took us on a tour of Malaysian hotels run by his friends, and treated us to the best Chinese food we've ever encountered—much to the dismay of Lisa, who on that trip was still searching for hot dogs and bologna. (Now she makes dim sum and kicks herself for not taking advantage of our gustatory opportunity.)

After a visit to Cambodia (Angkor Wat and Angkor Thom) and Thailand, where we were basically tourists, we went to Kashmir via New Delhi in search of high-altitude satyrine butterflies (like my favorite genus, *Erebia*). It was a mistake. On our way there, by reserving what was reputed to be the second best hotel in New Delhi, we'd ended up in a place with mice swarming across the lobby in the daytime, and that was just the beginning. Bad enough there, but the result of this cash-conserving strategy in Srinagar was an unmitigated disaster. To call the hotel we ended up in a dump would have been to lavish praise upon it.

I don't recall the details, but the next day we managed to rent a house-

Malay aborigine spirit sculpture of Hantu Makan Anak, a child-eating spirit. Author photo.

boat on the famous Dal Lake, complete with meals. We moved into the boat, which was clean and obviously recently constructed and quite pleasant. The lake itself was beautiful, and in the evening one of the staff from the houseboat took us for a lovely ride on a *shikara*—essentially a canoe with a roof and cushioned seating—through areas of the lake covered with water lilies.

The next day in search of more butterfly species we tried to get to Gulmarg, today a high-elevation ski resort but in 1966 reached only on horseback. In one of our family's famous reminiscences, when it became known that we needed three horses for the climb, we were almost trampled by dozens of local residents eager for us to rent their steeds. As in many of the third world areas we visited, the extent of poverty and poor nutrition was overwhelming. Even after we had hired the horses we needed, a crowd kept following us, hoping for tips "to keep the little girl [Lisa] from falling off her horse." (In fact, Lisa was already a more accomplished rider than Anne or I was.) After all that, Gulmarg itself was deeply disappointing: all the open areas were overgrazed down to stubble with no sign of any butterflies. Another example of nature desolated.

Things only got worse. We discovered that the dishes from our meals on the houseboat were being washed in the lake a full two feet from the outflow of the toilets. None of those complex parasite life cycles for us—direct anus-to-mouth transmission! We decided to flee back south and ended up in Delhi again, all with bacillary dysentery. Shankar Narayan, a wonderful Indian colleague from graduate school, and his wife rescued us by providing a local antibiotic, which worked, and taking us into their home, where we recovered. They were strict vegetarians and served us great yogurt and lentil dishes, which I loved. But I must admit that after a few meatless days any sacred cow that wandered near me was in mortal danger.

India, more than anywhere, made stark the tragedy of what Anne and I increasingly recognized as potentially catastrophic—overpopulation, hence the passages on famine, teeming streets, and the like in the beginning of *The Population Bomb.* Overpopulation of any animal, including *Homo sapiens,* occurs when there are so many that the capacity of their environment to support them in the future is degraded, or if average well-being would increase if there were fewer individuals. Sadly, the passages in the *Bomb* did not emphasize that overpopulation in high-consuming rich countries was worse for our life-support systems than overpopulation among the poor. We thus did not point out the entwined role of population growth and individual overconsumption in nature's diminishment and humanity's increasing peril. But that was a consequence of our naivete and our lack of the kind of analysis we later developed in response to our experiences on that sabbatical.

Although we certainly saw plenty of poverty in Southeast Asia, at least in the places we visited it was not with the same immense press of people or with the same depth of poverty or lack of sanitation we found in India. Our experience there really brought home to us how lucky we were. The same feeling of personal privilege, sorrow, and anger at injustice has followed us around the world over the years, and not just in Asia, Latin America, and Africa. Economic inequity has escalated globally since our experience of urban India in the 1960s. It has become intense in a different register in Palo Alto, especially since Ronald Reagan in his years as governor promoted the insanity of deinstitutionalizing the mentally ill—throwing many of them on the streets without adequate care. In the 1980s homeless people, often mentally disturbed, appeared begging in the streets of the Bay Area while the wealth of the local Silicon Valley rich continued to soar. The overall global dominance of wealth is, sadly, only likely to worsen for the foreseeable future. So is the situation of those ill, physically or mentally, even in the United States, which could easily give all its inhabitants good care.

From India we were all grateful to move on to Nairobi, which seemed an oasis of relatively cool climate and much less risky food. Our first experience with an African game park was Nairobi National Park, right at the edge of Kenya's capital city. There we saw our first free-roaming big African animals, including giraffes, zebras, and elephants. We rented a small car and the three of us ventured out to Tsavo National Park, about 160 miles southeast of Nairobi. We were rewarded with sightings of many more African animals, especially more elephants. On our way out of the park, however, we discovered that our rental car had an oil leak. The road was basically wide enough only for one car and, with dusk falling, we were dismayed when the two women in the car ahead of us decided that our honking, in an attempt to get by while the car was still drivable, was inappropriate and so decided to go even more slowly. Finally, they relented and let us pass; we barely made it back to the hotel before the oil ran out. Lisa reminds me that what followed was one instance in which she discovered her old man was capable of self-control. The two women went to some trouble to track us down based on the rental car license plates and found us later waiting for dinner at the hotel restaurant. Having listened to me invoke the Lord's name in vain in some detail while the women were blocking us, Lisa was expecting to watch me verbally eviscerate them when they confronted us. Rather to her disappointment, I calmly explained what our predicament had been and expressed sincere distress at having been forced to honk in the game park, hoping desperately not to be trapped there for the night. Given the explanation, they were quite understanding.

After that we flew south to Malawi. There we met up and went on safari with one of my first two doctoral students, Michael Soulé, and his wife, Jan, who were living on the outskirts of Blantyre while Michael helped found the first university in the country. In then Portuguese East Africa, we and the Soulés traveled around the fringes of the war between Salazar's Portuguese colonial dictatorship and the Frelimo (Frente de Libertação de Moçambique) then battling to free the country. We saw occasional villages burning, but most frightening was speeding along roads that consisted of two approximately six-inch-wide paved strips, resulting in spectacular games of chicken when vehicles traveling in opposing directions met.

In Southern Rhodesia (now Zimbabwe) we all committed the capital crime of criticizing Ian Smith's government, but because of our skin color we were not prosecuted and did not end up on death row as did others. When we were returned to our motel in Salisbury (now Harare) one night driven by the Black law professor and his attorney wife with whom we had dined, the motel owner intercepted us and explained how dangerous it had been for us because "they are just out of the trees."

That trip initiated Anne's and my long love affair with Africa. We've been there many times since and have become nostalgic about many of its people, places, and animals. We're actually hooked on watching some of the big five game animals (black rhino, African elephant, Cape buffalo, African lion, and African leopard), so called for their reputations to be the most dangerous to hunt on foot.

Visitors now have to see what they can and photograph fast, because elephants, rhinos, and lions are all being exterminated at frightening speeds. Elephants, of course, are prime targets for poachers servicing a strong market, particularly among rich Chinese and Vietnamese, for ivory. The story on rhino is even sadder in one way. Rhinos are greatly imperiled in part because of the putative aphrodisiac and other medicinal qualities of their horns (the chemical equivalent of human fingernail clippings). It was thought by many of us to be a problem that would be solved by Viagra (which actually works). But then I heard the rumor that the rhino horn dealers were adding Viagra to the ground-up horn, so that it, too, "works." How depressing is that? But the desire for rhino horn for other uses (carved into dagger handles, art objects, and so on) is much more broad-based and thus a more difficult market to end.

The first trip to Africa ended a stunningly interesting, educational, and active year that Anne, Lisa, and I will always treasure. One thing I brought home from the trip was the metazoan I've been closest to, a thirty-foot beef tapeworm acquired by my habit of loving beef extremely rare. The diagnosis and divorce from hermaphroditic Herman-Hermione is a medical saga in itself. The other thing I brought home was a much more global picture of communities of butterflies and other animals, especially human animals and, of course, the human predicament. At the very least it made us all more worldly and more aware of the great inequities in the human condition. It was really the start of my ever-deepening interest in international inequity and the global destruction of nature. The loss of natural habitat in Bethesda that later would stun me when I revisited old butterfly hunting grounds was a worldwide phenomenon.

EIGHT

The Population Bomb and the Carson Years

Science Meets Notoriety

The 1960s and early 1970s were a time of frantic activity for me and many others of our generation. For me, there was much turmoil in both science and politics—against a background of the Vietnam War and the influence on me of two of my heroes, Rachel Carson and Johnny Carson. The frantic activity, I must admit in retrospect, was partly rooted in my naivete. It was the era of my emergence as a public scientist-activist, addressing both what I thought science could contribute to understanding some large issues of the time and what I thought ought to be done to address them. In retrospect, from 2021 I can see that, although many considered me overly pessimistic, I was actually wildly optimistic about what would be accomplished if society's leaders and the public were alerted to the dangers ahead.

My early problems raising butterflies in New Jersey and early work on DDT with Robert Sokal had deepened my concern over the toxification of the landscape and predisposed me, a few years later, in 1962, to appreciate Rachel Carson's message in *Silent Spring.* The book was a brilliant exposé of the misuse of pesticides, introducing readers to the problems of toxification of the biosphere. It was written in Carson's lyrical style and carried the compelling image of the disappearance of birdsong from everyone's lives. It's a classic still worth reading. The general public, as well as many governments and corporate entities, had viewed synthetic organic pesticides as miracle compounds that were saving us from disease and pestiferous insects, and they paid little heed to the trend to soak the world with these substances or the actual implications of that toxic soaking. For instance, in the peak year of its application, 1959, nearly eighty million pounds of DDT were spread around in the United States alone—almost half a pound per person. Anne and I well remember that when we went to a drive-in theater in Lawrence a portable fogger blasted DDT through our open car window. Not good for our health, we were sure, but I was acutely aware of another downside in particular: development of pest resistance to the insecticide from overuse. DDT had been employed to virtually exterminate housefly populations around Topeka, Kansas. Local residents then grew more sloppy in such practices as disposing of lawn clippings in which the insects bred. No surprise, the flies soon became DDT resistant, and the fly plague came back worse than before.

When I was hired at Stanford in 1959, I was asked to teach a course in evolution. It was a ten-week course, and I spent the first nine weeks explaining where human beings had come from and the last week explaining where I thought humanity was going. The course was popular, and the students very much liked that last week of lectures. By the mid-sixties, attention to Rachel Carson's work had alerted much of the world about the problems with pesticide overuse and my work with Bob Sokal had given me a lot of lecture material on the evolution of pesticide resistance and, by extension, the sure-to-come problems of antibiotic resistance. It was also a time of increasing recognition of environmental problems related to population increases such as smog and urban sprawl and to practices such as the U.S. military's use of defoliants on some twelve thousand square miles of Vietnam's tropical forests, all of which brought evolution and ecology home to my students. This was the period of the most rapid growth rates of the human population in historic times—the world population was doubling in size about every thirty-five years; just during Anne's and my lifetimes to that point, from the early 1930s to the early 1960s, the number of people had risen from some 2 billion to about 3.3 billion. Students told their parents about my lectures, and soon I was asked to speak to alumni groups on the issue of the environmental future. Those audiences were generally supportive of what I had to say.

Through one such contact, I was invited to speak in 1966 to the Commonwealth Club of San Francisco, America's oldest and biggest public affairs forum. My address was entitled "The Food from the Sea Myth: The Biology of a Red Herring," and in it I contended that the then-current notion that human population could keep growing forever because the resources of the sea were infinite was nonsense. That was a position novel then, but what everyone knows today as stocks of species after species of fishes have declined from historic highs, many precipitously. What I hadn't realized was that Commonwealth Club speeches at the time were broadcast on several radio stations, and as a result I soon was getting requests to speak about population and resource issues on Bay Area radio and TV shows. Rachel Carson had stirred up the environmental movement but had not emphasized the key role of population growth and size in the growing crisis. As a concerned natural-born loudmouth, I could not resist taking the opportunity to address that by speaking to audiences of thousands of people rather than just dozens of students. For whatever reason, I did not share the common fear of public speaking; I actually enjoyed it—the bigger the audience the better.

Around the same time, Ian Ballantine (the inventor of the paperback book and founder of Ballantine Books) had been collaborating with David Brower, then Executive Director of the Sierra Club, in publishing on environmental issues. They came to me and asked if what I had been saying could be put down in a short book. They thought (a hysterically silly idea in retrospect) if such a book were published in early 1968, it might influence the politics of the presidential election that year and bring more attention to environmental issues.

I easily recruited the help of my scholarly partner, Anne, whose interest had fastened on the growing global environmental crisis and the poverty and hunger she had observed when we traveled in poor countries on our round-the-world sabbatical. Add to that my abundant lecture notes from seven years of teaching about evolution, and we were able to put the book together in about three weeks of evenings and an intensive weekend of editing. The book was very much a joint project, but Ballantine insisted that it should be single-authored, and Anne's name was removed from the final draft. Those were still the days of untethered sexism, I was too young and naive to refuse, and we had not yet acquired our wonderful agent, Virginia (Ginger) Barber, who would have advised us properly.

Anne has coauthored many Ehrlich books with equal billing subsequently, and she's received plenty of honors, including the Heinz Award, the United Nations Environment Programme/Sasakawa Environment Prize, and the Tyler Prize for Environmental Achievement, but in addition, at least half of anything I've accomplished, and any other awards I've received, I owe to her. She also took on many family chores that freed me to focus more on the science. But I'm still ashamed of caving in to Ian's demand. It was a poor decision on his part, too, because having a woman acknowledged as coauthor on a book like that would have been a real plus.

In many ways I can trace my entire career back to luck and to Anne. When Anne and I were young, we never questioned whose career would lead. In those days, careers in ecology and evolutionary biology were almost entirely the province of males (the brilliant Jane Van Zandt being the one exception I knew personally in our generation). The prevailing culture dictated that the man was the breadwinner and the woman raised the children. In fact, if Anne and I were young today, when female scientists are great leaders in ecology and evolution as well as in many other areas of human endeavor, our careers might well have turned out quite differently. She once told Lisa that as a child, she wanted to do fashion design. I knew she was a talented artist and illustrator, but I didn't realize what a gifted seamstress she also was. When Lisa was young, Anne made most of her clothes as well as her own, and those skills served her well in microdissection and illustration. I might have ended up a househusband supported by a top fashion designer.

Ian Ballantine not only demanded that Anne's name should not appear as coauthor but also thought that our proposed title, *Population, Resources, and Environment*, designed to meld our concerns with Rachel Carson's, was not sexy enough, and insisted upon *The Population Bomb* in its stead. The book was published in May 1968, and had no impact whatsoever on the election of Richard Nixon or the remaining months of Lyndon Johnson's presidency. The first edition cover (which we had nothing to do with)

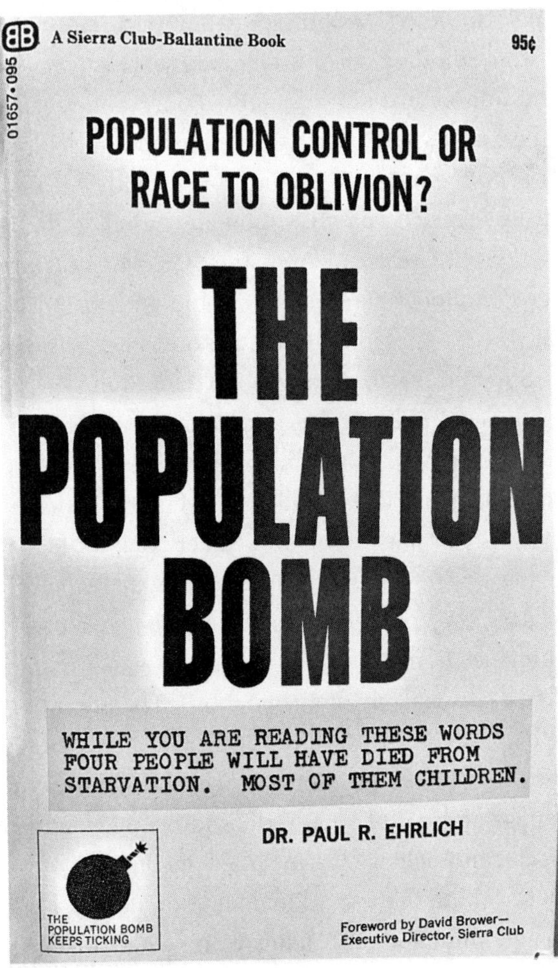

The cover for the first edition of *The Population Bomb*. Author photo.

had an amusing glitch, illustrated in the paperback edition depicted in the photograph.[1]

I learned a few lessons about being a public scholar right then and there. On the negative side, I got labeled a "population nut." That happened, even though practices such as misuse of pesticides played a major role in the book, in addition to its overall thesis of the importance of population size and growth for the environment and the human future, and its call to deal with that threat. From a commercial sales point of view, Ballantine was certainly not wrong on the title, though: the book has sold over two million copies—not bad for a book by two academics!

In general, academics are not great choosers of titles for popular books. My own bad judgment on titles was confirmed the following year in another instance. Lepidopterist Charles Remington at Yale University, New Haven attorney Richard Bowers, and I founded Zero Population Growth (ZPG). It was an organization dedicated to bringing the population problem to public attention, encouraging people in the United States to have smaller families and calling for an end to governmental progrowth population policies. The name for the organization was Bowers's idea, and I didn't like it a bit. I told him it would confuse people. But since he was the one who thought of starting an organization, we let him have his way. I was dead wrong. ZPG turned out to be an excellent name, and his argument was vindicated. Within a few years, it was ranked as the most effective lobbying group in Washington, D.C., and the term "zero population growth," meaning a "stationary" (that is, nonchanging) population size, actually infiltrated the technical demographic literature.

The Population Bomb received relatively few reviews, but enough to garner accusations of hating children, being antihuman and ignorant of human creativity (more people supposedly would provide more brains to solve civilization's problems), and on and on. A prominent criticism that persists to this day is that there isn't a problem of too many people with respect to needed resources, just too much consumption—when, of course, the number of people is a central factor in the amount of consumption, especially if any attention is paid to the importance of equitable distribution. The book also had me declared a "neo-Malthusian," tying me (and others like Bill Vogt, Garrett Hardin, and Lester Brown) to the economist who a century and a half before had called attention to the population problem. I must admit that in 2019 I was pleased to find an article in a history journal that credited us "neo-Malthusians" with stimulating "thinking of the planet as a whole and anticipating its future"—citing both *The Population Bomb* and my "food from the sea myth" lecture.[2]

The next big development in my career as a public scientist came in late 1968 when Arthur Godfrey, a major entertainment and aviation celebrity of the time, sent a copy of *The Population Bomb* to Johnny Carson, host of *The Tonight Show*. John was very interested in issues of population and environment, and he invited me to appear on the show. My first three appearances (out of twenty-some over more than a decade) with Carson occurred in the first few months of 1969. My first show was on January 7 and, as a newspaper account put it, "sparked an overwhelming viewer interest. Several thousand letters were received by the *Tonight* staff, as well as a number of telegrams. All but three of the letters supported Dr. Ehrlich's appeal for strict reduction in the number of births in the future."[3]

At the time of *The Tonight Show* invitation, ZPG was an organization of some six chapters and six hundred people, but John allowed me to mention ZPG's address in Los Altos, California, on each of the shows. By mid-1969, the organization had grown to six hundred chapters and sixty thousand members. A day or so after my first appearance on the show, Los Altos had the largest mail delivery to a single address in its history to that date. I learned a big lesson: you have a lot more influence talking to fifteen million people at one time than the few thousand people who listen to an average Bay Area radio show!

I had one outstanding attribute that gave me some success in the public arena—I've always enjoyed telling people about things that interest me regardless of the size of the audience. I really enjoyed my appearances on *The Tonight Show*; I loved working with John, who was extremely talented, and I got great satisfaction from it. John and I met briefly before I did the first show and found general agreement on topics—including talking about the need to improve access to contraception. The other guest on the show was a well-known singer, Julius La Rosa, who, ironically, had had a famous public dispute with Godfrey. After the first segment Julius jumped up, confronted John and me, and said, as I recall, "You guys can't talk about that stuff [contraception, I think] on TV." John said, "But we just did," and I chimed in

Johnny Carson and I discuss politics on *The Tonight Show* in 1979. I had been lecturing on a cruise in the Mediterranean and slipped getting back into a car at a field site in Israel. The car door slammed with me holding it, virtually amputating the end of the finger. It was sewn back together and splinted in an Israeli army hospital. It was my microphone hand, so for my subsequent lectures I was perpetually "giving the finger" to the passengers. NBC / Gene Arias / © January 1, 1979. NBCUniversal /Getty Images.

with, "Yeah, we just did." Julius, pointing at his chest: "It gets people right here." Me: "You're pointing too high, Julius." John: "Yeah, you're pointing too high." Julius: "I don't know what you guys are talking about." With that show, John and I had determined that we could work easily together. Subsequently, I would just send John a one-page cheat sheet with some suggested questions and a clue about how I would answer—but as far as I could determine, he rarely, if ever, consulted it. We just did my segments "off the top."

Publication of *The Population Bomb* and my exposure in the media, especially the appearances on *The Tonight Show,* changed our lives in many ways. Invitations to give speeches and seminars far and wide enabled me to do a lot of fieldwork in locations I wouldn't ordinarily have been able to consider. I was invited to places all over the world to talk about environmental issues, and that, in turn, allowed me to learn firsthand about environmental and political problems in many countries. Notoriety got me back to my favorite overseas destination, Australia, where (I recently learned) in 1971 I was the first scientist on that continent to discuss on television global warming.[4] Notoriety was also an in to the cruise-lecturing business, which, combined with Stanford Alumni Association Travel/Study cruise and air trips, meant that Anne and I have been able to travel the globe for virtually nothing—an extremely attractive price.

On the down side, with publication of *The Population Bomb* and appearances on *The Tonight Show* I got a lot more death threats, and John was getting them, too. One night in New York, John came back to the greenroom and said: "Paul, someone just called and said he was going to shoot me tonight with a .45 during the show. You've had lots of death threats—what do you think I should do?" I replied, "Seat me at the far end of the couch, in case the son of a bitch is a bad shot." John and I kidded around a bit—neither of us knew whether my announced presence on the show was a stimulus. It was around Christmas, a time when the mentally disturbed often come out of the woodwork, but the threat level to people in the public eye in that era was nothing compared to what such people must endure today.

We decided just to do the show, but then the crew refused to continue. Phone calls produced a ring of NYPD officers circling the theater. Anne was in the audience with my mother and LuEsther Mertz (more on her shortly), and they soon figured out what was going on. Ed McMahon announced the show, and John, forty-five minutes late, began his monologue. It started out weak and ran downhill from there. Finally, John turned to the camera, and for the benefit of me and the few others who knew, said, "If he's going to do it, now's the time." A fine display of the brilliant sense of humor of a real pro.

Anne's and my longest run with a mentally ill person was an experience with a bright young apparently paranoid schizophrenic named Linda. She had been a student of my former PhD student and then-postdoc Irene Brown. Irene had done her doctoral work in the 1960s and early 1970s on the population ecology of *Euphydryas chalcedona* on Jasper Ridge and how it differed from its sister species *E. editha*. It was part of my program to see what generalities might be induced from our long-term studies of *E. editha*. Irene was a determined and mature student who braved the heavy poison oak of *E. chalcedona*'s main habitat (it almost never showed up in the serpentine grasslands where *E. editha* flew) and produced a fine thesis. While a postdoc, she also taught at another Bay Area college, where Linda, a woman of medium size, had attacked Irene for no known provocation and given her a mild concussion. As I discovered in a conversation much later, Linda could be coherent and interesting when she wasn't suffering a bout of illness.

Linda developed a troubling fascination with me, which led to her showing up in our family life when we were all away at my sister Sally's wedding in 1973. Unknown to us, Linda had been living in our backyard for several days, hidden in a fence corner behind a tree and some bushes. When we left for the wedding, she broke into our house and started living in Lisa's room. She was discovered by Susan Gere, then as now Lisa's close friend and daughter of our wonderful next-door faculty neighbors at the time, Jim Gere (an expert on earthquake damage) and his wife, Janice. Susan, who had been coming in to feed our tropical fish and keep an eye on the place, saw that someone had been there, and notified the police. Linda (along with her little dog) was removed and ordered by a judge to stay off campus; we did not want to press charges on a clearly mentally ill person. Sometime later when we were out for an evening, however, the Geres spotted Linda at our house again, this time carrying a linoleum knife.

Those were trying days; Lisa started sleeping at friends' houses when she had not yet left for college at UC Davis, and I walked to work expecting Linda to spring out of the bushes at any moment. None of us got much sleep, and conversations with our friend and attorney John Montgomery and Stanford's very cooperative chief of police, Marv Herrington, taught us an important lesson: in the United States it is, in practice, very difficult to restrain stalkers until they actually try to injure or kill you.

The end came, from our viewpoint, on a warm Saturday afternoon in September 1973. Our old refrigerator had given up the ghost, and we had bought a new one. It turned out to be perfect except in one respect—it wouldn't keep its interior any colder than room temperature. Being a complainer, I complained, and that Saturday the refrigerator people swapped our old new one for a new one. When they departed, they left our front door open. A few minutes later the doorbell rang, and when I looked out, there was Linda, peering around the door jamb.

I can still picture it as if it were yesterday instead of almost fifty years ago. I went to the door but could not see if she had anything in her hands. "Linda, you are breaking the law!" I said, "The judge has a restraining order against you." "Tough shit," she said. I slammed the door in her face and called to Anne to set off the intruder alarm and to get Lisa and Page Kennedy (Don's daughter, visiting with Lisa now home from college) into a far corner of the house. Linda ran around the house, beating on various sliding screen doors trying to get in, and I got my Smith and Wesson .38 Chief's Special just in case she had the linoleum knife. Then Lisa yelled, "She's in the living room." Linda had broken through a screen door and was running at me in a rage. I raised and cocked the pistol but, fortunately, saw that her hands were empty. Linda paid no attention to the gun, which I lowered, and she stood a couple of feet away from me splattering me with spit and screaming that I had to stop sending her messages through her cat. Then she almost instantly became calm, and said, "I'm hungry, I'm going to get something to eat."

She walked past me into the kitchen, went to the refrigerator, and swung the door open. There was at least some comic relief. Having just been delivered, the fridge was bright, shining, and stark-staring empty. Unfazed, and knowing our house well from her previous residence, Linda went to the pantry, found a tin of tuna, got a can opener, and sat at our kitchen table to eat. By then our neighbors had started to arrive, attracted by our alarm siren. Jim Gere was one of the first—"It's Linda, isn't it?" Our other next-door neighbor, John Schwartz, a vice-provost in charge of university security, came by, and I asked him to hurry the arrival of the Stanford police. Jim and I stood in the atrium and through the screen door watched Linda eat while a large crowd gathered. Finally two giant Stanford policemen arrived, and the following dialogue ensued: "Young lady, you must come with us." "I'm not going anywhere." "If you don't come voluntarily, we'll have to remove you." "Just give it a try!" The cops moved toward her, but she jumped up and met them halfway, swinging viciously. They finally subdued her and carried her screaming past the crowd but being impressively careful not to injure her. Lisa will never forget how Linda's expression switched to a crazy grin as the police pushed her head down to get her into the patrol car. All in all, it was an unusual sight for a Stanford neighborhood afternoon.

Mercifully, no further action was required on our part, and Linda drifted out of our lives. She was imprisoned, apparently for violating the judge's order, and some months later was released because, we were informed, she "was too much trouble and kept attacking the guards" (I kid you not). The last we heard was several years later when, sadly, she was found dead on a southern California roadside. Linda's case was another legacy of Ronald Reagan and a tribute to a society that spends hundreds of billions of dollars on useless military buildups, destructive "development" and "nation-building" adventures, and greasing the palms of the already spectacularly rich but cannot sensibly take care of people in need. Several other incidents I'd rather not discuss have emphasized to Anne, me, and various colleagues the sad ridiculousness of trying to use the criminal justice system to deal with the mentally ill.

One benefit we received from all the death threats, encounters with Linda, and related traumas was getting to know forensic psychiatrist Don Lunde and his wife, Marilyn. Don was a leading expert on violent crime, and he gave me good advice on how to handle a series of threats, and Don and Marilyn and Anne and I quickly became social friends. We had many common interests in human behavior and also in good food, and for years we dined together several times a month. During that time Don was involved in a series of front-page cases, including the Patty Hearst kidnapping, the trial of Dan White for killing San Francisco Mayor George Moscone and Supervisor Harvey Milk, and the Jonestown massacre. One of the most horrifying evenings Anne and I ever spent was in the Lunde living room listening to the Jonestown tapes. The recordings were made while in Guyana in 1978 some nine hundred American men, women, and children in a religious cult committed suicide by drinking cyanide. I learned a lot about human behavior and the American legal system from Don, who had a long and distinguished career at Stanford.

A high point for me on *The Tonight Show* came one evening when the show was in Los Angeles. Craig Tennis, my talent coordinator, came to the greenroom and told me that John was sick. "He doesn't think he's up to an intellectual discussion tonight." "Sorry to hear it," I said, "I'll fly back up the coast." "No, hang around, and we'll see what happens." So John did the monologue like a trooper, and his first guest was Phyllis Diller. I still remember her routine—it was about her wedding night with a mythical husband she called "Fang." Sadly, Diller did only beautifully designed set pieces on Carson; she couldn't stretch her wonderful bit to fill some more of the time.

John's next guest was a starlet, doomed to remain nameless. John asked her what it was like working on her current movie. "Good," she said. It was the first of several monosyllabic answers. Craig came back and said, "We've got to pull her, and you're what's left. Get out there and talk!" By then John was in bad shape, so I went out and more or less asked myself questions by feeding them to John and then answering them. After the show, when I came out of make-up, John was walking slowly with Ed up a set of iron stairs away from me. "Paul saved the show," he said. I felt it was the best compliment I'd ever received.

My appearances on *The Tonight Show* taught me some important lessons about the corporate-controlled media. Talking about overpopulation, contraception, and abortion could then have been viewed as injurious to many corporate interests. But there were apparently some individuals high in the power structure whose population concerns were based on fear that increasing numbers of nonwhites and the poor might threaten their privileged position. Racist elements in the population movement (some still present today) remain a thorn in the side of trying to achieve a sustainable population. John was certainly not a racist, and he was likely the most powerful performer in the entertainment industry at that time. He could have on *The Tonight Show* any guest he wanted, and he genuinely wanted to make the world a better place.[5]

One of my best (and worst) characteristics is that I'm stubborn. Despite all the flak connected to *The Population Bomb*, I persisted in trying to spread news about what I saw as a looming environmental and human disaster if we didn't act. That led to more problems and led me to call on our attorney friend John Montgomery, who, along with his wife, Nancy, had been a critical reader of *The Population Bomb* manuscript. He was a great help—and gave us both some fun. Two incidents stand out in my memory. One was when I was invited to give several public lectures at the University of Arizona in the early 1970s. The governor was Jack Williams, an ex–radio announcer, who had recently shown his disdain for environmental issues by announcing that we need not worry about air pollution because early humans had survived smoked-filled caves and that his interest in vegetation was limited to greens on golf courses. In my first talk I quoted him, and said, "If you elect morons to public office, that's what you get." The governor's office contacted my hosts at the university and said if they let me give my second speech, the governor would destroy the university. My hosts said he already was doing what he could to undermine the university and urged me to give my speech. I did and he didn't. Sometime after that, one of Williams's assistants (I think an attorney) wrote demanding to know whether I had called the governor a moron. I turned the matter over to John Montgomery. John wrote back on his legal letterhead: "I don't know whether Professor Ehrlich called Governor Williams a moron and I don't care. Truth is an absolute defense against libel." We had dreams of interrogating Williams on the stand, but sadly, we heard nothing more from his office.

Even more fun was had with the Velsicol Chemical Corporation, a pesticide manufacturer that had notoriously threatened legal action against the publishers of *Silent Spring*. I published a scenario somewhere (can't remember where) in which in the future a president of the corporation ostensibly ate DDT on television to prove it was safe, but I added that it was actually powdered sugar. Velsicol's corporate lawyers demanded a retraction because I had libeled their future president. John and I opened a bottle of wine and wrote a retraction, the basic content of which was that we were delighted to hear that Velsicol planned to stop its program of poisoning Americans for profit and hire a president who was not a liar. We sent it to them and asked where they would like it to be published. Curiously, we heard nothing more.

Of course, corporate legal departments pursue a variant of such tactics today, most notoriously in some cases filing what are called SLAPP suits, strategic lawsuits against public participation. Their basic idea is to intimidate and silence critics with threats and/or high legal costs. That is just one of the techniques corporations have used to distort science, try to destroy the reputations of scientists who dispute their actions, and dominate agencies of the U.S. government.[6]

One of the perfectly expectable results of my discussing the dangers of overpopulation was an effort by racists to make the cure be stopping reproduction by so-called undesirables—poor people, immigrants, or, more explicitly, Hispanics or African Americans. Much of my subsequent work trying to counter such prejudices was done in collaboration with Shirley and Marc Feldman, particularly in dealing with the virulent anti-Black racism of Stanford faculty member William Shockley, who claimed that African Americans were hereditarily inferior intellectually to whites. His most famous statement was, "Nature has color-coded groups of individuals so that statistically reliable predictions of their adaptability to intellectual rewarding and effective lives can easily be made and profitably used by the pragmatic man-in-the street."[7]

Shockley's nonsense got great public attention because he had been awarded the Nobel Prize for his research group's invention of the transistor. He became a hero to white racists, and an embarrassment to Stanford and to science in general, and he was persistent. He was an especial pain to me, because I kept getting questions like, "To solve overpopulation shouldn't we stop those people Shockley says are inferior from breeding?" That's what stimulated Shirley Feldman and me to publish in 1977 a book explicitly debunking his ideas: the *Race Bomb* (a terrible title insisted on by the publisher—we wanted to call it *Skin Deep*). The book suffered from a scientifically silly review by a nonscientist in the *New York Times,* though it was thoroughly rebutted in letters from scientists, that hurt the book's chances for wide circulation.[8] It's a sad lesson, though, that because of my interest in population control, despite having documented the stupidity and damage done by racial and gender inequity in dozens of publications and many hundreds of public speeches and appearances in the media, and my single child and widely advertised vasectomy, I'm still often labeled a racist and/or a sexist.[9]

My political and social views were strongly shaped by my mother's liberal attitudes. She was a strong supporter of Franklin Roosevelt's New Deal, repeatedly warned me against racism, and always urged me to think about the feelings and situations of other people, from girlfriends to waiters. Pop was the same, but less articulate about it.

As my fear of nuclear war tracing to late 1940s nightmares persisted into the 1960s and 1970s, it gradually began to dawn on me that aside from the obvious U.S. propaganda we were subjected to during World War II, the government was hardly being truthful in its reports and claims about motivations for its foreign policy. Dwight Eisenhower's famous "military-industrial complex" warning in his farewell speech in 1961 was just one step in my education. By the height of America's involvement in Vietnam, many of my colleagues shared with me a deep suspicion of U.S. government rationales for the war and descriptions of its course.

The emotions stirred up domestically by America's Vietnam War, the first war brought home on television, made the late 1960s and early 1970s a horrible time on campus in general and for Anne and me in particular. Not only did we have to deal with a stalker who plagued the family, but there was the specter of bombings to worry about and other events connected with the general campus resistance to the war. For instance, one night the alarm we had installed went off, indicating someone was in our backyard (it was later concluded that it was someone thought to be on his way to "bomb" John Schwartz's house next door). I turned on our lights, moved Anne and Lisa to (relatively) safe places, got my .38, went out and nervously woke the rent-a-cop asleep in his car. He had been stationed there by the university to protect the Schwartz and Ehrlich families. He fortunately didn't start shooting, but when I said, "Let's go back there and get whoever it is," he said, "That's too dangerous, I'll call the police!" He may have been right, but none of the protestors making trouble on campus had been armed, and none of the bombs had, as I recall, been much more than firecrackers. I think the stupidest, most dangerous thing I did in that era was to awaken our armed "protector."

Most Stanford faculty were, I think, eventually opposed to the war, but they were also strongly opposed to disrupting campus as a way of stopping it. It was a tricky issue for all of us, as there *were* research and development activities on campus that clearly aided the U.S. war effort. My close colleagues and I were very disturbed about not only the war's horrendous human impacts but also the dangers to biodiversity of the widespread defoliation program. What could and should university scientists with such views do? Larry Gilbert, Peter Raven, and I wrote a letter to *Science* about defoliation in 1968. My memories are dim now, but I clearly remember one night Don Kennedy and I were on top of a computer science building talking to students sitting-in there. What made it stick in my memory a half century later was a demonstration of the impatience of youth. One student commented to us, "Do you realize we've been sitting in for twenty-four hours *and the war is still going on!*"

Many students, faculty members, and universities across the country were deeply involved in the political turmoil, as is oft reported. On one memorable occasion, I had just returned from a two-week-long, first Earth Day speaking tour in 1970, which, as best I can now tell from ancient scratches in a pocket calendar, consisted of addresses in Lafayette, Indiana; Allentown, Pennsylvania; Bowling Green State University, Ohio State, Minneapolis, Minnesota; Northwestern University, Illinois; Iowa State University, and several other places.[10] It was exhausting but also exhilarating; audiences were both friendly and also large and enthusiastic. Indeed, I was on a high—huge audiences showed interest in the environmental situation in general, the resource aspects of the war, and, especially, population.

I was about to crawl into bed when Richard Lyman, Stanford's president at

Plate 1. Ikurlik (right) and two other young Inuit friends, who grabbed flowers as a joke when they saw I was going to photograph them. Author photo.

Plate 2. Anne's painting of Muncho Lake, British Columbia. Based on a photograph I took on the Alaska Highway while Anne was home pregnant with Lisa in the summer of 1955. Author photo.

Plate 3. Cairn at Assistance Bay built in 1850–51 by the Penny-Ross Franklin search expedition. Author photo.

Plate 4. Bay checkerspot butterfly (*Euphydryas editha*) female feeding on nectar. Author photo.

Plate 5. Sue Thomas marking *E. editha* on Jasper Ridge in 1960. Butterflies were held alive in envelopes in cardboard box (right) until marked and released. Author photo.

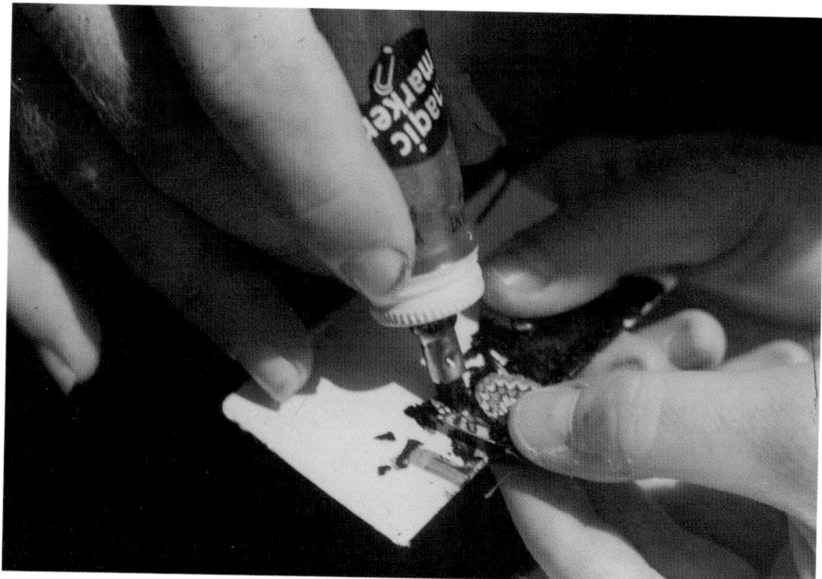

Plate 6. Marking a checkerspot butterfly in 1960 using an early felt-tip pen. Author photo.

Plate 7. Portion of a lighted sheet at Wau field station in New Guinea in 1966. Moth densities such as this are increasingly rare in many parts of the world. Author photo.

Plate 8. Aboriginal (Injalak) rock art above Gunbalanya (Oenpelli). DU Photography / Alamy Stock Photo.

Plate 9. Traditional bark painting of the Yolngu Aboriginal people of Arnhem Land depicting totemic animals of the Dhalwangu clan. Painting by well-known Yolngu artist Yangarriny Wunungmurra, with permission of the Buku-Larrnggay Mulka Centre.

Plate 10. Rajah Brooke's birdwing, *Trogonoptera brookiana*, with up to a seven-inch wingspread, one of the most spectacular butterflies Anne and I ever dissected fresh. Photo by Pavel Kirillov, CC BY-SA 2.0.

Plate 11. When Larry Gilbert and I studied *Heliconius ethilla* populations in Trinidad in 1969, we labeled marking stations with painted numbers on galvanized plates nailed on trees. When I returned in 2004, I found our number 7 location marker miraculously preserved. Author photo.

Plate 12. Tom Davis, Gretchen Daily, and me using a slingshot to shoot a bolt with string attached to hoist a butterfly trap high in the Costa Rican rainforest canopy. Photo by Tom Davis.

Plate 13. A large *Caligo* butterfly caught in a net trap, large enough to just write a number (B1) on the wings. Photo by Tom Davis.

Plate 14. Life-size models of butterfly fishes (*Chaetodontidae*) created by Frank Talbot's staff in the exhibits department of the Australian Museum. Author photo.

Plate 15. Schooling actual butterfly fishes (*Chaetodon falcula* and *C. unimaculatus*) on the Great Barrier Reef. Author photo.

Plate 16. I "tick off" my first Florida jay—a lifer, or a bird species (*Aphelocoma coerulescens*) I had not previously seen. Photo by John Ogden.

the time, called. It was early May, and President Nixon had just announced the start of America's Cambodian incursion (read "large-scale ground invasion"), a widening of the Vietnam War that his administration hoped would give more time for their program to equip and further train Vietnamese forces to allow U.S. forces to quit the war without appearing to lose it. A protest group of faculty and students from Stanford was going to Washington, Dick said, and he asked if I'd join it to help keep a constructive focus and show the students that they had faculty support. Very sleepy, I reluctantly said yes, and Dick said I should go to the alumni center, where the group was getting organized because a problem had arisen.

At the alumni center I found an intense argument in progress. The delegation that had been organized was dramatically short of minority students. Bill Miller (later provost) had just arrived, too, and we both suggested that we simply expand the group. But, we were told, the academic senate had only authorized twenty-five students (the number as I recall it, possibly not exactly right). We said, forget the academic senate, a notoriously ineffectual body; this was an issue that had to be settled now. "But where would the extra money come from?" We replied that we'd find it. I can still see a colleague leaning over the table and wagging his finger at Bill and me, warning us, "Do you realize that if you exceed the authorized size, you'll bring down on your heads the wrath of the academic senate!" Bill and I almost fell out of our chairs laughing—the threat was equivalent to saying that the Brownies would no longer give us a discount on their cinnamon cookies. So we took a larger group with several minority students, and neither Bill nor I got a much-desired academic senatorial condemnation to hang framed on our wall.

On the flight to Washington there was another incident. The California grape boycott was under way, and the airline showed the movie *Viva Max!* on the flight—a comedy some thought demeaning of Mexicans. Students protested loudly, and I found myself standing between them and a crew-cut copilot who clearly wanted to depressurize the plane and chuck the students off. Somehow the faculty managed to get things calmed down.

Events were hectic in Washington, D.C., over the next few days; I remember only bits and pieces. We persuaded a couple of senators we knew to come to our motel and meet with the students, though a few of the students refused to meet with them and walked out. I accompanied a congressman over to a critical vote on Vietnam; he said he agreed with me completely, and then voted the opposite way. What I remember most is getting into a shouting match with Henry Kissinger in front of the students in the war room of the White House. I claimed the incursion was crazy, and he insisted I'd agree with it if I knew what he knew. It turned out we all knew what he knew, but that made no difference.

In addition to Johnny Carson, someone else who greatly helped me spread the word as I saw it in a mass medium, well after publication of *The Population Bomb*, was a world-class NBC News journalist, Sam Hurst. He invited me to lunch one day in 1989, two decades after I began appearing on Carson's *Tonight Show*, and asked if I would like to work with him as a special correspondent producing a series of Assignment Earth segments for the *Today Show*. He had taken time off from being a journalist to study evolutionary biology and was obviously super-smart. I liked him immediately, quickly agreed, and he (we) launched the first coordinated effort by NBC News to focus on the emergence of *global* environmental issues: climate change, biodiversity and extinction, population, energy, consumption, and so on.

Thanks to Sam, our focus in Assignment Earth was never the toxic-dump-in-a-neighbor's-backyard, which was basically how the environment had been covered up until then, but the central global problems as seen from the perspective of an environmental scientist, not an environmental activist. I had to be careful to maintain my reputation in the scientific community, and Sam was totally on board with that. I was the *Today Show*/NBC News special correspondent from 1989 to 1992, doing roughly two five-minute segments a year, spending a week or more on each. Sam and I traveled extensively in search of the most revealing stories. We had a great time, working with a wonderful cameraman, Keith Hathaway, who insisted that each shot be perfect and, if possible, artistic.

One of our great adventures was shooting a segment on overgrazing in the American West. We were filming in Arizona, and Keith wanted me to do a stand-up (little set-piece speech) in front of a herd of cows. Every time the cows were facing me and the camera, I blew the stand-up. Every time I got it perfect, the cows were all anus-on. The piece didn't get into our show.

On that shoot we were working in an arroyo, having dragged all our equipment through a barbed-wire fence with a "No trespassing" sign. The location was spectacular: so overgrazed there wasn't a bit of living vegetation visible. As we started to work, a genuine cowboy came riding along, Stetson on head, six-shooter on hip, followed by a pit bull. My instinct was to run. Sam, having been in tight spots in Vietnam, gave him a hearty "Howdy!" and said we were making a movie of the wildflowers (there wasn't a wildflower as far as the eye could see). "Really?" "Would you like to be in it?" Sam asked. "Sure." "Then just slowly ride off into the distance in that direction" (pointing). Keith faked filming, and the cowpoke (and pit bull) disappeared into the distance.

We received many good comments on our shows, and our segments were nominated for an Emmy Award in 1990.

One of the main dilemmas of becoming a public scholar was obvious to me from the very start of my life in the media. When I first went on television and radio, I was concerned that my scientific colleagues would write me off as a mere popularizer. How could I maintain a scientific reputation while communicating with the public in terms that were divorced from those used when publishing in the technical literature? If one approached a TV interview prepared to mimic the structure of a scientific paper—introduction, materials and methods, results, and discussion—the interview would be over long before you even got to materials and methods. Concise statements of basic conclusions are what is required. But I needn't have worried. When addressing the public, the answer is to use sound bites in plain English, making them as scientifically accurate as possible, and to keep up your scientific work so that people cannot accuse you of having left science behind. Fortunately, many of my colleagues in ecology and evolution would become as concerned as I was about the presentation of science in the media.

For example, the Aldo Leopold Fellows program, led by marine ecologist Jane Lubchenco (later administrator of NOAA and, under Biden, deputy director for climate and environment); Pamela Matson, dean of earth sciences at Stanford; and others, was specifically designed to train midcareer professional ecologists in how to work with journalists and others in informing the public about environmental issues. For several years around the turn of the century, I trained fellows in how best to deal with news crews wanting interviews at various events.

My colleagues at Stanford were always extremely supportive of my Bay Area activities and writing of *The Population Bomb.* It turned out that many evolutionists and ecologists, not only at Stanford but elsewhere, were extraordinarily concerned about the neglect of the population problem and the evidence they were uncovering on the deteriorating state of the natural world. They were delighted to support me and my efforts. They were equally pleased that I was able to present their concerns on *The Tonight Show* to a wide audience.

Early on, Anne and I and many of those colleagues recognized the great need for a textbook that would present a comprehensive view of the human predicament and the many connections among topics as diverse as demography, mineral resources, silent springs, human nutrition, pollution, biogeochemistry, condoms, religion, and nuclear war. Human practices were not going to change, we knew, unless bright young people in large numbers learned how the world worked. With the enthusiastic collaboration of our friend William Kaufmann, then president of W. H. Freeman and Company publishers, in the late 1960s Anne and I began working on what turned out to be the first modern environmental science textbook, *Population, Resources, Environment.* It not only brought together many previously never-connected issues in one place, it also took a neo-Malthusian worldview on resources and population. The first edition came out in 1970 and sold very well as many of our colleagues adopted it for class use. It went through three editions, the last of which, published in 1977 under the title *Ecoscience,* was coauthored with John Holdren, then at UC Berkeley. *Ecoscience* established a pattern of analysis of environmental problems in college textbooks and popular volumes that persists to this day—dealing with biophysical and sociocultural issues in the same volume.

The president of the organization that owned W. H. Freeman and Com-

Anne, Bill Kaufman, and me working on the illustrations for *Population, Resources, Environment.* Author photo.

pany in those days was Gerard Piel, a science writer who had played a major role in revitalizing the magazine *Scientific American.* Piel was a conservative Catholic who told Bill Kaufman that the first edition Ehrlich manuscript, because of the way it covered demographic issues, made him sick. It was a highlight of my life when, in 1989, twenty years after Gerry was sickened, I was awarded the AAAS/Scientific American Gerard Piel Award for Service to Science in the Cause of Humankind. With Anne, John and Cheri Holdren, and Bill attending, Gerry had to hand the prize to me in person.

Arthur Godfrey did me another great favor in addition to getting me on *The Tonight Show.* A couple of years after *The Population Bomb* was published, he invited me to a luncheon on population issues and sat me next to a very nice woman, LuEsther Mertz (who, among many other things, was later a backer of the Broadway show *A Chorus Line*). She was a delightful companion, and we had a wonderful lunch. I only found out how much she'd enjoyed it when months later she sent my research fund at Stanford a check for $50,000 from her foundation (the equivalent of more than $300,000 today), saying she'd been following what we were doing and wanted to help; I should spend it as I thought wise and no reports were necessary. Such no-strings-attached support is the very best thing a scholar can receive, especially one involved in what were then some relatively controversial activities. And the next year LuEsther increased it to $100,000—allowing me to support much of my graduate students' research, money for which was a problem through much of my career.

LuEsther, it turned out, had founded Publishers Clearing House with her ex-husband, Harold Mertz, and her daughter, Joyce. She was obviously wealthy, brilliant, funny, and liberal. Anne and I soon developed a firm friendship with her, spending time with her whenever possible and talking on the phone whenever it wasn't. She and we shared with many colleagues a taste for off-color jokes, of which she turned out to be an excellent source. Dennis Murphy and I were able to name a California checkerspot butterfly subspecies, *Euphydryas editha luestherae*, after LuEsther in 1980, and in 1983, Mike Singer, Phil DeVries, and I named a new species of tropical satyr butterfly, *Cissia joyceae*, after Joyce, who had died prematurely of cancer.[11] We also became friends with her close companion and colleague Larry Condon, a delight-filled bond we have kept up since LuEsther passed away in 1991 at the age of eighty-five. As she wished, her foundation's support continues, and it has been a major factor in allowing Anne and me to keep working on analyzing the human predicament and what can be done about it.

We have been especially lucky because our other major source of no-strings long-term support also evolved into a wonderful friendship. At a lunch in 1977, I had asked Bill Miller, by then Stanford's provost, not to appoint me to a named chair, something that was then becoming commonplace. A named chair was a fundraising ploy by the university, which meant little to the recipients ("recognition," an uncomfortable symbolic wooden chair, and free special stationery). I didn't want one, because I was hoping to get Johnny Carson to donate a chair for me, but to add to it an endowed research fund (that would have meant a lot!). That same year Anne and I were traveling to Australia again for fieldwork when I received a telegram from John Thomas congratulating me on becoming Bing Professor of Population Studies. I was really irritated; no Carson chair and research fund would now be possible even had John been willing. I sulked for a while, but three years later, in 1980, at Don Kennedy's inauguration as Stanford's president I briefly met Peter Bing, whose family I assumed was responsible for the chair.

Shortly thereafter, I took the bit in my teeth and called Pete, asking if it was his family that had endowed my chair. He said it had indeed been him. I said that, if he'd like, I'd take him to lunch and tell him what our research group was up to. He accepted the offer immediately. I started the lunch by telling him of my original disappointment, and my disappointment that Stanford had not informed me of the source of my chair and gotten us together then. He said he was equally annoyed by not being informed how and why his money was being spent. This led to a rather bad day for Stanford's then-director of development (actually a good guy) when Pete and I showed up at his office together and asked for much more coordination between chair donors and recipients. Pete was chairman of Stanford's board of trustees and its most valued alumnus. Happily, the director immediately initiated a program to do that, and even today, more than forty years later, when Anne and I publish a book, we're contacted and asked whether we've told "Dr. Bing."

Pete is a physician who, among other of his activities, was an official in Lyndon Johnson's administration and as a young doctor practiced on Indian reservations. We quickly found much common ground, partly because, in addition to shared political, academic, and Stanford interests, Pete, Anne, and I are all pilots, and Pete's artistic wife, Helen, tolerates pilot talk. A long-term friendship quickly developed, and the Bings for years joined us at RMBL each summer for talk and hiking. In addition, Pete and Helen have supported our work in a way a Johnny Carson chair never could have. We owe debts that can never be repaid to the Bings, LuEsther, and other friends of means who have worked to make the world a better place and who were willing, early on, to support public science. Other nonbiologist good friends have contributed by helping us in tough fieldwork in the steaming tropical forests and cowpat-steeped meadows of Costa Rica, especially George and Yvonne Burtness and Ellyn Bush and her husband, Tom Davis.

I incurred another debt in the 1980s as well. The Center for Conservation Biology was running out of money. I had set it up in 1984 to examine *all* the factors that were leading to the disappearance of biodiversity, which included virtually the entire human enterprise as it was being conducted. The CCB's financial troubles were thus hardly surprising. I was about to shut it down when our friends the Burtnesses suggested we invite to dinner two friends of theirs who shared interests with all of us. They were John and Sue Boething, owners of a huge tree farm, a business dedicated to regreening the cities of America, and with an abiding interest in regreening the world. We had a delightful dinner, with much talk of trees and conservation, and as they left John handed me an envelope containing a check for $50,000. It saved the center, and in 1989 we established the Boething Lectures on Trees and the Human Predicament, given annually in honor of John and Sue.

Many of my colleagues in science have now gone public on environmental issues. Indeed, a number had preceded me, notably another longtime friend unafraid to castigate stupid ideas and a pioneer at alerting the public to climate disruption, George Woodwell, founder of the Woods Hole Research Center, recently renamed, in his honor, the Woodwell Climate Research Center. As I write this he, at ninety-two, is still a powerful force for environmental sanity.

The enthusiastic support of my colleagues has been a wonderful aspect of my career as a public scholar. Especially in the early days of my media career, I suffered many (verbal or written) attacks—and of course they continue. But like most scientists, I care not what Rush Limbaugh, Ann Coulter, Ross Douthat, or random commentators on the editorial pages of the *Wall Street Journal* or the Fox "News" Channel think about me personally or my environmental views. Scientists value first and foremost their reputations with their scientific colleagues, not with the ignoramuses that so often pop up on op-ed pages, airwaves, and the web. So they don't hurt me personally, since I care mostly about the views of other scientists, but I hate reactionary views that are widely disseminated and darken the future for all our descendants. To protect our scientific reputations, Anne and I have always tried to have our public statements and policy publications carefully refereed by the best scholars we know to be sure they are as accurate as possible. This is, of course, especially important when one is doing interdisciplinary work and speaking out in areas not considered part of one's disciplinary background.

A pressing problem for public scholars is how to make it clear when you're speaking as a citizen-scientist and when you're speaking only as a citizen. Several of my colleagues, especially Steve Schneider, and I developed a formula for this, which I try to follow. First, inform people of the scientific consensus on an issue. Within your own discipline scientists generally know what this is. For instance, I know that the scientific consensus is that biodiversity has been generated by organic evolution, not specially created by some supernatural figure. So I feel that telling people about evolution is something I can responsibly do—it's a consensus in my own discipline that I agree with. On the other hand, if I differ from that view in my own area of expertise, Steve and I decided it would be ethically correct to give my opinion but to make clear its degree of departure from the scientific consensus. Of course, if I found good evidence the consensus was wrong, I would happily tear it apart—sending a manuscript to *Science* or *Nature* immediately.

That human activities are causing climate change is another instance of scientific consensus, but for someone trained as I have been it is different. I'm no atmospheric physicist, so how can I freely discuss that notion? The answer is that I can understand many of the technical issues, and I also know a group of atmospheric scientists whose competence, ethics, and motives I can judge. I also can personally judge many of the effects of climate disruption, such as changing patterns of butterfly distributions. And I can participate in policy research to look at options open to society to solve or ameliorate the crisis of climate disruption. I can cite that consensus to the public, making clear my level of knowledge. Here, as in the case of evolution, I can speak as a scientist on what *is* supported by the evidence as opposed to what those lacking the training, effort, and contacts simply *believe* is the case.

Those are rules for scientists, but should scientists give the public their opinions on environmental issues? Steve and I thought it was important to do that as citizens who have put a great deal of effort into studying an issue. For example, although I have no training in climatology, besides knowing the scientific consensus, I have studied it intensively, read the literature over the years, and discussed it frequently with experts like Steve, John Holdren, John Harte, Kirk Smith, Peter Gleick, and Michael Mann. Therefore, in my opinion, it is okay for me to express views publicly on what I believe society *ought* to do about issues of climate change, as long as I make clear that I am transmitting opinions that are the result of study and discussion with experts who know the area well. Obviously, there often are not firm lines between various levels of expertise. One can, however, strive to inform audiences and readers how far your views are from scholarly consensus and what cultural baggage you may be bringing to the discussion. I do try; sometimes I fail.

Convincing others is another matter. I can still picture Steve Schneider, Anne, and me having a long argument in the 1980s with Ben Bradlee, then the executive editor of the *Washington Post*, about the poor coverage of environmental issues at the time in his newspaper. Why didn't they, for example, have a box on the front page giving statistics on population size, amounts of carbon dioxide in the atmosphere, production of toxic chemicals, and the like? People aren't interested in numbers in newspapers, Ben explained. "Did you ever look at the sports and stock pages?" we asked. Ben said that was different. We also asked him why he didn't have trained science reporters at the time. Because Ben wanted his science reporting to be fair and balanced. "To be fair and balanced do you have baseball reporters who don't know a strike from first base?" No reply. Our failure to convince him came as no surprise to us, because by then we were all aware of the role that sports, Wall Street, and the mainstream media played in supporting the wealthy class that ran the nation, a class not anxious that the public be well informed about what corporate rentier capitalism and its growth-crazed allies were doing to civilization. Ben clearly was very bright, but he was also educated in the persistent and fanciful beliefs of that class.

Being a public scholar carries with it many burdens, but it also provides (especially for a field biologist) many benefits. As I said above, invitations to speak around the world and on cruise ships have allowed me to carry out fieldwork in areas that would have been financially impossible for me otherwise. That wide-ranging work has also been a huge personal pleasure. It has given me the chance to observe environmental conditions directly in many places. And most important, going public has given me a chance to get feedback from people who normally are not part of a scholar's world—from the attitudes of military officers on weapons of mass destruction (discovered during our research on nuclear winter) to farmers' attitudes on biodiversity loss (for example, in a joint meeting of ecologists and farmers in the Western Australian wheatlands), to callers to talk radio shows who are enraged by the idea that there is no evidence of genetically determined intellectual differences among "races."

The reactions of the public to scholarly outreach and the failure of most decision-makers to take the necessary steps to ameliorate the human predicament have long been gradually shifting my research to trying to understand *cultural* evolution—that is, how and why humanity's nongenetic information changes over time. Anne and I have long believed that society must find ways to shape deliberately that dimension of evolution so that the views of those who study humanity systematically can more readily be brought to public attention, evaluated, and, where appropriate, incorporated into policy.

My first research excursion into that area was generated by one of the reactions to *The Population Bomb*. In response to our argument that the world was becoming overpopulated, colleagues frequently pointed to psychologist John Calhoun's famous work in the 1950s and early 1960s on behavioral sinks in rats. Calhoun and his colleagues had put some rats in a large pen, given them abundant food and water, and let them breed. As the rats got more and more crowded, unusual behavior showed up, the frequency of homosexual behavior increased, and some ate their young. These results were interpreted in two ways relative to human crowding. One was, we needn't worry about human crowding as our population grew—it would naturally stop growing when enough of us turned gay and ate our young. The other was, we needed to worry about human crowding for as our population grew, people would turn gay and eat their young.

A literature search revealed no studies showing that either homosexuality or cannibalism were more common among human New Yorkers than

Iowans. More surprising, there were essentially no studies of the effects of crowding on human beings: *no* studies of how many soldiers could be crowded onto troop ships, prisoners jammed in cell blocks, sailors added to the crews of nuclear submarines, and so on. So at Stanford I recruited a psychologist colleague, Jonathan Freedman, and in 1968–69 we ran some experiments. For ethical and also logistical reasons these experimental sessions had to be of relatively short duration—basically, groups of recruits from a high school student population spent four hours performing various tasks in rooms that were either highly crowded (no room for another desk) or sparsely populated. In our first experiments we found that, on tasks like crossing out sevens on sheets of random numbers, memorizing words, or counting clicks coming from a loudspeaker, people did as well under crowded as under uncrowded conditions. In later experiments we had groups of high school students, either all female or all male, get to know each other, first discussing topics and then playing mechanical games requiring partners to coordinate. Then, in the final hour, the partners got to choose either a cooperative or competitive strategy in a prisoner's dilemma type of game. The results were interesting—in the crowded room, boys were more competitive, in the uncrowded room less competitive; the results for girls were the opposite.

In another experiment, adults of diverse backgrounds were recruited through newspaper ads, allowed to get to know each other in either crowded or uncrowded conditions, and then watched a courtroom tape and served as a jury. They also filled out questionnaires on such issues as how they liked the experiment and how they liked their fellow jurors. The results were somewhat like those in the previous experiments—but women showed stronger preference for close company, giving more lenient sentences when having close company, whereas men were harsher when more crowded. Men were also more negative about the experience and their fellows when more crowded, and they thought they made a lousier jury. Women were exactly the opposite. But nobody ate their young. I concluded that physical crowding was not nearly as important a problem as was human numbers exceeding available supplies of needed resources and overwhelming the capacity of waste sinks (such as the atmosphere for dumping carbon dioxide and other greenhouse gases or the oceans for plastic debris). Nonetheless our paper created quite a stir, and Jonathan continued to do research on the topic and wrote a book about it.[12]

Perhaps the biggest single academic advantage of being a public scholar for me has been the opportunity to meet and work with people in numerous disciplines—economics, psychology, political science, history, the law, aviation, military intelligence, medicine, and dentistry, to name a few. Besides encounters with a mob of economists, I've benefited greatly, for example, from interactions with psychiatrist Don Lunde; psychologists Robert Ornstein (with whom I wrote two books), Jonathan Freedman, and Lee Ross; political scientist Dennis Pirages (who became my postdoc and later wrote a controversial book with me, *Ark II*, on environmental politics) and his wife, Suellen Pirages (who earned her PhD with me on butterfly genetics and went on to work for several organizations in the field of toxic substances disposal). Then there were lawyers (especially John Montgomery, Meg Breinholt, Paul Brest, Mary Ann Hurliman, and Paul Perret), politicians (notably Colorado senator Tim Wirth, California congressman Pete McCloskey, Colorado governor Dick Lamm, and Australian foreign secretary and former premier of New South Wales Bob Carr), people in the arts (Tony Angell, Karole Armitage, and Darryl Wheye, for example), and an orthodontist, Sandra Kahn. This has been great for broadening horizons, becoming educated in new areas, dealing with tough criticism, and finding fine friends.

The good news is that disciplinary boundaries in academia are gradually breaking down even though the stultifying disciplines themselves persist. Also declining are prejudices about scientists speaking out on issues of public policy. Many senior environmental scientists are working to change our own disciplinary culture, which once was summarized by the old saying, "Shoemaker, stick to your last." When I was trained, the emphasis was on doing research and then letting fellow scientists know what you had discovered. Your science was not completed until, as Mich pointed out repeatedly to me when I was a student, you had "informed other researchers of your results by publishing them." Now many scientists are working to add to that dictum ". . . and explained their importance to the general public."

In 1969, I got into an argument in the *Stanford Daily* (the student newspaper) about population with Dudley Kirk. A distinguished demographer, Kirk, in the still-continuing tradition of some in that profession, failed to grasp issues at the population-environment interface. He was also able to bear the sufferings of the poor with a stiff upper lip. Kirk did not see something I felt was obvious (and still is obvious)—that bringing down population numbers is a key to justice and equity and creating a world with any chance of sustainability over at least centuries.[13]

At that time, a graduate student in the Department of Aeronautical Engineering, John Holdren, would come home from the lab each night and tell his wife, Cheri, that Ehrlich was right and Kirk wrong. Cheri would suggest that he call me up and talk to me. One day, John, after writing me a letter, did just that, and I asked him to meet at noon the next day for a sack lunch in the Twitty Room.[14] At 6:30 that next evening John left. In the intervening hours we had already outlined the first of many joint publications and started what would become a lifelong friendship between Anne and me and John and Cheri.[15] Cheri, as noted in chapter 6, would eventually do her PhD with me, starting that long-term field experiment testing whether *Euphydryas gillettii* could survive if introduced to the vicinity of the Rocky Mountain Biological Lab. Aside from agreeing on almost everything, John and I had strongly complementary backgrounds and expertise. John was a brilliant mathematical physicist and aeronautical engineer, while I had trouble counting to eleven without taking off my shoes. The combination worked well (as did my collaboration with botanists), and it has worked well ever since. We published a long series of papers and articles, focusing early on population-related issues.

Perhaps our most utilized contribution was the basic concept of ecosystem services. It was introduced initially as natural services—the benefits (such as crop pollination and shoreline protection) and products (like food from the sea) that humanity gets from natural ecosystems—and developed in a joint 1974 paper, "Human Population and the Global Environment," led by John; it later formed the basis of the rise to prominence of our joint student Gretchen Daily.[16]

A second often-cited joint contribution was the IPAT (I=PAT) equation.

Put forth in 1971, in a *Science* paper entitled "The Impact of Population Growth," the equation stated that the negative impact (I) of a society on its own and the global environment is simply the product of its population size (P), how much the average person in the society consumes (A, for affluence), and the technologies and social arrangements employed to service the consumption (T). Our motive in publishing it was to counter two misleading ideas that still persist. One was that promoted by cell biologist Barry Commoner, who basically blamed all environmental problems on faulty technologies and said that population growth was unimportant. One does not need to be a genius, however, to see that a billion people deploying a faulty technology would do more environmental damage than a thousand people deploying the same technology. Commoner had once done important work in calling attention to the impacts of nuclear fallout, but he ended up doing incalculable damage to the human future by crusading on a platform that misled people into ignoring the environmental costs of population expansion and overconsumption. He may still turn out to be sort of right, however, since increases in population and a thirst for resources to support them (A) could lead to massive use of that faultiest of technologies, thermonuclear weapons.

In front of the President's Commission on Population Growth and the American Future in November 1970, established partially in response to Anne's and my efforts, Commoner stated, "If a ship is sinking, some [gesturing at me] would throw the passengers overboard; I prefer to man the pumps." I replied, "If the sinking ship is tied up at a dock and passengers are boarding, I'd prevent any more from coming on board, *while* I manned the pumps." The laughter of the commissioners was gratifying. The commission concluded that it was important to reduce unwanted pregnancies and to slow population growth to improve the quality of life.[17]

Commoner famously orchestrated another attack on me at the United Nations Conference on the Human Environment in Stockholm in 1972, using his students as surrogates to harass me and later stole a paper by John and me that had been accepted but not yet printed in the *Bulletin of Atomic Scientists*.[18] He published it and a critique in his own journal without our permission or any opportunity to proofread it.[19]

The second reason to develop the I=PAT equation was to counter the still-too-common notion that the population problem is one of too many poor people, when too many rich people is more to the point. Poor people don't ordinarily fly on jet aircraft, own several automobiles, sleep in air-conditioned five-bedroom homes, eat steaks nightly, and buy endless gadgets and sets of clothes. Of course, both rich and poor must consider the technology factor. Walking on shoe leather puts less carbon dioxide into the atmosphere than transporting yourself in a car; high-rise dwellings are generally less damaging for biodiversity than suburban sprawl.

Our contribution has come to be seen by many as simple, straightforward, and educational, and it has been much utilized. It is more than a mathematical equation: it is still in our view a great way to organize thoughts and analysis about large-scale environmental impacts.[20]

John Holdren's long series of joint publications with me also included a monthly column in 1970 and 1971 in the *Saturday Review of Literature* at the request of its editor, Norman Cousins, who was dedicated, as we were, to nuclear disarmament. And besides collaborating on papers and columns, John was a great help to Anne and me in writing the second edition of *Population, Resources, Environment*, especially in areas requiring physical science expertise.

John soon figured as well in a number of my other activities and a bit later started coming to RMBL in the summers. In 1970, in part out of gratitude for John's huge contributions to the writing of *Population, Resources, Environment*, we invited the Holdrens on a trip to Bora Bora, where my fascination with reef fishes had been born in 1965. We all got scuba certified before we left and delighted in the glories of the Hotel Bora Bora with its cabins on stilts over the reefs (where Anne and I would later investigate fish responses to mirrors). At the outset, we intended to investigate cleaner fish behavior (small fishes that make a living by picking parasites off large fishes). Our only notable scientific experience, though, occurred when we saw a bluestreak cleaner wrasse entering a coral-encrusted beer bottle, which we capped with our fingers and extracted from the reef. To get some good pictures of the captive fish, I focused our Olympus SLR on John's upturned

Sabre-toothed blenny, or false cleaner fish. I'd been fooled frequently by snake mites with teensy brains, but all four of us had been conned by the blenny with its larger brain. It promptly took a chunk out of John Holdren's hand and was quickly released. Author photo.

hand, and Cheri dumped the fish into it. It immediately bit a nice chunk out of one of John's fingers.

We amateurs had been fooled by a cleaner mimic—a sabre-toothed blenny with exactly the cleaner's color scheme, which lures big fish to be cleaned with a cleanerlike display and, when the big fish strikes an "I want to be cleaned" pose, snatches a big bite out of the victim and flees. The picture I had taken of John's bloody finger became a fixture in years of lectures on animal behavior, coevolution, and reef ecology.

John went on to become one of the world's top scientists in his own right. He became well known as, among other things, the lead author on a critical study of nuclear safety, founder of the energy and resources group at UC Berkeley, adviser to the U.S and Russian governments on nuclear issues (especially the likely environmental impacts of fusion power), and acceptor of the Nobel Prize for the Pugwash movement (a global organization working to avoid large-scale wars). As President Barack Obama's science adviser and head of the Office of Science and Technology Policy, John was very influential in moving the administration toward dealing with climate disruption and other existential threats.

The opportunity to collaborate with John has been one of the most important experiences in my life. I only outsmarted him once in the half century we've been friends, in an area where he soon far surpassed me. Early on, we began to introduce the Holdrens to good wines. John thought it was all nonsense and decided to demonstrate that once and for all. He refilled a Bordeaux bottle with a California jug wine and served it to us, using the Ehrlich sock method to conceal the label. Then he asked me what I thought. In those days, unhappily for John, California jug wines tended to have a very characteristic odor, which gave away the game immediately. I automatically responded that I thought his horse had diabetes. Now John produces a professional-quality annual guide to hundreds of wines, using an algorithm that evaluates quality against price, much to the amusement of Barack Obama and his other friends.

It has been a long time coming, but with the help of many colleagues, especially John, Anne and I have gradually seen the population issue working its way back into public and professional discourse in recent years, which has led me to reevaluate *The Population Bomb* in retrospect (chapter 12). My favorite example is a 2017 paper by scientists Seth Wynes and Kimberly Nicholas showing that having one fewer child in a developed nation would reduce greenhouse gas emissions as much as twenty-four people permanently giving up driving cars.[21] It reduced Anne and my possible guilt for our greenhouse gas emissions, especially with all the flying, because we had limited ourselves to a single child (when we would have loved to have two). Gradually population as a key issue is blending into that global view of population, resources, and environment that the neo-Malthusians have been credited with originating. Population as well as butterflies changed my life, and ironically my life is fading just as the SARS-CoV-2 virus should be making everyone intensely interested in demography. Human population size, density, and movements are key elements in the spread of viruses, as is the exponential growth of virus populations.

The sort of global view of the human predicament engendered in part by the neo-Malthusians (especially *The Population Bomb*) and Rachel Carson, among others, as well as the development of nuclear weapons, satellites, and the World Wide Web, seems to have made the world ready to do something about the demographic elements of human resource, environment, and political problems. I just hope civilization will manage it.

NINE

Global Fieldwork

Butterflies (as well as both many other creatures and being a public scholar) have taken me repeatedly all over the world. It has been another aspect of born-in-1932 luck; just as Anne and I were in a position to begin serious traveling, jet aircraft came along and made it easy. And in the 1960s, when we started, there was still a fair amount of relative wilderness rich in biodiversity around the globe to explore. In subsequent decades we have gone far beyond the travels associated with that wonderful 1965–66 sabbatical year Anne, Lisa, and I spent largely in Sydney, Australia, with Charles Birch. Charles and I published several papers together and became fast friends, exchanging visits virtually every year until his early death in 2009. Until Covid-19 intervened, we still returned to Oz, typically about once a year, to see other old friends, collaborate with colleagues, and census birds in the Sydney region.

It was also on that first trip to Australia that we became friends with Hal Wagner, as I've mentioned, who had joined us for dinner in Sydney that sabbatical year every time the *Mariposa* sailed in. He was a San Franciscan, so we could keep up our socializing together after Anne and I returned to Stanford. One night when I remarked on how much we had enjoyed our year in Oz and hoped we could get back there, Hal responded that if I would be willing to give a couple of lectures each week on board, Matson Lines would be happy to take Anne and me out and back. Thanks partially

(I suspect) to the notoriety the Carson show had brought me, my career in cruise lecturing was thus launched in the late 1960s and soon was not confined to travel to Australia; it would later be supplemented by lecture cruises run by the Stanford Alumni Association.

Cruise lecturing had benefits beyond allowing us to do fieldwork in exotic places that otherwise we could never have reached. Often—though not always—the dinners on board were with inquisitive, intelligent people and occasionally with those who took great and enduring interest in our work. On a side trip from a South American cruise, for example, we went to Machu Picchu in a train compartment with Max and Isabell Herzstein from Houston, Texas. We had a great time, and after we returned they came up to San Francisco and introduced us to Max's brother Stanley and his wife, Marion, who lived there. We shared many common interests, and Stanley became a tireless advocate at the Koret Foundation for supporting our group's work—all traceable to our sharing a train compartment with shipmates in Peru.

My earliest research support had come from the National Science Foundation, starting with the grant that David Keck had arranged. For a time I had two distinct NSF grants, one for my long-term studies of Bay checkerspot populations on Jasper Ridge and one for coevolution. Eventually, the NSF decreed that no investigator could have two simultaneous grants, so I gave up the one for our coevolution work in order to maintain continuity on the other. The level of support was seldom adequate, however, and I still needed funds for our social science and political outreach. That's where private donors such as Stanley and Marion Herzstein have made all the difference. Most of the money always went to salaries for grad students, postdocs, and assistants, and their travel and ours. Fortunately, little of the research in my career had high equipment expenses, except for a few years when our group ran a biochemical (electrophoresis) lab. It was then that I really came to appreciate the funding problems that my colleagues in, for example, molecular biology, complained about. The financial situation for most of science improved in the first decades of my career, the 1950s and 1960s, but it deteriorated somewhat in more recent years even though the need, especially in environmental science, had vastly expanded. Fortunately, private donations and money from prizes I've been given and donated to our program at Stanford buffered my own research group from the worst of it, especially as we became more politically involved.

Our travels for research and other pursuits took us to the Caribbean to study fish schooling, Panama, Trinidad, and Peru (butterfly ecology), Costa Rica (bird flocking), Tanzania's Gombe Stream (chimp behavior) and Ngorongoro Crater (education), Gunbalanya in Australia's Arnhem Land (Aboriginal art), the Galápagos (evolutionary history), Antarctica (ecotourism), and many other places and activities. Diverse as these seem, there was, however, a common theme. The distribution of the diverse animals, ecosystems, and human cultures that were our main items of research interest were generally global. Our extensive travel started with the 1965–66 trip to Australia and around the world that allowed us to dissect fresh specimens of the full taxonomic diversity of butterflies. The various subsequent trips helped to inform us about the environmental state of the world, and we translated what we found into scientific papers, articles, and books that were part of our broader education efforts. When we were accompanied by others we were always adding to that education through lectures. And travel always seemed to open up opportunities for research. I couldn't study dominance relations among tropical birds, the behavior of reef fishes, or the dynamics of long-wing butterfly populations in Palo Alto, California. But truth be told, despite loving those research, observation, and education activities, Anne and I always had a travel bug.

After our experiences with reef fishes on our sabbatical, Anne and I became interested in pursuing reef research in the Caribbean. My uncle and aunt, Gordon Rosenberg (my mother's brother) and his wife, Connie, were great swimmers and sailors and had discovered (actually, helped establish) a small resort, Palm Island, in the Grenadines. One year around 1970, on our way home from fieldwork in Trinidad, we stopped at Palm Island and discovered a nice snorkeling reef right off the beach with a daytime school of French grunts (*Haemulon flavolineatum*; the "grunt" name comes from the oink-like sound those fish make if taken from the water).

What exactly the grunts were doing was an obvious question. And it was that question which launched our grunt research program and established about-once-a-year expeditions to the Caribbean that would continue for several years. When flying ourselves down from Palo Alto on those trips we'd typically stay over with friends in Fort Lauderdale, Florida, and then the next day check in with customs in the Bahamas before overnighting in the Admiral's Inn, located on a hilltop next to an airstrip on South Caicos in the Turks and Caicos Islands. The scene in the inn's bar was much like the famous bar scene of *Star Wars*. The place was a center of drug distribution for the entire area, and all night long we would hear light aircraft overhead and cigarette boats roaring around. The next morning we would fly to Saint Croix to do research on grunts with my former student and still good friend John Ogden (and his biologist wife, Nancy) for several days at the West Indies Marine Lab. We'd then head down to Palm Island to check out the grunts there, and meet Connie and Gordy.

Reef research can have bracing moments, like pulling on a cold, dripping wetsuit at 4:00 a.m. For me, a most memorable day was my fortieth birthday (May 29, 1972). In the morning John Ogden and I had entertained ourselves dogfighting with scuba scooters (self-propelled torpedolike vehicles that pulled you around fast). That evening I did my first night dive, weighed down by cameras and lights. Idiotically I forgot to inflate my buoyancy compensator (which should be adjusted to offset the weight of any equipment one has) before going over the side. My light beautifully illuminated the bottom as I plunged toward it, showing in detail a solid carpet of *Diadema antillarum*, the long-spined sea urchin. Fortunately I didn't suffer any deep punctures, but I was rubbing vinegar into my legs and butt for days afterward (a locally recommended treatment). But even the long-spines didn't reduce my pleasure in the beauty of cruising over the bottom in moonlight with John, phosphorescent diatoms rising in the wake of our flippers.

John, Anne, and I collaborated in subsequent years in grunt research. We

Anne and I doing research in oenology as we approach middle age. Author photo.

ended up with a couple of papers on the convergent coevolution of color patterns and how they led to similarity in the daytime resting patterns of grunts and goatfishes and likely added thereby more predator protection to the schools.

One year, George and Yvonne Burtness joined us in our grunt investigations at Saint Croix. We led off with some wine research. Just before departing Palo Alto, we sampled four bottles of midrange Bordeaux and made notes on them. Then Anne and I flew down by ourselves to Saint Croix and George and Yvonne came by a commercial flight, bringing a set of exactly the same wines. We sampled them again in the tropical setting; warm, humid weather, ocean view, low cumulus clouds. To us they tasted entirely different. That expedition in addition gave us a fine war story. John, George, and I (Anne and Yvonne didn't scuba dive) would lie on the bottom waiting for dusk when the resting schools would break up and the fish would leave the reef for the seagrass beds to feed. It was thrilling, almost otherworldly, just to wait, along with large, hungry groupers and, one time, a barracuda hoping to make a meal of an unsuspecting grunt or goatfish. Right on cue, the fish would stream off the reef en masse, and we would follow them into the seagrass, dropping strips of yellow plastic tied to small pieces of rebar (reinforcing bar) along the way. The next day we could return in daylight and chart their routes by the rebar trail. The trail confirmed our view that the grunts rested on the reefs in the daytime and foraged in the seagrass beds at night.

One night when the seas were a little rough, George did not return to the boat with us. Long after John and I figured George's air must have been exhausted, he still hadn't returned, and we were very worried. When we saw a flashing light we didn't understand on the distant beach, we decided to return to the lab and drive down the beach to investigate. We eventually found George, along with mutual friend (and later colleague) Darryl Wheye, who with her husband had a home down the beach. George had borrowed a flashlight and was trying to signal us in Morse code—a hopeless task since neither John nor I knew it well. In the rising chop of the sea, George had not been able to spot the boat's small light when he surfaced and so wisely headed in the direction of the island. So all was well that ended well.

Such adventures and research expeditions were really possible only because of 5352S. In 1971 through the Pirages we had met Paul and Iris Brest. Paul was a professor in (later, dean of) Stanford's law school and Iris a practicing attorney. They owned a Cessna Skymaster 337—the famous high-wing push-pull twin-engine airplane that had the front end of a Cessna 210 with a second engine in the rear between two booms that extended back from the wings and supported an elevator and two rudders. The idea behind the design was to avoid the asymmetrical thrust that caused problems if an engine failed in a conventional twin with one engine mounted on each wing. We sold our share in a single-engine 899F we had purchased after our sabbatical year in Australia to George Burtness and bought half of the Brests' Skymaster, call sign 5352S. It was an ideal vehicle for our fieldwork. Taking aerial photos was easy without wings and engines in the way, and the plane was faster than our old one and safer in design, roomy and comfortable for long trips and well equipped for instrument flying, with a simple autopilot that saved Anne, who now had a pilot's license as well, a lot of boring effort.

Anne with N899F, our first airplane, a Cessna 182 Skylane. Author photo.

It was returning from Saint Croix reef fish research in January 1973 when we had one of our few "exciting" times with 5352S. We had stopped in Baton Rouge to see LSU economist Herman Daly and his lovely Brazilian wife, Marcia. Herman was a great pioneer, one of the first of the few economists interested in the question of how to have a successful economy without endless growth. After a delightful evening, we departed for home on a miserable rainy morning heading for a stop in Austin, Texas, to visit two old friends. We were on instruments in driving rain within a few seconds after takeoff, but with no thunderstorms predicted, we proceeded routinely.

After a couple of hours or so, however, water started to come into the cabin around an access hatch in front of the windscreen and cascade over the radios. Then abruptly we lost our directional gyro, an important gadget for flying on instruments, which was even more worrying. We were north of Houston, and I called air traffic control, declared an emergency, and asked for a no-gyro emergency approach into Houston. They began to vector us toward the airport, giving us instructions of when to start and stop turns. I was scared: if we lost our increasingly soaked radios, our only option would

In this painting by aviation artist Frank Wootton, Anne and I are flying our second plane, Skymaster 5352S, over Union Island in the Grenadines. Author photo.

be to let down blind and hope we broke out below the clouds and could see around us before we hit something.

Air traffic control took me in too close to make a smooth turn onto the localizer, which provides right-left guidance to the runway, and asked if I'd like to try it or be vectored around to a better position for the approach. Hoping the electronics would last, I chose the latter and was able to make a smooth approach, breaking out of the clouds at about two hundred feet with the approach end of the runway straight ahead of us: the happiest sight Anne and I had seen in a very long time.

For over two decades, being pilots was a big part of my life, and of Anne's. Obviously a problem only for the privileged, it was nevertheless one of the saddest days in my life in 1986 when skyrocketing insurance costs and the looming costs of replacing the worn engines of 5352S forced us to give up our Skymaster. Stanford's salary couldn't safely carry the load. We gave her to a group of flying doctors to help poor people in Latin America, and there were tears in Anne's and my eyes as she taxied away.

One of my first field trips after the sabbatical in Oz was to Central America in 1969 with graduate students Larry Gilbert and Michael Singer, both of whom had done pioneering work on *Euphydryas editha*. The trip included many memorable hours crawling around with headlamps on dark forest floors looking for caterpillars of a large complex of satyrine butterflies. One couldn't help expecting to meet the deadly bushmaster snakes, which would, we imagined, strike us between the eyes. A visit to Barro Colorado Island in Panama was a highlight. During our stay, a near-continuous downpour was accompanied by the loud cries of some captive howler monkeys, who increased their volume with the intensity of the rainfall. Despite the downpour, and largely because of Larry's and Mike's keen powers of observation, we found and photographed the little satyrine butterfly *Euptychia westwoodi* ovipositing on a lycopsid, one of the very few examples of a caterpillar feeding on a nonseed plant.[1] The paper on that got one of Larry's pictures of the egg-laying act onto the cover of *Science* magazine.

On that first Central American trip we were joined by a young postdoc of Peter Raven's from England, Andrew Beattie, as well as Larry's wife, Christine, and Maggie Sharp, another graduate student and now a long-term friend. We had a wonderful Christmas at the New York Zoological Society's Simla field station in the mountains of northern Trinidad. Lisa accompanied us (age fourteen) and thrilled the whole gang when she poured a pitcher of water over my head when I made an inappropriate comment about her mother.

We had started a research program at Simla at the request of the zoological society to give the organization an excuse to keep the station open. An old estate, Simla had been bought in 1949 by William Beebe, perhaps the most famous tropical ecologist of his day, and named after the hill station in India he had visited and loved. It was a magnificent old house where the gang could stay, with a small bedroom outbuilding where Anne and I (the old folks, at ages thirty-six and thirty-seven) slept. The station's library had a copy of the American butterflies volume of Adalbert Seitz's *Macrolepidop-*

tera of the World—an invaluable resource for making our early ecological investigations of tropical butterflies. A highlight for all of us, however, was the excellent meals the staff served us, preceded by wonderful rum drinks known as Simla Specials.

Michael Singer had joined our group at Stanford from rainy-foggy England, and I had immediately set him to work on *E. editha* on Jasper Ridge in California's wet season, to which he was clearly preadapted. He and I hoped to uncover the secrets of the caterpillars' lives—critical to understanding what controlled the size of their populations. In Trinidad he focused on small satyrine butterflies, tropical relatives of the boreal *Erebia* I had studied in my youth. Jasper Ridge and Trinidad had started Mike on a career focused on the food-plant relationships of butterflies, and he still continues his research on checkerspots as the world's expert on diet choice in herbivorous insects.

In Trinidad Larry Gilbert and I did research on the structure and size fluctuations of a population of the longwing butterfly *Heliconius ethilla.* Our results contrasted greatly with what we were finding on Jasper Ridge with *Euphydryas editha.* Females of the latter emerged with almost all their eggs—many hundreds—mature and ready to be fertilized and laid. But being a caterpillar is a dangerous business in the tropics, where voracious ants constantly patrol the leaves. Anne's dissections showed Larry and me that female *Heliconius* emerged with only a handful of eggs ready to lay, gradually maturing and laying more over many weeks. The *Euphydryas* lived something like ten days on average as adults and, like most insects, never coexisted with adult offspring. The *Heliconius* adults were very long-lived for butterflies (or most insects), however. Adults sometimes flew with their grandchildren! We recaptured one *H. ethilla* an extraordinary 162 days after it was first marked, suggesting a possible active adult life span of six months.

Larry made an important discovery at Simla. The female *Heliconius* actually collected pollen from certain species of plants to produce clumps of pollen on their "tongues." They then secreted digestive enzymes into the clumps and sucked up the resulting amino acids, the building blocks of proteins. This provided them with the proteins they needed to continue egg production through their long adult lives. I had seen the special structures on

Heliconius tongues that allow them to collect pollen but had totally missed their significance.

Larry and Mike were great examples of a huge benefit I have enjoyed at Stanford, access to brilliant graduate students from whom—if one were so inclined (and too many are)—one can steal both ideas and credit. What more could a professor want?

In traveling to Australia about once a year and spending a couple of part-year sabbaticals at Macquarie University, we became close friends with Andy Beattie and his biologist wife, Christine Turnbull. In the mid-1990s they gave Anne and me one of the most wonderful days of our lives. We had been exploring Kakadu National Park near Darwin in the Northern Territory, seeing many interesting birds and the gigantic "salties" (crocodiles) and were planning a trip to Oenpelli (Gunbalanya) to pursue our joint interest in Aboriginal art (ours stimulated by our 1965–66 experience with bark painting and church missionary censorship). I wanted to get some pictures of the famous Kakadu Aboriginal rock art but had not found good, properly lit sites. I went into the Kakadu Park Center shop to see if I could buy some slides of the paintings to use in the "Art Not Ours" lectures I was giving on cruise ships in those days. I found a set of six slides and handed the clerk my credit card. Surprisingly, he asked if I was Ehrlich the ecologist. I confessed, and he turned out to be married to the teacher at the Oenpelli school, who in turn was an employee of one of Andy's colleagues in Darwin. Small world came together, and the clerk, who said the Kakadu rock art was inferior compared to that at Oenpelli, arranged for his wife to give us a tour late that afternoon, after school was out.

We hopped in our snorkel-equipped vehicle, forded the river that separated the Aboriginal-controlled area from the park, and met up with her. She led us on a great tour of a hundred yards or more of the Injalak Hill rock shelters decorated with the art of the Kunwinjku people. The fantastic ocher (earth pigment—mostly yellow, brown, and red) paintings of human figures, game, totemic animals, food plants, abstract designs, and other depictions of an ancient way of life cover large areas of the ceilings of overhanging rock (plate 8). There was much overpainting and mixture of themes. The paintings had been done over many thousands of years by one of the truly sustainable societies of *Homo sapiens.* They had the same feel as our favorite bark painting by Yangarriny Wunungmurra, which we had purchased from a Sydney dealer in 1965 (plate 9). It depicts a billabong, the Aboriginal name for an oxbow lake, in a design that is sacred to the Dhalwangu clan. The design shows totemic tortoises, fish, and crayfish, spiritual emblems of the clan or of individuals, while the cross-hatching represents the mud and weed of the billabong. Without a written language, the Aborigines used body decoration, rock art, painting on slabs of bark, and the like to record the significant stories of their culture, their history, their land, and their beliefs, especially about their origin in the dreamtime. The origins of modern Aboriginal art go back less than a century, and Anne and I, in our interest in the art being sold by the Church Missionary Society in 1965, were there near the beginning. As you can see in the color plates (I hope), Aboriginal art has a near universal appeal to human aesthetic senses. In the 1970s Aboriginal artists developed a new way of basically coding their stories in "dot art," producing paintings of (to Anne and me) extraordinary beauty.

At the time of our visit to Oenpelli, viewing the rock art was highly restricted by the village elders, and Anne and Chris, being women, were asked not to look in certain directions. We were stunned by the beauty and diversity of the art and amazed at how the rock floors on which the artists sat to paint on the low overhangs had been polished smooth by thousands of years of human posteriors. After our tour of the art we went into the small settlement of Oenpelli, where the lineal descendants of the artists were still painting, but now on special paper imported from England.

Andy and I have written several papers together, and Chris, a talented artist, illustrated a book we published with Yale University Press in 2001, *Wild Solutions,* on the ways in which natural products can enhance human well-being. Andy and Chris are the glue that holds our Aussie gang of colleagues and dear friends together since Charles Birch's death in 2009. When I get depressed unable to visit Oz because of the pandemic or other reasons, I like to imagine going again to our favorite café at Bobbin Head, a beautiful

Yolngu painting now done on special paper imported from England. Bruce Nabegeyo, *Namarladj Djang* (*Orphans Dreaming*), early 1990s. © Bruce Nabegeyo / Copyright Agency. Licensed by Artists Rights Society (ARS), New York, 2021.

anchorage in Ku-ring-gai Chase, where Chris once showed me a lifer—my first long-sought glossy black cockatoo.

But Chris's greatest triumph of many attempts at helping me to see rare organisms in the remaining wonderful diversity of life occurred on that dismal day in November 2016 when an anti-environmentalist and climate change denier was elected president of the United States. We had spent much of that day searching shoreline woods around Cairns seeking a life bird for me, the beach thick-knee (also known as the beach stone-curlew—*Esacus magnirostris*). That bird eluded us, and we had to quit the search so I could give a speech for a leading tropical conservation biologist, Bill Laurence, at James Cook University. Bill and his wife, Sue, took us all out to dinner at a restaurant with fine wines on the Cairns esplanade. Chris and I staggered out at the head of the group, going through a closed bar that shared an entrance area with the restaurant. Then Chris announced, "There it is!"

Also known as the stone-curlew and classified as "near threatened," *Esacus magnirostris* is one of the heaviest shorebirds and feeds on crabs and other small invertebrates, foraging both by day and by night. Photo by JJ Harrison, CC BY-SA 4.0.

Out from under a bar stool marched a beach thick-knee, one of the largest shorebirds (standing more than a foot tall), classified as near threatened by the IUCN (the International Union for the Conservation of Nature—the closest humanity has to an official global body to protect biodiversity). Our thick-knee marched proudly ahead of us, displaying so Andy and Anne, following us, could see its distinct markings. It became the first bird I'd long searched for and then found when I was drunk (for good reason). Little could I have imagined a relationship that started in jungle butterfly research in Trinidad would lead, many decades later, to a Trump-night avian triumph in Oz.

In doing field studies of biodiversity in the Americas, any evolutionist would have a strong urge to see the Galápagos Islands because of Darwin's classic visit there. I was no exception. Our first expedition to the Galápagos took place in 1979. The trip was courtesy—though obliging me to lecture along the way—of the Stanford Alumni Association's Travel Study program, which periodically invited me to lead and lecture on trips all over the world.

On that 1979 trip, I got to photograph Galápagos penguins on land from the water with my ancient though still-functioning Nikonos camera. I also was anxious to get pictures of a marine iguana feeding on the seafloor. With a buddy (I can't remember who), I snorkeled perhaps a mile out—stupidly too far—searching for one. When a storm started building on the horizon, we headed back toward our cruise ship anchored in a cozy harbor behind a breakwater. But the storm built faster than we could have imagined, and by the time we were snorkeling along the sea side of the breakwater toward the harbor entrance, large waves were breaking over it. One picked my companion up and deposited him in the calm water beyond, but the one that picked me up carried me into the rocks of the breakwater itself. My snorkel was ripped from my mouth and I started to panic. Then my religion saved me. Remember, I've always been a coward, and orthodox. As a result, unlike many snorkelers, I'd always worn a life vest while snorkeling, and it occurred to me that that was exactly the sort of situation I wore it for. I popped the carbon dioxide cartridge, the vest inflated, and the next wave boosted me into the calm harbor.

The ship for the Stanford Galápagos expedition was an ancient (and dangerous) tub called the *Bucanero*. I sat next to a guy in the bar one night who said he was a marine (ship) surveyor and added he couldn't wait to get off the *Bucanero*, which he thought was a candidate for sinking soon. The lifeboats were metal, not the rubber Zodiacs used by most expedition cruise ships, and loading passengers into them in rough seas to visit the islands gave us some near misses. On the good side, the *Bucanero* voyage introduced me to Jack Grove, a dive guide who took great care with his clients and had an encyclopedic knowledge of fishes. Jack later obtained a PhD in biology, though he continued to work on expedition ships. I've sailed and dived with him many times since our Galápagos adventures.[2]

I was not lucky enough to see giant tortoises in the wild on the Galápagos in our travels there. They have been driven to extinction on some islands, very much reduced on others, and threatened everywhere. That was to my deep regret because their island-to-island differences are a classic of the geographic variation that is a way station on the road to speciation—the evolving of different kinds of organisms. Anne and I did get to see giant island tortoises on another great Stanford trip, though. It was in 1994, this time on a trip co-led by Gretchen Daily, then a joint postdoctoral fellow with John Holdren at UC Berkeley and me. A highlight of that expedition to the Indian Ocean was a visit to the isolated atoll of Aldabra with spectacular clear water and great reefs, but also beaches cluttered even then with flip-flops from the beaches around Perth, Australia, more than four thousand miles distant. Aldabra giant tortoises grew shells to some four feet long and had total weights of well over five hundred pounds, close in size to Galápagos tortoises. Giant tortoises once evolved, as far as the fossil record shows, on all continents except Antarctica and Australia, and had reached many islands, especially in the Indo-Pacific. But extinctions have expunged them from most of their distributions, largely, it is suspected, because they were easy sources of food for a spreading voracious predator, *Homo sapiens.*

One of Darwin's contributions to the understanding that organisms evolved and were not specially created was pointing out that species on islands tended not to be as closely similar to each other as they were to species on the nearest land. Thus Aldabra giant tortoises are most closely related to smaller tortoises on Madagascar, not to the superficially similar Galápagos giant tortoises. The latter, in turn, are closely related to tortoises on the South American mainland.

Why should the memoir of a butterfly scientist include a section on Hawaii? After all, that state has only a few native butterflies. The answer is obvious—it's a wonderful place to write books and articles and grade class papers. Anne and I have always had a soft spot in our hearts for Hawaii. We first ventured out there in the late 1960s shortly after our return from that first sabbatical year in Oz. Dick Holm had seen an ad in a Bay Area magazine for an apartment for rent on Maui, near Lahaina, and we thought the three of us (Anne, Dick, and me) could leave Lisa in the care of my graduate student Maggie Sharp, whom she luckily adored, and go out between winter and spring quarters to see if it would be a suitable place. We went first to Hilo on the Big Island. The warm tropical air, low cumulus clouds, and mai tais had me relaxed and immediately entranced, and the Japanese food at Kai Kai Tai restaurant added to the joy. Next stop was Maui. That apartment Dick found right by Honokowai Beach Park was very comfortable, and we vowed to return to the area. While we occasionally went elsewhere in the islands, for the next couple of decades we were hooked on Maui. Typically, we went out for a few weeks between quarters, renting a second-floor apartment in the same development right on the water with a view in one direction over the channel to Molokai, and in the other a view over Honokowai Park. Each morning we would walk a couple of miles down the beach to Kaanapali Point and back.

Dick would then prepare special hamburgers for us, and we'd work until lunch, take a nap, work some more, and then go out for dinner—a great routine that even resulted in some books, articles, and graded exams and term papers. Many friends came to visit, often including John and Cheri Holdren and another couple, Kirk Smith and Joan Diamond, especially when we had sabbatical leave and could stay five to six weeks. Kirk was John's first graduate student; in the first years we knew them, Kirk was based at the East-West Center in Honolulu and Joan was climbing to executive vice-president of Hawaiian Electric. We couldn't have imagined what the future held—Kirk and Joan moving to Berkeley in 1990, Kirk becoming one of the world's most honored public health scientists, demonstrating, among other things, that the world's worst air pollution problems could be found in third-world huts due to the emissions from inefficient cooking and heating stoves. He was also arguably the funniest world-class scientist. Joan became one of my closest colleagues running the Millennium Assessment of Human Behavior (MAHB), and remains a close friend and colleague of ours after Kirk's sudden and premature death in 2020.

Hawaii provided us not only a relaxing place to write and grade papers but also a chance to observe various tropical organisms—especially reef fishes, which I sometimes enjoyed in the company of the guy who virtually invented their study, Jack Randall. My most adventuresome dive was with him at Molokini, where we went down about 120 feet, deep for me but nothing for Jack. I came up with a nearly empty tank; Jack's was still 80 percent full. Jack had a great reputation as an anaerobe. He had transformed understanding of the taxonomy and ecology of reef fishes, but we couldn't get him elected to the National Academy of Sciences in later years because of the strong bias in favor of experimental scientists (Darwin would be unlikely to be elected today).

Despite Hawaii's fine fish fauna, and my interest in it, my biggest biological surprise in the islands was terrestrial. One day in February 1976 I saw a swallowtail butterfly. I thought I must be hallucinating—it looked like a Japanese species I was familiar with, but as far as I knew there were no swallowtails in the Hawaiian Islands. I dashed to a sporting goods store, bought a fish net, and went butterfly hunting. I soon had a specimen, saw that my "on the wing" identification was correct: it was *Papilio xuthus*, a species whose caterpillars feed on citrus. I notified the Hawaiian Department of Agriculture; they told me they were already aware of its presence—first seen on Oahu in 1971 and on Maui in 1975. I published a short note letting the community of butterfly aficionados know that Hawaii now hosted two large butterflies species (the first was the monarch). For me, as a butterfly person, it was great fun—maybe not so much for citrus farmers.

I can't leave Hawaii without mentioning that it supplied me with great earth science thrills. Wendell "Duff" and Ann Duffield have been friends of long standing, and Duff had a great career in the US Geological Service. Once when we were together on the Big Island (Hawaii), Duff took Anne and me on a hike on a cooling lava flow and we got to look into the throat of an active vent. Even more exciting, with my colleague Peter Vitousek, whose family was prominent in Hawaii, I once got to spend several hours watching a lava flow pour into the sea. We were actually seeing Hawaiian island land being formed as the Pacific tectonic plate marched northwestward over a hotspot in Earth's mantle. The beauty of the red-white hot lava being repeatedly submerged by waves and then emerging unsnuffed was mind-boggling. Water often streamed off of fire, as if defying everything I thought I knew about physics. After a couple of hours we had to leave, but I noticed that

Peter, born in Hawaii and having seen such displays many times before, backed away as we departed, like me unwilling to tear his eyes from the spectacle.

A further connection with islands of the Pacific and another nonexperimental science also came to me in an unexpected way. My interest in cultural evolution, and my collaboration in that domain with Princeton mathematical ecologist and long-term friend Simon Levin, had led me late in the last century to seek a system in which to test a simple idea. It seemed to me that culture evolved much more rapidly in domains where technologies important to survival were being developed and tested against the environment than in areas such as philosophy or ethics. Alfred North Whitehead once observed, for instance, that Western philosophical traditions were just a series of footnotes to Plato's writings. If alive today, Plato, upon learning the appropriate spoken language and history, could no doubt immediately participate in a contemporary philosophy department seminar. In contrast, Isaac Newton would be lost in a seminar on nuclear physics or evolution. I was looking for a system to study the idea of different rates of cultural evolution in different domains of culture, and I started looking to the islands of the central Pacific. They were the most recent parts of the planet our ancestors had occupied—some five hundred to fifteen hundred years ago, it's believed—and had had only one great acculturation event, which occurred when the Western world swept through the islands in the seventeenth century and later.

I started trying to compare the evolution of a technological and a nontechnological cultural domain by comparing island cultures. For technology, I tried agriculture, to determine which crops were grown; for a philosophical cultural element with close to zero impact on survival, I tried to tabulate which gods were prayed to. Male anthropologists attracted by the bare-breasted women Gauguin made famous wrote ethnographies of virtually every island group, but they were lousy at taking data. They would mention some crops but not give ranked lists by area planted of different species, and transliteration differences in gods' names made it tough to tell whether the people of two islands thought they were worshipping the same gods or even how many they imagined.

I was tempted to give up, but then I discovered the magnificent two-volume book *The Canoes of Oceania.*[3] It presented some difficult problems of analysis, but I solved that by the standard professor's strategy of bringing into the research a really smart graduate student. Deborah Rogers was over fifty when she applied to work in our group. Conventionally, that's very old to enter graduate school, but her experience, ambition, and obvious intelligence led us to take a chance on her. Boy, did it pay off. In one of my first conversations with her, arguing for the speed of technological change, I pointed out that if someone invented a six-sided wheel, and then another invented an eight-sided one, the second would replace the first almost instantaneously. But, Deborah responded, if the next invention were circular, change stops. Smart graduate students can really make you feel stupid.

Deborah shotgunned the study in which we compared structural characteristics of the seagoing canoes (outriggers) to symbolic ones (decorations). It turned out she was on the right track. Technological change in this case was conservative, slowing when something works well in the environment. Symbolic features may change rapidly, especially when they can differentiate groups (think clothing styles, types of music). In any case Deb's and my paper on this was well received; *Discover* magazine named it as one of the hundred most important scientific stories of 2008.[4]

Anne and I went to Antarctica the first time in 1975, along with Dick Holm and Hal Wagner on the Lindblad *Explorer.* It was one of our greatest travel experiences. Walking through colonies of thousands of gentoo and chinstrap penguins while pairs signaled to each other with calls and visual displays, watching individuals steal pebbles from neighbors' "nests" (small patches of pebble-surrounded bare ground), and hearing their deafening combined calls, was a never-to-be-forgotten experience.

For me the highlight of the trip came when we were cruising down the Lemaire Channel, a narrow passage of black water with huge glaciers on each side. Suddenly there was the shout of "Killer whales ahead!"—and everyone rushed to the bow to see. A pod of orcas was approaching a small

A pod of orcas attacking a Weddell seal in the Lemaire Channel, Antarctica, 1975. Note the seal on the ice pan just behind the head of the lead orca. Author photo.

ice floe on which a Weddell seal was perched. The pod rushed toward the floe, creating a substantial wave that washed over the seal. As the ship sailed past they repeated the act, finally washing the seal off and devouring it. Kodak made a fortune that day, as all you could hear besides the tourists' shouts was the click and whirr of camera shutters, including mine. Over forty years later, reading Carl Safina's magnificent book *Beyond Words* I was taken back to that day as he described this behavior so vividly.[5]

On this and a subsequent trip to Antarctica and South Georgia Island, we were thrilled by close encounters with humpback whales, leopard seals, elephant seals, king penguins, and gorgeous scenery. We even visited Elephant Island, where twenty-two of Ernest Shackleton's men were stranded in 1916 for almost five months awaiting his return and that of five others who were attempting to sail to South Georgia to arrange a rescue. Those left behind lived in a makeshift shack made from the remains of two wrecked lifeboats and some sail, hunting the occasional seal or penguin and trying to find comfort on a frozen beach of baseball-sized rocks. We were hardly comfortable in the hour or so we spent there! After an incredible, nearly eight-hundred-mile open-boat voyage and an amazing climb over the mountains of South Georgia Island, Shackleton made it to a whaling station and arranged the rescue, saving all of his men, an epic of polar exploration.

Later, I read a book by the famous red-bearded evolutionist George Gaylord Simpson in which he claimed the Antarctic was likely the best tourist destination on the planet. But, he remarked, he wasn't sure, because he hadn't been to the Himalayas. At the end of the book there was a "note added in proof": "I've now been to the Himalayas. The Antarctic is the best tourist destination on the planet." Antarctica has now, more than forty years after our first visit, become a huge tourist destination. That's a mixed bag—more people getting to see its beauty and diversity and, to appreciate both, more tourist-related damage.

On our way back with Dick Holm from Antarctica in 1975, we visited my sister Sally and her husband at their home in Lima, Peru. A skilled linguist, Sally had a wonderful career as a UNICEF officer in Peru, Zambia, Kenya, and Bangladesh, doing both good and interesting work. That trip was our first visit to her on the job and was marked by two particularly memorable events. First, I wanted to visit the Chanchamayo Valley on the eastern side of the Peruvian Andes, the putative home of that most unusual of butterflies, *Styx infernalis*. That's the one of which Mich had borrowed a specimen for me to dissect from the British Museum twenty years earlier. The exact evolutionary relationships of *Styx* were then in doubt (as to a degree, they still are) even after my research on butterfly higher classification had demonstrated its lycaenid affinities.

Sally's husband, Steve, drove Anne, Dick, and me over the Andes to the valley. At Ticlio pass, almost sixteen thousand feet above Lima, which is at sea level, with another five thousand feet of mountains above us, I got out of the car to look for alpine butterflies. I felt so dizzy from the altitude that I immediately got back in the car. I felt even dizzier as Steve drove us along the two-way, only one-car-width dirt road that switchbacked down into the valley with a thousand-foot drop on one side. With inches of road on the drop side and the only barrier being the occasional wooden cross marking where previous cars had gone over, Steve insisted on driving twenty to thirty miles an hour. I finally insisted that he stop driving and allow me to take the wheel. Even if he had been a superb driver, one lost drag-link spring could have sent us all to our deaths. We survived the trip down and back up, although in the lowlands a passing truck threw a rock and utterly destroyed our windshield, making the return in occasional rain truly miserable. We saw no *Styx*.

The other memorable event of our Lima visit came as we went out to dinner one night. A motorcyclist going the wrong way on a one-way street zoomed by us from behind, snatching Anne's purse off her shoulder. It was lucky that she wasn't inadvertently killed, but even though guarded carefully, the purse came away smoothly. Our passports, air tickets, and some money were gone. Sally had diplomatic status as a UNICEF officer, and the next day we started getting our passports replaced. But then, fortunately, the purse reappeared. The thief had tossed it over a hedge from an alley when he was done with it, and it had landed in the backyard of a teacher in a naval college. He noted that I was a professor, and with Sally's phone number in the purse, called, and we retrieved it (and gave him some expensive booze). The purse had been ransacked to the extent of unwrapping some tampons, but only the money and some keys were taken; blessedly we got our passports and tickets back!

Luck played a huge role, again in South America, in a different way a few years later when Anne and I were watching birds at Iguazú Falls, in Brazil. There, on earth wetted by spray from the falls, a variety of butterflies were mud-puddling. That's a way that some insects, most notably butterflies, gain needed nutrients such as salts and amino acids, sucking up available fluids from wet soil, decaying corpses, sweaty skin, or other substrates. At Iguazú, sizable lizards were attacking the butterflies and provided us with the opportunity to do the first systematic studies of predation on butterflies in the field. We were able to get hints, from the patterns of which species were attacked, of the protective value of distastefulness in some species that serve as mimicry models.[6] Caterpillars of some species sequester plant defensive compounds that make the adults taste bad to predators. As a result, other species may evolve to mimic those adults, fooling birds and lizards into not attacking them. We managed some five hours of observations on two consecutive days, the second ending only when a group of teenagers, seeing what we were doing, started throwing rocks at the lizards and scared them away.

Around 1970, Stanford's Human Biology Program for undergraduates, which David Hamburg and I had cofounded, made an arrangement with Jane Goodall to, among other objectives, get Stanford students and faculty to do research at the Gombe Stream Research Centre in Tanzania, the site of Jane's classic chimpanzee studies. There was already huge interest in Jane's chimp work, and I thought it would be a good place to set up a long-term study of butterfly populations as well. Similar plans I had drawn up had been thwarted in Trinidad when the New York Zoological Society decided to close the Simla station. When I returned to Trinidad decades later, the steep forests had mostly been cut down to grow chayote, a favorite local squash, showing me how vulnerable to destruction were even topographically difficult systems of biodiversity. I did find a few live *H. ethilla* and evidence of our ancient research (plate 11). The irony of the Tanzanian choice is what happened subsequently at Gombe, as I'll describe.

Working around the chimps was always fascinating and led to some adventures as well. I had first gone to Gombe largely out of curiosity and to see if it was suitable for both our butterfly work and the Stanford Human Biology student program. I was determined to look at the primates themselves "scientifically"—as was the commandment of animal behaviorists in the 1960s and 1970s: "Don't anthropomorphize!" My determination lasted a few minutes until a chimp toddler, frightened by a stick (I figured it mistook the stick for a snake), screamed and leaped into its mother's arms, to be comforted there with head patting and hugging. Modern neuroimaging and studies of behavior and neurotransmitters have shown that not just so-called higher mammals, such as chimps, have brain structures and emotional responses very similar to those of humans. Octopuses and even fruit flies are now seen by many scientists to have feelings very similar to ours. The old "don't assume that just because it looks like fear, or joy, or whatever, it is" approach to ethology seems to have been largely wrong.

On another occasion Anne and I were standing in a clearing with Jane and Anne Pusey (then a student, now the James B. Duke Professor of Evolutionary Anthropology at Duke), when Humphrey, then the dominant male chimp, entered the clearing in a rage. His hair was erect, and he was throwing large rocks around as if they were tennis balls. Humphrey picked up a palm frond and used it to thrash first Anne Pusey and then Jane. He approached us, and Anne Ehrlich quickly moved behind me. I stood as tall as I could, raised my shoulders, clenched my fists, and glared at him. He contemplated me for a moment, then dropped the frond and left.

I was probably supremely stupid—Humphrey easily could have grabbed my arms and torn me in half. Jane had wisely forbidden all physical contact with the chimps, lest they discover how much stronger they were than people. But no scientist could long observe them and cling to the Cartesian view that they were mindless automata. To appreciate the death of that fantasy, which I partially shared when I first arrived at Gombe, Carl Safina's *Beyond Words* is again a wonderful guide.[7]

One of the most interesting sets of behaviors we saw occurred on a subsequent trip to Gombe I later described in *Human Natures* (2000). A chimp mother from a group Jane Goodall had not accustomed to human presence wandered into the territory of Jane's group and "was brutally attacked, and the infant she was carrying was injured. The . . . males took the infant into a tree, killed it, and began to eat it. Then, according to the observers, [they] 'seemed to think they were doing something wrong,' and one of them took the body some two miles to Jane's camp and left it on the laboratory porch."[8] I still hesitate to interpret this most interesting sequence. But I can explain Anne's and my subsequent behavior.

We were leaving Gombe the next day to lecture at the University of Dar es Salaam. Jane asked us to take the dead baby chimp to Professor Msangi there, who routinely cooperated with Jane by autopsying all dead chimps she recovered. We started with a four-hour, hot, open-boat trip to Kigoma, where we waited at the airstrip for our charter flight to the city. A Cessna 210 finally arrived, and a semicompetent pilot flew us to Dar in the heat and turbulence below the convergence layer. We finally reached Dar only to discover that Professor Msangi's father had died and Msangi had returned to his home village. As a result, we (and the chimp) ended up in a modern, air-conditioned hotel, where Anne and I showered and dressed for our first "fancy" dinner in a long time.

Life's darkest moment: before leaving for dinner we began to realize that the dead baby chimp was sending out strong olfactory signals. The trip had been too hot and too long. What to do? The closet would not contain the growing stink. The door leading to a balcony was screwed shut. The room got ever more redolent. I considered sneaking out of the hotel and depositing the corpse in a garbage can. Anne suggested that, if I were caught at it, the rotting baby might be thought human and I might spend an unpleasant time in the Dar es Salaam jail.

I ended up going to the front desk and announcing, "I am Professor Ehrlich, and I want to see the manager." I settled for the assistant manager and told him, "I have a biological specimen for Professor Msangi at the university. I need some plastic bags and space in a freezer to keep it overnight." I returned to the room with plastic bags and an extremely curious bellboy. Anne and I did the famous "re-bag the dead baby chimp keeping your bodies between it and the bellboy" dance. When the job was done, the bellboy took me to a freezer where the cadaver was to spend the night. We finally had a nice dinner.

The next morning it was gone from the freezer. Anne and I decided to skip breakfast, fearing the bagged baby might have wandered to the kitchen. Finally, I found it in another freezer many floors from its previous resting place. When I arrived at the university for my lecture, it was an immense pleasure to hand the package to my host (a very disconcerted botanist!) with instructions to pass it on to Professor Msangi.

At Gombe, Anne and I started a project looking at the joint dynamics of the members of a butterfly mimicry complex, intending to track fluctuations in the populations of different species that had evolved to resemble each other—and to gain insight into those evolutionary processes. At the very start of our time there, I made one of those lucky observations that often lead to new insights or research projects. A small blue butterfly, *Zizula hylax*, was common along the stream where we were working. It had unusually narrow, elongated wings, and as a pilot I assumed that the wings' high aspect ratios

Zizula butterfly crawling into *Asystasia* flower to get nectar. Butterfly wing length is less than an inch. Illustration by Darryl Wheye.

were related to the butterfly's flight behavior. But its flight was weak and it didn't glide much. Then, to my surprise, I noticed it visiting flowers of a common *Asystasia*, a bloom with a deep corolla. The butterflies were crawling inside to get nectar, and when folded, their wings just fit. Evolution in action once again!

We took Lisa to Gombe in 1972, on our second trip there—an experience she will never forget. At sixteen, she was watching out for cobras and crocs while swimming in Lake Tanganyika, and the mamba (large, fast, extremely venomous snake) ricocheting around the dining hall impressed her as much as the ever-present chimps. So did the baboons who peed on her homework (an excuse her teachers later admitted was "original"), the one hour of electricity a day, eating the same eland (the most cowlike of the antelopes) for a week (baked eland, fried eland, eland burgers, spaghetti with eland meatballs), and sieving the ants from the honey. At Gombe, the main source of light was a primitive version of a Coleman lantern, and lighting these was made almost farcical because the matches in Tanzania were "fire retardant" for "safety" (and literally labeled as such)!

Anne's big moment came when she was taking a sponge bath in our hut. She had hung a towel on the rebar antichimp screen for privacy, and it was gradually disappearing. She discovered Humphrey carefully pulling it away. Disappointingly, it was a shipboard romance—afterward he didn't write, he didn't call. . . . But she enjoyed our stays at Gombe nonetheless.

Our butterfly mimicry studies and chimp adventures at Gombe ended grimly in 1975 when Congolese rebels under Laurent Kabila (who later became president of the Democratic Republic of the Congo) kidnapped three Stanford students and a Dutch colleague from the site. Fortunately for us, neither Anne, nor Lisa, nor I, nor any of my students were there then. It was a hideous long time for the students, who were beaten at first and threatened with death for months. It was heart-rending for their families and for the faculty of the Human Biology Program. Eventually a group of us, led by a wealthy parent, paid a ransom of $460,000, and to our great relief, the hostages were released alive.

In our efforts to study and enjoy biodiversity we've had many wonderful adventures and some, as just recounted, not so great ones. Our most disastrous trip in the field occurred in January 1984, when Anne and I and John and Cheri Holdren were coleading a Mother Earth expedition of about thirty people to East Africa, with the eventual goal of visiting the mountain gorillas in Rwanda. On the way to Rwanda, our group stopped in Ngorongoro Crater, a reserve in Tanzania still famous for game viewing. Well aware of the potential problems of falling tree limbs, we advised camping away from two gigantic fig trees that dominated the campsite. Unfortunately, the local game guards instructed people instead to keep their tents close to the trees, assuming there would be less risk there from encounters with lions, hyenas, or other potentially dangerous animals. After a morning game drive, John and Cheri were preparing lectures in one of the two gigantic canvas-covered Bedford safari trucks, and I was stretching my miserable back on one of the truck's long bench seats. Anne went to take a shower.

Just before noon a gigantic thunderstorm built up and it began to pour; then suddenly the rain stopped, but the wind grew to gale force. As John and I peered out from under the canvas to see whether our group needed help holding down their tents, we heard a loud "crack." We both yelled, "Get down," and dived for the truck floor. One of the fig trees, with a trunk perhaps sixteen to twenty feet in girth, came crashing down on the camp, missing our vehicle narrowly but smashing the cab of the other truck and breaking a rib of the driver inside. The whole world seemed transformed by the toppling of the giant tree, which demolished several of the tents. John and Cheri and I leaped from the truck and dived into the mass of branches to help anyone who had been in the tents. We were immediately attacked by African honeybees, which attack in swarms and sometimes sting people so many times they die, that had a nest in the fallen tree. Fortunately, a downpour started again and suppressed the bees before I and others could be stung more than a few times. I was so stunned by the event that at first I didn't realize the person I was trying to free was actually someone I knew well. I had to check the pinned woman very carefully, after breaking away the restraining branches, before daring to move her for fear she had broken her neck or back. Finally, John and some others arrived with a door that they had wrenched off a shack; we determined the injured woman had certainly painful but probably not life-threating injuries, and we managed to remove her. A second injured person we found, an older man, was also in apparently bad, if not serious, shape. Another victim, a young woman, just short of her twentieth birthday, had been struck squarely by the trunk of the falling tree, crushed, and killed outright. She had come on the trip with a young male friend she had been somewhat reluctant to accompany, but he escaped unscathed.

The storm cleared, and John went to see if he could find a vehicle in the crater to evacuate the injured. Cheri, a nurse, and Anne cared for the injured, but the safari company's first-aid kit was nearly empty, and with no book to tell us what analgesics (we only had aspirin and Tylenol, as I recall) we could use on people who we were afraid might go into shock. Some of our passengers, including our old friend Darryl Wheye and an ex-marine helicopter pilot named Richard Garbaccio, helped people, others sat stunned and helpless, and one man ran in circles screaming and shouting, disturbing everyone. I told him to shut up, which he eventually did; he later sued *Mother Earth News* because the trip hadn't worked out as he wished.

Then the assistant safari leader, fresh out from Britain, who had been about to start an affair with the unfortunate young woman who was killed, announced that he was going to cut her body free from the downed tree. I told him he wasn't; the bees were now back in their nest, and disturbing them would put everyone, especially the injured people, at risk of death. "I'm not afraid of bees," he said, and started toward the tree. Apparently, he was unaware that honeybees from Africa can be extremely dangerous when aroused. I blocked him, saying I *was* afraid of them and that he'd have to go through me to get to the tree. He probably could have forced his way through but thought better of it and turned away.

I asked one of the park guards to give me his .303 British (the Lee Enfield rifle of my polar bear search that was then ubiquitous around the world as surplus); I was going to seek help at the lodge visible on the crater rim about two miles away. He said it was too dangerous and didn't want to give me the rifle. I tried to explain that I would be cautious and that the local predators were clearly well fed. Before our argument ended, John returned. He had run down the last tourist Land Rover in the crater (others had left because of the storm) and went to get medical help.

The doctor from the crater clinic who, with some assistants, followed John to the accident site seemed highly competent but was utterly without modern equipment (Tanzania was dead poor then); the clinic didn't even have a blood pressure cuff. John went to call the Flying Doctors in Nairobi.

He found the radio powered by a stack of automobile batteries and successfully contacted the group, who promised to fly in the next morning (too tricky without runway lights at night and possible large animals on the airstrip).

The injured and other passengers were evacuated from the campsite to the rim lodge. After the last passengers were taken to the hotel and the two safari leaders left to stay with our trucks on the crater floor, I took the Land Rover up to the lodge about 8:00 p.m. As I went through the door, a man who I soon learned was the manager greeted me as I'll never forget. He said, "You must be Professor Ehrlich—my goodness, you look tired." He turned to his assistant and said, "Open the kitchen and make Professor Ehrlich dinner!" The Tanzanians at the clinic and the lodge did everything in their power to help us.

The next morning the Flying Doctors plane arrived and took away the two injured people; both survived after some weeks in a Nairobi hospital. Anne, Cheri, John, and I held a meeting with the other passengers to see what they wanted to do. The safari company said they would send another Bedford truck if we wished to continue, and the group decided unanimously to go on. Several had spent their life savings on the trip and all felt that the disaster had bonded them together. The young companion of the dead girl even said he wanted to go, too, but I said he couldn't. I told him, "You are going back to see her folks and explain exactly what happened; you'll never forgive yourself after you took her along and then just continued the trip after she was killed." He finally agreed to stay behind and to help arrange for taking care of her body. As it turned out, he rejoined us at Lake Victoria despite my advice: the poor girl's parents had decided (wisely, in our view) to have their daughter buried in Tanzania.

In Rwanda we arranged for everyone in the tour to have a small-group experience with mountain gorillas, and the Holdrens and Ehrlichs got extensive small-group experience with human beings. It included seeing gorilla poachers being tortured (beaten on the soles of their feet; we couldn't intervene) and bribing rangers to get our group's turn to hike to visit gorillas, visits that previously had been properly booked, with the richest members of the tour demanding special treatment. On the more positive side, the opportunity to sit a few feet from a silverback, have him jump over my legs to

I am being "brave" in Africa, courtesy of the foreshortening effects of a telephoto lens. Author photo.

punish an upstart teenager who was molesting a juvenile, or having Cheri virtually knocked head over heels by a female's fart (impressive, gorillas eat leaves), was incredible.

All this came a decade before the hideous Rwandan genocide, although the ecological foundations of Rwanda's distress were everywhere visible, from the rivers earth-brown from erosion, the ubiquity of coppiced trees (trees trimmed of branches to provide firewood), and the steep hills plowed to the top, an open invitation to soil destruction.

The disaster at Ngorongoro, our adventure with a white colonialist when on safari with Michael Soulé in Zimbabwe, and having reports of my speeches censored in the press when our friends Brian and Merle Huntley were taking us around South Africa in the days of apartheid—these were the only events that have really marred the joy that has characterized Anne's and my relationship with the human home continent. In perhaps twenty-five visits as researchers, tour leaders, and late-in-life scientist ecotourists, we have, above all, been thrilled by our contacts with African people and Afri-

A young lion with its "kill." Luckily, it chose to snatch the coffee container rather than one of us! Author photo.

can wildlife and by the opportunity to look back into the Pleistocene when herds of large herbivores roamed over much of the planet—preyed upon by lions and other large cats.

Many Africa trips after the Ngorongoro disaster, in the summer of 2017, Anne and I were back once more, this time to seek the ground pangolin. At a private reserve (Londolozi) near Kruger National Park in South Africa, we ran into the largest lion pride we had ever seen: four adult lionesses and twelve young, nine females and three males, all one to two years old. This pride was returning from a kill at the margin of their territory, moving like a herd around our vehicle, which was trying to keep up with it. As our Land Rover was crashing through the shrubbery, one of the young lions snatched the coffee box from the vehicle's back, scattering thermos bottles and other

The thrill of seeing this wonderful ground pangolin, a mammal about three feet long, was possible in Tswalu Reserve in South Africa because it was being radiotracked by a young biologist (the transmitter is visible on its back). The eight species of pangolins (aka "scaly anteaters") live in Asia and Africa and are all endangered because of poaching, their scales commanding high prices for their culinary and putative medicinal value. Author photo.

paraphernalia, trying to kill it by biting and thrashing it, and eventually running away with it. Very exciting, our first observation of a lion "kill," and luckily, not one of us traveling in a wide-open Rover had been chosen as a tasty morsel.

In the Tswalu Reserve in the southern Kalahari on that same 2017 visit (with our friends John and Aileen Hessel and my zoologist colleague Gerardo Ceballos and his family), we finally did get to see the ground pangolin. That was a special thrill since the twenty-some species of pangolins, beautiful scaled mammals, are globally threatened, primarily to satisfy the culinary and medical desires of an increasing population of rich Chinese. Ironically, emergence of the Wuhan coronavirus disease of 2019 (Covid-19) with a possible pangolin connection may indicate that the pangolin has, so to speak, bitten back. China has been the world center for the evolution of lethal emerging diseases, in part because it's a center of illegal wildlife trade, though finally, it seems, steps are being taken to curtail that doubly lethal activity.

Beyond the pleasures of wildlife biology, we have also been heartened in our travels by the trend in some nations to enable the local people to develop great ecotourism operations, giving hope for both the fauna and for the future of their economies. Botswana is an outstanding example. In addition, more and more game guides have been happy to consult with us on conservation issues and have welcomed the raft of papers on conservation we've sent them. We always requested African guides who were not primarily interested in chasing around to show you examples of the fabled Big Five but who were quite familiar with and were happy to seek out unusual birds, reptiles, insects, flora, and the like. Even beetles have given us some wonderful experiences there. In Namibia, for example, we were fortunate to find the spectacular huge sand dunes at Sossusvlei covered with *Stenocara*, the desert beetle famous for standing on its head and collecting moisture from fog by allowing it to condense on its body and run down into its mouth.

I can't finish the account of our love affair with Africa without mentioning a spectacular day in South Africa we spent in 2008 with Stuart Pimm. A leading conservation biologist and activist and world-class birder (I'm not well-equipped for it—color-blind, tone-deaf, and impatient) and great scientific protector of biodiversity, Stuart had taken us on a multiday birding trip.[9] Its highlight for war buffs like Stuart and me, though, was a full day spent on an extraordinary tour, complete with fine lectures and sound effects, of Isandlwana and Rorke's Drift. Isandlwana is the site of South Africa's 1879 equivalent of Custer's Last Stand, when brilliantly organized Zulu impi (regiments) all but wiped out a large British force—the only time a native army inflicted a major victory on the British imperialists. And the story of the survival, at the time, of a small British unit at nearby Rorke's Drift (ford) is a classic of military history. It was made into a largely accurate and spectacular movie, *Zulu*, in which Michael Caine, in his first big role, played Lieutenant Gonville Bromhead, second in command of the British detachment.

We may have had our last African eco-trip in September 2019 where, in South Africa, we had great luck watching leopards and lionesses hunt. In the most spectacular incident, a female leopard had killed an impala and, as is routine, dragged the antelope's body up into a small tree to keep hyenas from stealing it. While we watched, a big hyena walked up, surveyed the situation, and clearly concluded that the leopard hadn't lugged the impala high enough in the tree. It went to the base of the tree and leaped up, trying to grab the impala's dangling leg. It missed by a couple of inches, and the hyena tried twice again with the same failure. We don't know much about leopards' senses of humor but suspect that this one's was great. Seeing the hyena's near miss, the leopard didn't lug the impala carcass much higher—it just raised it a couple more inches and calmly watched the hyena finally walk away empty-jawed.

In many areas around the world, efforts are under way to preserve wildlife, such as those in South Africa to prevent poaching of local rhinos by partly sawing off their horns to reduce a rhino's value as a target. Nonetheless, work I've been doing with my colleagues Gerardo Ceballos and Rodolfo Dirzo on the escalating rates of population extinctions occurring throughout biodiversity has often made me despair over the chances that our descendants will have a chance to observe wonderful incidents on land like the hyena's defeat. Underwater is no different. The Australian government, for example, has been in the hands of people who, judging from their policies, apparently value short-term economic benefits from coal over long-term value from fish harvests, biodiversity tourism, and, of course, the survival of civilization. As a result, it seems likely that Anne's and my great-grandchildren will never peer into the depths of the Coral Sea from the edge of the Great Barrier Reef trying to identify a nearby giant sea turtle from the pattern of barnacles on it or to wonder at sharks and huge groupers barely discernable far below. With climate disruption I'm not even sure many places in the United States will remain in which our descendants could wander through fields dense with flowers and admire many beautiful butterflies nectaring on them or wake to the songs of abundant birds on spring mornings. Our descendants may well face a natural world so stripped down that it no longer presents anything like the complex, tangled bank of mysteries that Darwin described and that even my generation has thrilled in trying to untangle and interpret.

TEN

Great Affairs, and Some Great Birds

My pursuit of big issues and a growing infatuation with birds took me to diverse places from sunny Santa Barbara (constitutional change and sea birds) and gloomy Glasgow (nuclear winter weather but no birds) to Cairns, Australia (Trump and the beach stone-curlew), amazing New Guinea (Chinese forestry, many great birds), and Costa Rica, with stunning flocks of tanagers and often stunningly good environmental laws. Biology and policy can make an interesting mix.

My interest in world affairs, discussed early on in many articles, on *The Tonight Show* with Johnny Carson, and in numerous other media appearances, as well as my scientific standing, prompted an invitation in 1969 to join a review committee for the Center for the Study of Democratic Institutions. A well-known public policy think tank at the time, the center was run by famous educator and ex-president of the University of Chicago Robert Maynard Hutchins.

Our committee was charged with evaluating the center's entire operations. The other reviewers were a great group; I especially remember Jerome Wiesner and Bertrand de Jouvenel. Jerry was a terrific scientist (electrical engineer, ex-president of MIT) and a wonderful guy. In the early 1960s he had headed John F. Kennedy's President's Science Advisory Committee.

On one memorable occasion Jerry told me about that advisory committee's work responding to a Kennedy request to estimate the number of intercontinental ballistic missiles that the United States should build to deter a Soviet attack. Kennedy had campaigned against Nixon claiming a serious U.S.-USSR missile gap. The gap (putatively in favor of the USSR) later turned out to be purely fictional, and Kennedy probably knew that from the start. In 1961, when the Soviets had but a single nuclear warhead on an ICBM (intercontinental ballistic missile), the U.S. Air Force accidentally dropped two hydrogen bombs near Goldsboro, North Carolina—fortunately, they didn't explode. Jerry joked that there was no sign of a gap but that his committee programmed their computers to give an estimate of the number of needed missiles that would "fly on the Hill."

Bertrand was a different kettle of fish. He was famous as a political philosopher, as a Frenchman who had flirted with fascism (I saw no sign of that), and for an exotic sex life—he had an affair with the novelist Colette when she was his stepmother and some three decades older. Added to this gang was Alex Comfort, famous author of *The Joy of Sex*, even more famous for his escapades than Bertrand was. He was accompanied to all our meetings by a "niece" or some such several decades his junior (but far from underage). I'll know we're making progress on the gender equity front when distinguished senior female scientists feel comfortable bringing their "nephews" to scientific meetings. Hutchins himself was the very picture of a mandarin—so distinguished looking and upright that one almost got the urge to press money on him to help save the world (since Anne and I were nearly broke, I restrained myself). His organization was housed in a Spanish-style hilltop castle with a glorious view of the California coast near Santa Barbara. Posh, truly the leisure of the theory class.

When we discussed the future of the center, Hutchins had repeatedly asked the group if we thought the center should be relocated. One evening sipping drinks around the swimming pool, Jerry and I came up with a suggestion. The next time Hutchins asked the moving question, we would answer, "Yes, indeed, the center should be moved." Each of us would come up with a suggestion of some miserable spot. Mine was to be Gary, Indiana, where I would point out the center would be close to the problems of agriculture as well as the urban slums of Gary itself and nearby Chicago. We rehearsed over many drinks, but unfortunately Hutchins never again raised the issue.

When I was associated with the center I participated in a project examining what needed to be changed to make the U.S. Constitution a better instrument for governance in the twenty-first century. The study was run by Rexford Tugwell, a liberal economist who had originally been a member of Franklin Delano Roosevelt's brain trust. Before I could make any real contribution, however, the project was dropped. The reason: it quickly became obvious that so many changes were needed that to make them would require a constitutional convention.[1] What was true then is even more obvious today. Instead of dealing with such governance issues as those that have become so pressing now, a convention would all be about hot button issues such as abortion restrictions, gun laws, immigration reform, LGBTQ rights, and the like. I and the others feared then, as I do today, that a convention now would result in an even more defective document—especially in view of the now-revealed failure of the American educational system to inform people adequately not just about the Constitution itself but also about the endlessly fascinating debates, federalist versus antifederalist, that preceded its ratification and are so pertinent today. Just as thirteen distinct states needed to find a way to deal with their common problems in the 1780s, almost two hundred distinct nation-states need to find ways to deal with their common existential problems today. But even our most prominent universities show little consciousness of it.

Internal dissension and funding problems reduced the influence of the center; it became affiliated with a couple of universities and eventually closed. I faded out of it in the early 1970s—mostly because I was much too busy at Stanford, RMBL, and elsewhere. At that time Dennis Pirages and I were working on a book, *Ark II: Social Response to Environmental Imperatives*, on reform of the political system.[2] It floated a number of ideas that might be useful to consider if there is a reboot of American civilization.

No longer associating with the Center far from ended my interest in and engagement with policy issues. But in the mid-1970s I was trying not only to keep active in broad affairs, almost all of which inevitably involved ecology, but also to conduct considerable fieldwork. The 1970s and 1980s were a great time for fieldwork, and I devoted much to it in those decades, but it was also the time of a campaign to bring the existential threat of nuclear winter to public attention, and Anne and I became pioneers and ongoing participants in that.

We had first discussed the likely ecological effects of a large-scale nuclear war (based largely on World War II firestorms) in *The Population Bomb* and in *Population, Resources, Environment*; then John Holdren, Anne, and I had dealt with it in *Ecoscience*.[3] At the time we tried to persuade Jeremy Stone, then head of the Federation of American Scientists, to take up the issue of even a limited nuclear war's likely ecological impacts. Previous volcanic explosions in Indonesia, specifically Mount Tambora in 1815 and Krakatoa in 1883, had lofted gigantic amounts of debris into the upper atmosphere, as was well known. In the case of Tambora, the average global temperature is estimated to have dropped about a degree Fahrenheit, and agriculture suffered severely in many parts of the world. What might be thought of as a preview nuclear winter caused crop failures and livestock deaths that resulted in famines and worsened plagues. In the northern hemisphere, 1816 was known as the year without a summer. Krakatoa was a smaller event, but it, too, led to global climatic cooling, and both events should have taught humanity a lesson. Smoke and debris from a global nuclear exchange could have a similar effect multiplied many times over—greatly damaging agriculture in a world already failing to supply many hundreds of millions with adequate nourishment.

We lost that one: Stone rigidly refused, it not being one of *his* ideas. But a paper by atmospheric chemists Paul Crutzen and John Birks in 1982 finally brought the topic to the attention of a significant portion of the scientific community. The paper indicated with a quantitative analysis that a nuclear winter was a possible result of a large nuclear exchange. The huge fires that would result in so much debris being spewed into the atmosphere meant that sunlight would become partially blocked and global temperatures would plunge, with devastating effects, especially on agriculture. That publication regenerated interest in the ecology of nuclear war, and after much maneuvering, a group of us, including Peter Raven, John Holdren, Thomas Eisner, George Woodwell, and Thomas Lovejoy, started organizing to disseminate these findings widely to the public.

To what degree should we involve Carl Sagan, we wondered? Carl was noted for his massive ego but also for his brains, communication talents, and connections. We decided to invite him to join us, and I thought our decision to do so was correct, even after we had an awful meeting with him in mid-1982. The low point was his insistence that we cancel a public relations extravaganza on the impacts of nuclear war that we had planned (and paid a lot for in advance) in Washington, D.C., and move the whole operation to Boston. It took an exhausting day to persuade him that would be a mistake, but fortunately we managed to do so, and preparations then moved ahead.

The exhausting planning meeting was followed by an incident that became famous among my close colleagues. Tom Lovejoy, in addition to his Grand Canyon wine-rafting skills, is a terrific environmental scientist who both invented debt-for-nature swaps (a great idea on conservation financing) and conducted a large-scale experiment on the impacts of reducing forest habitat area on biodiversity.[4] I visited his field site near Manaus in Amazonia and still remember a night in a hammock in a crude forest shelter, listening to jaguars coughing in our vicinity. My back has never forgotten the night in that hammock, either.

Tom is also a great host, and he invited his friends on the nuclear winter committee to dinner after the meeting. Tom lived in the Virginia countryside, in a spot difficult to reach by taxi. It was a tiny house and could fit only about ten people at the dinner table, so he invited a few graduate students to drive us out to his place, telling them that although he could not feed them, they could stay for drinks before dinner and mix with the "distinguished scientists." We assembled in Tom's living room and were treated to a superb chardonnay. The grad students were anticipating something like $E = mc^2$, and leaned in to listen to one of the world's most distinguished scientists, Tom Eisner, the father of chemical ecology. Tom started the conversation with, "Have you guys heard . . . ," followed by a middle-school-level *very* obscene joke. Things went on in that vein, and no word of science escaped to enlighten the students. But they had a great time and got rid of, in one quick session, the idea that scientists were all serious stiffs in white lab coats.

That sense of humor was well illustrated by Gerardo Ceballos. He was driving Gretchen Daily and me to a field site at Chamela in the wilds of Jalisco, Mexico. He led us to believe that we would be staying in a rough, waterless shelter and feeding ourselves. We stopped at a shabby bodega a half hour before arrival, early in the evening. There we bought a sack of rice, some very old boxes of breakfast cereal, and some other minimal supplies for our stay. Then we arrived travel-worn at a locked and guarded gate. We were admitted and found ourselves at the door of a huge mansion owned by Gerardo's friend, millionaire financier Jimmy Goldsmith (and younger brother of our old acquaintance Teddy Goldsmith, founder and first editor of *The Ecologist*). Cleaned up, the three of us were served a magnificent dinner, with great wines, and with a servant standing behind each of us to tend to any needs. Our quarters matched the splendor. The rice and ancient cereal lived on only in legend. Some "shelter." I still plan to get my revenge on Gerardo. In any case, in the world I've lived in, keeping one's sense of humor has been essential.

The public meeting our gang had organized on nuclear winter went off well, with good organization and good press coverage, the latter in no small part because of Carl's connections. It brought the environmental consequences of nuclear war to public attention and to the attention of the military in the Soviet Union and the United States. I personally gained great respect for several of the field-grade officers that worked with us. They were imbued with a basic rule of military ethics—minimize damage to civilians. Indeed, I've always remembered the comment to me of one officer discussing war in central Europe: "You've got to realize that towns in Germany are only a kiloton apart."

I must make one correction here. There was actually one glitch in our public relations extravaganza. I was so exhausted I fell asleep while participating in a U.S.-Soviet TV discussion of the impacts of nuclear weapons, a "first" of which I'm almost proud. But my sleeping image on the giant TV monitors in the large hall wasn't the only one; the time zone was even worse for the Russians.

The next year, in 1983, Carl Sagan and four of his students (known familiarly as the TTAPS team (Turco, Toon, Ackerman, Pollack, and Sagan) published a study in *Science* magazine detailing the likely climatic effects of the clouds of smoke and dust in the atmosphere for months following such an attack, a finding that Steve Schneider independently confirmed.[5] In the same issue of *Science*, nineteen colleagues and I published a paper that discussed the likely biological effects of such a nuclear winter.[6] All told, especially because of the strong cooperation of military people in both the United States and the Soviet Union, I think the nuclear winter educational efforts we and many others made at the time damped down the enthusiasm for actually fighting nuclear wars. Nevertheless, despite the continued efforts of a substantial portion of the scientific community and civil society, the threat of a nuclear Armageddon may be larger today than ever before.

It is important to remember that all of the talk about nuclear weapons, about such actions as modernizing the triad (spending even more money on the first leg—our worse-than-useless silo-based ICBMs—and improving the second leg, land-based bombers, and the third, submarine-based ICBMs) is done in a context of complete insanity. One night during the nuclear winter days John Holdren and I decided to figure out how many Hiroshima-size fission bombs would be required to end the United States or Soviet Union as functional entities. We came up with twelve to destroy the United States and a few less for the Soviet Union. In the former, hitting Washington and New York would cripple government and the economic system and then hitting the main rail and road hubs (Chicago and Los Angeles, for example) would end the critical distribution of food and other essential resources and shrink aid-sheds. If a single city is wrecked, aid can flow in from the rest of the nation, as in any ordinary disaster. But with a dozen simultaneous disasters and the electric grid going down, keeping food from being processed and preserved and gasoline from being pumped, overwhelming medical and emergency-response systems, deaths from trauma, starvation, lack of care, and likely pandemics would escalate. Fewer detonations would have crippled the Soviet Union because there were fewer hubs to hit. Compare that requirement for, say, twenty-two small warheads with today's possession by the United States and Russia of more than ten thousand warheads, most of enormously more destructive power. Thus the United States and Russia keep the potential sources of a nuclear winter in strategically useless superabundance and quite vulnerable to accidental use. In 2020, the United States had over five thousand nuclear warheads, roughly three hundred times as many as would be required to end Russia as a functioning entity. Russia returned the favor with slightly more warheads, and China moved into the insane asylum with several hundred nukes, so any one of that competitive triad was capable of destroying civilization as a whole—a situation I call "mutually agreed imbecility."

Anne's and my original discussion of Dunkirk had signaled to me her strong interest in international affairs and conflict. That was reinforced by her contributions to a late fall tour, I think in 1983, of England with a Soviet colleague, the three of us lecturing on nuclear winter. She then served on the London City Council Commission that produced the GLAWARS (Greater London Area War Risk) report on what the effects such a war would have on the greater London area. That and her subsequent tireless work on important policy issues led to her election as a fellow of the American Academy of Arts and Sciences.

Our joint work on nuclear winter in the mid-1980s earned us a most interesting trip to a 1988 meeting in Sochi, Russia, sponsored by the Pugwash Conferences on Science and World Affairs. It was the time of Perestroika, and there was a lot of ongoing Mickey Mouse behind the scenes with old-line Soviet operatives trying to interfere with interpersonal collaboration between American delegates and our Russian colleagues—some of whom we had gotten to know during the nuclear winter campaign in the United States and on our nuclear winter tour in Britain a few years before. Indeed, in 1985 one of our nuclear winter colleagues, controversial Soviet physicist Vladimir Alexandrov, disappeared mysteriously at an international meeting in Spain. He possibly was murdered. It was a hopeful but nasty time. In any case, Anne continued to attend Pugwash conferences as an environmental scientist for a decade or so thereafter.

On the personal side, nuclear war seems almost always to have been on my mind since I first learned about nuclear weapons in 1945. My fear that they would be used again started early and continues today. In 1945, like most Americans, I was thrilled by the news of the atomic bomb and the surrender of the Japanese. The good guys had won. That joy was, however, slowly dampened by the fear in my teenage years that accompanied learning of the developing Cold War and the unexpected news, in 1949, that the Soviets could also manufacture nuclear weapons. In a popular magazine in the late 1940s or early 1950s I read a story about New York being A-bombed and gigantic mutant rats roaming the ruins in its aftermath. One night, when I was living in northern New Jersey, I was awakened in the middle of the night by a violent thunderclap. I was terrified—was that the sound of a nuclear explosion over Manhattan? I was especially distressed later by how the potential catastrophic effects of a nuclear war were routinely underrated by analysts like Herman Kahn, who seemed ridiculously calm about projected monstrous death rates and never mentioned ecological devastation and its consequences.

My focus on the potential environmental consequences of nuclear weapon use grew in part out of my interests in aviation and the havoc wreaked by the conventional bombing campaigns of World War II. I read voraciously on the subject, and had been horrified especially by the descriptions of gigantic firestorms created by the combined high-explosive and incendiary bombing of German and Japanese cities, most notably Dresden, Hamburg, and Tokyo. That's why in scenario 2 in *The Population Bomb* we wrote what is probably the first projection of what the environmental impacts of a nuclear conflagration would look like.[7] But in subsequent years nuclear arsenals and the power of individual weapons kept growing, delivery systems kept increasing in sophistication, and the military-industrial complex continued to profit greatly. At least initially Ronald Reagan believed the stories of con men that nuclear wars were "fightable." He proposed a space-based antimissile system, nicknamed Star Wars, in the early 1980s. If built, it would have proved a bonanza for the armaments industry, even though honest scientists pointed out that it wouldn't work as a robust defense system, the most basic reason being that incoming warheads from MIRVed ICBMs (ones with multiple independently targeted warheads) from the Soviet Union would always be cheaper to produce and could be made more numerous than defensive missiles. The nonsense persists—the triad modernization of the U.S. nuclear forces was started by President Obama and continues today.[8] The cost of this great reduction in American (and world!) security was estimated at more than a trillion dollars. Meanwhile, we can't seem to afford medical care and healthy diet for all, a decent educational system, or enough well-paid and socially conscious police officers.

Not all my policy travel was on topics as grim as nuclear war. One memorable trip still had an element of personal grimness, however. It came just after a failed intervention trying to deal with Dick Holm's alcoholism in 1985. I had to go to Gland (near Geneva), Switzerland, for a meeting of World Wildlife Fund International, where I was to speak and receive an award for my efforts in conservation. I was very upset over Dick, who had been taken to the hospital. Anne dropped me off at the airport. As I got into the appropriate British Airways line at SFO, I discovered (despite what I thought had been great care) that I had by mistake picked up Anne's passport, not mine.

I dropped my bags over the counter, shouted I'd be back to the ticket agent, and dashed outside. Luckily, a taxi was just going by, and I threw myself in front of it. "I'll give you $200 if you can get me back here from Stanford in an hour." Off we raced, with me watching out for the police. When we pulled into our driveway I realized Anne was not home yet and I had no key (I always left my keys at home to simplify security inspections when flying). I tried to get in by vaulting over the atrium wall, but only succeeded in splitting my pants in two. The taxi driver, a young, athletic man, jumped over the wall and opened the door, and I rushed in to exchange passports. At that moment Anne arrived home to see a cab in the driveway, the house door wide open, and a strange man (the cabbie) standing in the doorway. As she got out of the car to ask what was going on, I appeared, yelling I needed new pants (because I'm color-blind, Anne has always been in charge of my clothes). We went roaring back to the airport with me changing in the back seat of the cab. The driver got $200 and a set of torn pants. The ticket agent said she thought I wouldn't make it. I agreed.

That, it turned out was only the start of my adventure. London was fogged in, so our plane landed at Manchester and we were loaded onto an ancient bus with tiny seats. I reached Heathrow in pain, to the expected news that I'd missed my original flight to Geneva and several subsequent ones. I finally got a flight and arrived very late and disconsolate in Geneva. And who was waiting for me, having worked out what had happened, but my old friend Tom Lovejoy. He took me out to a (wonderful) late dinner and took me to my hotel—a friend indeed!

The WWF meeting sessions dragged on, as such group meetings almost always do, but I was mightily impressed by Prince Philip, who was president then of World Wildlife Fund International and ran the meeting with great patience. I was impressed, as I have been before by some individual wealthy people, like Prince Philip, who, rather than just enjoying themselves, work hard for a cause they believe in. And Philip worked hard for five days. During the breaks, cocktail hours, and meals we got to know each other a bit and hit it off, sharing many interests. He was the only British Royal I ever had personal contact with, but because Tom Lovejoy was a friend of Prince Charles, another strong supporter of green causes, and Charles later gave wonderful support to Anne and me on the inaugural paper we wrote for my election to the Royal Society in 2012.[9]

I got the news that Dick Holm had died the morning I spoke at that WWF conference—the end of a wonderful friendship and collaboration. Dick was, sadly, prepared to go—he spoke often of his desire to "drink myself to death." I was never prepared for his departure, and never will be. But he would have approved that Tom and I dined one night soon after at "the best French restaurant in the world," whose name and location we've both forgotten (we were unimpressed). After that meeting outside Geneva, we turned from trying to save biodiversity to more pleasurable activities. Tom and I flew to Paris, where Sir Valentine Abdy, European representative of the Smithsonian Institution (where Tom then was assistant secretary), arranged for us to have an incredible lunch at Jamin, the first restaurant of Joël Robuchon, considered by many the best chef in the world. Then Tom and I took the Concorde—a special treat for a pilot—to attend Lisa's wedding to Tim Daniel in Washington, D.C.

Now to a more pleasant subject than death and destruction that's been on my mind for only about forty years. All during the early 1980s while active on issues surrounding nuclear winter, I of course had not abandoned my more conventional ecological research interests. In fact, I had added to them. That was thanks in part to an old friend, the great ecologist Jared Diamond, at UCLA. Anne's and my relationship with Jared and his wonderful wife, Marie, a clinical psychologist, goes way back, so far that I can no longer remember when it started. For a long time we've met at least once a year, to talk science, World War II, and book projects. Jared and I often read and comment on each other's manuscripts. He is one of the writer friends and relatives whose literary skills I greatly envy (others include John Holdren, Robert Sapolsky, Mary Ellen Hannibal, and my granddaughter Melissa Daniel). Jared holds a special place in that pantheon for his refusal, at least until now, to use a computer. Despite his inability to get jokes via email, he has a fine sense of humor and a prodigious memory, especially of the history of the Japanese navy in World War II.

One day in 1980 Anne and I were visiting Jared and Marie in their home near UCLA, and I described how my research group was mapping the distribution of birds in montane islands in America's Great Basin. I said that I would like to participate but couldn't because I was color-blind. It hadn't been a problem with the few bird species and open terrain in the Arctic, but I didn't think I'd be very good at censusing birds in forest or brushland. Jared claimed that was nonsense, gave me a pair of binoculars, and took me out in his backyard. Almost immediately I saw a Bewick's wren and a phainopepla, and I was rehooked on my Arctic interest in birds. Today, more than 4,300 twitches (of lifers—species seen for the first time and ticked off a world list) and a lot of research later, I'm still at it, despite the inborn handicaps I mentioned above (plate 16). For one who loves nature, observing birds makes a great supplement to studying butterflies. I discovered that one can even go out and enjoy them on a cold spring dawn before giving a seminar at an East Coast university, when there is no chance of even *seeing* a butterfly.

Jared's recruiting me into the ranks of birders led to one of Anne's and my most memorable field trips. It was to New Guinea in 1985, a location central to Jared's legendary research on the structure of bird communities. With Jared, Anne, and me were Dick (Sir Richard) Southwood and Frank Talbot. The putative purpose was twofold. One was to dedicate a new field station established by the Christensen Fund at Madang, on the northeast coast of Papua New Guinea. The other was to establish a research program there, especially one testing some of the ideas on reef fish ecology that Frank and I had developed at Lizard Island. One of my sub-rosa purposes was to see if Jared could really identify mobs of tropical birds from the calls alone. My answer came fast—the first time we birded together in a New Guinea forest, he identified some two dozen species by ear before I managed to see even one of them and determine that he was correct.

The scuba diving turned out to be spectacular at Madang, with an especially rich anemone fish fauna. Frank and I started to set up long-term studies of the fish communities, and Jared, Dick, and I negotiated with locals to investigate bird and butterfly communities on their land. At the reception dedicating the station, I was telling the wife of the Canadian ambassador of Anne's and my plan to drive up to Mount Hagen in the highlands to see what changes there had been since we first visited twenty years earlier, in 1965. She urged me to talk to her husband before venturing out. He in turn warned me that the locals along the road would likely roll rocks in front of our vehicle to stop us and then roll more behind it to keep us from backing up. They probably wouldn't kill us, he said, but would take everything we had. We changed our plans and returned to Port Moresby with Jared.

In Moresby I went on a long birding hike with Jared. When we were a few miles from the hotel, I felt really sick with nausea and a headache, and we returned. At dinner I felt even sicker; I was getting a fever and had to leave the table. I was pretty miserable that night and went to see a doctor the next morning. He took one look, and said *falciparum* malaria, and recommended a heavy dose of Fansidar, then a commonly prescribed antimalaria drug. I insisted on getting a blood slide, since I was worried that it might be scrub typhus because of a massive chigger attack I had suffered some days earlier birding in the Atherton Tablelands of Queensland. Scrub typhus, a rickettsial disease, can be fatal unless treated with antibiotics, but Fansidar would not cure it. I also had been on chloroquine, the locally recommended antimalarial. A slide to check for malaria was taken, but I didn't get a chance to see it (I'd studied malaria parasites as an undergrad), and it was declared negative. Anne and I decided that we would flee to Australia, where Charles Birch could hook me up with the Sydney University's excellent tropical medicine group.

We got a flight right away, which involved changing planes in Brisbane. I was increasingly sure I had malaria (slides are tough to read—the parasites are scarce at the start), and by then I had markedly cyclic symptoms. I was sitting in the Brisbane airport with Anne and Jared, absolutely soaked in sweat and barely conscious, when a scantily dressed woman jiggled by. I showed no signs of noticing. Anne really got worried; later, she said, "I knew the danger signs of death." In Sydney, Charles met us and took me directly to the tropical medicine center, where blood was drawn for examination.

A couple of hours later I was diagnosed as having *Plasmodium falciparum*, just as the doctor in Moresby surmised. It's the deadliest of the four species of protozoan that cause malaria in people but one that has no stage outside of the red blood cells and so does not relapse. You either kill it or it kills you. A tough chemotherapy involving Fansidar, quinine, and doxycycline eventually killed it, but it was a difficult few months. I saw the *Challenger* shuttle crash from my bed on January 28, 1986, and many more times on reruns. The long recovery transformed my attitude about malaria from an intellectual fear to an emotional one. But I still can't stay away from the tropics.

And my fascination with birds endures despite my encounter with *falciparum*. To stimulate myself to learn more about them, in the 1980s I began writing a column about avian biology for *American Birds* and I started to teach a class in bird biology (it was always a challenge to learn new information faster than bright Stanford undergraduates could keep up with). In teaching, it became clear that the standard bird guides then available told you pathetically little beyond how to identify a species, where it lived, and (as part of identification) its song. This led two colleagues, Darryl Wheye and David Dobkin, and me to write *The Birders' Handbook* (1988). It tried to tell what the standard guides didn't say about such aspects of bird life as parental care, hunting techniques, preferred foods, and nest type. It was followed later by a European version prepared by ecologist and conservationist Stuart Pimm—with whom Anne and I have had great birding adventures, as mentioned earlier. *The Birder's Handbook* has since been emulated and largely replaced.

One day, Terry Root and I, both of us by then dedicated birders, were trying to figure out why we kept looking for birds we'd never seen before (lifers). What was the attraction? Our answer was, first, that we were both inveterate collectors, and we could collect lifers without their adding to the piles of stuff in our homes. Beyond that, birding took us to obscure places we'd never ordinarily visit, often with interesting results.

On one such occasion, I found myself tromping through New Zealand fields on that nation's little-known southernmost island with two women at night in search of a famed species. The excursion had come about in a roundabout way. One of my scientific heroes was Allan Wilson, an evolutionist who, along with Mary-Claire King, did seminal work showing how critical gene regulation was in evolution, how, for instance, the tiny differences between the DNA of people and chimpanzees resulted in the great differences between us due to changes in how our and their shared genes are turned on and off. Allan died young in 1991, and I was invited to give a series of lectures in 2013 to honor him in his native New Zealand. Two wonderful women, Glenda Lewis and Wendy Newport-Smith, gave Anne and me a sensational tour, including more than a week of fine dinners washed down by Marlborough wines and a few days on Stewart Island at the south end of the country, where I lived on the splendid oysters found there. I had been enjoying bird watching for the entire trip, but the pinnacle came one of those Stewart Island nights. Glenda, a guide, and I marched through streams and fields in a freezing rain (Anne and Wendy had the good sense to remain in the warm hotel) for what seemed like forever. Then, around midnight, as it started to sleet, we were rewarded. A genuine kiwi virtually ran between our legs!

Another example, this one including Terry herself: On a road along a river in the island of New Britain, west of Rabaul, where Anne and I had adventured decades before, Steve Schneider, Terry, Tom Lovejoy, Anne, and I were following superguide David Bishop looking for owls one evening. We rounded a bend and were confronted by an approximately twenty-foot tree coated with fireflies (lampyrid beetles). They were, stunningly, flashing synchronously. Shining our lights over them broke up the synchrony, but when we turned off the lights, it was reestablished in a few minutes. A speeded-up version of the McClintock effect, or girls' dorm phenomenon, in which women living closely together putatively find their menstrual cycles synchronizing—or was it? Unlikely. That's actually a very controversial claim about women, and I have no explanation for the firefly phenomenon.

Birding, besides leading us to places we might not otherwise have visited, has also been a wonderful way of cementing friendships. Several trips with David Bishop added him to our gang—especially a birding tour of Bhutan that included tea with that country's queen and learning about the nation's goal of gross national happiness, as well as an introduction to a fascinating avifauna. David was originally a London bobby who had taken up protecting English nature reserves. He started doing the same in South Asia, taught himself ornithology, and became a wonderful friend. Anne and I often reminisce about one incident in particular that occurred on a birding side trip. We were driving from the Kanha Tiger Reserve in Madhya Pradesh, India, where on elephant back we had been lucky to approach a Bengal tiger lazing near its kill. It had been a sensational experience—though I kept wondering when a tiger would figure out that those weird protuberances on the elephant's back were hors d'oeuvres and sample them. We had also been lucky enough to have a long, good look at a sloth bear. But it was that primate David that we recalled most. We had driven into a sizable town on our way to an airport to fly to Bhutan. There we were blocked by a gigantic traffic jam, mostly of trucks, all trying to get past a five-way junction. Bobbyism struck. David leaped from our vehicle, and waving his arms and loudly whistling, he directed traffic. In a few minutes traffic was moving and Indian truck drivers were applauding.

In a somewhat different context, whenever Anne and I go to Oz, Graham Pyke and I plan in advance an outing to see some special bird and to have long talks as we, for example, drove far up the Cape York Peninsula. It was with him that I first saw the malleefowl, the fabled bird species in which the male incubates the eggs in a huge mound of rotting vegetation, males controlling the incubation temperature by opening and closing the mound to regulate the rate of decomposition. The females lay eggs in the mound, but neither sex sits on them—and the young hatch ready to fly. That mound-building behavior can now readily be seen around Sydney. A program of poisoning imported foxes has permitted an explosion of brush turkey populations. The birds look like turkeys but are actually relatives of the mallee-fowl, both species being in a group called megapods in honor of their big digging and scratching feet. The mallee gets the attention the way Darwin got over Wallace—there was a good book written describing the mallee.[10]

Graham, who we first got to know one summer at RMBL, is one of the most distinguished living ecologists, having been a founder of optimal foraging theory (explaining, for example, how honeybees judge when to stop getting nectar from a plant and move on). He suffered brain damage in the early 1980s when another driver died at the wheel and crossed into Graham's lane, front-ending the Pyke car. Recovery took more than a decade out of Graham's professional life and eventually ended his marriage. But Graham came back strong and still (2021) develops brilliant ideas about plant-animal interactions.

When I think of Graham, though, I start remembering our times together spotting less common birds such as inland dotterels in a pasture in far outback New South Wales, the spotted quail-thrush that may well have been my last lifer—seen near Sydney on our fourth try (2018) over as many years—and the entire surviving wild population of orange-bellied parrots in the spectacular unpopulated southwest corner of Tasmania. *Neophema chrysogaster* is one of only three species of parrots that migrate, moving from Tasmania, where it breeds in the southern summer, to the south coast of mainland Australia in the winter. It may soon be extinct in the wild; there is a captive breeding program with several hundred birds, but even if successful, it is not clear where a strong population could be reestablished in the wild.

Graham is one of the most dedicated scientific birders I know, but he is outdone by one of my former students, Çağan Şekercioğlu. Çağan may have twitched more birds globally than almost anyone, but that has not kept him

In the southwestern corner of Tasmania I was thrilled to see virtually all the surviving wild population (fifty or so individuals) of the gorgeous but critically endangered orange-bellied parrot. Author photo.

from, like Graham, having a spectacular career uncovering the causes and consequences of bird extinctions and in other ways helping to advance the field of conservation biology.

But for bird-watching thrills, nothing will ever match for me my adventures with the sunbittern—*Eurypyga helias*—a shorebird placed in its own separate family and famous for its gorgeous displays. Early on in my birding career I was in the last Zodiac (rubber boat) taking a group of Stanford alumni tourists on the Amazon when all the boats ahead of us saw a displaying individual on the shore. I didn't even get a glimpse. After that it was a sunbittern drought—my most wanted bird. I thought I almost saw one fly away on the Río Jaba (the stream flowing through the field site at which our group did research in Costa Rica), but I couldn't be sure. Then one day I was visiting my friend Álvaro Umaña, once Costa Rica's first secretary of the environment, at his butterfly-raising facility near Braulio Carrillo National Park outside of San José. We were hiking to a stream far below, and I casually asked Alvaro if he had ever seen a sunbittern there. "What the hell is that?"

he responded. We hiked a way along the beautiful stream and then started back. Just as we were about to climb the trail back up, a sunbittern zoomed beneath my nose, landed on the rocks of the stream, and proceeded to treat us to its wonderful display. Later I saw it commonly in Venezuela, transformed in birder lingo into a garbage or trash bird, one so commonly seen as to no longer be of interest.

Having broad concerns and doing research on rapidly deteriorating complex systems can lead to substantial shifts in interests and activities. In the 1980s the fieldwork of our group at Stanford was moving increasingly toward issues at the low end of the population-size spectrum—toward the dynamics of small endangered populations. In addition to wanting to understand population dynamics in general, I had realized that the few acres of serpentine grassland on Jasper Ridge were unlikely to be able to sustain populations of *Euphydryas editha* permanently. Our group's focus and that of many other biologists was shifting to the decline of species diversity and the growing problem of extinction, which Anne and I had focused on increasingly as we worked on our 1981 book of that name.[11]

It had long been clear that, since the tropics were the center of species diversity, understanding more about population processes and community structure among species there would be important. Larry Gilbert and I, working out of the Simla field station in Trinidad, for example, had managed in the early 1970s to show that a population of longwing tropical forest butterflies (*Heliconius ethilla*) was quite constant in size over time. This possibly was a function of seasonal constancy in the tropics compared to seasonal change in the temperate zones. That fit our preconceptions of how tropical herbivorous insects would differ from temperate ones, such as checkerspot populations, which classically showed dramatic fluctuations in size.

My original intention with the Bay checkerspot system had been to look simultaneously at the butterfly's ecology and its evolution. I wanted to answer such questions as, "Would the populations become less diverse genetically if they shrank in size?" Shrinkage in size could lead to more accidental loss of gene variants (genetic drift), but it also could lead to selection favoring new variants. The mark-release-recapture technique gave me a tool for estimating population sizes, but no easy way of looking at their genetics existed when I started the research. Michael Soulé and I had a shot at using measurement of their wing pattern elements as a possible indicator of genetic change (population phenetics), but the results were unenlightening. With the help of Steve McKechnie, Maureen McReynolds, Larry Mueller, Dave Heckel, and others, I set up a gel electrophoresis lab in the early 1980s, inspired by classic work done by Richard Lewontin and Jack Hubby. Electrophoresis uses electric currents passed through a special gelatinlike substance to separate molecules and let us examine biochemical variation in the *Euphydryas*. That produced some interesting results showing that natural selection was operating on the system (those were the days of debates about the neutrality hypothesis—that most genes in natural populations were not under selection), but the sorts of questions I wanted to answer were beyond our technical ability. Forty some years later, with modern molecular genetic techniques, answering those questions would have been a relative cinch.

But in the mid-1980s, we were able to take advantage of Stanford's diversity of ecologists to get at issues of species decline in another way. Anne and I were looking for a measure of humanity's impact on global ecosystems—*Homo sapiens*'s life-support apparatus. We wanted to investigate how close our species was coming to a serious limit in how much in aggregate it could consume, and how that would influence both civilization and other consumers—our fellow animals and the threat to their extinction. One possibility was to figure out how much of Earth's net primary production (organic material created by photosynthesis minus that used by the green plants themselves) is used by *Homo sapiens*. Fortunately, one married couple among our young Stanford friends, Peter Vitousek (with whom I had watched lava from a Hawaiian volcano flow into the sea) and his wife, Pamela Matson, were experts in that area and were happy to collaborate. The result was a 1986 paper showing that humanity was using or coopting nearly 40 percent of Earth's entire food supply generated on land.[12] The results can now be seen dramatically in that human bodies and those of our big domestics (cows and pigs, for example) in the early twenty-first century constitute an estimated

96 percent of the biomass of mammals on Earth. Ironically, as so often happens, the manuscript was first sent to *Science* magazine and was rejected on the basis it wasn't important enough. It led to one of my favorite scientific memories. I was so annoyed at the rejection that I got up about 4:00 a.m., unable to sleep, and fired up my computer to reformat the paper to submit it to *BioScience*. At about 6:00 a.m. the phone rang, and it was Peter Raven to tell me I'd been elected to the National Academy of Sciences. Weirdly, the first thing that went through my mind was that if *BioScience* turned it down, I'd send it to the *Proceedings of the National Academy of Sciences*. In those days (1985), *PNAS* had to publish any manuscript submitted by a member! *BioScience* did accept it, it appeared in 1986, and as of 2019 it had been cited 2,268 times. Even better, in less than a decade, Peter and Pam were both elected to the academy.

Just as visits to and research in Hawaii and Colorado had become habit-forming for Anne and me, so Costa Rica in the early 1990s became my favorite place to do tropical research. My colleagues and I at the Center for Conservation Biology had been looking for a good place for doing more fieldwork in the tropics, and Costa Rica seemed an ideal place to consider. It had a stable, conservation-oriented government and was a relatively safe place for students to work. It had well-known bird and butterfly faunas, thanks to good field guides and the activities of the Organization of Tropical Studies (OTS), a consortium of some fifty universities that then promoted education and research in the tropics and ran several field stations.

Before I developed a relationship with one of those OTS stations, the Las Cruces Research Station in southern Costa Rica, I got involved in fieldwork in Costa Rica in the 1970s with Mike Singer and a little bit in Costa Rican politics. I was a fan of the president at the time, Daniel Oduber Quirós, who was a pioneering political environmentalist. Mike and I made some presentations in the country in his support, and Oduber and I had one nice conversation. Anne and I much later took another good Tico politician, President Oscar Arias, to dinner. Arias was totally relaxed, without security, and happy to discuss the environmental situation in his nation in terms with which we totally agreed.

In the late 1980s, when we first started to establish a program in the country, I paid a visit to Jardin Botanico Wilson at the Las Cruces station, a beautiful spot about at three thousand feet elevation in the southern part of the country near the Panama border. I was anxious to get to know the local avifauna because we could use visual censusing (no need to mark birds, as was necessary for our work there with butterflies) to study trends in tropical avian biodiversity in the face of global change. At Las Cruces I was delighted to find an abundantly fruited cecropia tree growing so that its crown had just about reached the height of the main lab building. One could just sit in the lab and count woodpeckers, thrushes, warblers, and, especially, a colorful array of tanagers feeding on the cecropia fruits.

Anne and I took my then-graduate student Gretchen Daily there for a research session in 1991. One of our first projects was to see if we could work out the dominance relationships among different species of tropical forest birds. Observations had been made of squabbles high in the treetops, but little was known about how avian communities were structured. The issue was of some pertinence to their conservation (Would dominant species be more likely than subordinates to persist in fragmented forests?). The cecropia gave us an ideal study site, soon supplemented with an exotic fig tree that bore its fruit on the trunk and major branches. In both cases we were able to video the visiting birds' interactions, capturing such details as how long individuals of different species kept their heads down in fig fruits while feeding. Unsurprisingly, individuals of subordinate species looked up more often than dominants to see if someone was coming to displace them. Unhappily, just an hour or so of filming resulted in many hours spent tediously analyzing the tapes frame by frame. Such are the thrills of tropical fieldwork.

Soon after the dominance study at the Wilson Botanical Gardens, our group started a butterfly research program there, led by Gretchen. She had started in the late 1980s as an undergraduate working at RMBL with our group on butterfly population structure and community relations. There we got lots of exercise dashing across high-altitude fields with nets. In Costa Rica our research routine was more relaxed; we used butterfly traps to help

A scarlet-rumped tanager, one of the gorgeous tanagers that were central players in studies by Gretchen Daily and me of tropical avian dominance hierarchies. Photo by Becky Matsubara, CC BY-2.0.

us understand how butterflies used a landscape of forest patches mixed in with farm fields. It was some of the first work in what became known as countryside biogeography, a new approach that Gretchen pioneered, focusing on the fate of biodiversity in highly human-disturbed habitats.

Our Center for Conservation Biology group had great times at the Jardin, and we made fast friends with Ana Hera, one of the campesinas employed there, and her family. George and Yvonne Burtness often joined our group working as volunteers there, as did Ellyn Bush and Tom Davis, and I had some of the most wonderful times in my life (plate 12). I always felt super-relaxed when our gang arrived at what became my favorite hotel in all the world, the Bougainvillea in the San José suburb of Santo Domingo. Among my favorite memories of the Bougainvillea was getting a life bird my first time in its bar (a buff-throated saltator, *Saltator maximus*, pecking at its reflection in the bar window) and one very special dinner. The latter occurred after the center started doing research at the Jardin with Gerardo Ceballos and his students from the National University of Mexico (UNAM). Our work had expanded to the countryside biogeography of mammals, and Gerardo had ordered dozens of mammal traps from a biological supply house. On the afternoon we arrived and drove our rental cars to the hotel, he went to customs to pick up the traps. Disaster. Instead of the usual collapsible wire traps Gerardo had ordered, the company had mistakenly sent rigid ones—a gigantic pile that would have required a road train to transport over the dangerous Cerro de la Muerte (hill of death) highway south to the Jardin. Gerardo brought the gang the bad news, which led to by far the most unforgettable dinner we ever had in the restaurant of the Bougainvillea. Fortunately, the Bougainvillea had an ample supply of good, inexpensive wine and tolerance for boisterous good customers. Fortunately also, Gerardo and Gretchen had sufficient scientific friends in Costa Rica that we were able to borrow enough traps to actually carry out our planned mammal research program.

Perhaps here's the place to point out that Gretchen, who started as a shy undergraduate in my lab, is now my boss (as a Stanford professor with a named chair, she must sign off on any financial commitments I make as a professor emeritus). She is now director of the Center for Conservation Biology and among the most distinguished conservation biologists in the world. She has earned many international prizes for her work and was elected a member of the American Academy of Arts and Sciences and the National Academy of Sciences at unusually early ages. Among her many honors, the most recent was the Tyler Prize, awarded in 2020. I'm very proud of both Gretchen and another of my students who also was elected to the National Academy, plant ecologist Susan Harrison; they represent an important trend of recognition of the increasing leadership of female scientists in all disciplines, but especially in ecology, evolution, and behavior.

Gretchen's Natural Capital Project (NatCap) is, in my view, the most important global private conservation effort today. Natural capital is the assets nature provides humanity at no charge—such as fresh water, soils, and pollinators—and which are even more important than manufactured capital (buildings, machines) and human capital (educated and experienced workers). NatCap is working in countries around the world to find ways to simultaneously preserve biodiversity and ecosystem services while improving human welfare—often using novel computer tools to figure out where and how. Gretchen has been a close friend of Anne's and mine for decades and is notorious for being a nice and helpful person (despite having trained with me), and also for working too hard (ditto). I couldn't break her of that habit, and neither could her friend Pete Bing nor her supremely supportive physicist husband, Gideon Yoffe. Maybe her son and daughter, now entering adulthood, will have better luck.

Working in Costa Rica with Gretchen on our butterfly research I got a thrill that reminded me of sugaring for moths when as a kid I used bait of rotten bananas, molasses, and rum to attract *Catocala* moths to tree trunks in New England nights. We used the same kind of bait in Costa Rica to trap gorgeous butterflies: morphos, caligos, and charaxines (leafwings) in rain forest patches (plate 13). The bait was placed on plates hung under net cylinders. The butterflies could land on the edges of the plate, walk under the net to the bait in the center, get drunk, and then fly up and be trapped inside the screen cylinder. They rarely figured out how to escape and were extracted and marked through a Velcroed slit in the side of the cylinder and then released. The memories of handling those gorgeous critters makes me feel good to this day.

In the course of that work, which also involved a lot of slogging through hot pastures often paved wall to wall with cowpats (a professional hazard), we realized that to get a complete picture of the distribution and abundance of biodiversity in southern Costa Rica, we'd need to look at the distributions of other kinds of organisms. That led to a lot of further fun with moths, birds, mammals (once we solved the trap problem), reptiles, amphibians, and even plants.[13] The results are sets of data that will allow scientists to follow the fate of a tropical biota as environments change with expansion of the human enterprise and resultant increasing climate disruption. Our entire group really loved the work at Las Cruces, and many students also got rewards in the form of publications. Gretchen and some other colleagues still do research there. I wish I could.

That's because I guess I'm a quintessential hypersocial naturalist. For instance, when in my dotage I think back on Costa Rica, I get a flood of joy from remembering the great colleagues I worked with and the wonderful local people who befriended us. I wish I could be dining once again in the home of Ana Hera and watching with her family a bootleg video of a movie. Fond as I am of Lepidoptera, people beat butterflies every time.

ELEVEN

The Crafoord Prize and Projects of the New Millennium

In the academic careers of field scientists, including mine, there tend to be four stages. The first is training and gaining a position. Then there is setting up a research program, recruiting graduate students, building a reputation in a research area, and attaining tenure. Third, if you work hard and/or are lucky, you become established, stop worrying about making it, and spend time doing the research and teaching you enjoy, and going to places where you want to do fieldwork or you've been invited to give lectures, or occasionally to receive awards. Sometimes, even, you could found organizations. That third stage, which Peter Raven and I used to call playing distinguished scientist, typically generates a richly assorted bag of stories about science, politics, and the foibles of scientists and politicians. Peter and I had big egos, but I hope we also managed not to take ourselves too seriously. During the years that seemed to be going particularly poorly politically and environmentally, I often thought of what Peter used to say when bad news reached us while having coffee at the round table: "Let's go down to the garage, idle the motor, and talk it over." The fourth stage? That's the one I'm in now—doddering, unsuccessfully fighting being a has-been, but still engaged in a multitude of projects, doing what I can to draw attention to the dangers we face as a civilization and as a species and what we can do to address them, enjoying old friends and old wine, and revising a memoir (some might say, in the latter, imitating my old colleague Gary Luck, who, thriving on his farm in Tasmania, is doing conservation and writing fantasy).

There have been a lot of prizes given to ecologists and evolutionists since the world discovered the environment. I've gotten more than my share of them; there have been a lot of ceremonies for which I had to put on ties, and substantial amounts of money that have gone into the Center for Conservation Biology and other of my research and political activities. I've been extremely lucky and very grateful. The best of all probably was sharing the Crafoord Prize with E. O. Wilson in 1990—best for me because of a special guest I invited to accompany me to the ceremony (a woman, but not Anne). It was great to share it with an old comrade-in-arms: Ed was a brilliant scientist, fine illustrator, and splendid writer, and he knew more about ants than anyone else in the universe. That we differed on various issues of sociobiology had not interfered at all in our common goal of saving biodiversity.

The Crafoord was better than a Nobel Prize; it was created deliberately to be the equivalent of a Nobel in areas not favored with Nobels. It is awarded in ecology by the Royal Swedish Academy of Sciences only every three years, not annually like the Nobel. Ed and I agreed that was appropriate since in our unbiased view ecology, evolution, and behavior are now so much more important than the scientific fields recognized by the Nobel that "gongs" in our fields should be harder to get.

In addition, instead of a mob scene, Ed and I had the ceremony all to ourselves, including the king and notoriously beautiful queen of Sweden. I committed, as always, a faux pas. When the group photo was being taken, the photographer said, "Could you move to the right, Professor Ehrlich, because the queen's face is blocking yours." Naturally I said, "That's fine, she's so much prettier." The protocol mice gasped, but the queen laughed.

Ed brought his mother to the ceremony, and I brought mine—my special female guest, Ruth Rosenberg Ehrlich. Anne, Lisa, and Sally came as well, but ceremonies are especially great for mothers. Mom got to sit and talk with the king for perhaps fifteen minutes while the queen poured tea for them. I felt sorry for Mom's friends; after that whenever she and they shared tea or coffee, Mom always told them, "It reminds me of when the queen of Sweden poured tea for me."

The Crafoord ceremonies were fun, but the biggest prize it brought me was an invitation to join the founding board of the Beijer Institute of Ecological Economics of the Royal Swedish Academy of Sciences. I had once thought that ecologists and economists were natural enemies, even though our daughter Lisa has a PhD in economics, as does her husband, Tim. But meeting Herman Daly, the father of ecological economics (which might be defined as economics that includes attention to natural capital, equity, and knowledge that the human enterprise can't grow forever), had altered that view.

Anne and I have always remembered the day in 1973 when Herman took us boating in the bayous of Louisiana. Though he had had one arm amputated when polio had made it useless, he refused help in driving, towing the boat, getting the boat off the trailer and into the water, or roaring around the bayous, where he proceeded to cast a line for fish while steering our vessel.

He was as independent mentally as he was physically, opposing all the standard growth-as-unmitigated-good ideology that, alas, is still dominant in macroeconomics. Herman and I once (in 1997) had long philosophical discussions while sharing a voyage around the Black Sea with the eastern pope (the archbishop of Constantinople) and his associates and assorted scholars interested in saving the environment. Bartholomew I, the "green patriarch," had been a pioneer among religious leaders in trying to defend "the creation," for which I greatly admired him despite our small doctrinal differences. If most of the people in the world believe in the supernatural, it's good to have leaders who say that wrecking Earth's human life-support systems for fun and profit is a sin.

Anne's and my most exciting adventure related to Herman and his wife, Marcia, occurred when we were staying in a luxury hotel south of Ipanema Beach in Rio after field research in Brazil. The Dalys had invited us to dinner at a distant restaurant to which we would take a taxi. They instructed us to leave all money (except for cab fare), passports, jewelry (outside of Anne's wedding ring and a zircon ring I inherited from my father, we had none of value), and so on in the safe deposit box in the hotel lobby. Robbing tourists was a popular pastime in Rio then. We were greeted at the door of the restaurant by two guards with sawed-off shotguns and had a wonderful dinner with Herman and Marcia. A cab deposited us back at the hotel without incident, but a chaotic scene greeted us in the lobby. A gang was bent on robbing the safe-deposit boxes, and a firefight with the police had ensued. Apparently no one had been killed, but the place was a mess. Fortunately, our valuables were untouched.

After our adventures with Herman Daly, I had the great pleasure of getting to know another economist, Partha Dasgupta, when he was briefly on the faculty at Stanford. He, too, helped transform my view of economists. We were introduced at a dinner party, where he noted I was the author of *Ecoscience* and said he'd read it from cover to cover. Welcome words to any author, of course. He's probably the only economist in history actually to have read all of Anne's, John Holdren's, and my thousand-page textbook. Both Herman and Partha would become involved in Beijer, as did many other economist friends and colleagues, including Larry Goulder, Karl-Göran Maler, Roz Naylor, Scott Barrett, Steve Polasky, and the amazing Ken Arrow. Partha is now considered one of the world's leading economists, recently crowning his monumental contributions with a magnificent study of the economics of biodiversity for the British government—showing the way for all social scientists to take on the really big problems.

Most major universities have a collection of bright people in their economics departments, many of whom unfortunately have little or no training in the natural sciences. They often remain so ignorant of how the biophysical world works that they miss what is important in the underlying conditions of their field. Thus key issues such as how to construct a viable steady-state sustainable society, how to design a monetary system not dependent on growth as is today's fractional reserve banking system, and how indeed to alter the view that finance should be the central theme of civilization are all still topics largely going begging for serious research.

The Beijer Institute has had many meetings designed as workshops to produce papers in ecological economics (which it has done most successfully), held together by a fine group of Swedish executives and colleagues.

Many of the get-togethers have been held annually on the island of Askö in the Stockholm Archipelago. Intense discussions have been punctuated in evenings by great food and some alcohol, leading to Swedish songs that featured beating one's head in rhythm on the table (I skipped that; my chore was to sing the "La Marseillaise," which for some reason I had memorized, and with my voice I simulated head beating).

One of my favorite old Turk "heterodox" moments came from an Askö meeting more than four decades after Dick Holm and I published the controversial 1962 *Science* paper "Patterns and Populations." In 2004, economics Nobel laureate Ken Arrow and other Beijer Institute colleagues (including me) sent a paper entitled, "Are We Consuming Too Much?" to the *Journal of Economic Perspectives.* That journal was the preeminent economics journal in North America; I once published an analysis of its macroeconomic content showing that it essentially never published on a truly significant topic (unless you count the economics of college football).[1] To my eternal joy it was reported to us that one editor said, "We have to publish this article by Ken Arrow and his communist friends." They did publish it, and ever since I've been announcing my pride in having been one of Ken's "communist friends."[2]

In early September of 2001, after an Askö meeting dealing with existential issues humanity faces, I joined Carol Boggs on a trip to Finland. Carol had long been involved in checkerspot research, and together we visited our European checkerspot colleague Ilkka Hanski in Helsinki. He and I had been working on a checkerspot book, *On the Wings of Checkerspots,* to which Carol had been contributing heavily. It was a chance for the three of us to work face-to-face. After our meeting with Ilkka, Carol and I took the train "to the Finland Station" (the title of Edmund Wilson's classic book on the history of revolutionary thought up to Lenin's arrival at that station in 1917), and both Carol and I had our first visit to Saint Petersburg. There we met Gretchen Daily, who had just been with me at the Askö meeting in Sweden, and the three of us enjoyed the city's famous museums and the fabulous

Amber Room, which had been destroyed by the Nazis but has since been successfully restored. We even saw a ballet; Anne, who would have loved it, sadly missed that part of the trip.

Anne wasn't sad to miss the rest of it, though. Just as those born before the middle of the 1950s all remember where they were when they learned President Kennedy had been shot, everyone born before the early 1990s remembers where they were on September 11, 2001. I am no different.

On September 10, I flew from Russia to Washington, D.C., to lecture in an Aldo Leopold Fellows meeting and see my grandkids on my way home. Early that evening, I went to see older granddaughter Jessica perform in a tap dance recital and then took Jessica, Lisa, my son-in-law, Tim, and Wren Wirth (Tim Wirth was in New York) out to dinner at Asia Nora, then one of my favorite restaurants and now gone. It was our last dinner in the old world.

The next morning I was lecturing to the fellows on how to give "ambush interviews" to television reporters when someone announced that an airplane had just hit the World Trade Center. We all rushed down to the hotel bar, just in time to see on the screen the second plane hit the towers.

The new world where terrorism became central in security thinking thus began with a bang for me, stranded (like so many) far from home. Washington was soon a shambles of sirens and rumors, among which one turned out to be true: the crash of American Airlines Flight 77 into the Pentagon. I was watching the TV with Tom Sisk (a former student), Jack Liu (a professor at Michigan State University who was about to start a sabbatical with me at Stanford), and another colleague, John Largier from Scripps Institution of Oceanography. I said I didn't think the airlines would be back up for weeks and suggested we rent a car to drive to the West Coast. Jack said Michigan State had a special deal with a car rental company, left the hotel, and returned a few minutes later having rented a Kia van. Little did we realize at first how lucky that was; in very short order there was not a car or van rental to be had in the Washington metropolitan area. We agreed to wait a day or so to see what would happen, although we were concerned that more strikes on Washington might follow, including possibly a dirty bomb.

That night there was supposed to be an Aldo Leopold Fellows banquet that Tim Wirth was going to address, but he was stuck in New York, and the entire banquet staff had gone home. With Stuart Pimm, who had also been lecturing at the Aldo Leopold event, Jane Lubchenco, and my editor (and good friend) then at Island Press, Jonathan Cobb, we went to see if we could get dinner at the fine restaurant in the Tabard Inn. As we went through the lobby, where small groups were clustered around TV sets, we heard, "Paul, Jonathan." It was Jean Thomson Black (who had edited a book at Yale University Press for Andy Beattie and me) and my friend Susan Solomon (of Antarctic ozone-hole fame).[3] They joined us, and the six of us strived to drink the Tabard's restaurant's wine cellar dry. Later that night I spent about $100 through my hotel's switchboard trying in vain to get through to United Airlines, still holding out the hope of eventually flying home, despite the grounding of all air traffic for an as-yet-to-be-determined period. So I moved from my downtown hotel to Lisa's house in suburban Bethesda, where I found that my terrified granddaughters (Jessica, not quite thirteen, and Melissa, not quite ten) had built "forts" under their captain's beds to hide from the terrorists. Our family had dinner that night with the Wirths, Tim having made it back from New York. He had seen the World Trade Center buildings come down and was understandably almost in shock.

I think it was Thursday or Friday when Jack, Tom, John, and I decided the airlines were beyond hope. The others drove the Kia to Bethesda to pick me up, Lisa threw a load of snack food, pillows, and blankets into the van, and we took off. It was some hegira. We were roaring through Kentucky when a state trooper pulled us over for speeding. "Where are you gentlemen going?" We told him, "We were at a scientific meeting in D.C. and we're trying to get home without airlines." "You have a safe trip now and try not to kill yourselves."

The real danger was the food (roadside fare being what it was) as we drove day and night, taking turns at the wheel, stopping only to refill the van's gas tank and fill and empty ourselves. We did find some decent food in a café somewhere in New Mexico. The family at the next table were trying to get back to the East Coast, and the man introduced himself as a state trooper (I think from Maryland). He then proceeded to brief us on how far we could go over the speed limit in each segment back to Palo Alto.

We dropped Tom off in Flagstaff near midnight of the second day and gulped down some wonderful split pea soup his wife, Helen, had made for us. Then it was my turn to take the wheel. It was a scary over-the-mountains drive in the dark on a newly surfaced U.S. 40 with no white lines. Around dawn we left John Largier sitting on a curb near an open McDonald's in Barstow with his cell phone, waiting for his wife to drive up from San Diego to pick him up. Jack and I zoomed up U.S. 5 to the Bay Area, pulling into my driveway early in the morning, forty-nine hours after leaving Lisa's driveway. Anne had been tracking us via my phone calls and briefing in turn worried friends and family via email. She greeted us, turned a hose on Jack and me, and all was well.

That trip formed a bond with Jack Liu that strengthened over his sabbatical year, where he led some fine research with Gretchen Daily and me, showing, among other things, how important household size (as well as brute population size) was in human environmental impacts.[4] Our friendship has continued through a wonderful trip to China sponsored by the Chinese Academy of Sciences and hosted by their great conservationist Zhiyun Ouyang. Jack, a top panda expert, showed us through China's famous panda research facility and continues to do great things with Gretchen and Ouyang for Chinese-U.S. cooperation in trying to preserve biodiversity and ecosystem services *and* increase human well-being. Jack increases Anne's and my well-being with fairly frequent visits and has increased human well-being by pioneering the analysis of environmental issues in a world full of long-distance, connected biophysical and social (telecoupled) ecological systems. The global nature of rapid climate change itself and its origins in human sociopolitical systems and impacts upon them is an outstanding example of telecoupling. So, of course, was the 9/11 sequence and the "war on terrorism," which transformed the world.

With a friend in 2010 at China's Chengdu Research Base of Giant Panda Breeding. Photo by Jack Liu.

Flash forward fifteen years: the Beijer Institute celebrated its twenty-fifth anniversary in 2017, and the meeting's topic was not only global in scope but directly population-related. The institute has managed to bring world-class economists and ecologists together year after year and bond them into a group of friends that tries to bring the understandings of the two disciplines together to bear on the human predicament and its teleconnections. Other people have been much more responsible than I for the success of the enterprise, especially economists Partha Dasgupta, Ken Arrow, and Karl-Göran Maler, ecologists Carl Folke and Simon Levin, and a brilliant organizer, Christina Leijonhufvud, but I've loved attending the meetings—I've probably been to at least twenty—with these and other increasingly good friends. I can still picture Ken Arrow banging his head on the table as part of one of the Swedish songs—he was even there in 2016 at the age of ninety-five! Some six months later, though, Ken died peacefully and painlessly in his sleep.

Ken, noted for solving incredibly difficult mathematical problems, felt that he could learn by listening to almost anyone. I can never recall him indicating in any way that he thought himself special, even though he may have been the most special male human being I've ever known well. I'll always remember being jet-lagged, trying to stay awake in Askö meetings, and watching Ken doze. Then he'd open his eyes and give the most insightful comment of the meeting. In a conversation the day before he died, when he had come back from the hospital and was described to me as "confused," we were comparing Richard II to Donald Trump, and I quickly realized that, of course, Ken knew a hell of a lot more even about the Plantagenets than I did. Brilliant and sweet is such a rare combination. I hope I can remain as "confused" as Ken as I head for Fiddler's Green.

That twenty-fifth-year celebration of the Beijer Institute in September 2017 was our first meeting since Ken's death a few months before. The theme of the meeting was human migration, an obviously hot topic with many demographic, environmental, and economic aspects. Anne and I had learned a great deal about its complexity and many ethical dimensions in the 1970s when we wrote *The Golden Door* with our good friend (who had been our best man), Loy Bilderback, and I worked with the politicians on the President's Commission on Population Growth and the American Future. Since no one else at the Beijer meeting had much on-the-ground experience with the issues of migration, I made several comments about what I thought would make a good and useful paper. They were largely ignored, and the discussion became (in my view) interminable and irrelevant. I never managed to learn from Ken Arrow how to hide my arrogance (or how to be totally without it, as he might have been). So I finally announced impatiently to the group that it was wasting its time—a paper such as the group was planning would have no impact and would be unlikely to be published in any case.

It was a dumb thing to do, and I've often made similar mistakes when disagreeing with colleagues. I think it's a tribute to science that I haven't been drummed out of the club; I consider myself a living example of how scientists can have vigorous debates and still remain friends. But I've also used mechanisms to keep my arrogance and sense of self-assurance from getting out of hand, and they work, sometimes. One such mechanism is named Anne. I've also always leaned on colleagues to tell me when I'm full of it, in reviewing my papers, ideas, and behavior. I loathe being criticized, but as I've often said, I'd rather be shown to be a jackass by my friends in private than by, say, the *Wall Street Journal* in public. I also have a nasty habit of being pompous and not realizing it. Several of my friends don't hesitate to point that out, but I find that tougher to correct than simply being wrong.

That Askö meeting gave me a chance to be arrogant. What I said about the group paper under discussion was unpopular, but I knew in advance that several of my colleagues agreed. One of the advantages of being an ancient curmudgeon is that your comments can be worded very frankly and you often can get away with it. Besides, since writing this I've seen a draft of the paper that may come out of the migration meeting, and it's better than I expected. Wrong again, but right in my continuing view of the uniqueness and great example for human organization the Beijer represents—no holds-barred discussion and cooperation sans worrying about disciplines.

While on the topic of arrogance, it might be of some interest to say how such a self-assured scientist might evaluate his or her own work. So here's an attempt to evaluate mine so far, what it meant to me, and what it might have meant to the world. Others can judge my opinion's accuracy.

Much of the research that gave me great pleasure over the years now seems to me of little scientific value. Discovering that the unusually narrow wing shape on a little lycaenid butterfly at Gombe Stream was probably not an issue of "aspect ratio" involved in its flight patterns pleased me greatly. The wing shape was, apparently, an evolutionary adaptation to slipping into the narrow corolla of a local flower to feast on its nectar. A clever, even correct conclusion perhaps, but cutting-edge science it was not.

Neither were such efforts as showing that the poster colors of reef fishes were not territorial signals nor that surgeon fish schools were structured by dominance hierarchies and that the fish used their "scalpels" to attack rivals nor that coral reef fish communities varied in ways similar to communities of terrestrial animals. It was science done within the already accepted paradigm, but still, conventional or not, working on coral reefs was one hell of a lot of fun. So was working on dominance hierarchies in tropical bird communities (leaving aside the hours analyzing videos frame by frame). All such research I believe helps humanity to understand the world better—the increments to human knowledge are miniscule, but in aggregate such contributions create an evidence-based world. Important in that sense, but in individual research results, not earth-shaking.

The same could be said for my early work sorting out the evolutionary relationships of butterflies. Still, I was thrilled to find that when the scales were removed from specimens (and my eyes) and their exoskeletal features made accessible by boiling in potassium hydroxide, their evolutionary relationships became quite clear. Previous taxonomic conclusions based largely on the structure of the wings had been muddled. I felt that wonderful patterns in nature had been revealed to me. Who, however, really gives a damn about the taxonomic position of *Styx infernalis*? The insights my butterfly work brought to the theory of systematics might be seen as but another example of a life of failure to make a significant difference, since much scientific effort is still largely wasted as far as society is concerned on taxonomic revisions that may, in some cases, slightly improve humanity's picture of biodiversity. In light of the looming crisis that is beginning to overtake us, I now feel that the major efforts of every taxonomist should be devoted to saving biodiversity—the more that can be accomplished there, the more future taxonomists can have the pleasure of working out the details of the relationships of Earth's fascinating biota and the joy of arguing interminably over the nonissue of how to define species.

Studying butterflies can be great sport, and more knowledge of them can add to the general scientific view of life—all especially worthwhile if humanity manages to make the moves necessary to sustain itself and the scientific enterprise. My *favorite* paper of the past decade, though, was one of a different order and led by my colleague Darryl Wheye, a science artist. She noted that certain parts of the color pattern on the wings of adult butterflies resembled caterpillar patterns. At first I thought it a crazy idea, but the more we looked, the more I became convinced she was on to something. To make a long story short, we decided to put the question to the community of butterfly people: Were butterflies, in essence, warning away predators by displaying pictures of distasteful caterpillars on their wings? We were able to publish a paper in *News of the Lepidopterists' Society*, presenting the idea and showing color pictures of putative examples.[5] Considering the great popularity of butterflies, and especially of butterfly photography, the whole area seems ripe for citizen-science projects. How widespread is the phenomenon? How do the adults with the pictures on their wings match up with the species of caterpillars illustrated? Are adult-larval pairs sympatric (that is, do they occur together in the same areas)? Since the article was published only in 2015, there's not been much time for feedback and I haven't a clue—but it sure was fun working on it![6]

My all-time *sentimental* favorite paper (as opposed to the most scientifically important one) was that one described in chapter 2 on bees and forest habitat led by Taylor Ricketts and published in 2004 under the title "Economic Value of Tropical Forest to Coffee Production" on which Mich, Gretchen Daily, and I were coauthors.

Without a doubt, the 1964 paper Peter Raven and I wrote on the coevolution of butterflies and their food plants (described in chapter 6) had more impact on the scientific community than anything else I was involved with in evolutionary biology. It created the field of coevolution and has at least partially motivated thousands of articles and many books. A plant ecology text written in 1960 would likely have had a few pages on herbivory; in a plant ecology text written today, coevolution with plant-eaters would occupy a major portion of the book.

In my work, the only scientific competitor for the coevolution studies in impact has been more than forty years of studies in the ecology and evolution of checkerspot butterflies (*Euphydryas*) that I pursued with many colleagues. Among other aspects, we documented early on that there was a real metapopulation structure—a regional collection of interconnected small populations with some going extinct and others being reestablished—a phenomenon my colleague and friend Ilkka Hanski expanded on brilliantly. He established the field of metapopulation biology and made significant contributions to it before his tragically early death in 2016. My research group also discovered that if one were designing a reserve for an herbivorous insect, topographic heterogeneity in the reserve was often likely to be of more importance than the size of the area set aside. A variety of slopes and exposures meant that in virtually any year some areas on Stanford's Jasper Ridge Biological Reserve had an ideal microclimate (topoclimate) for the butterflies.[7] Overall we learned a hell of a lot, but I'm disappointed that the conservation community is not often using what we learned to actually conserve butterfly or other populations, which are being mowed down as the human enterprise grows. An exception to this is my once-student Stu Weiss, whose Creekside Center consulting firm continues to be a savior of the Bay checkerspot, helping protect surviving subpopulations of *Euphydryas editha* in the San Francisco Bay Area. Another of my ex-students, Nick Haddad, has written a book (*The Last Butterflies*) that describes other exceptions.

At the sociopolitical level I suspect Jonathan Freedman's and my crowding experiments helped put to death the notion that people would have a simple ratlike reaction to crowding. Anne's and my paper on human use of Earth's production of animal food with Peter Vitousek and Pamela Matson helped show the serious scale of human impacts on humanity's life-support systems. The nuclear winter study, and our work with John Holdren and others on the human population problem, clearly were very significant as judged by numbers of citations, but many were too far ahead of their time to be readily accepted.

My greatest public impact doubtless has come through Anne's and my *The Population Bomb* (to be reexamined in chapter 12), my roles in Zero Population Growth and on the Carson show, our subsequent writings on the demographic drivers of the human predicament, and our roles in Earth Day and publicizing that predicament. Maximum scientific impact in that area probably came from John Holdren's and our early post-*Bomb* work on the IPAT connection (there has been much attention to that simple equation in the social science literature). Even so, half a century (and some three thousand citations) after John Holdren's and my "Impact of Population Growth" article in which the IPAT equation and its significance were first described, many people still deny the role of overpopulation in creating existential threats to civilization. In short, our policy research, I would guess, has had substantial impact on the scholarly and public views of some of those threats, but far from enough, given the magnitude of the problems. It is cheering, however, as we'll see, that some of our most recent policy work has attracted much media attention—especially on the importance of population extinctions.

When I look back on my career at Stanford University, saving Jasper Ridge as a biological reserve and starting the unique interdisciplinary Human Biology undergraduate program with Dave Hamburg were probably the best endeavors in which I was deeply involved. But the one I'm most proud of was something I did at one meeting in the early 1960s of the university library committee. Fred Terman had sent me on a personal mission to find out what was wrong with the Stanford library and then put me on the university library committee. He was dedicated to making Stanford a world-class university, and among the faculty and graduate students worries were legion about the paucity of the library's holdings. I was especially distressed that Stanford's holdings in entomology and agriculture were so poor.

Schools like Harvard and Texas had much larger libraries. Not only did both have multitudes more books than Stanford had then, but those institutions were buying many more books annually. The only solution to the problem that potential librarians (I was also on the search committee for a new librarian) and the library staff could come up with was simply to buy more books. In a flash of unbelievable brilliance (or fantastic luck in a passing thought), I said, "Why not take $30,000 out of the book-purchase budget, hire a driver, buy a car, and have it drive back and forth all day between our library and Berkeley's, and reduce interlibrary loan time from weeks to hours?"

Al Bowker, a statistician, then graduate dean, and Dick Lyman, who would later become Stanford's president, backed me to the hilt, and the Gutenberg Express was born. In effect, our book taxi added UC Berkeley's millions of volumes to Stanford's then medium-sized library. It was used extensively in its first decades, but interest in it declined with the growth of the electronic age. I recently Googled "Gutenberg Express Stanford" and found this posted in 2007 (sob!): "In the *old days* there was a special bus that ran between the Cal and Stanford campuses, called the Gutenberg Express—probably for library exchanges, hence the name" (my emphasis).

When you're an ancient but once successful scientist, you are frequently asked if you can explain that success. A straightforward answer would be genes for pure genius, but unfortunately, I would have to ignore my knowledge of the interactions of genetic and cultural evolution to make such a response. One likely part of the answer would surely be my mother's support of my early scientific interests; unlike my father, she wasn't afraid that my interest in butterflies and tropical fishes would override my interest in girls.

When I was in high school and college, I came to a purely selfish decision that turned out to be correct. Should I go into business or medicine and make money, leaving me a couple of weeks' vacation each year to fool around with butterflies? Or should I go into entomology professionally, study butterflies, evolution, and environmental problems all the time, and potentially suffer penury? I picked the latter. I had a lot of fun in college doing things like microdissecting butterfly genitalia that positioned me well to do microdissections of a butterfly's entire skeletal anatomy, allowing me to rapidly complete a complex dissertation that I would even enjoy doing again. That choice meant that I could be very efficient—I could "work" ten to eighteen hours a day and love it. And I could spend my nonworking hours on wine, women, and novels, and love that, too.

More specifically I've often been asked, especially by students, how I've managed to maintain my productivity. I suppose a memoir is a good place to answer the question, and Lisa has urged me to do it. The obvious answer for me to give would be that I'm a workaholic. Sadly, that's not correct. One reason I've been productive was luck—I picked a profession that, luckily, I've always loved, and I continued my work in a direction that gave me great satisfaction. I was also lucky enough to land a wife who enhanced my life and career in every way. I also like finding out new things, things previously unknown to science or little recognized, and I like telling people about what I've learned. And I'm egotistical enough to think people want to hear my views and the results of my investigations, and even, maybe, read a memoir about them. Of course, there are many people who would prefer me to shut up, but as I've indicated, I'm incapable of doing that. I just have too much fun talking and writing.

Another reason I got things done is that I try never to waste time. When I'm not playing I want to be doing something useful (sleeping is one example, reading another). I've always told students who complained that they needed a couple of peaceful hours to get something written, that they were likely doomed to failure. Instead, they should train themselves to fill the inevitable short chunks of empty time they face daily with productive work or joyful play. I always took books or printouts of papers to a doctor's appointment or a doctoral dissertation defense seminar, so I could do something productive when the doctor made me wait until twenty minutes after the appointed time or the defense was deeply boring. And I often worked on manuscripts a few lines at a time between student appointments.

For years I have listened to tapes of courses (*The Great Courses*), podcasts, and books while I walked to and from work—an hour a day of continuing education (which for me was entertainment). In earlier days, I used some of that time walking to dictate whatever I was writing to be typed up later by an assistant. I've been lucky to be able to walk to work almost every day, given California's mild climate, for almost sixty years. I have also learned, on Stanford's ever-expanding campus, to loathe back-up beepers and leaf blowers, two of civilization's greatest curses. (The beepers would be fine if they could not be heard for more than a few yards rather than a couple of miles; the leaf blowers are useless.) "Audible" on my iPhone has replaced the tapes of yore and extended this ability to make use of those isolated chunks of time, since I always have the phone on me. For example, it took six months, but I listened to the four volumes published so far of Robert Caro's *Years of Lyndon Johnson*, arguably one of the best works ever produced in political science.

This may also be the place to mention one of my greatest failings—selfishness. Among the most successful of my close scientific friends—Don Kennedy, Hal Mooney, Peter Raven, John Holdren, Gretchen Daily, and Joan Diamond—all were builders. I wasn't. Don rose through the academic ranks to university president, ran the Food and Drug Administration on the way, and ended his career bringing the journal *Science*, on which he served as editor-in-chief for almost a decade, into the new age of science. Hal was determinedly unassuming as he organized the global scientific response to the environmental crisis. Peter made the Missouri Botanical Garden into a world-class institution, oversaw the globalization of plant taxonomy and evolution, and ran the National Academy of Sciences as home secretary for years. John ran a series of studies on nuclear issues and became de facto one of Bill Clinton's main science advisers and de jure Barak Obama's. Joan made the MAHB into a world-class organization despite great difficulty in getting it financial support. Gretchen organized and ran the Natural Capital Project, a superb academic-business-government consortium trying to improve the human condition and preserve ecosystem services. None of that was for me. I hated administration and did as little as possible because it took me away from the research and organisms I loved. I was delighted to delegate hiring, firing, begging for funds, and dealing with bean counters (as Joan Diamond and biology's brilliant administrator Bettye Price would testify). If I had taken any of the major administrative or political jobs I might have, that would have made months each summer at RMBL, research and great fun in Costa Rica, yearly trips to Oz, and dozens of long cruises difficult or impossible. For me a university presidency would be a terrible fate, just as it would have been for the university. It wouldn't have worked despite my legendary ability to suffer fools gladly. I reached the ultimate goal of my professional career when I became a full professor at Stanford.

As that account indicates, I never have remotely been a workaholic. Alcohol and women were my main entertainments as an undergraduate; not once did I cancel a social engagement to write a paper or study for an exam, as my grades clearly demonstrated (I hated taking exams as much as I, for fifty-six years as a professor, hated giving them). Anne and I have followed my tradition—we've never canceled a social engagement to do more work, and on average we probably socialized three or four nights a week, and still did, remotely, during the pandemic. We never berated Lisa to study more, and we urged her to live her life to enjoy it, although she did accuse us of setting a difficult standard by "working so much." We did what we loved doing, but I don't think Lisa realized how much I loved dissecting butterflies and berating bigots and fools.

Of course, I was able to get so much done because to a degree I didn't pay enough attention to raising a daughter. One accomplishment of which I am proud, but that I am less arrogant about because I am under no illusions about my contribution, was raising Lisa. Like many American dads of the 1950s and 1960s, I focused primarily on my career and left most of the child-rearing to my spouse, as I've mentioned before. My temper would be tough on any child, though. Lisa has been quite clear that she would have appreciated more (positive) attention from me growing up. Nonetheless, she has credited me and her mother with raising her to be independent from an early age and with allowing her to largely make her own decisions and suffer (or benefit from) the consequences.[8]

Lisa had plenty of complaints about my child-rearing style, mostly legitimate, I fear. But despite it all, Lisa grew up to be a close friend, so close that I felt comfortable letting her help with this book, confident that she would not try to remove my voice or non-PC attitudes. She's a pleasure to work with, and she raised her three daughters (one a stepdaughter—she had read our books) to be wonderful, productive adults and fine company, not just for her but for Anne and me too. If your granddaughters become drinking buddies, I contend you must have done something right!

Lisa's existence ironically contributed to my relative neglect of her. As an old man and a public scientist, I've often been asked what has inspired me to continue the struggle for a sustainable society despite virtually no progress on that front and a growing sense of foreboding about the future. The main factor that has given me continuing inspiration to keep going has been concern about the world that our generation was leaving to our descendants: one of reduced biodiversity, deteriorating environment, increased probability of nuclear disaster, and so on. This was an especially strong motivation when Lisa was a little girl. When she got old enough to say, "Get stuffed, Daddy," that motivation diminished somewhat, but then she presented us with two wonderful granddaughters and, through her husband, with a brilliant step-granddaughter. It was reinforced by the charming and wonderful kids of many of our friends and recently by their equally charming grandchildren. They all deserve a better future than they are going to get.

Knowing what I do, I can't just do nothing and enjoy the end of my life while young people today are unable to have anything like my opportunities, just as it's been difficult throughout my life to enjoy things I've known were not available to billions of other people.

I had a difference of opinion with a valued colleague, Jim Brown, the world's top biogeographer, when Anne and I in the early twenty-first century thought there was about a 10 percent chance to avoid a collapse of civilization. Jim thought it was only about 1 percent. But we agreed that it was worth it for me to work hard to increase the chances of civilization persisting to 10.1 percent and for him to struggle to make it 1.1 percent. In light of the political situation, especially the rise of far-right autocrats utterly unaware of or unconcerned about the existential threats they and their supporters were worsening at home and abroad, I now suspect Jim was right.[9]

So Anne and I in our dotage have decided to do whatever we can to avoid or ameliorate a collapse, either as a bang or as a whimper. In 2016 we traveled first to Vancouver for a conference on the impact of overpopulation on children set up by old friend and ex-Stanford student Sally Otto, and then to Europe for a series of speeches and conferences. The trip was a change in many ways since we rarely spend a lot of time traveling among cities. We had an intense conference in Crans, Switzerland, over the organization of the Fan Initiative, a network of concerned scholars and communications experts founded by another old friend, Pete Myers, and a bright activist named Margaret Calantzopoulos. Pete once did great work on shorebird ecology and was a coauthor of *Our Stolen Future*, a pioneering book on the toxification of Earth. Now he does great work as head of Environmental Health Sciences, especially in alerting people to that toxification. Participants in the Fan struggle to find ways to soften what many see as a coming collapse and/or making possible at least a partial recovery to a sustainable society.[10]

I happened to be lecturing in Leipzig a day or so after Trump wrapped up the Republican nomination, and I broke the unspoken rule of not comparing American politicians with Hitler. In fact, I went into the parallels in some historical detail. Hitler had gained power in the NSDAP (Nazi party) in part through his virulent anti-Semitism; Trump gained support among Republicans in part by making Mexicans and Muslims the "new Jews." Hitler had encouraged his followers to be violent, forming the SA (*Sturmabtei-*

lung, Storm Detachment, Brownshirts), as did Trump with less immediate success in his own dog-whistle way.

I was surprised that my German audience appreciated the discussion, and several thanked me personally afterward because it turned out many of them did not know in much detail how Hitler rose to power in a weakened Weimar Republic. In retrospect, I'm glad I made the then-disapproved-of comparison, especially in light of events such as the invasion of Michigan's legislative building by right-wing protestors armed with AK-47s and later still by Trump's January 6, 2021, incitement of what amounted to a coup attempt and what was revealed afterward about it.

After a brief stop in Berlin, we moved on to Cambridge, England, where, hosted by Partha Dasgupta, I was invited to give a speech to the Centre for the Study of Existential Risk on the forces that threaten human extinction or the collapse of civilization. Cambridge, of course, is very impressive old England. Anne and I stayed in the Judge's Room, and dined at Trinity College high table.

Circumstances had certainly changed since the 1960s, the last time I had dined at high table, then at All Souls College at Oxford at the invitation of the famous evolutionist Henry (E. B.) Ford. Not only were British universities stuffier then, but Henry was a caricature of an upper-class Englishman. Once when we were walking together through Oxford, the clocks struck noon, and I mentioned that they were a little off. Henry's response, said in all seriousness: "My dear boy, Oxford is not on Greenwich Mean Time, it's on God's time." On another walk then, a very well dressed gentleman came up to us and said, "My watch has stopped—could one of you gentleman please tell me the time?" Henry's response: "My dear man, how dare you accost me on a public thoroughfare?"

Henry's work on checkerspots and his close relationship with Sir Ronald Fisher (father of modern statistics) had made him one of my heroes, but associating with him could be disconcerting—like being at high table and hearing a discussion of the '14 port, and realizing they were talking about the 1814 port. My friend Miriam Rothschild was a close friend of Henry's (she campaigned with him for the legalization of homosexuality), the world's expert on fleas, and a fine all-around naturalist. Quite naturally, being vastly wealthy, she was accustomed to getting her own way, and with me she usually did. She was an impressive lady in whom I only detected one major flaw—when she entertained and I was there, she never served the good stuff.

Some of the happiest times of my life have been spent with nonhumans, as I've mentioned before: diving on the Great Barrier Reef, gathering data on the behavior of gorgeous butterfly fishes, watching aardvarks forage in the South African night, seeing a pair of endangered golden-shouldered parrots on the Cape York Peninsula of northeastern Australia return to the home they'd bored in a termite nest, or discovering that patterns on many butterfly wings appear to be representations of caterpillars. Appreciation and discovery of the beauty, intricacy, and relationships of the animals and plants of our planet have continually inspired me to keep doing all I could—and can—to preserve biodiversity, and thus the life-support systems of humanity and the rest of nature. And in that cause I've also had an opportunity to collaborate in recent years with a wonderfully diverse group of scientists who share that appreciation.

Corey Bradshaw, a youthful (to me) leading global ecologist is one such scientist. He came to visit Gretchen Daily at Stanford early in the new century, and we met largely by accident. Corey and I almost immediately hit it off in many dimensions—especially in comparing the biodiversity situations in Australia and the United States. That led to our 2015 book *Killing the Koala and Poisoning the Prairie: Australia, America, and the Environment.*[11] At the suggestion of Corey's partner, Karah, we had applied to work on a subsequent book as residents at the Rockefeller Foundation Bellagio Center. Corey and Karah and Anne and I ended up spending a month living with a couple dozen spectacular and diverse scholars, in great comfort, in a palace on a beautiful hilltop overlooking Lake Como. We actually got a lot of work done on how our nations dealt with the problems of the human predicament, resulting eventually in our leading, with the help of Dan Blumstein, a large group of scientists to publish on humanity's likely "Ghastly Future" if it pursued its current foolhardy course.[12] Corey, Dan, and I with more than fifty other scientists have followed that up by working on another paper on how the future might be made less ghastly.

Anne and I and our colleague Gerardo Ceballos used our gang's inspiration a few years ago to produce what, in a fit of self-promotion, I will describe as "a beautiful book," *The Annihilation of Nature* (2015), illustrated with photos taken by Gerardo, by other colleagues and friends, and a few by me. It was designed to introduce people to the birds and mammals that are disappearing and to raise money to support our Navjot Sodhi memorial fund established for training and inspiring at RMBL young conservation scientists.

Annihilation actually had its genesis in a conversation between Gerardo and Navjot Sodhi, a brilliant and funny guy who was a leading conservation biologist in Southeast Asia. Navjot and I coedited a book called *Conservation Biology for All* (2010), which was widely distributed gratis in poor countries. From my perspective, Navjot, with his vast knowledge of the tropics and the practitioners of conservation biology, was an ideal coeditor—especially since he did most of the work. Navjot had been at Harvard but had moved to the National University of Singapore when he, Gerardo, and I started writing *Annihilation*. When we had barely begun, though, Navjot was diagnosed with a lymphoma, which at first seemed to go into remission but then suddenly killed him. He was only in his forties and was (and is) badly needed for tasks like battling palm oil barons. *Annihilation* for me is full of nostalgia for him, and triggers more when I see in it again my photos of one of the last orange-bellied parrots and of a stream of wildebeest crossing the Mara River in Tanzania.

Aside from my passion in defense of the human environment and the natural world, what keeps me going on various projects, as you may have figured out from comments like those on Gerardo and Navjot—indeed, from many of the projects described in preceding chapters—is the pleasure of friendships with wonderful coconspirators. Hal Mooney, for example, has been my colleague in Stanford's eco-evo group for half a century. The world's leading plant physiological ecologist, he's also a wonderful guy with a genius for organizing people. I continue to do him one big favor—he's four days younger than I am, and so I serve as his early warning system. If and when a terrible sign of aging shows up, I promise to tell him he's got four days left. We've spent a lot of time lunching together, frequently accompanied by Anne and by Hal's wife, Sherry, and talking department, university, national, and global politics—usually grim subjects all. Hal has also been the behind-the-scenes mover and shaker of many of the significant efforts the scientific community has mounted to try to preserve the natural world. Find a weird acronym like IPBES (Intergovernmental Science-Policy Platform on Biodiversity and Ecosystem Services) or a massive effort like the Millennium Ecosystem Assessment (MEA), and you'll find Hal behind it, gently manipulating his colleagues to join in and steering the effort. This is so well known that when Hal calls a colleague, they always fear they'll get assigned what is known by another acronym, the HRT (Hal-Related Task).

One of the biggest of many favors Hal has done me was to suggest to a mammalogist and ecologist colleague of his that he spend a sabbatical with me. That was Gerardo. A young man on the faculty of UNAM in Mexico, he showed up at Stanford at the end of the last century with his wife, Pupa (Guadalupe), son, Pablo, and daughter, Regina. Gerardo later claimed (falsely) that I wouldn't pay enough attention to him. But we soon discovered great mutual interests; Gerardo and I have now coauthored, in addition to *The Annihilation of Nature*, many papers, and we've done fieldwork together in Mexico and South Africa and (with Gretchen Daily) in Costa Rica.

Another brilliant member of our faculty (and a friend of Gerardo Ceballos) who has become a collaborator on my late-in-life projects, is Rodolfo Dirzo, who, along with his wife, Guille, and son, Arturo, have joined our growing circle of Mexican friends. Don Rodolfo is, like Gerardo, a foreign member of the U.S. National Academy of Sciences. Rodolfo is the world expert on defaunation—the phenomenon of forests being emptied of their mammal and bird faunas, creating the widespread "empty forest syndrome." Rodolfo joined Gerardo and me in our work on population extinctions (or perhaps, more accurately, we joined him in his pioneering work on defaunation). In 2017 the three of us published in the *Proceedings of the National Academy of Sciences* a definitive paper on "Biological Annihilation via the Ongoing Sixth Mass Extinction Signaled by Vertebrate Population Losses and Declines" showing that Earth's sixth mass extinction was under way.[13] We did that by documenting widespread declines in the numbers of individuals within vertebrate populations and by showing that many of the component populations of species were already going extinct. With Gerardo, Rodolfo, and my old buddy Peter Raven, I've continued in my old age to publish warnings that by destroying biodiversity, civilization is sawing off the limb upon which it is perched.[14]

Species extinctions are generally preceded by such declines in the number of individuals in populations of the species, and then by loss of component populations of that species themselves. Loss of populations without their replacement can signal an extinction epidemic in progress, as does the disappearance of some *E. editha* populations in California without new ones appearing. The loss of Bay checkerspot populations is thus part of the sixth mass extinction even though the species has not gone extinct and most of its California populations seem still to be hanging on. In other words, population extinctions are often signs of approaching death of a species, just as difficulty breathing and high fever are often signs of a person's approaching death. And just as some moribund people can linger on the brink of death for a long time, so can some moribund species.

I had been observing population extinctions of checkerspots at Jasper Ridge and butterfly populations elsewhere all through the 1970s and 1980s. Then, in the 1990s, two of my graduate students at the time, Jennifer Hughes and Gretchen Daily, and I decided to look at the overall problem of population, as opposed to species, extinction. How did the extinction of one of the populations of *E. editha* on Jasper Ridge, for example, relate to the disappearance of all populations of that species, such as had occurred to passenger pigeons in the nineteenth century? Jen led the study, and it turned out to be the first of its kind, published in *Science* in 1997. It made the first very rough estimate of the rate of population loss in the sixth mass extinction—about eighteen hundred an hour out of a total of some one to seven billion globally.[15]

The findings of Gerardo, Rodolfo, and me on population extinctions were thus no surprise after what we had been observing in our own fieldwork or to other scientists who had been studying the loss of biodiversity elsewhere. But what was a surprise was the great attention our joint 2017 *PNAS* paper received from the mass media globally: a full page in *Le Monde*, articles in the *New York Times*, *Washington Post*, *Guardian*, and many other periodicals, and much coverage in major television and radio programs in many nations. We're still not sure why, but we were certainly pleased with the attention given to the critical subject, and pleased again when a subsequent paper on the same topic in which Gerardo and I were joined by Peter Raven got great press coverage. That paper, focusing on the large number of vertebrate species on the brink of extinction, reinforced the urgent need for the kind of remedial steps we had urged in our earlier work.

Both Gerardo and Rodolfo were students at UNAM of José Sarukhán, who had personally helped to put Mexico ahead of the United States in the battle to save biodiversity. He did it by establishing (and still running) the Mexican government's CONABIO (National Commission for the Knowledge and Use of Biodiversity), an agency charged with evaluating, conserving, and advising on the condition and use made of Mexico's rich natural capital—its plants and animals. José is a brilliant ecologist who ran UNAM, one of the world's largest universities, from 1989 to 1997, and in the administration of Mexico's president Vicente Fox he served as commissioner of the social and human development cabinet. I know no other person who has had such success in science and politics and in generally making the world a better place. José and his wife, Adelaída, have made Anne's and my world a better place—by being wonderful friends to us.

It certainly is a small world. Gerardo changed my life as a close colleague in ecology, but he also transformed my life in another small-world way, one that ultimately led to another late-in-life project. Gerardo has always been very active in Mexican conservation, being personally responsible for preserving more biodiversity-rich habitat than any scientist I know, and he became particularly involved in efforts to preserve the jaguars of the Calakmul Biosphere Reserve at the base of the Yucatán Peninsula. In connection with the organization Rain Forest to Reef, he got to know David Leventhal (raised in Mexico) and his wife, Sandra Kahn (born in Mexico, now a U.S. citizen), and later introduced us to them.

Sandra (an orthodontist) and David (an entrepreneur) opened a wonderful tiny eco-resort called Playa Viva on the southern Pacific Coast of Mexico near Zihuatanejo. Anne and I loved it, and I helped by putting together a butterfly guide to the area. Sandra had been trained and had practiced extensively as a conventional orthodontist, but she had decided that some orthodontists were doing more harm than good. Her view of the profession altered rapidly when her six-year-old son began snoring and mouth breathing (especially at night) and losing his cute appearance. She concluded that a small group of dentists and orthodontists were onto something when they claimed that malocclusion (crooked teeth) and mouth breathing were by and large an epidemic disease of modern lifestyles. She then got to know Dr. John Mew in Great Britain, the guru of this way of thinking.

Since I had for decades been deeply concerned with the world food problem, the epidemiological environment, and public health in general, I began discussing it with Sandra, and I became more and more convinced that she was right. I was also embarrassed that, as an evolutionist, I hadn't asked myself why myriad children had braces and I and others had unerupted third molars (wisdom teeth). How could human beings have evolved such defective anatomy? An especially interesting question, since our hunter-gatherer ancestors virtually never had crooked teeth or impacted wisdom teeth. In the end, a meeting with John Mew and my discussions with Sandra led the two of us to write a popular book designed to bring the problem, and how to avoid it, to the attention of decision-makers and the public, especially the parents of young children. It took a while, but after I had read something like five hundred papers in the dental literature to try to catch up with Sandra, we finally completed the text and illustration program, and *Jaws: The Story of a Hidden Epidemic* was published in 2018 by Stanford University Press.

Its basic message is that human jaws are shrinking and causing massive problems, not just crooked teeth and lack of room for the third molars, but much more seriously disturbed breathing during sleep (sleep apnea), and an array of diseases related to the stress of disturbed sleep.

Perhaps the most interesting reaction to *Jaws* in the dental community has been to persist in the claim that jaw shrinkage is "genetic." As the book explains, jaw shrinkage seems clearly a response to the massive environmental changes flowing from agriculture and industrialization and concomitant changes in diet and other practices, especially oral posture—how kids hold their jaws when not eating or speaking and how they swallow. Human beings have brought Stone Age genes into a McDonald's world, with an entirely new environment (more liquid diet, more stuffy noses and mouth breathing, different swallowing patterns, sleeping postures, eating utensils such as spoons and chopsticks, and so on).[16]

One conclusion that became obvious as the scientific consensus on climate disruption, destruction of biodiversity, and other assaults on human life-support systems became firm and empirical evidence readily available to those willing to look: simply telling people what the science said by itself was not leading many people to change their behavior (or often even their minds). It also did not cause institutions like Stanford University to change their curricula to reflect an utterly transformed world, the National Science Foundation to alter its priorities, or even the *New York Times* to focus much more of its news on existential threats and actually deal with such issues as overpopulation, overconsumption, and growthmania itself. Growthmania is especially important as an underlying principle of today's human culture, related to, but even more basic than, greed. It is the universal notion of the daydream believers running society that the human enterprise can and must grow forever.[17] Finding approaches to encourage humane and equitable shrinkage of that enterprise and our interest in human behavior (*Human Natures* again) were main reasons for Anne's and my founding of the MAHB.

The MAHB had its origins in the Millennium Ecosystem Assessment, on which several thousand ecologists cooperated to produce at the turn of the millennium a global analysis of humanity's life-support systems and what was sustaining and undermining them.[18] Its broad conclusions substantiated what those who had been tracking humanity's assault on those systems had long recognized: many of those life-support systems (such as the oceans and tropical moist forests) were in deep trouble. Soon after release of the assessment, Anne and I suggested that the basic need then wasn't so much further understanding of the biophysical situation but understanding why societies were taking few if any significant steps to end the destruction. With Don Kennedy's help, we pushed the idea that what was needed was a Millennium Assessment of Human Behavior to explain the lack of action and, building on the work of social scientists, figure out how to generate pressure from civil society on governments to take action aimed at dealing with existential problems.[19] Psychologists such as Lee Ross and Robert Cialdini, for example, understand a great deal about human behavior, but too little attention is paid to their findings and to those of others trying to delineate what behavior was actually occurring and what trajectories that behavior might lead to.[20]

After a series of false starts at Stanford, the MAHB began to take hold with a broader audience. One of the spark plugs was Gene Rosa, a leader in the social sciences and a key member of the MAHB steering committee. Gene discovered that one barrier to the participation of social scientists in the MAHB was, amazingly enough, the use of the word "behavior" in the name. Gene hypothesized that the problem was memories of B. F. Skinner's manipulative approach to psychology, called radical behaviorism. On

Gene's advice we held on to the acronym but changed the name of the organization to a (mostly meaningless) Millennium Alliance for Humanity and the Biosphere.

Starting in 2013 MAHB has been headed by our colleague Joan Diamond, deputy director and senior scenarist, Nautilus Institute for Security and Sustainability. The MAHB strives to get civil society to focus on the basic issues—population, consumption, environmental quality, and equity.[21] Rather than reaching out just to the scholars and elites known for responding to the human predicament, the MAHB attempts to bring all of progressive civil society into the conversation. Since the challenges facing humanity have been and are those of understanding, responding to, and getting ahead of the ever more complex and interdependent stressors on civilization—stressors that often threaten the values and institutions upon which a just future relies—we believe that all citizens of the world should have the opportunity to participate in developing solutions. The MAHB has provided a much-used forum to discuss existential threats, and it has aided many people and NGOs (nongovernmental organizations) in this enterprise. In essence the MAHB has been working toward the conscious cultural evolution Robert Ornstein and I described in our books *New World: New Mind* (1989) and *Humanity on a Tightrope* (2010) as necessary to provide hope of avoiding a civilizational collapse.

Participation in the MAHB has come from unexpected and welcome places. Karole Armitage, for example, was one of the great dancers and forward-looking choreographers of the twentieth century, dancing with Merce Cunningham, choreographing for Mikhail Baryshnikov, and later leading her own companies.[22] She had already choreographed a dance about climate change when she read an article by Anne and me entitled *The Culture Gap and Its Needed Closures* (2010), and mentioned she'd like to do a dance about environmental science based on that as well.[23] We worked on a script for me to narrate, and she went through the long process of designing a dance, *On the Nature of Things*, and perfecting it with her company of dancers. Karole arranged for it to be performed in 2015 at my old stomping ground, the American Museum of Natural History in New York.

Although the museum's butterfly collections had been totally rearranged since my days with Mich and Fred Rindge (the latter was curator of Lepidoptera from 1949 to 1994), the director when I visited in advance of the dance performances found someone to lead me to the *Erebia* and I spotted a specimen I remembered well. It was an *Erebia fasciata avinoffi* that I had rescued from a discard drawer at the Academy of Natural Sciences of Philadelphia in the early 1950s. It was being tossed then because it was mangled, but I knew that the mangling resulted from having been chewed by an Inuit for its fat content—and for me that just added interest to what, back in those days, was a very rare specimen.

Being at the museum brought back many memories. There I had met Vladimir Nabokov when I was a child. Our brief acquaintance was ended by him when I was a graduate student at Kansas and sent him a printed departmental reprint card requesting a copy of *Lolita*, which I filled in on the appropriate line. Another character at the museum when I was young was a wealthy businessman, Cyril S. Dos Passos (author John's second cousin), with strong views on butterfly taxonomy to which he was dedicated. He lived to be ninety-nine and donated his vast collection to the museum. I also met the émigré artist Andrey Avinoff, author of an interesting study of *Karanassa* butterflies, satyrines, in Central Asia. I was sixteen and he was gay and not primarily interested in my (then very limited) expertise on satyrine butterflies. He blew his approach, however, by saying he wanted to give me the gift of a butterfly for my collection. His hand hovered over a very interesting *Papilio machaon*–group swallowtail from Central Asia, and I wondered if my already very deep commitment to the opposite sex would hold. But then the hand moved on to give me a common *Morpho* from Brazil, removing any temptation to make even a temporary switch. Such was butterfly life in the AMNH in the olden days.

Karole's three dance performances, all of them sold out, took place in March 2015, under the life-size model of a blue whale in the Milstein Family Hall of Ocean Life. It was the most nerve-wracking of all my public appearances: I had to read the narration because the dance was cued to it—and I *never* read speeches. If I missed a cue, I would ruin the show. Karole had added cues for me of the "when key of C turns to E" sort to my script, but I didn't know a key from a chord (color-blind and tone-deaf, I'm potentially the perfect aesthetic blank). She solved that by seating one of her colleagues next to me on the stage to tap me each time I was to start talking.

The shows all went well, and I was astonished by the quality of the dancing, although after three nights of narrating, I came down with pneumonia (glad there are antibiotics). The reviews were great—except for the *New York Times*, which was lukewarm, accusing us of trying to change the world (well, true) and hadn't (true as well, but we hadn't expected to). It did not shake my confidence in the importance of the arts in contributing to understanding of our current situation, eliciting empathy for nature, and developing a vision of what we could do.

TWELVE

The Population Bomb Revisited

It has now been over fifty years since *The Population Bomb* was written. The book sold some two million copies, was translated into many languages, and changed Anne's and my lives, as well as Lisa's. Whether a person agrees with it or not, *The Population Bomb* helped launch a worldwide debate that continues today. It introduced millions of people to the fundamental issue of the Earth's finite capacity to sustain human civilization. Anne and I believe that, despite its flaws, it still provides a useful lens through which to view the environmental, energy, pandemic, and food crises of the present time.

On a more personal level, the book's publication led to my being labeled the "population bomber" and categorized as someone who thought overpopulation was the sole problem of humanity, which I surely did not—and do not. To this day when I lecture or appear in the media, I am pursued by inaccurate or out-of-context quotations from the book. Despite the intervening half century, such statements are frequently assumed to represent Anne's and my *current* thinking on many topics, including ones on which we have subsequently written many articles and entire books.[1]

The Population Bomb was written in response to a request that I summarize arguments I had been making in the media in the mid-1960s that the population issue should be taken up by the growing environmental movement. That movement, as I noted in chapter 8, had been triggered in no small part by Rachel Carson's *Silent Spring*, published only a few years earlier, in 1962. The record rate of global population growth occurred near that time (2.2 percent annually in 1962–63). I could then jokingly say that I had been the two billionth human being to be added to the population, since that was its approximate size in 1932. Then I could add that just in my short life, by 1968, the number had ballooned to three and a half billion—an *addition* the size of the entire global population in 1900.

The book has been seen, at the very least by some on the lunatic fringe, as of enduring importance. It was listed by the *Intercollegiate Review* (a periodical that claimed to provide "the best of conservative intellectual thought") as one of the fifty worst books of the twentieth century, along with John Kenneth Galbraith's *Affluent Society*, John Maynard Keynes's *General Theory of Employment, Interest, and Money*, and John Rawls's *Theory of Justice*.[2] In another conservative periodical's list of the "Ten Most Harmful Books of the Nineteenth and Twentieth Centuries," it came in eleventh ("honorable mention"); even so, it bested such other listed books as Darwin's *Origin of Species* and Carson's *Silent Spring*, though it was outranked by Keynes (again), Marx's *Das Kapital*, and the Kinsey Reports, among others.[3] What company we've kept!

The basic mainstream criticism of *The Population Bomb*, just like the later criticisms of the Club of Rome's 1972 publication of their computer study of the future, *Limits to Growth*, came from economists whose fairytale ideas these books threatened. After all, in the typical assumptions of mainstream macroeconomists, population growth, expanding per capita consumption, and free markets would surely keep the human enterprise forever expanding, along with human happiness. Entrepreneurial sorts in free markets traditionally focus on exploiting resources such as oil, rare earths, or fishes, and depleting such resources as cheaply as possible by hook or by crook. They especially enjoy pushing the costs of depletion off on others who do not share in the profits. They then try to use these resources to provide the most attractive possible products for the highest possible price to an ever-expanding population of consumers, supplied both by population growth and by imperialistic expansion of markets. So, by this logic, population increases mean more customers and thus more profits, and since GDP (gross domestic product) is the total value of goods and services being bought and sold in a nation, GDP would grow as well. What could possibly go wrong?

The reason this picture can be made to look so rosy is that corporations are able to externalize so much of the true costs of their production and market expansion, including those of imperial expansion (taxpayer-funded military), and ultimately, the potentially civilization-ending negative effects of population increase itself. Externalities are an activity's side effects that influence costs or values of other economic actors. If you paint your house you may create a positive externality for your neighbors by increasing the value of their homes, now in a more attractive setting. If a corporation dumps carbon dioxide into the atmosphere when manufacturing its product, that is a negative externality affecting everyone by increasing the costs suffered from (or of combatting) climate disruption. Many corporations that I think of as murder incorporated—gun manufacturers, cigarette merchants, big pharma producing opioids, oil companies, and the like—for example, are specialists at passing costs they should pay off on society as a whole. Those costs of their production processes and products often include disease, injury, and death. In addition, GDP, as conventionally defined, does not take into consideration depreciation of a society's capital; especially ignored is the recent plummeting of our critical natural capital—soils, pollinators, groundwater, the capacity of the atmosphere to absorb greenhouse gases safely, and so on.

It was of course the growing environmental externalities and the decline of natural capital that have most concerned me as their continuation threatens to lead us toward a collapse of the human enterprise. A substantial increase in the numbers of incredibly poor people would make only a trivial difference in most environmental externalities; a very small increase in the very wealthy, on the other hand, is a boost toward disaster. And then there's the likely result of the most desirable goal, of giving everyone around the world a decent standard of living. It's not rocket science. A larger, better-off population increases the negative externalities of more carbon dioxide and methane dumped into the atmosphere, more toxic substances released into the global environment as more products are manufactured with little attention to costs and benefits, of a higher probability of global epidemics, of increased chance of accidental nuclear war, and on and on. More people increases the depreciation rate of virtually all natural capital from fisheries to stocks of rare earths. Small wonder that ecological footprint studies indicate that *Homo sapiens* is already in overshoot—demanding more ecosystem services than Earth can sustainably supply.[4] A way of summarizing humanity's situation is to calculate Earth Overshoot Day, which is the date when the human demand for ecosystem resources and services in a given year exceeds what the biosphere can regenerate in that year. In 2021, Overshoot Day was July 29.[5]

Many years ago, I think, economist Herman Daly succinctly summarized a major failure of the perpetual growth structure beloved of academic macroeconomics, which goes something like this: "If the survival of your civilization is external to your model, you probably need a new model." But academic macroeconomics just marches on, with those in power rewarding academics who invent rationales for economic rape, plunder, and life-support system destruction.

Demographer Nicholas Eberstadt and others have called people the "wealth of modern societies."[6] Trained people, of course, can be regarded as productive assets (embodying, as economists put it, "human capital"), but it is a major error to consider increases in human *numbers* as automatically expanding either that capital or real (inclusive) wealth—that is, the aggregate of all forms of capital that contribute to well-being. Given the growing scarcity of natural resources, population growth normally *reduces* per capita genuine wealth in the long term, and can even shrink a nation's total wealth, as Kenneth Arrow and "his communist friends" pointed out in 2004.[7] If wealth were a function of population size, China and India each would be three to four times as wealthy as the United States and more affluent than all the nations of Europe combined, Africa's wealth would outstrip that of North America or Europe, and Yemen would be more than three times as well off as Israel.

British scientist James Lovelock, whose invention of the apparatus that allowed discovery of the threat to the ozone layer helped to save humanity from that existential peril, has stated: "We have grown in number to the point where our presence is perceptibly disabling the planet like a disease."[8] When *The Population Bomb* was written, there were roughly three and a half billion people in the world. A little over five decades later there are some eight billion people, meaning that the world population has more than doubled since copies of the book first rolled off the presses.

Despite this growth in world population, there have been some remarkable advances on the population front in recent decades. Birthrates have dropped in much of the world, partly in response to government-sponsored programs in education, especially of women, enabling them to take advantage of job opportunities in place of reproduction and making contraceptive information and materials accessible, and to economic factors such as a reduction in demand for offspring as farm labor. Even though the *rate* has dropped, the annual addition of people has remained considerable, around eighty million people were added in 2020. Examples of the good news include: in southern Europe the total fertility rate (completed family size) is 1.4, way below replacement reproduction (which is a fertility rate of about 2.1 children per woman), and in Bangladesh almost two-thirds of married women are using contraception. If such current trends in reproductive behavior could be globalized and maintained for a couple of centuries, the prospects for humanity would brighten considerably. But I'm scared stiff that we don't have more than a couple of decades to change our ways as the biophysical and social existential threats, virtually all exacerbated by population growth, are increasing rapidly. We are, after all, already in overshoot.

Some of the world's lowest birthrates are now found in the rich, fully industrialized nations of Europe and in Japan, and their populations are on the verge of decline. That's fortunate in one respect, because it is people in the high-consuming rich nations that place the greatest pressure on humanity's staggering life-support systems. The big exception to this pattern is the United States, which is a center of overconsumption and whose population continues growing because of relatively high (though diminishing) birth and immigration rates in recent years. Immigration aside, if current trends continue, the U.S. population will soon cease growing because death rates will catch up with birthrates (thanks to an aging population), and there will be no natural increase. Further population growth would then depend on how much immigration keeps exceeding emigration. But that still means the U.S. population, which in 2020 stood at some 330 million, could well be creeping toward 400 million around midcentury.

Such projected increases in the population of the United States must be seen in the context of a desperate need for population *shrinkage*. That is necessary if any semblance of sustainability on a world scale is going to be achieved. Earth already has several times more people than the number that likely can be sustained at a reasonable standard of living. That sustainable number at the moment, it appears, is somewhere between one and a half billion and two and a half billion, the size of the world's population in the early twentieth century.[9] Whatever the number in that range, if human civilization is to survive, lower birthrates and redistribution of wealth (perhaps including a universal basic income) and perhaps near ubiquitous participatory budgeting, where community members help determine how to spend a public budget, seem inevitable features of a viable future in which there is equity within and among nations.[10]

The United States has been in the strange position of vigorously debating immigration policy without discussing population policy—one measure of the dumbing down of American politics since the report of the President's Commission on Population Growth and the American Future appeared in 1969. And during Republican administrations since Ronald Reagan's the United States has, in effect, encouraged high birthrates on a world scale by limiting aid to developing nations that would allow women access to contraception and safe backup abortion. Even so, the majority of developing countries have adopted population policies, and many have substantially reduced their birthrates as the perception of children as valued farm labor has changed with urbanization to one in which children do not join the labor force early and are recognized as being expensive to educate.

That Japan's and several high-consuming European populations are starting to shrink in size has ironically triggered complaints about aging populations. That change in age distribution is mathematically inevitable: population growth stops when people age out of the reproductive years and are not replaced with equal numbers of new reproducers, so that deaths eventually balance births. With planning, the change to an older age composition of the population could be managed in ways to benefit collective well-being (changing retirement ages is an obvious example). On the plus side would be the vast benefit of lessening pressure on our already battered life-support systems, and with a more mature age structure, lessening the chances of crime sprees and wars because those tend to be activities of young males. There also would be the potential of even greater gains if birthrates could be reduced even further for a time to provide a reduction of population size to a level that might be sustained.

The goal of *The Population Bomb*, to encourage the adoption of policies that would gradually reduce birthrates and eventually start a global decline to a sustainable level, is thus being partially achieved, and some analysts credit the book with helping make progress toward that vital goal. Rather than doubling the population in thirty-five years, as continued growth at the 1968 rate would have done, the world did not reach that level—seven billion—until 2013, forty-five years later.

Yet recognition of the impact of population growth for our overall well-being is only gradually, faintly, and confusedly working its way back into the public and political consciousness today, as suggested in chapter 8. That's perhaps aided by results such as those mentioned there of Seth Wynes and Kimberly Nicholas on the benefits of smaller families in the reduction of greenhouse gas emissions.

Even with some such good news on the population front, if more concerted effort is not made, humanity may add some three billion or more people to the population before its growth levels off and a slow (we hope) decline begins. With unwanted pregnancies still common, that demographic result could probably be averted by a major effort to give every human being access to modern contraception and safe backup abortion, but that effort doesn't appear to be on the horizon at the moment. All that, of course, assumes that a great change or even collapse of civilization does not intervene soon. The most recent update of the Limits to Growth scenarios certainly suggests some such may occur.[11]

Unfortunately, the addition of those three billion people would have a disproportionately negative impact on our life-support systems. The reason for the disproportionality is that our ancestors naturally farmed the richest soils they found and used the most accessible resources first.[12] Those soils, where people first settled as they took up farming, have often been eroded away or paved over, and people are increasingly forced to turn to marginal land to grow more food. Even with artificial fertilization, soils in many fields under cultivation are producing crops increasingly poor in vital micronutrients and require better soil management.[13] Ores are now found farther from convenient transportation and point of use, and they are mined and smelted at ever-greater energy environmental cost. Water and petroleum now more often come from lower-quality sources and deeper wells and have to be transported over longer distances, while massive use of the one-time bonanza of fossil energy must be stopped as fast as possible. The impacts of past and future population growth will be with humanity for a very long time as people struggle with what William Rees has called our population "plague phase" and the related need for disproportionately more energy and materials on a planet whose natural capital is depreciating at a rapid rate.[14]

A typical example of the confusion in the mass media about population was a 2015 column in the *New York Times* by environmental journalist Fred Pearce.[15] Pearce declared that although *The Population Bomb* that concerned Anne and me was being defused, there remained a "consumption bomb." According to Pearce, we shouldn't do anything more to limit population's quantity despite the outstripping of resources that population's increase will inevitably entail. Such depletion would occur even if everyone had opportunities for only a Mexican-style standard of living, which itself would be sufficient to lead to the eventual destruction of civilization with continued population growth. According to Pearce, our one remaining hope lies in improving our technologies servicing human consumption to reduce the rate of depletion—such as doing better with solar power and manufacturing imitation meat from vegetables. Humanity's record in the area of adopting more environmentally sound technologies is not entirely encouraging (think plastics, hormone mimics, nuclear weapons, artificial intelligence, leaf blowers, processed baby food, billionaires launched on space vacations), but maybe a miracle technology will appear.[16]

An international crash effort to educate and give equal rights and economic opportunities to women around the world and—to repeat for emphasis—make modern contraception and safe backup abortion universally accessible, might not only improve the well-being of millions of women (surely a worthy goal in itself) but also give global society a hundred years from now (if there still is one) several billion fewer people to care for and thus a better chance of reaching some level of sustainability.

Aside from its general emphasis on the perils of population growth, *The Population Bomb* also drew early attention to overconsumption, pointing out statistics on how much each American baby on average would consume in a lifetime, adding up to a nation of superconsumers, even if many individuals had far too little to live adequately. That overconsumption we regarded even then as a problem is now increasingly seen as a pattern that may be more difficult to alter than overreproduction.[17] It, of course, became more of a problem on a world scale as people in a number of countries began to enjoy a life beyond rock-bottom subsistence. China is a classic example, where eating meat has escalated with consequences ranging from endangering biodiversity to increasing the chances of lethal pandemics.[18] I think *The Population Bomb* also did a pretty good job for its day in drawing attention to many of the elements now pushing us toward a global collapse, such as climate disruption, toxification, deterioration of the epidemiological environment, and the threat of nuclear war.

From a personal point of view, the worst aspect of the book was its title. We called the manuscript *Population, Resources, and Environment* (and soon wrote a text with that title). Ian Ballantine's choice of *The Population Bomb* was perfect from a marketing perspective, but it led me to be miscategorized as solely focused on human numbers, despite my interest in all the factors affecting the human trajectory and how they are related to one another.

Perhaps the most serious flaw within *The Population Bomb* was that it was too optimistic about a business-as-usual near future. When it was written, carbon dioxide was thought to be the only gas whose greenhouse effect might cause serious global heating, and perhaps not for a century or so (the roles of methane, nitrous oxide, and chlorofluorocarbons were not recognized until years later). When the book was published, some climatologists thought that any warming from carbon dioxide emissions would be counteracted by anthropogenic dust and the contrails from high-flying jets, which would have a global cooling effect by reflecting solar energy back into space, or by regenerating forests, thriving on carbon dioxide as they sucked it out of the atmosphere. As a result, we could only write that exploding human populations were tampering with the energy balance of Earth, and the results globally and locally could be dire, especially since any rapid climate change would likely greatly reduce agricultural production.

Since *The Population Bomb* was written, scientists have learned much more about the assaults our species has unwittingly made on our life-support systems. In 1968 Sherwood Rowland and Mario Molina had not yet discovered the potential of chlorofluorocarbons to destroy the ozone layer and make life on Earth's continents impossible, for example; that came in 1974. It may have been cured by reductions in the guilty gases under the 1989 Montreal Protocol in which nations agreed to phase out their production—at least I hope so. Norman Myers was a decade away from calling world attention to the destruction of tropical rain forests when *The Population Bomb* was written; the possibility that the tropical moist forests of the Amazon basin, Africa, and Asia might be destroyed was essentially unimaginable before that time.[19] And it was a half century later before our research group could nail down the critical importance of extinctions of populations.[20] Also unknown when *The Population Bomb* was published were the threats of endocrine-disrupting contaminants (pollutants that mimic human hormones), compounds with nonlinear dose-response curves that may be more dangerous in trace than in high concentrations. Polar bears were not having reproductive difficulties blamed on pollutants then, nor were they losing their habitat due to melting sea ice. There were no big concerns over the likely related declines in human sperm counts. Wide recognition of the problem of rapid ocean acidification was still some four decades in the future, and coral reefs appeared to be permanent features of Earth. We did not anticipate the disaster of plastic pollution.

There were flaws as well in *The Population Bomb*'s analysis of known threats. The first lines of the prologue proved to be among the most troublesome in the book: "The battle to feed all of humanity is over. In the 1970's the world will undergo famines—hundreds of millions of people are going to starve to death in spite of any crash programs embarked upon now."[21]

We are often asked what happened to the famines *The Population Bomb* predicted, as if the past four decades were a period of abundant food for all. But, of course, there were famines, more or less continuously in parts of Africa. Perhaps three hundred million people overall have died of hunger and hunger-related diseases since 1968. But the famines *were* smaller than our reading of the agricultural literature at the time had led us to anticipate, and our description of undeveloped countries was too harsh and monolithic (as was soon recognized in international affairs literature and the characterization replaced with developing nations).[22] What actually happened? The central factor was the success of the green revolution (the transference of agricultural technologies, especially new high-yielding crop strains, from rich to poor nations) in expanding food production at a rate beyond what many, if not most, agricultural experts believed likely. In addition, the United Nations and other organizations began to establish a network of agencies to move food to famine-struck regions when needed. As a result, there wasn't a general rise in the death rate from hunger, although there have been periodic regional rises in South Asia and Africa.

The analysis of the food situation in *The Population Bomb* was thus wrong in that it underestimated the short-term impact the green revolution would have. At the same time, it did recognize that serious ecological risks, such as the danger of huge pest outbreaks due to planting large stands of single crop strains and problems of overuse of pesticides, would accompany the spread of that revolution, although missing the overdrafts of groundwater, reductions in the genetic variability of crops, and some other problems that arose.[23]

The *Bomb* emphasized the importance of both curbing population growth and attempting to expand food production, and it is worth noting that in recent decades falling population growth rates in the rich nations of Europe and the United States may have played a role in the extent of agricultural surpluses in those countries. Nevertheless, the absolute numbers of hungry people (around eight hundred million today, discounting the great increases in hunger being wrought by the spread of Covid-19), are somewhat less than they were in 1968 despite a far larger population now—a cheering result.

Unfortunately, the basic pessimism of *The Population Bomb* about the human nutritional future does not seem misplaced today. A 2016 report by an independent panel of food and agriculture experts led by the former president of Ghana (John Kufuor) and the former chief scientific adviser to the U.K. government (Sir John Beddington) stated that while eight hundred million people were hungry, "two billion people lack the range of vitamins and minerals in their diet needed to keep them healthy. The result is an increase in heart disease, hypertension, diabetes and other diet-related illnesses that undermines productivity and threatens to overwhelm health services. These non-infectious, chronic diseases have been associated with the fatty, highly processed diet of the developed world. But most new cases are appearing in developing countries. The panel has warned that if current trends continue, the situation will get far worse in the next 20 years. It says only a global effort similar to that used to tackle HIV or malaria will be enough to meet the challenge."[24]

In the early twenty-first century the reason that so many people are inadequately fed is primarily economic inequity—enough calories are available to supply everyone adequately, but many people can't afford to gain access to them. The same is likely for micronutrients. The basic food problem in the early part of this century is one of maldistribution traceable largely to economic inequity and lack of public education. But current trends in population growth, the deterioration of arable land and the need for more, the disruption of climate critical to agriculture, declining pollinator availability, reduced nutritional quality of crops thanks to carbon dioxide fertilization, and the changing ecology of the oceans and their projected spread over low-lying farm fields suggest that the overall availability and quality of food could change dramatically for the worse in the not-too-distant future for many, many people.[25] Indeed, the world now seems to be on the brink of a major rise in harvest shortfalls that may outstrip the global emergency food supply.[26] But the real crunch between food supply and high population numbers may come when one assumes that everyone should have not simply (at best) minimal nutrition but diets that approach those in, say, parts of Europe. Numbers and equity need much more attention. The focus of *The Population Bomb* on human numbers versus quantity of available resources instead of numbers and inequity is something I wish we had handled better.

The Population Bomb was also somewhat misleading in stating that the birthrate in the United States might soon rise as the post–World War II baby boomers matured into their reproductive years. Instead, that rate actually dropped a little over time. One interesting question raised by this shift is how much of that change was the result of rising concern about overpopulation generated in part by *The Population Bomb* itself. Further, in 1968 the critical importance in lowering birthrates of providing women with education and job opportunities, as well as providing access to contraception and abortion, was not widely recognized by us or by others. Those factors, with some notable exceptions, generally improved around the time the baby boomers came of age and clearly helped prevent a new baby boom.

The biggest tactical error we made in *The Population Bomb* was to use scenarios, stories based on different assumptions designed to help one think about the future. Although we explicitly stated that the scenarios were not actual predictions and that "we can be sure that none of them will come true as stated"—their failure to occur has often been cited as a failure of prediction.[27] In honesty, the scenarios were *way* off, especially in their timing (we underestimated the resilience of the world food system and overestimated the likelihood of nuclear war). But they did highlight future issues that more people in 1968 and subsequent years should have been thinking about: the potential for widespread famines, pandemics, water shortages, climate disasters, resource wars, and nuclear war devastation—all issues more relevant today than ever.

The essential point made about population growth by *The Population Bomb* is as valid today as it was in 1968: "Basically, there are only two kinds of solutions to the population problem. One is a 'birth rate solution,' in which we find ways to lower the birth rate. The other is a 'death rate solution,' in which ways to raise the death rate—war, famine, pestilence—*find us*."[28]

That fundamental point of *The Population Bomb* is still self-evidently correct. Anne and I believed and still believe that the capacity of Earth to produce ample food and provide a reasonably healthy environment for people is finite. Worse yet, it is declining in the face of ever-expanding demand and, increasingly, assaults on the environment wrought by greenhouse gas emissions, habitat loss, release of huge amounts of plastic wastes and toxic chemicals, and other results of the activities of an expanding human population.

One of Anne's and my personal strategies has, as I've indicated, always been to have our work reviewed carefully by other scientists, and *The Population Bomb* was no exception. As I pointed out, it was reviewed prepublication by a series of scientists, including some who became top leaders in the scientific enterprise. That is one reason that long ago the fundamental message of *The Population Bomb* moved from a somewhat unorthodox view to a nearly consensus view of the scientific community. More and more scholars have realized that as our population, consumption, and technological skills expand, the probability of catastrophic change looms steadily larger. Already in 1992, fifty-eight of the world's academies of science stated, "Continued population growth poses a great risk to humanity."[29] In the same year, seventeen hundred independent scientists, including more than half of the Nobel laureates in science, produced the "World Scientists' Warning to Humanity" saying essentially the same thing.[30] In a second endorsing statement by a much larger group in 2017, more than fifteen thousand scientists basically endorsed the fundamental positions Anne and I and many other colleagues have taken—that population growth is one element that has placed humanity on "a collision course with the natural world."[31]

THIRTEEN

Combatting the Forces of the Endarkenment

As I've aged, I've found myself increasingly diverted from my great interest in human achievements in science to increasing distress at certain features of modern human culture that I believe threaten us all, and by all I mean the natural world, not just ourselves. I, of course, have lived in an amazing time for a scientist. When I was first fooling around with butterflies, scientists knew nothing about DNA. We thought humanity's prehistory was a pretty straight line from a chimplike ancestor, through Australopithecus, to *Homo erectus*, to Neanderthals and *Homo sapiens*. Only later did scientists uncover the great diversity of our ancestors and the evolutionary relatives with which they interacted. Doctors had just begun using catheters to diagnose problems in beating hearts, electron microscopes had just been developed, nuclear power and nuclear proliferation were still in the future, computers did not then control much of human activity as they do now, no artificial satellites were circling Earth, and no human being had ever ventured above the atmosphere. That we now know so much more about how organisms function and evolve and how ecological systems work than was known when I caught that *Euphydryas phaeton* in Bethesda at the age of fifteen I find mind-boggling. At a more plebeian level, when I started at Stanford in 1959 we had no Xerox machines, no smartphones, no desktop computers, and, of course, no word processing and no email.

On the cultural front, as noted earlier, I might have been able to write a similar screed of social and political accomplishment for America if I were writing this in, say, 1980, before the Reagan presidency set us on the *facilis descensus Averno.* In 1980 the situation of African Americans compared to twenty-five years earlier had improved greatly—lynchings had died out in the South, no facilities in Lawrence, Kansas, were still segregated, and increasing numbers of people were realizing that those with darker skins could be top scholars and excellent politicians. Women were well on their way to penetrating niches once reserved for men, and I had taken much of my instrument training from a female pilot. People in religious minorities were infrequently at risk of violence. Further, official notice of and action on environmental problems was, if inadequate, in existence and cheering, bolstered by some landmark legislation. Much of that was reversed by Reagan, and since Reagan, socioculturally it's been at best a roller-coaster of destruction of environmental safeguards and social safety nets followed by the reinstitution of these safeguards, greater acknowledgment of the threat of fossil fuel–induced climate change, and attempts to increase access to affordable medical care and the like. Nevertheless, inequality has continued to grow, and there has been a decline generally in American indirect democracy, epitomized by the nearly successful Trump putsch of January 6, 2021, a set of events virtually inconceivable a decade or more before. To cope with the crises of biodiversity loss, climate change, overpopulation, and threats to the provision of life's essentials, far more is needed than scientific reports that are too often largely ignored. To rescue the human enterprise in the long run requires strong action in the short run directed toward saving biodiversity and bringing the human enterprise within sustainable limits.

There are, of course, concerned people the world over actively attempting to deal with such elements of the human predicament, including many among the religious. My admiration for the bravery of Pope Francis in particular greatly increased after I was invited in 2016 to speak at a meeting on species extinction hosted jointly by the Pontifical Academy of Science and the Pontifical Academy of Social Sciences. I was somewhat apprehensive at the thought of taking my invited place at their workshop at the end of February 2017. Through right-wing Catholic websites that were loaded with outrage and lies in response to news of my invitation and that of John Bongaarts from the Population Council, more than ten thousand people had signed petitions to get me (or us) excluded from the meeting.[1]

My apprehension was unnecessary. The view of the academies, backed by the Vatican, was that all voices should be heard. The workshop, arranged by my old friends and colleagues Peter Raven and Partha Dasgupta, was one of the most productive and informative I have ever attended. It was an assembly of scientific stars, and everyone was treated with dignity, respect, and fine hospitality. The presidents of the two academies, Werner Arber and Margaret Archer, and their chancellor, Monsignor Marcelo Sánchez Sorondo, were open and friendly. The papers that were delivered at the meeting, now available as a commercially published book, were generally excellent, as was most of the discussion.[2] Everyone emphasized both the grave danger extinctions pose to human life-support systems and the ethical duties of humanity to preserve "the creation"—the only life-forms we know of in the universe. There was essentially complete agreement among participants that the drivers of the now under way sixth mass extinction were human overpopulation, overconsumption by the rich, and extreme inequity.

The only issue that was carefully avoided was contraception. Everyone there, like virtually everyone in the world, wanted abortion to be extremely rare. Since it was not in our charge, there was no point in having a discussion of methods of birth control, but everyone was aware of the view, which I share with all of my colleagues (including many Catholics), that contraception should be available to all, as a major tool in both the needed reduction in birthrates and avoidance of abortion.

All in all, it was an encouraging experience. The Catholic Church is the only religious organization with scholarly academies charged with providing unbiased information. As a result, for example, it has helped Pope Francis to become a leader in the battle against climate denial with his encyclical on ecology, *Laudato Si'*, and the church accepted the overwhelming evidence for evolution almost a century ago. In a civilization facing existential risks, the church should be praised and supported for this attitude toward science. I only wish that all religious people (indeed all people) did so—the world would be a much safer and happier place.

The agreement in the Vatican academies was especially pleasing given Anne's and my long-standing deep concern about the extinction problem. The first book we published on the demise of species, *Extinction*, appeared in 1981, soon after the appearance of Norman Myers's pioneering work *The Sinking Ark* (1979). One of the questions I have been repeatedly asked when speaking to the public about extinctions is, "What difference does it make if some bird or butterfly goes extinct?" Anne and I developed an answer, first published in *Extinction:* Suppose you are boarding an airliner and notice a mechanic popping rivets out of the wing. "What are you doing?" you ask. "I'm removing rivets so the airline can sell them. Don't worry—there's plenty of redundancy, and it lets Idiot-Air have cheaper fares." If you are sane, you of course change airlines. You never know when metal fatigue or severe turbulence might overwhelm the redundancy and make the wing fail and ruin the passengers' entire day. There is also redundancy in ecosystems, and removal of a single species may not cause any discernable change. Then again, it might cause a catastrophic loss of desired functions. For instance, the extinction of the passenger pigeon led to ecosystem changes that are thought to be a major reason for the nasty plague of Lyme disease in the United States many years later. The rivet-popper metaphor emphasizes a common biological principle: small, seemingly inconsequential destructive acts piled up one after another can eventually lead to disaster. Think smoking cigarettes over decades and then dying of lung cancer after months of agony.

The great interest in the findings of science in the Vatican under Pope Francis was heartening. But my concern over the human predicament has nevertheless deepened in recent years by what I worry are social and political symptoms of a coming collapse, which you may remember Jared Diamond described as "a loss of socio-political-economic complexity usually accompanied by a dramatic decline in population size."[3] On its face, that might sound like a white nationalist dream: back to the simple, rural life, without all those big population centers around, filled with godless democrats and other people of the wrong colors and religious beliefs. But a little thought about migration patterns, for example, or potential competition under conditions of breakdown for basic food and other necessities of life, shows that it more likely would be a nightmare. The symptoms of a potential coming collapse include the extreme fractionation of information channels brought on by the proliferation of social media and other sites that make it easier for groups to have just their own views reinforced, in turn making needed cooperative action with others of a different persuasion more difficult. The symptoms also include years of seemingly unwavering political support for ultraconservative politicians among evangelical Christians (largely, I suspect, because of the right's war on women), white supremacists, conspiracy theorists, and some other destructive segments of the American population. Indicative, too, of the growing potential for breakdown is the rise in virulent assaults on aspects of science that interface with social dilemmas and increased attacks on evidence-based reasoning more generally.

The rejection of evidence-based policy positions by a substantial minority of the U.S. population is reflected in the active antivaccination and antimask movement that developed quickly during the first year of the Covid-19 pandemic, the kind of pandemic against which public health scientists had long warned and which Anne and I warned against in *The Population Bomb* and subsequent speeches and publications. I can't recall a major scientific issue where the recommendations of action coming from the public health as well as the knowledgeable scientific communities were more uniform, more directly consequential to individuals and their loved ones, more amenable to individual action, and more widely ignored. Even in some instances sensible actions undertaken (such as mandating vaccinations and mask-wearing indoors) were actively thwarted by, variously, the federal government, some state governments, and segments of the public. That cost hundreds of thousands of lives, and subsequent lying and quackery on the issue of immunization, face masks, and social distancing killed many more.

The politicization of these issues of public health and basic social responsibility indicates some serious shortcomings of the American educational system, including lack of adequate discussions of key aspects of governance and provision of the analytical tools students need to recognize and dismiss media disinformation. Yes, as many claim, requiring people to wear masks restricts their freedom. But so does forcing them to drive on the right and to not shoot neighbors who play loud music—surrenders of liberty that are prices of enjoying the benefits of an organized society. And the failure of many educational systems globally to inform their populations adequately about the existential threats we all face and the reasons people organize politically makes it seem likely that superstition may continue to undermine many efforts based on scientific understanding for years to come.

Aside from the pandemic, the next most obvious area in which science has been blatantly disregarded, and for a much longer period, has been the widespread denial of the threat of human-caused climate disruption, But disregard has been only the leading edge of the antiscience movement in this realm.[4] Recent Republican administrations have gone out of their way to promote policies, such as reversing automobile efficiency standards and leaving the Paris Climate Accords, whose overall effect is to make future climate-caused death and destruction worse and develop more rapidly than it would have otherwise. Rising temperatures and increased extreme weather events make it increasingly hard to deny climate disruption outright, prompting strategies to minimize the problem, claim that technological fixes are just around the corner, or advocate a go-slow approach and overestimate the costs of mitigation, ignoring that the costs of failure will be near infinite.

The general assault on science among some segments of the American population has extended far beyond climate disruption and the Covid-19 pandemic to denying the effects of toxics, to general antivaccine propaganda, and to overconcern about genetically modified foods (mixed with too little concern about industrial farming and food overprocessing), to say nothing of those peddling pseudoscientific claims of products to treat short-term memory loss or cure-alls for many other ailments. Above all, the repeated warnings of the scientific community on the dangers of our population overshoot rarely hit even the back pages of today's newspapers. Science, of course, is by definition evidence-based. Its adversarial structure, where practitioners are encouraged to check the findings of their colleagues and where articles are typically subject to peer review before publication, is part of the reason that airplanes fly, cell phones work, and vaccines and kidney transplants save lives. Humanity will not enjoy such benefits for long if faith-based assaults on reality continue seriously to degrade public attitudes toward scientific findings—or, worse yet, to reduce support for the scientific enterprise because its findings on overpopulation, pandemics, climate disruption, biodiversity loss, and other threats are distasteful to some. Those findings, in fact, may be the most crucial in the history of civilization for informing effective remedial action. It's important for scientists to recognize that it is not enough in this day and age simply to do research and publish findings; when they are pertinent to the human predicament, one has to take an active role in bringing those findings to the public and indicating their implications. In this respect, researchers should follow the magnificent lead of Rachel Carson and *Silent Spring* in bringing the toxification problems to public attention and motivating more research, research that has subsequently uncovered critical factors such as hormone mimicry. It is crucial to learn broadly what scientists can show, even if they don't necessarily agree exactly with what other scientists think should be done. Scientists need to pay more attention to the "ought" part of the is/ought dichotomy while being clear about which half they are dealing with in any specific case.

In corporate-sponsored media the views of conservative and middle-of-the-road commentators predominate, and quite strict rules prevail on what the boundaries should be of acceptable discourse. A truly progressive viewpoint, such as that of Noam Chomsky, is simply placed outside the bounds of discussion in American mainstream media. Chomsky, whom I greatly admire, has focused on the international behavior of the U.S. empire and as such has been viewed as a threat to much of the American power structure. More recently he has also chimed in on the importance of working to forestall further future climate disruption. The role the powers-that-be play in what Anne and I could write and say with much hope of a substantial audience has always been near the top of our minds. I got to appear on *The Tonight Show* with Johnny Carson even though some NBC bigwigs and sponsors hated it, as I noted in chapter 8, because John agreed with me, and his financial influence in Hollywood overrode their opposition.

To me, the greatest immediate question facing humanity is whether a governance system can quickly be devised that will be humane, reasonably democratic, evidence-based, and sustainable. A foundational requirement for the establishment and maintenance of such a society is that the government and the governed share a basic body of agreed-upon information and ethical norms such as criticizing views and not persons, not deliberately cherry-picking data, and pointing out when your views are heterodox (and why).

How might it be possible to reconstitute society with more broadly shared reasonably reliable information and modern ethical norms—one in which equity is a major goal? That's going to require a huge effort in a society in which misinformation and ignorance of existential threats are rampant. It's a tough but urgent question to answer, deserves wide discussion, and perhaps evangelism for a new pseudoreligion without doctrinal supernaturalism—perhaps something along the lines of Unitarian Universalism, to satisfy the apparent human needs for spiritual comfort and social interaction.[5] At the very least, people could be helped to understand the reason gods were invented by primates that had evolved genetically coded cause-and-effect recognition programs, as Albert Michotte demonstrated more than a half century ago.[6] They were nearly forced to find an instrumental cause for mysterious effects like thunder, sunrise, and natural death. On this basic physiological fact our ancestors evolved the vast and diverse arrays of supernatural entities and ideas that afflict and comfort human beings today.

In a world where, at the moment, profoundly stupid and/or self-aggrandizing wielders of power control and kill vast numbers directly or indirectly through their policies, various forms of wider participation in governance clearly ought to be tried, in my view. It may, however, be that state power and a manufactured consensus are necessary now for survival; much more is at stake today than there was in the late eighteenth century when the Founders were contemplating modes of governance. But of course it all depends on who holds state power and in the name of what a consensus is manufactured. A despot who is benevolent may be appealing in the abstract, but what happens if you end up with rulers, all too common in the twenty-first century, who hold state power and try to manufacture consent but are heading in directions that are designed mainly to enhance their own positions and that exacerbate a rush toward collapse?

Noam Chomsky has, from my viewpoint, surely been right in arguing that discussions of how to meet the existential threats we face, and address flagrant abuses of power and equity, should take place openly within the bounds of socially acceptable discourse. That now can happen on a broad scale only if the corporate elites who exercise much control over the government, the universities, and the media decide that widening the bounds of discourse is in their interest. That occurrence seems unlikely from today's perspective, since members of these elites are trained in schools like Stanford. There, the basic dominant cultural assumptions of the corporate elite rule, including embrace of growthmania and a finance-centric world view. Business schools represent the essence of this problem, as the department of management, University of Bristol professor Martin Parker's devastating critique *Shut Down the Business School* applies pretty much to the entire university system. Universities are, in Parker's words, "too busy oiling the wheels to worry about where the engine is going." According to Parker, business schools "are places that teach people how to get money out of the pockets of ordinary people and keep it for themselves." To the degree students are taught business ethics, the public cost of corporate externalities, distributional equity, and such at all, it tends to be as an afterthought.[7]

The roles business schools in particular and universities in general, as currently constituted, play in failing to challenge the momentum toward destruction of global society are seldom touched on. Symptomatic is the current paucity of public intellectuals among university presidents and the relative absence of their voices on such issues as their institution's refusal to divest from fossil fuel stocks and their failure to institute massive revision of their curricula and departmental structure to meet the dramatic new challenges civilization faces. University administrators and faculty rarely include existential threats in their everyone-should-know curricula or protest government bungling of responses to events such as (in Australia) the bushfires of 2019 or (in America) the coronavirus pandemic of 2020–22. University administrators seldom even call attention to the erosion of belief in the value of scientific evidence and its replacement by crackpot ideologies.[8]

Universities will, as in the past and as in other countries than the United States, become centers for change only when many young faculty and students demand it. That seems increasingly likely as it begins to dawn on the young what a dismal prospect we are passing on to them and they face the desperate need for leadership in planning rapidly for a reboot of contemporary civilization.

Even more telling has been the frequent discussion in the media and elsewhere of a return to normal after Covid-19, indicative of the failure of the educational system—as well as governing institutions and the media itself—to point out that what people hoped to return to was, from a historical perspective, in no sense normal. Ours has been an extremely abnormal period, roughly only one-thousandth of human history, based on a one-time energy bonanza from fossil fuels.[9] In that tiny three-hundred-year stretch in its roughly three-hundred-thousand-year history, modern *Homo sapiens* expanded some fifteenfold in numbers, fouled the air so that it often became lethal to breathe, began to disrupt greatly the climate on whose stability the human food supply rested, wiped out most of the other large animals and replaced them with domestics, depleted much of our planet's soils and underground freshwater stores, spread novel poisons everywhere, managed to kill in a single war more than five times the number of people that existed on the planet when our species invented agriculture, and developed and used weapons with the potential to kill everyone.

Pointing out a need for more and better education is, of course, what one would expect from a lifelong compulsive learner and long-term teacher like me.[10] Throughout my adult life it has been crystal clear that to establish a sustainable sociocultural foundation for the human enterprise and the viability of the biosphere, growth of both the physical economy and the human population need to be halted and reversed, carefully and equitably. In recent decades the necessity of population shrinkage and resource redistribution has become more evident than ever. With the existential environmental crisis building and the serious possibility of nuclear extermination persisting, these moves would clearly be advantageous for the rich in the long term as well as the poor immediately. But in my view, the current higher education system is by and large designed to reinforce the dominant ideology, avoid criticism (or even discussion) of the power structure, and turn out obedient "leaders" for the "normal" growth machine. The proof of the pudding is the failure of faculty to get organized and push administrations to focus curricula much more strongly on existential threats. Fear of losing grant support from the fossil fuel industry, or of displeasing other donors and politicians, who often are those running civilization over a cliff, guides many academics at Stanford and elsewhere. Gradual changes in curricula seem less dangerous financially than the kind of rapid and dramatic change that might help alter humanity's course for the better.

Many—but not all—scientists have yet to adjust their activities to match the urgency of the environmental and sociopolitical crises upon us. While watching the reaction to the Covid-19 pandemic, I was struck by a failure of many scientists, who obviously knew better, to explain to the public the seriousness of the issue and its connections to other existential threats like overpopulation, biodiversity loss, and climate disruption. A group of colleagues and I were increasingly impressed with what well-known climate scientist James Hansen called the problem of scientists being "dangerously reticent" by not fully expressing their level of concern for the fate humanity is facing.[11] One result was publishing the first of what may prove to be a series of papers (see chapter 11) discussing the likelihood of a "ghastly future" if dramatic changes are not made.[12]

Part of the problem lies again with universities and the siloed nature of scientists' education. An instance especially close to me involves my home institution. It gives me a (possibly irrational) feeling of personal failure. Stanford University, in my view, is one of the best universities in the world despite manifest flaws that characterize many large institutions. Like most other first-line universities, it's plagued by persistence of an antique structure based on the ideas of Aristotle and saddled with a series of old-time "disciplines" or "subjects" that for convenience fracture the continua of human knowledge. Yes, there increasingly are interdisciplinary programs, but as I've mentioned, the main problem is with the disciplines themselves. No existential problem can today be solved within the boundaries of a single university department, yet universities cling to departmental structures.

Leave it to the flexible Finns to recognize the serious consequences of the rigid "learn your subjects" approach. In Finland they are trying a new system of teaching: "In Phenomenon Based Learning (PhenoBL) and teaching, holistic real-world phenomena provide the starting point for learning. The phenomena are studied as complete entities, in their real context, and the information and skills related to them are studied by crossing the boundaries between subjects."[13] Could Stanford, Harvard, Yale, Princeton, the University of California, and the others ever catch up with Finland's middle schools?

Historians delight in chronicling the crumbling and disappearance of past civilizations from the Maya and Aztecs to the Greeks and Romans. What, if anything, suggests that today's situation is different from that of those collapsing civilizations in the past? First, the civilization faced with collapse is, for the first time, global. In addition, many stresses on today's civilization are building at once, and they involve highly developed and nearly ubiquitous modern technologies, including fossil fuel–powered energy mobilization, artificial intelligence, computerization, synthetic chemicals, electric grids, and nuclear and biological weapons. They have created novel risks (of rapid climate disruption and/or nuclear winter and their attendant effects on the world's food production and transport) unknown in past catastrophes. Unlike previous civilizations that have disappeared, today's civilizations possess the means of rapid self-destruction, and each is subject to much the same external existential threats as one another. Second, humanity is now tied together by global trade, instant communications (which can generate global panics), rapid transport of people and pathogens, and the ability of countries to alter the environments of distant nations—all in addition to common vulnerabilities of civilizations. Mayan civilization could collapse and the Egyptians didn't even know it. If the Indians and Pakistanis go to war using nuclear weapons, other societies around the world would be threatened with collapse themselves from a combination of the environmental and sociopolitical impacts. Third, global trade has left many fewer communities self-sufficient if cut off from interaction with other communities.[14] So, for the first time it could be a global society that is collapsing, unevenly, in fits and starts, but with few if any people likely to be left relatively untouched.

A fourth major difference of the present compared to past collapses is the rate of change. Governments are not accustomed to dealing with major problems on time scales of decades or less; the more than two centuries of struggle over race in the nominally democratic United States is illustrative. There is no question that in less than a decade many things *could* be done, for example, to ameliorate the impact of climate disruption on the food system, including dietary changes, reduction of waste, making distribution more equitable, improving yield forecasts, and so on.[15] And, of course, nations could move away from fossil fuels on an emergency basis. But the central question is: *Will* governments get their acts together themselves—or at least be forced to by popular movements—in time?

I am convinced that a major task of progressive members of society, in addition to addressing directly issues raised above, is to persuade governments (especially local and regional ones) to start preparing for the various forms a collapse might take, planning for how postcollapse societies in their area might function, what the goals should be for a postcollapse life-style, socioeconomic organization, and governance. They should, in my view, be addressing questions such as the following in San Francisco: How will San Francisco operate when paper currency is inadequate to handle financial dealings and there is no internet because electric current is available only two hours a day and food flows to the city are cut by 50 percent? How can the need for policing be reduced and the residual need supplied safely and equitably? What kind of economic relations should be developed in place of the old, so that necessary exchanges can continue?

Broad examination of such questions might, if undertaken almost immediately, lead to steps that would at least somewhat ameliorate the impact and consequences of any kind of collapse short of that caused by a nuclear war. It also might lead to contemplation of how to design a reset that would forestall or at least not lead inevitably to another growth-collapse cycle. It might also make the issues real enough that people would redouble efforts to avoid a collapse in the first place. After all, why shouldn't it become a movement right now? I agree, for example, with Joel Bakan's view of corporations as psychopathic engines of social and environmental destruction.[16] This includes the heavily greenwashed "new corporations" that largely are the same old rapacious wolves in sheep's clothing.[17] One feature of a reset might be to do at the start the sort of review of the U.S. governance system the Tugwell committee at the Santa Barbara center abandoned. If the nation miraculously changes enough for the results of a careful review to be implemented, one step might be to outlaw the creation of for-profit corporations with limited liability as a way of increasing the social responsibility of individuals and avoiding heedless growthmania. As a start toward preparing for a reset, how to redesign civilization to avert or at least ameliorate renewed collapses should be a major topic not only in university curricula but also in the media and in public forums. Above all, if we are to have a viable, even brighter future, civil society must get beyond its present tendency simply to rearrange the deck chairs on the *Lusitania.*

Many of our problems seem traceable to *Homo sapiens* being a small-group animal, most comfortable in collections of under 150 people or so, the so-called Dunbar's number. It was proposed by anthropologist Robin Dunbar based on studies of primate brain size and group size. That's roughly the maximum size of most hunter-gatherer groups, as it is today of typical groups of colleagues, lengths of Christmas card lists, and so on.[18] We're now a species trying to get "comfortable" in groups of thousands, millions, or in some peoples' minds, billions. And we're clearly often doing a lousy job of it. Religion is one way we've found to develop in-group versus out-group distinctions that can make our perceived groups smaller, as are race, gender, patriotism, political parties, soccer team support, corporate loyalties, fraternities, sororities, and on and on. Many of these groups go far beyond Dunbar's number and could be a rich research field for social scientists interested in the causes, connections, and consequences of group-size variation. Almost all of these entities carry the same seeds of believing in myths, failing to have as much as possible an evidence-based world view, and promoting intergroup dissension and even violence.

So as a species, we apparently evolved genetically and culturally to live in groups of 50 to 150 people.[19] That means that for most of modern *Homo sapiens*'s hundreds of thousands of years of history we associated mostly with close relatives with the same general appearance, same language, same genes, same environment, and same culture. Such limitations still show up in our societies.[20] No doubt this is a major reason we have both a fascination with diversity (is it novelty?) and a problem with diversity (the others?). Sadly, we don't have wide discussions of topics like "Is there an optimal level of diversity for a given society?" or "Considering the uneven global distribution of resources, and the virtual absence of serious efforts to reduce global inequities, are borders ethical?" It is, of course, still not clear whether *any sustainable* social system can be devised for a small-group animal like *Homo sapiens*, struggling to live in groups of millions and even billions.

In summary, the biggest question is: How to get from where we are to where we want to go? That means the first task is to get a substantial portion of society to understand humanity's current situation and to recognize the growing barriers we've created to our own sustainability. Then, if we can agree we want to create a peaceful and equitable future world where everyone has a reasonable level of well-being, we need to change the direction of our efforts, discourse, and institutions to make determining how best to respond to the human predicament society's collective primary goal. This is obviously an extremely daunting challenge, demanding revision of many of the most basic assumptions of today's maladaptive cultures.[21] Once that's generally agreed upon, if it can be, the next goal is even tougher—making the changes. But it has long seemed to me that the very least we should do is try. Nothing is more impractical for humanity than *not* developing a massive and clever response and instead plunging on to experience a ghastly future.

FOURTEEN

The End of *Life*

As happens to all who live to old age, long-established patterns must be changed and finitude finally faced. Three huge "end of life" changes have greatly altered Anne's and my trajectories. I can take credit for one because I'd been smart enough to marry Anne, and she talked me into the change. That was moving, when I was seventy-four, into a retirement complex. We took up residence in an apartment in the Vi at Palo Alto, which I often have referred to as the Drool Farm (in honor of Stanford being colloquially known as the Farm, so nicknamed because the land had originally been Senator Leland Stanford's farm). More appropriate would have been to name it Casa de Baba (House of Drool), since so many non-Hispanic Californians love to apply wherever possible the language of those with whom they prefer not to socialize. I hated to admit I was aging, but because we had superstressed our family economy by purchasing a house in 1962 soon after we arrived in the area, the insane rise in housing prices over forty-two years made it financially possible to sell the house and move into the Vi. As we had seen with older friends, in the San Francisco Bay Area it is difficult to get help in the home if you need it as your body deserts you. If you can afford it—and unfortunately, not many can—contracting with a Vi-like establishment that can supply increasing levels of aid is, we believe, a good idea and often best done before significant decline sets in.

Anne was right; the Vi is a great place to live, free of the pains of maintaining a house, free of security worries, and, best of all from my viewpoint, with a fine swimming pool. As an additional advantage, the other inmates include many well-educated, interesting people, some of whom have become good friends. Although I'm an inveterate complainer, the Vi staff handled the pandemic problems highly competently from our perspective.

The second huge change was the end of my long career of doing physically adventurous fieldwork. The end came abruptly in a flurry of rank stupidity while chasing rare birds in Hawaii in early 2016 when I was eighty-three. Accompanied by Kirk Smith and Joan Diamond, we drove up Mount Haleakala to meet Laura Berthold of the Maui Forest Bird Recovery Project. She had agreed to take us down the trail from Hosmer Grove to one of the few remaining patches of native forest where we might see the Maui parrotbill or another endangered bird, the crested honeycreeper. Anne wisely decided to give it a miss, but at 8:00 a.m., Kirk, Joan, and I joined Laura and one of her colleagues and started down the two-mile trail that drops five hundred feet to the forest site.

At first the trail was easy, but eventually it became steep, narrow, often muddy, and root-strewn. I was being *very* careful. As we started down the last drop, with my hiking poles solidly placed and my feet on what appeared solid ground, suddenly my feet went out from under me. I crashed down, wrenching my shoulders trying to keep myself upright on the poles. I got a nasty, agonizing injury of my left rotator cuff and hurt the right one as well. My left arm was useless. We discussed helicoptering me out, but it was clear that would mean winching me up at a hover, since there was no opening on the trail where it would be safe to land a helicopter. Finally, with Kirk just behind and Joan in front of me, ready to try to catch me if I fell again, I inched my way back up in a couple of hours. Better friends are impossible to find. It's more than five years later as I write this, and I'm still suffering occasional nasty pain and weakness in my left shoulder.

The parrotbill and other spectacularly interesting Hawaiian birds are still racing me to extinction, however. Climate disruption is making it easier for introduced mosquitoes to carry lethal avian malaria into the birds' high altitude habitats. Plans are being made to translocate some of the roughly 150 surviving parrotbills to once-occupied habitat patches, but the principal hope of saving the Maui population is in a new technique of genetic control

I am in front of our cabin at 9,600 feet, at the Rocky Mountain Biological Laboratory in the West Elk Mountains of Colorado. Author photo.

that has proven very effective against mosquitoes in a few other situations. Basically it involves inserting genes that lead to sterility and will spread in populations because they are overrepresented in the formation of eggs or sperm.

A bigger blow for me than learning by demonstration that I was no longer a young Turk was the third big change. It came at RMBL in July 2017. The previous summer Anne had had sufficient trouble breathing at 9,600 feet elevation that she had begun using an oxygen concentrator at night. In the summer of 2017, though, she needed it for substantial times during the day as well when we were there. RMBL is not a place to be if you can't do a little hiking, so we decided it was time to give up the cabin after fifty-six years. We soon had confirmation of our decision. Although I had made the climb to a favorite site called the "first crossing" (of Copper Creek) some two miles from the cabin and about four hundred feet higher, it had taken me three hours for a round trip that only a few years earlier had taken only an hour and twenty minutes. Aging is not linear. My usual hiking companions, John and Mel Harte, he a youth of seventy-eight and she even younger, stuck with me, but I was clearly a drag. I hated the thought of losing their company on these excursions—Mel knew the flowers like the back of her hand, and John, a relapsed particle physicist, taught me a lot, and we collaborated on exploring many issues, especially the global problems of undernutrition and malnutrition. Their brilliant daughter Julia worked with Anne and me for a week when she was thirteen to fix a totally bungled computer index for *Human Natures* (sample original entry: "Why, the question of"). Julia is now a star investigative journalist for Reuters.

Then on July 3, 2017, just below Judd Falls, about ten minutes into our traditional hike, I had a TIA (transient ischemic attack). I grabbed hold of John's hand and tried to tell him what was happening; my mind was clear, but it was perhaps twenty to thirty seconds before I could make the words, "I just had a TIA," come out. It scared the shit out of me. A colleague, Erica Newman, was hiking with us, and she and I did the standard symmetry checks; all were negative and I had no headache. Just the brief awful episode of "expressive aphasia"—the inability to turn my thoughts into words. It took about twenty minutes for my friends to help me back to the Harte cabin. By then I was essentially normal, I felt, but terrified. Mel drove me to the Gunnison hospital an hour away, Anne followed, and I was thoroughly checked out by a highly competent and considerate staff. Old age, as Bette Davis said, "ain't no place for sissies."

So our days at RMBL were over, which gives me a well-earned but mild situational depression. Have I mentioned how beautiful it is there? And how many old RMBL friends we miss?

Among the population of bright, well-educated seniors at the Drool Farm, some have become good friends, including molecular biologist Lucy Shapiro and her physicist (and talented artist) husband Harley McAdam.[1] Proof of the concept: Ken and Selma Arrow were also inmates. During the pandemic Lucy and Harley, Anne and I, neurobiologist Carla Shatz, and immunologist Pat Jones became Zoom mates, and discussions with them were enormously helpful in understanding issues in the pandemic. In the fall of 2020 I watched Pat's Zoom lectures in her graduate immunology course and remained as convinced of her brilliance as I had been in 1978 when I helped to hire her as the first female faculty member on campus in the Stanford biology department.

One of the pleasures of my life has always been reading, another wonderful way to expand one's experiences, and that pastime becoming ancient hasn't changed. I read all the time, often technical tomes or histories, especially histories about the two World Wars (which I, following many historians, have long viewed as two acts of the same horrible play). I think one learns a lot about human behavior when people are under stress. In addition to reading about it voraciously, Anne and I often arranged research travel to include visits to battlefields—the Wilderness, Rorke's Drift, Verdun, Belleau Wood, Pearl Harbor, Singapore, Wewak, Guadalcanal, Lae, and others. Once we planned a trip with Loy Bilderback to France explicitly to pursue historic battle sites. One of the most emotional was Verdun, the site in 1916 of the longest battle of World War I, one that cost a combination of over seven hundred thousand French and German lives. Shell holes and battered forts can still be seen, and one can have the stunning experience of looking through a window at an ossuary holding the bones of more than a hundred thousand soldiers.

After Verdun we moved on to Normandy. My biggest surprise of that trip came as we drove toward a war-famous Normandy village. I saw what I thought was a piece of white plastic trash caught on a church steeple. Trash it was not, and recalling my reading about D-Day I quickly made the connection. The night before American troops landed on Omaha Beach, Private John Steele and his fellow paratroopers of the U.S. 82nd Airborne Division jumped into the area behind the beach. Steele's parachute hung up on the steeple of the church in Sainte-Mère-Église, the first village to be liberated. Steele survived, and the village has turned the site into a tourist attraction, with the "trash" on the steeple being a mock parachute from which a dummy of Steele dangled. Depictions of paratroops occupied the stained glass of

In the 1990s, half a century after World War II, the horrors of D-Day are not obvious in this French tourist attraction I photographed.

the church windows, souvenir stands surrounded the area, and even road signs testified to the commercialization of slaughter.

I also read war novels and other novels that transport me to other places and times, as well as a lot of page turners (mostly crime) and, of course, a wide range of nonfiction. I still vividly recall how, more than half a century ago, reading Erich Maria Remarque's *All Quiet on the Western Front* altered my view of war. In the excellent original 1930 film version, the hero, named Paul, was a butterfly collector who was killed by a sniper as he reached to catch a lycaenid with his hand. For some reason that has stuck with me. Mary Doria Russell's *Epitaph* introduced me to life in the Old West, and my favorite novel of all time, Michael Shaara's *Killer Angels*, evoked pathos over the careers of Civil War officers. Wilbur Smith's *The Burning Shore* gave me a feel for the life of San Bushmen, as Katherine Boo's *Behind the Beautiful Forevers* did for slum life in modern India. Recently I was reading our friend

Dummy representing U.S. 82nd Airborne trooper hung up on the steeple of the church in Sainte-Mère-Église. Author photo.

Bob Carr's *Diary of a Foreign Minister* and discovered that he also was a fan of novelist Alan Furst, whose gripping novels gave me a greater feel for the run-up to World War II than any history text ever did.

Reading nonfiction books that give detail on past events or unfamiliar locales and circumstances seems to give me a deeper understanding of things I was familiar with as well. Reading Robert Caro's classic *Power Broker: Robert Moses and the Fall of New York*, for example, gave me even more insight into how the world works. Reading Ayaan Ali's *Infidel* gave me a new depth of appreciation of some key ethical issues in gender equity, especially those of male responsibilities when large numbers of women are horribly abused on religious grounds—and are frequently brainwashed to think that it is acceptable. But when it comes to equity issues I can't remember anything that struck me so hard as Jennifer Eberhardt's extraordinary book *Biased: Uncovering the Hidden Prejudice That Shapes What We See, Think, and Do.* After a lifetime of wrestling with issues of racial prejudice and sexism, it led me once again into an examination of my own biases (not always a pleasant task). It reinforced what I've learned, in part through my friendship with Lee Ross, the enormous value (at least to me) of social psychologists. Finally, philosophers have often contributed to my thinking, even though some of their musings have left me cold. A recent outstanding exception was Susan Neiman's *Learning from the Germans*—which pretty much changed my mind about the wisdom of reparations for our country's reign of terror on Blacks and Native Americans.

One of my greatest regrets at the prospect of dying is that I'll never get through all the books stacked by my bed or on my iPad and iPhone (Audible) or finish watching future great television series like those I have such as *A Place to Call Home* or *A French Village.* Caring for pseudokin is a powerful human attribute—attested to by the great popularity of soap operas. That may hint at a source of hope for a small-group animal, since constant exposure visually or in print to strangers can convert them to in-group members. And, of course, a love of books and videos and, through them, caring for pseudokin, has been a psychological life-saver during Covid-19 lockdowns.

As others of our gang have realized that, with the extinction crisis, increasing climate disruption, and other existential threats looming, civilization as anything like we've known it may well collapse, some have asked why I don't give up. The biophysical signs, abundantly documented in the scientific literature, were so clear that friends wanted to know why I was wasting my time with the struggle to improve the human future. My standard answer, largely true, was that I cared enough for my grandkids and the children and grandchildren of friends, and even the billions of innocent people who will suffer and miss so many joys that, as Jim Brown and I agreed, even if the chance of significant positive change were only 1 percent, it was worth trying to effect it. But to be honest, I'm sure I had (have) an egotistical motive. It was well expressed in a joke line a friend sent me: "Sometimes I feel like giving up; then I remember I have a lot of mother——s to prove wrong." In any case, I've found that being a has-been is much more fun than being a wannabe.

People have also often asked how I manage to keep my spirits up when I spend so much time on downbeat topics. My standard public answer is, I drink good wine so as to keep my internal environment in good shape while the external environment goes down the drain. Another aspect of staying sane I mention is *not* to try to ignore your emotions. I found this easy any time Donald Trump or any of the legions of those like him who are bent on throwing our collective future under the bus appeared gibbering on the tube. I follow my emotions and instantly switch channels. Still another part of the answer is related to my lifelong interest in gender interactions: my life would be must less pleasurable if there were no way to maintain a sense of humor, especially about sex.

I don't think any of us are obliged to put 100 percent of our time into attempting to save civilization from itself. Anne and I are still writing books and papers on the human predicament, maintaining a mailing list to associates on related issues, meeting with colleagues when we can, struggling to raise funds to support the MAHB and participate in some of its projects, and otherwise following old habits to the extent that an ongoing pandemic and gathering decrepitude allow. But we only have one life to live, and I've been lucky enough to devote much of it to the pursuit of pleasurable activities. In addition to working with the MAHB, research, and writing, there's been walking (still try to put in two miles a day), more reading, dining, and wine drinking with friends when not locked down, and enjoying nature in all its facets, especially still learning what's going on with butterflies, fishes, and birds. Anne and I have been lucky to enjoy most of these into old age—fortunate indeed.

Involved as I became in global issues, I never lost my fascination with organisms, and especially with butterflies. I've mentioned that the paper I most enjoyed working on in my later years I owe to my science-artist colleague Darryl Wheye, one of my coauthors on *The Birders' Handbook*. Our paper on the possibility that butterfly wing patterns echoed the patterns of distasteful caterpillars raised some fascinating questions of evolution and could provide an interesting system for training citizen scientists—but I also just enjoyed the discovery. Like a discovery Larry Gilbert made decades ago about the feeding habits of *Heliconius*, it was something I should have spotted but totally missed. As I said earlier, I could start another butterfly collection tomorrow!

Despite some low moments, I can hardly begin to remember all the natural history sights my early interest in butterflies—and, to a lesser extent, in tropical fish and birds—has led me to enjoy. I've watched butterfly fishes jockeying for resting positions at dusk on Australia's Great Barrier Reefs; a nearly all-white male Truk monarch (a flycatcher) flicking its tail above me near the lagoon that was a graveyard of Japanese ships in World War II; a group of kagu, one of the world's rarest and most unusual birds, displaying in the Rivière Bleue tropical forest of New Caledonia; thousands of wildebeest madly swimming across the crocodile-infested Mara River in the Serengeti; schools of grunts mixed with goatfishes resting over the coral reefs of Saint Croix in the Caribbean; tinamous and giant hummingbirds abundant in the high Andes of Argentina; handsome diademed sandpiper-plovers breeding in a marsh formed by glacier runoff in a bowl at sixteen thousand feet surrounded by high peaks in Chile; a gigantic saltie (saltwater crocodile), its head more than a yard long, lounging on a riverbank in Kakadu National Park in the Northern Territory of Australia; that Ross's gull on Cornwallis Island in the high Arctic; elephants playing in a pond in the Okavango Delta of Botswana; and wading in penguin shit in Antarctica (the only butterfly-free continent).[2]

As an old man, I probably should say something about what has happened to my genes, if only briefly. As a young woman, Lisa acquired the best son-in-law in the world, Tim Daniel, who has since become a close friend and colleague. Lisa and Tim have been great professional help over the years as we've gotten more and more into economic issues. They both have doctorates in economics and met while being fingerprinted for their then-new jobs at the Federal Trade Commission (FTC) in 1984. Tim has spent his career as an antitrust and consumer protection economist. Lisa left the FTC in 1998 to stay home with her two girls. Then, in 2006, she discovered her true passion. She is now happy as a professional dog trainer. It turned out that associating with biologists for her entire life had given her some insight into animal behavior; she now constantly marvels at the many dog owners who either expect their dogs to behave like humans or, worse, like stuffed animals.

My unbiased view is that my granddaughters are all brilliant. Mara, Tim's daughter from his first marriage, is a theoretical physicist with a doctorate from Yale. At her job at Ball Aerospace, she developed antijamming devices for U.S. Navy airplanes. In her spare time, Mara got married and has produced four children. If it sounds like Mara hasn't taken my advice, that would be correct. Her mother took Judaism quite seriously, and Mara grew to be quite religious—eventually marrying an Orthodox chemist, Josh Baraban, and becoming Orthodox herself.

Jessica, Lisa's firstborn, completed her PhD as a social epidemiologist at Harvard and took a job at a consulting firm. As a graduate student she produced a series of first-authored papers, one of which included some complicated genetic issues. A senior professor coauthoring the paper said, "Boy, this is complex. Too bad we can't get Marc Feldman to look at it for us, he'd be perfect." Jess, who knew Marc as a longtime family friend (Marc early on had been my postdoc), said, "Actually, I think I can arrange that." And she got "Uncle Marc" to do it. In August of 2013, Jess married her long-standing boyfriend, Aaron Marden, now lead data analytics developer for Mathematica, Inc. They now have two beautiful, brilliant girls, Ada and Liv. That has the horrifying (to me) effect of making my daughter a grandmother!

Meanwhile, our youngest granddaughter, Melissa, is an economic consultant, until recently living in Los Angeles and now in Boston to get an advanced degree in data analytics at Boston University. From an early age, she was a gifted writer, so I sometimes think she is wasted on economics. She's also a wonderful traveling companion, and in one of their sensible acts, economists love paying her money for her advice.

The one prediction I can make with total confidence is that I'm going to die soon. Now that I am ninety, with heart disease, back pain, slowly failing eyesight and hearing, on blood thinner after two TIAs, my thoughts too frequently turn to death. Declining unto death is really boring, as your abilities and pleasures gradually desert you, and I'm scared witless of having a major stroke: "There's Ehrlich, the poor drooling old fool doesn't even recognize his own wife" is the sort of thing that haunts me. So the fears I have now are largely of losing my mind so fast I don't have time to take the pills, and the great sadness I feel at the prospect of leaving Anne, Lisa, and the rest of my family and friends. But as Weston La Barre put it in *The Human Animal*, "Only those who haven't lived, long for immortality."[3]

There's also the sadness of realizing I'll probably never know the fate of today's civilization—how it will react to the existential threats. And I'll never see the answer to big questions such as, "Is there life on the sure-to-be millions of Earthlike planets, and if yes, what's it like?" or that biggie I mentioned before: "Why is there anything at all?" or even knowing if that's a sensible question. I used to worry that I wouldn't get to do all the things I wanted to, but I've led a full life, done most of them, and have few regrets. I agree with La Barre: the thought of living forever has no appeal and being dead itself holds no fears, since I know exactly what that's like. I experienced it for at least fourteen billion years before I was born, and it didn't seem so bad—I had neither nightmares nor the need to stumble out of bed to pee. How long I was nonexistent before that, as some Bible-thumper would say, "God only knows," but I'm certain she doesn't. The best statement I know on this general topic came from my old butterfly acquaintance Vladimir Nabokov: "Common sense tells us that our existence is but a brief crack of light between two eternities of darkness."[4]

NOTES

1. The World of My Childhood

1. Ty Seidule, *Robert E. Lee and Me: A Southerner's Reckoning with the Myth of the Lost Cause* (New York: St. Martin's Press, 2021).
2. For Americans' belief in ghosts and demons, see H. Allan Scott, "More Than 45 Percent of Americans Believe Demons and Ghosts Are Real: Survey," *Newsweek*, October 19, 2019; for their belief in hell, see "How Many Americans Believe in Hell?," *Policy Reformation Institute*, www.prophecyrefi.org/our-teachings/introduction-2/how-many-americans-believe-in-hell/.
3. On why Senator Inhofe believes only God can change climate, see Elizabeth Bruenig, "Why Do Evangelicals Like James Inhofe Believe That Only God Can Cause Climate Change?," *New Republic*, January 29, 2015.
4. Anne and I (she in Iowa and I in New Jersey) were both fascinated by the war and asked our respective parents whether newspapers would still be published daily after the war. Our parents laughed, but we couldn't figure out what would be in them with no war news.

2. A Passion for Butterflies

1. Taylor H. Ricketts, Gretchen C. Daily, Paul R. Ehrlich, and Charles D. Michener, "Economic Value of Tropical Forest to Coffee Production," *Proceedings of the National Academy of Sciences* 101 (2004): 12579–82.
2. "Dodic" is what I called him once we became friends, as did Tim Prout and other friends, but everyone I heard speaking of him casually called him "Doby"—I follow "Doby" here to avoid confusion.
3. The reference is to geneticist George Beadle, who, along with Ed Tatum, was awarded the Nobel Prize for the one-gene, one-enzyme theory.

4. Our RMBL colleague geneticist Eddie Novitski had pointed out such an error, much to his later regret. Ironically, he eventually wrote a book that dealt with the Dobzhansky-Sturtevant split, a complex and sad affair triggered by something as silly as what constituted a "good species."
5. Paul R. Ehrlich and Ilkka Hanski, eds., *On the Wings of Checkerspots: A Model System for Population Biology* (New York: Oxford University Press, 2004).
6. General Douglas MacArthur's "Old Soldiers Never Die" address to Congress, April 19, 1951, Manuscript/Mixed Material, Library of Congress, www.loc.gov/item/mcc.034/.

3. To the Arctic

1. Nunavut is the name of a new territory carved from Canada's Northwest Territories in 1999 as a result of Inuit efforts and changed attitudes toward indigenous rights in the general Canadian population.
2. "Inuit" simply means "people" and is used in Arctic Canada. "Eskimo," which was a name given to the Inuit by others, is considered pejorative by many Inuit but is accepted in much of Alaska.
3. Helen Epstein, "The Highest Suicide Rate in the World," *New York Review of Books*, October 10, 2019.
4. One of the delightful Arctic stories I heard by palling around with the 408th concerned a pompous wing commander who landed his Lancaster on an airstrip bulldozed in the sea ice at Coral Harbour. He climbed down the ladder from the aircraft, stomped on the ice, and noticed an Inuit standing nearby. He approached him and asked, "How thickee icey?" The Inuit was a well-known hunter and guide I had met named Harry Gibbons. Harry had been adopted and raised by an upper-class English couple at Fort Churchill. He replied in perfect Oxonian English: "As a matter of actual fact, it's about six feet, three inches thick right heah!"

   The Arctic was a widely dispersed small community in those days—a few thousand people at military bases, villages, Hudson's Bay Company posts, and so forth—but it was united by an informal radio network. In a matter of days the story was everywhere; and whenever the wingco entered a mess, everyone would shout, "How thickee icey?"
5. Years later, in 1988, when Anne and I revisited the Arctic while leading a Stanford Travel Study trip, I met up with Santianna again. Our ship stopped at Eskimo Point (now Arviat) on its way to Fort Churchill. I took a walk alone out of town in the tundra, feeling very nostalgic once I had passed the garbage and Pampers zone. I was rewarded with my first sighting ever of a glorious species: a pair of snowy owls sitting on the tundra, ones that allowed me to get close enough for full-field views in my binoculars. A fitting farewell to a biome I had learned to love.

6. Botanists Dot Brown, Ann Oaks, and Barry Irvine, DRB officers Cec Law and Jim Easterbrook, Canadian Army sergeant Joe Bigras, and me.
7. Driftwood runners and crossbars bound in place with walrus hide gave the komatik sleds great flexibility for travel over rough ice or rocky ground.
8. Taxiing in circles to make small waves, then starting a takeoff run; when the plane was traveling fast enough to create lift, rocking onto one float, and then bouncing from wavelet crest to wavelet crest until we could remain airborne.
9. Actually "person"—Inuit is the plural "people."
10. Ryan Schuessler, "Indigenous Cooperation a Model for Walrus Conservation," *Hakai*, March 29, 2016, https://hakaimagazine.com/news/indigenous-cooperation-model-walrus-conservation/.
11. W. Gillies Ross, *Hunters on the Track: William Penny and the Search for Franklin* (Montreal: McGill-Queens University Press, 2019).
12. My mother, ever the intellectual, started searching the medical literature when her husband got Hodgkin's disease. She told me she had pointed these potential treatments out to his physicians; whether they would have discovered them on their own I have no idea. Ironically, vinblastine and vincristine were defensive compounds of the Madagascar periwinkle plant—a weapon in the plant-herbivore coevolutionary wars I discuss in chapter 6.

4. Evolution in Kansas . . . and Chicago

1. Before I got married, for reasons I can no longer remember, I had been sharing an apartment at KU with Loy. Almost exactly my age, Loy was an undergraduate history student, and we quickly started a close friendship that lasted until his death in 2004. He also happened to be a friend of Anne's, and when I wrote to Anne in the summer of 1954, I mentioned that we were roommates. Anne says she might not have answered that letter if I hadn't mentioned her friend. Loy was super smart and later did a PhD dissertation on the Council of Basel, possibly the first computer-based dissertation in the field of history. He showed that the degree of conservatism of that multiyear set of Roman Catholic Church meetings in the fifteenth century could be predicted by looking at the places from which delegates were coming and their proximity to centers of a heresy, Bohemian Hussitism. Loy, Anne, and I later wrote a book together, *The Golden Door*, on international migration, especially that between Mexico and the United States. Among his many gifts, Loy had a devilish sense of humor and, according to Lisa, was the rare alpha male who really took children seriously: the kind of guy one could be happy confiding in.
2. Paul R. Ehrlich and Peter H. Raven, "Differentiation of Populations," *Science* 65 (1969): 1228–32, took a more heterodox view.
3. Today many split the metalmarks from the Lycaenidae into a separate family,

Riodinidae. It's likely a mistake, overemphasizing the differences, but not a serious one.

4. For such comparisons there are N × (N–1)/2 possibilities. If one was comparing just three species, A, B, and C, the possibilities would be AB, AC, and BC, that is 3 × 2/2 = 3 combinations.
5. Charles D. Michener and Robert R. Sokal, "A Quantitative Approach to a Problem in Classification," *Evolution* 11 (1957): 130–62.
6. Paul R. Ehrlich, "Problems of Arctic-Alpine Insect Distribution as Illustrated by the Butterfly Genus *Erebia* (Satyridae)," *Proceedings of the Tenth International Congress of Entomology (Montreal)* 1 (1958): 683–86.
7. Edward O. Wilson and William L. Brown, "The Subspecies Concept and Its Taxonomic Application," *Systematic Zoology* 2 (1953): 97–111.
8. Nicholas W. Gillham, "Geographic Variation and the Subspecies Concept in Butterflies," *Systematic Zoology* 5 (1965): 110–20.
9. Paul R. Ehrlich, "Has the Biological Species Concept Outlived Its Usefulness?," *Systematic Zoology* 10 (1961): 167–76; Robert R. Sokal and Theodore J. Crovello, "The Biological Species Concept: A Critical Evaluation," *American Naturalist* 104 (1970): 127–53. For a recent article, see Susan Milius, "Defining 'Species' Is a Fuzzy Art," *Science News*, November 1, 2017, www.sciencenews.org/article/defining-species-fuzzy-art.
10. See note 9, above.
11. Interestingly, Peter Raven's and my heterodox 1969 *Science* paper on the mechanisms of speciation, arguing that selection regimes were more important than reduction of gene flow, was published, but few paid any attention to it.
12. Paul R. Ehrlich, "Some Axioms of Taxonomy," *Systematic Zoology* 13 (1964): 109–23.
13. I actually had learned something of Hall's ways earlier, when I took a course from him in which he demonstrated that he was a jackass. He was already known as not just a second-rate scientist but a third-rate teacher and a mean-spirited person.
14. John Keats, *The Crack in the Picture Window* (New York: Ballantine, 1956).
15. Joseph H. Camin and Paul R. Ehrlich. "Natural Selection in Water Snakes (*Natrix sipedon* L.) on Islands in Lake Erie," *Evolution* 12 (1958): 504–11.
16. J. H. Camin, C. Triplehorn, and H. Walter, "Some Indications of Survival Value in the Type 'A' Pattern of the Island Water Snakes in Lake Erie," *Chicago Academy of Sciences, Natural History Miscellanea* 131 (1954): 1–3.
17. Now called sacahuista or sacahuista beargrass.
18. Hall wrote: "It would seem to be far better for all of us, as with any kind of truth, to recognize the biological differences between the subspecies of man and by providing some areas in which citizenship for one subspecies alone will obtain, apply the available zoological knowledge so as to promote harmony instead of discord and so lengthen the present interval of peace." E. Raymond Hall, "Zoological Subspecies

of Man at the Peace Table," *Journal of Mammalogy* 27 (1946): 358–64. For an early refutation, see Paul R. Ehrlich and Richard W. Holm, "A Biological View of Race," in *The Concept of Race*, ed. Ashley Montagu (New York: Free Press of Glencoe, 1964): 153–79.

19. It was not until a few years after we left Lawrence a second time, however, that the Lawrence swimming pool was desegregated. Interestingly, when I tried to find newspaper accounts to fill in details of our restaurant efforts, none could be uncovered despite the help of Kansas historian and good friend Katie Armitage and a university librarian, Barry Bunch. My mistake was to wait too long—Mich remembered the events only vaguely, and those I knew, including Ralph, who had been directly involved, had died. In general, the sit-ins in the Midwest were ignored by the press. Ronald Walters, "The Great Plains Sit-In Movement, 1958–60," *Great Plains Quarterly* (1996): 85–94.

5. Joining the Only Junior University

1. Joseph H. Camin and Paul R. Ehrlich, "Natural Selection in Water Snakes (*Natrix sipedon* L.) on Islands in Lake Erie," *Evolution* 12 (1958): 504–11.
2. Paul R. Ehrlich and Richard W. Holm, "A Biological View of Race," in *The Concept of Race*, ed. Ashley Montagu (New York: Free Press of Glencoe, 1964): 153–79. Dick and I had taken up the same basic point in *The Process of Evolution* in 1963.
3. Paul R. Ehrlich and Richard W. Holm, "Patterns and Populations: Basic Problems of Population Biology Transcend Artificial Disciplinary Boundaries," *Science* 137 (1962): 652–57.
4. I was reminded of this sequence fifty-five years later by a visit from Frank's son Lou Pitelka—a distinguished ecologist in his own right.
5. I got this quotation from Herman E. Daly and use it a great deal in speeches. Gaylord Nelson apparently did as well: see Nelson's *Beyond Earth Day: Fulfilling the Promise* (Madison: University of Wisconsin Press, 2002).
6. Peter Raven also became home secretary of the National Academy of Sciences and has garnered more honors and prizes than any other scientist I've known personally. His autobiography, *Driven by Nature: A Personal Journey from Shanghai to Botany and Global Sustainability*, documenting an astonishing career, was published in 2021 (Missouri Botanical Garden Press). I suspect readers will find there are both similarities and differences in our respective interests.
7. Susan and Anne and I maintained the Saturday lunch tradition through its fifty-seventh year, to December 30, 2017. Days later Sue, who had just turned eighty, suffered a nasty fall and died within hours in the hospital. Thus ended sadly a most pleasant era.
8. Jens Clausen, David D. Keck, and William M. Hiesey, *Experimental Studies on the*

Nature of Species III: Environmental Responses of Climatic Races of Achillea (Washington, D.C.: Carnegie Institution of Washington, 1948).

9. Damon Linker, "No, Condoleezza Rice Is Not a War Criminal," *The Week*, January 10, 2015, theweek.com/articles/446657/no-condoleezza-rice-not-war-criminal.
10. Bob had pushed me for the position at his institution when I was at the Chicago Academy of Sciences working with Joe Camin and Bob.
11. Dirk Johnson, "Yale's Limit on Jewish Enrollment Lasted until Early 1960's, Book Says," *New York Times*, March 4, 1986; Wikipedia contributors, "Yale Program for the Study of Antisemitism," *Wikipedia*, last edited January 26, 2021, https://en.wikipedia.org/w/index.php?title=Yale_Program_for_the_Study_of_Antisemitism&oldid=1002804661.
12. "Breckinridge Long," *Americans and the Holocaust, United States Holocaust Memorial Museum*, https://exhibitions.ushmm.org/americans-and-the-holocaust/personal-story/breckinridge-long; Daniel A. Gross, "The U.S. Government Turned Away Thousands of Jewish Refugees, Fearing That They Were Nazi Spies," *Smithsonian* November 18, 2015, www.smithsonianmag.com/history/us-government-turned-away-thousands-jewish-refugees-fearing-they-were-nazi-spies-180957324/.
13. Marc was very helpful to me in reconstructing the Bridging the Rift story.
14. Jason R. Rohr, "The Atrazine Saga and Its Importance to the Future of Toxicology, Science, and Environmental and Human Health," *Environmental Toxicology and Chemistry* 40 (2021): 1544–58.
15. Rebecca S. Lowen, *Creating the Cold War University: The Transformation of Stanford* (Berkeley: University of California Press, 1997).

6. Coevolving with Botanists and Butterflies

1. Paul R. Ehrlich and Peter H. Raven, "Butterflies and Plants: A Study in Coevolution," *Evolution* 18 (1964): 586–608.
2. Paul R. Ehrlich and Ilkka Hanski, eds., *On the Wings of Checkerspots: A Model System for Population Biology* (New York: Oxford University Press, 2004).
3. Patrick P. Edger et al., "The Butterfly Plant Arms-Race Escalated by Gene and Genome Duplications," *Proceedings of the National Academy of Sciences* 112 (2015): 8362–66.
4. Nick Davies, *Cuckoo: Cheating by Nature* (New York: Bloomsbury, 2015).
5. Thomas R. Neil et al., "Thoracic Scales of Moths as a Stealth Coating against Bat Biosonar," *Journal of the Royal Society Interface* 17 (2020), https://doi.org/10.1098/rsif.2019.0692.
6. Mothers Out Front website, www.mothersoutfront.org.
7. G. C. Daily, P. R. Ehrlich, and N. M. Haddad, "Double Keystone Bird in a Key-

stone Species Complex," *Proceedings of the National Academy of Sciences* 90 (1993): 592–94.

8. C. L. Boggs et al., "Population Explosion of the Transplanted Checkerspot *Euphydryas gillettii*: A Response to Climate Change?," *Journal of Animal Ecology* 75 (2006): 466–75.
9. Paul R. Ehrlich and Anne H. Ehrlich, "Can a Collapse of Civilization Be Avoided?," *Proceedings of the Royal Society B: Biological Sciences* 280 (2013), https://doi.org/10.1098/rspb.2012.2845.

7. Australia and a Trip around the World

1. Heather Tallis and Jane Lubchenco, "Working Together: A Call for Inclusive Conservation," *Nature* 515 (2014): 27–28.
2. Paul R. Ehrlich and Anne H. Ehrlich, *Extinction: The Causes and Consequences of the Disappearance of Species* (New York: Random House, 1981).
3. On John Muir as a racist, see Alex Fox, "Sierra Club Grapples with Founder John Muir's Racism," *Smithsonian*, July 24, 2020, www.smithsonianmag.com/smart-news/sierra-club-grapples-founder-john-muirs-racism-180975404/.
4. I kept paying my dues to the Royal Aero Club of New South Wales (RACNSW) for years because I loved being a member. As I grew older I joined many scientific societies to get their journals, and often when I was to be introduced at seminars or meetings, the hosts would ask which society they should mention. I always said the Royal Aero Club, explaining that the qualification for the others was the ability to pay the subscription price each year, but for the RACNSW, one also had to be able to fly an airplane.
5. Patricia A. Labine, "Population Biology of the Butterfly, *Euphydryas editha*. I. Barriers to Multiple Insemination," *Evolution* 18 (1964): 335–36.
6. RCAF serial number 260697.
7. That trip was to be my last adventure with John—he died tragically young in 1976 at the age of fifty-six. Anne and I gave Dick Roughsey's paintings (along with much of our art collection) to the California Academy of Sciences in 2005 when we gave up our house and moved to an apartment.

8. *The Population Bomb* and the Carson Years

1. Paul R. Ehrlich, *The Population Bomb* (New York: Ballantine Books, 1968). In the lower left-hand corner is a picture of a bomb and the statement "*The Population Bomb* keeps ticking." But the bomb has no clock timer, only a burning fuse. No one has ever called this to my attention.

2. Fabien Locher, "Neo-Malthusian Environmentalism, World Fisheries Crisis, and the Global Commons, 1950s–1970s," *Historical Journal* 63 (2020): 187–207.
3. See www.tumgir.com/tag/paul%20ehrlich, a newspaper Tumblr message posted by thepopculturearchivist and run down by Darryl Wheye.
4. Bob Carr, "'Everybody's Scared': The First Mention in Australian Media of Global Warming Could Only Gesture to the Future," *Sydney Morning Herald*, August 30, 2021.
5. After I had done *The Tonight Show* a few times, I was asked to join the television performer's union, AFTRA (now SAG-AFTRA). It's a membership I am proud of, and one of my more recent regrets has been the weakening of the American labor union movement, a pillar of what's left of our democracy.
6. For a fine example, see Jason R. Rohr, "The Atrazine Saga and Its Importance to the Future of Toxicology, Science, and Environmental and Human Health," *Environmental Toxicology and Chemistry* 40 (2021): 1544–58.
7. See "William Shockley," Southern Poverty Law Center, www.splcenter.org/fighting-hate/extremist-files/individual/william-shockley.
8. Letters to the editor, *New York Times*, October 16, 1977, www.nytimes.com/1977/10/16/archives/letters-race-bomb-murder.html.
9. On my writings, see, e.g., Paul R. Ehrlich and Richard W. Holm, "A Biological View of Race," in *The Concept of Race*, ed. Ashley Montagu (New York: Free Press of Glencoe, 1964): 153–79; and Paul R. Ehrlich, *Human Natures: Genes, Cultures, and the Human Prospect* (Washington, D.C.: Island Press, 2000). On labeling as racist and/or sexist, see, e.g., Jedediah Purdy, "Environmentalism's Racist History," *New Yorker*, August 13, 2015, www.newyorker.com/news/news-desk/environmentalisms-racist-history.
10. For Bowling Green, see "'We May Not Make It'—Ehrlich," *BG News* (Bowling Green, Ohio), April 23, 1970, available at http://scholarworks.bgsu.edu/cgi/viewcontent.cgi?article=3449&context=bg-news.
11. Honoring LuEsther, "LuEsther T. Mertz: Theater's 'Angel of the Arts,'" *New York Community Trust*, April 8, 2019, www.nycommunitytrust.org/newsroom/luesther-t-mertz-theaters-angel-of-the-arts/.
12. Paul R. Ehrlich and Jonathan Freedman, "Population, Crowding, and Human Behavior," *New Scientist and Science Journal* 50 (1971): 10; Jonathan L. Freedman, Simon Klevansky, and Paul R. Ehrlich, "The Effect of Crowding on Human Task Performance," *Journal of Applied Social Psychology* 1 (1971): 7–25.
13. Megan K. Seibert and William E. Rees, "Through the Eye of a Needle: An Eco-Heterodox Perspective on the Renewable Energy Transition," *Energies* 14 (2021), https://doi.org/10.3390/en14154508.
14. Named after the biology chairperson who had hired me, Victor Twitty; he later contracted Parkinson's disease, which prevented him from doing delicate op-

erations on chick embryos, and eventually drank a glass of cyanide solution in his lab.

15. Paul R. Ehrlich and John P. Holdren, "Population and Panaceas: A Technological Perspective," *BioScience* 19 (1969): 1065–71.
16. For example, G. C. Daily, ed., *Nature's Services: Societal Dependence on Natural Ecosystems* (Washington, D.C.: Island Press, 1997); John P. Holdren and Paul R. Ehrlich, "Human Population and the Global Environment," *American Scientist* 62 (1974): 282–92.
17. C. F. Westoff, "The Commission on Population Growth and the American Future: Its Origins, Operations, and Aftermath," *Population Index* 39 (1973): 491–507.
18. Andrew Feenberg, "The Commoner-Ehrlich Debate: Environmentalism and the Politics of Survival," in *Minding Nature: The Philosophers of Ecology*, ed. David Macaulay (Guilford Press, 1996), 257–82. I was also excoriated for suggesting that Kenya could get its income from the tourist trade, not by industrializing. Norman J. Faramelli, "Toying with the Environment and the Poor: A Report on the Stockholm Environmental Conferences," *Boston College Environmental Affairs Law Review* 2 (1972): 469–86. It would still be a good idea if exchange rates were right and the people of the world took seriously the issue of the ethics of borders! Is it ethical, for example, for a nation to keep control over a vital commodity simply because a natural accident resulted in a large quantity within its frontiers?
19. In 1993 John Holdren wrote, but did not publish, a summary of our battle with Commoner. It can be found in the MAHB library. "A Brief History of 'IPAT' (Impact= Population x Affluence x Technology)," https://mahb.stanford.edu/library-item/a-brief-history-of-ipat-impact-population-x-affluence-x-technology/.
20. Paul R. Ehrlich and John P. Holdren, "Impact of Population Growth," *Science* 171 (1971): 1212–17. Amusingly, helpful critics have often pointed out that the three factors are not independent. If they had bothered to read the paper, they would have discovered that we pointed that out.
21. Seth Wynes and Kimberly A. Nicholas, "The Climate Mitigation Gap: Education and Government Recommendations Miss the Most Effective Individual Actions," *Environmental Research Letters* 12 (2017): 074024, is one of the most useful papers detailing the great importance of population growth as a driver of environmental destruction.

9. Global Fieldwork

1. Michael C. Singer, Paul R. Ehrlich, and Lawrence E. Gilbert, "Butterfly Feeding on Lycopsid," *Science* 172 (1971): 1341–42.
2. Don Kennedy and I arranged to have his book *The Fishes of the Galápagos Islands* published by Stanford University Press (1997).

3. A. C. Haddon and James Hornell, "Canoes of Oceania," in *The Canoes of Oceania* (Honolulu: Bishop Museum Press, 1975).
4. Deborah S. Rogers and Paul R. Ehrlich, "Natural Selection and Cultural Rates of Change," *Proceedings of the National Academy of Sciences* 105 (2008): 3416–20.
5. Carl Safina, *Beyond Words: What Animals Think and Feel* (New York: Picador, 2015). Safina also reminded me of a magnificent day on Puget Sound with our nature sculptor and environmental educator friend Tony Angell—much of it spent with the J-Pod of orcas.
6. Paul R. Ehrlich and Anne H. Ehrlich, "Lizard Predation on Tropical Butterflies," *Journal of the Lepidopterists' Society* 36 (1982): 148–52.
7. Safina, *Beyond Words.* If you think nonhuman animals are automata, this is the book for you. One of my very favorites that I wish were required reading for all college freshman (even though I didn't write it).
8. Paul R. Ehrlich, *Human Natures: Genes, Cultures, and the Human Prospect* (Washington, D.C.: Island Press, 2000), 207.
9. Stuart Pimm is president of Saving Nature, an NGO that is working hard to do just that.

10. Great Affairs, and Some Great Birds

1. For the direction the Tugwell group was going, see www.maebrussell.com/Articles%20and%20Notes/New%20Constitution.html.
2. Dennis C. Pirages and Paul R. Ehrlich, *Ark II: Social Response to Environmental Imperatives* (New York: Viking, 1974).
3. Paul R. Ehrlich, *The Population Bomb* (New York: Ballantine Books, 1968), 77; Paul R. Ehrlich and Anne H. Ehrlich, *Population, Resources, Environment: Issues in Human Ecology* (San Francisco: W. H. Freeman, 1970); Paul R. Ehrlich, Anne H. Ehrlich, and John P. Holdren, *Ecoscience: Population, Resources, Environment* (San Francisco: W. H. Freeman, 1977), 690.
4. The Minimum Critical Size of Ecosystems project.
5. R. P. Turco et al., "Nuclear Winter: Global Consequences of Multiple Nuclear Weapons Explosions," *Science* 222 (1983): 1283–92.
6. Paul R. Ehrlich et al., "Long-Term Biological Consequences of Nuclear War," *Science* 222 (1983): 1293–300.
7. Ehrlich, *Population Bomb*, 77.
8. David Vergun, "Nuclear Triad Modernization the Nation's Highest Priority, Admiral Says," *U.S. Department of Defense*, April 21, 2021, www.defense.gov/News/News-Stories/Article/Article/2582206/nuclear-triad-modernization-the-nations-highest-priority-admiral-says/.

9. Prince Charles also furnished a comment for the monarchy's website that begins: "Paul and Anne Ehrlich's report is a timely and urgent reminder of how the collapse of civilizations has, in the past, been caused by the degradation of Nature's services, and how that process is now being repeated on a global scale."
10. If you want fascinating stories of brush turkey behavior (or that of other feathered creatures), there's a great book by Jennifer Ackerman called *The Bird Way: A New Look at How Birds Talk, Work, Play, Parent, and Think* (New York: Penguin, 2020).
11. Paul R. Ehrlich and Anne H. Ehrlich, *Extinction: The Causes and Consequences of the Disappearance of Species* (New York: Random House, 1981).
12. Peter M. Vitousek, Paul R. Ehrlich, Anne H. Ehrlich, and Pamela A. Matson, "Human Appropriation of the Products of Photosynthesis," *BioScience* 36 (1986): 368–73.
13. On moths, see G. C. Daily and P. R. Ehrlich, "Nocturnality and Species Survival," *Proceedings of the National Academy of Sciences* 93 (1996): 11709–12.

11. The Crafoord Prize and Projects of the New Millennium

1. Paul R. Ehrlich, "Key Issues for Attention from Ecological Economists," *Environment and Development Economics* 13 (2008): 1–20.
2. K. Arrow et al., "Are We Consuming Too Much?," *Journal of Economic Perspectives* 18 (2004): 147–72.
3. Andrew J. Beattie and Paul R. Ehrlich, *Wild Solutions: How Biodiversity Is Money in the Bank* (New Haven: Yale University Press, 2001).
4. Jianguo Liu, Gretchen C. Daily, Paul R. Ehrlich, and Gary W. Luck, "Effects of Household Dynamics on Resource Consumption and Biodiversity," *Nature* 421 (2003): 530–33.
5. Darryl Wheye and Paul R. Ehrlich, "Are There Caterpillars on Butterfly Wings?," *News of the Lepidopterists' Society* 57 (2015): 182–93.
6. Thirty years earlier Darryl and I published on another fun project. At Darryl's suggestion we studied mating patterns in a natural population of *Euphydryas editha* by dusting the external genitalia of males we caught and released with fluorescent dye microparticles, different colors for males from different groups. We then examined mated females we netted under UV light. The fluorescent dye worked as a tracer, but we decided not to expand our research into its obvious applications to human behavior. Darryl Wheye and Paul R. Ehrlich, "The Use of Fluorescent Pigments to Study Insect Behavior: Investigating Mating Patterns in a Butterfly Population," *Ecological Entomology* 10 (1985): 231–34.
7. Paul R. Ehrlich and Ilkka Hanski, eds., *On the Wings of Checkerspots: A Model System for Population Biology* (New York: Oxford University Press, 2004).
8. There were a couple of memorable occasions, however, when I intervened. One

day when Lisa was in first grade, she came home crying. The principal had made her and some other children stand up in assembly, and he bawled them out in front of the whole school because their parents hadn't come to a parent-teachers event the night before. Anne and I had been busy, and I had little interest in interfering with what then had the reputation of being an excellent public school system.

Despite being a calm and patient man, I decided it was time for me to go to school. I went to the principal's office and told his secretary that I wanted to see him. She said he couldn't be disturbed. I said he would be, and went in past her desk. The guy was maybe five foot seven, and then I was six foot two; he was startled by my sudden appearance. Rather loudly, and in no uncertain terms, I explained that if he ever did anything like that to my daughter again, he'd regret it (I think the actual explanatory phrase was "I'll beat the shit out of you"). By pure coincidence, our good friend Don Kennedy, whose daughter (then in kindergarten) had also been in the group of shamed and terrorized kids, came into his office and repeated my performance a short while later. Some years later the school system let the principal go for some similar moronic act.

My next memorable school adventure took place in Sydney, Australia. Anne took Lisa, aged nine, to enroll her in the Double Bay (an upper-class suburb—our U.S. salary went a long way in Oz then) public school. In the registration process (handled by the vice-principal) Anne was asked "what scriptures" should Lisa go to. Anne asked Lisa what her choice would be, but Lisa wasn't paying attention, and the vice-principal was shocked: "We don't ask the child! Has she ever been to church?" Lisa had once accompanied a friend to an Episcopalian service, so Lisa got signed up for Church of England.

Lisa was oblivious to all this, and when her homeroom teacher said, "It's time to go to scriptures," Lisa was clueless. "What's your religion?" the teacher asked. We'd always told Lisa she was, like me, "Jewish, but for purposes of persecution only." She didn't know what "persecution" meant when she was nine, so she said "Jewish" and ended up hearing that sect's indoctrination stories. All was well until a Jewish holiday came along and the teacher who told the Jewish stories bawled Lisa out for coming to school that day; Lisa then came home and announced that she "had" to stay home for the next one coming up. Anne turned the case over to me, and I wrote a letter to the teacher. On reading my letter, the teacher went to the vice-principal, who thought Lisa had been going to Church of England scriptures for months. A very uncomfortable vice-principal finally asked Lisa where she'd prefer to be. Lisa asked, "What do they do in Church of England?" The principal said she would "learn all about our Lord Jesus Christ." Lisa said, "I think I'll stay where I am." Problem solved.

One other memorable example I'll mention. When she was seventeen, Lisa asked my permission to ride to San Diego with her boyfriend on his motorcycle.

That was a no-brainer. "Honey, I can't really stop you at this point, but if you want to sleep with your boyfriend in San Diego, I'll buy you an airline ticket." Anne gave a similar answer. A couple of years later, Lisa told us she was thrilled by our response—she was scared by the prospect of the long ride (and of being alone far away with a somewhat sketchy boyfriend), and we had given her an excuse to refuse.

9. Curiously, with a totally different analysis two physicists came up with our original estimate of a 10 percent chance of avoiding collapse: Mauro Bologna and Gerardo Aquino, "Deforestation and World Population Sustainability: A Quantitative Analysis," *Scientific Reports* 10 (2020): 7631. For a recent, less optimistic view, see Bill Rees's classic article, "The Fractal Biology of Plague and the Future of Civilization," *Journal of Population and Sustainability* 5 (2020): 15–30.
10. The Fan Initiative, www.faninitiative.net. "The FAN Initiative brings to one place powerful narratives describing the system vulnerabilities; reflections by leading thinkers on the power to meet the challenge; and the ways some are responding to shift us from collapse to a compelling future."
11. Corey J. A. Bradshaw and Paul R. Ehrlich, *Killing the Koala and Poisoning the Prairie: Australia, America, and the Environment* (Chicago: University of Chicago Press, 2015).
12. Corey J. A. Bradshaw et al., "Underestimating the Challenges of Avoiding a Ghastly Future," *Frontiers in Conservation Science* 1 (2021), https://doi.org/10.3389/fcosc.2020.615419. This paper was written to point out that scientific reticence was giving the public a falsely optimistic impression of the future of civilization.
13. Gerardo Ceballos, Paul R. Ehrlich, and Rodolfo Dirzo, "Biological Annihilation via the Ongoing Sixth Mass Extinction Signaled by Vertebrate Population Losses and Declines," *Proceedings of the National Academy of Sciences* 114 (2017): E6089–96.
14. Gerardo Ceballos, Paul R. Ehrlich, and Peter H. Raven, "Vertebrates on the Brink as Indicators of Biological Annihilation and the Sixth Mass Extinction," *Proceedings of the National Academy of Sciences* 117 (2020): 13596–602.
15. When Jennifer Hughes came to Stanford, she was easily the shyest grad student ever to join our group. To help her with that problem, I signed her up to lecture at a major biodiversity conference in Washington, D.C., speaking on a panel with the likes of Peter Raven and Norman Myers. She was nervous but gave a very good talk. After receiving her doctorate, she shifted into investigations of the ecology of microorganisms—an incredibly important area that was then only thinly populated with investigators. Now, under her married name of Jennifer Martiny, a leader in that field, she recently gave a presentation at the Stanford Woods Institute for the Environment; it was one of the best seminars I have ever heard.
16. With Marc Feldman and Robert Sapolsky, Sandra, Simon, and I now have a long

peer-reviewed article on "The Jaw Epidemic: Recognition, Origins, Cures, and Prevention," *BioScience* 70 (2021): 759–71.

17. Megan K. Seibert and William E. Rees, "Through the Eye of a Needle: An Eco-Heterodox Perspective on the Renewable Energy Transition," *Energies* 14 (2021): 4508.
18. Millennium Ecosystem Assessment, *Ecosystems and Human Well-Being: Synthesis* (Washington, D.C.: Island Press, 2005).
19. Paul R. Ehrlich and Anne H. Ehrlich, *One with Nineveh: Politics, Consumption, and the Human Future* (Washington, D.C.: Island Press, 2004); Paul R. Ehrlich and Donald Kennedy, "Millennium Assessment of Human Behavior: A Challenge to Scientists," *Science* 309 (2005): 562–63.
20. If you want a clue to work of Lee Ross and Robert Cialdini, see Thomas Gilovich and Lee Ross, *The Wisest One in the Room: How to Harness Psychology's Most Powerful Insights* (New York: Free Press, 2016).
21. See the MAHB (Millennium Alliance for Humanity and the Biosphere) website with many resources, https://mahb.stanford.edu.
22. Karole is the daughter of Ken and Katie Armitage, whom we met after Ken joined the faculty of the zoology department of the University of Kansas when I was a grad student (he joined my committee) and a good friend whom we later saw frequently in the summers at the Rocky Mountain Biological Laboratory. Ken died peacefully with his family around him at the turn of 2022, age ninety-six.
23. Paul R. Ehrlich, "The MAHB, the Culture Gap, and Some Really Inconvenient Truths," *PLoS Biology* 8 (2010): e1000330. What is the culture gap? In hunter-gatherer groups, ordinarily all adults were in possession of the vast majority of their society's culture—its nongenetic information. Even the best-educated person today does not have one millionth of 1 percent of the culture of a modern industrial society. And that near total ignorance is a major factor in the failure of most people to grasp the existential threats to society.

12. *The Population Bomb* Revisited

Author's note: This chapter is based on Paul R. Ehrlich and Anne H. Ehrlich, "*The Population Bomb* Revisited," *Electronic Journal of Sustainable Development* 1 (2009): 65–71, www.populationmedia.org/wp-content/uploads/2009/07/Population-Bomb-Revisited-Paul-Ehrlich-20096.pdf.

1. For a partial bibliography, see "Ehrlich, Paul R(Alph) 1932– ," *Encyclopedia.com*, www.encyclopedia.com/arts/educational-magazines/ehrlich-paul-ralph-1932.
2. Mark C. Henrie, Winfield J. C. Myers, and Jeffrey O. Nelson, "The 50 Worst Books of the 20th Century," *Intercollegiate Studies Institute*, July 21, 2014, https://isi.org/intercollegiate-review/the-50-worst-books-of-the-20th-century/.

3. Human Events Staff, "Ten Most Harmful Books of the 19th and 20th Centuries, *Human Events,* May 31, 2005, https://archive.humanevents.com/2005/05/31/ten-most-harmful-books-of-the-19th-and-20th-centuries/.
4. "What Is the Ecological Footprint?," *Earth Overshoot Day,* https://www.overshootday.org/kids-and-teachers-corner/what-is-an-ecological-footprint/.
5. Earth Overshoot Day homepage, www.overshootday.org.
6. Nicholas Eberstadt, "China's One-Child Mistake," *Wall Street Journal,* September 17, 2007.
7. K. Arrow et al., "Are We Consuming Too Much?," *Journal of Economic Perspectives* 18 (2004): 147–72.
8. Quoted in Crispin Tickell, Foreword to James Lovelock, *The Revenge of Gaia: Earth's Climate Crisis and the Fate of Humanity* (New York: Basic Books, 2007), xvi.
9. Gretchen C. Daily, Anne H. Ehrlich, and Paul R. Ehrlich, "Optimum Human Population Size," *Population and Environment* 15 (1994): 469–75.
10. It can't be emphasized too much that some form of redistribution of wealth internationally is essential if a state-based global system is to be even medium-term sustainable; it's what John Holdren, Anne, and I called de-development of overdeveloped countries. Paul R. Ehrlich, Anne H. Ehrlich, and John P. Holdren, *Ecoscience: Population, Resources, Environment* (San Francisco: W. H. Freeman, 1977).
11. Gaya Herrington, "Update to Limits to Growth: Comparing the World3 Model with Empirical Data," *Journal of Industrial Ecology* 25 (2021): 614–26.
12. Paul R. Ehrlich and Anne H. Ehrlich, *One with Nineveh: Politics, Consumption, and the Human Future, with a New Afterword* (Washington, D.C.: Island Press, 2005), 102.
13. Rattan Lal, "Restoring Soil Quality to Mitigate Soil Degradation," *Sustainability* 7 (2015): 5875–95.
14. William E. Rees, "Ecological Economics for Humanity's Plague Phase," *Ecological Economics* 169 (2020): 106519.
15. Fred Pearce, "Overconsumption Is a Grave Threat to Humanity," *New York Times,* June 8, 2015, www.nytimes.com/roomfordebate/2015/06/08/is-overpopulation-a-legitimate-threat-to-humanity-and-the-planet/overconsumption-is-a-grave-threat-to-humanity.
16. This ignore-the-population-problem view has persisted. George Monbiot, who rightly thinks that a major element in the human predicament is overconsumption by the rich, doesn't pursue the fact that the amount the wealthy consume is a function of, not just per capita consumption among them, but how many wealthy people there are. He has been correct that a half century ago Anne and I wrote some things that sadly gave ammunition to those who thought the population problem was too many poor people, and he likes to cite those ancient statements. Yet in a

2020 *Guardian* article he cites the I=PAT equation by Anne, John Holdren, and me published in the early 1970s that we developed explicitly to counter the notion that environmental degradation was just the fault of too many poor people. But he did not cite any of our many attacks on the idea that environmental problems were the particular fault of the poor. In an era in which ignoring the science on existential environmental issues is one of the most pressing human problems, it seems to us tragic that some voices for environmental sanity persist in devoting scant attention to serious, perhaps catastrophic demographic problems.

17. Paul R. Ehrlich, *The Population Bomb* (New York: Ballantine Books, 1968), 133.
18. Melinda Liu, “Is China Ground Zero for a Future Pandemic?,” *Smithsonian Magazine*, November 2017, https://www.smithsonianmag.com/science-nature/china-ground-zero-future-pandemic-180965213/. Old but interesting. Regardless of the source of Covid-19, China remains an important site for virus evolution.
19. Norman Myers, *The Sinking Ark* (New York: Pergamon, 1979).
20. Paul R. Ehrlich and Gretchen C. Daily, “Population Extinction and Saving Biodiversity,” *Ambio* 22 (1993): 64–68.
21. Ehrlich, *Population Bomb*, xi.
22. For example, William Paddock and Paul Paddock. *Famine, 1975! America’s Decision: Who Will Survive?* (New York: Little, Brown, 1967).
23. Ehrlich, *Population Bomb*, 108.
24. For the report, see Global Panel on Agriculture and Food Systems for Nutrition, *Food Systems and Diets: Facing the Challenges of the 21st Century* (London: International Food Policy Research Institute, 2016). Robert Pigott, “Poor Food ‘Risks Health of Half the World,’” *BBC News*, September 25, 2016, www.bbc.com/news/science-environment-37450953.
25. On reduced crop nutrition, see Matthew R. Smith, Philip K. Thornton, and Samuel S. Myers, *The Impact of Rising Carbon Dioxide Levels on Crop Nutrients and Human Health* (London: International Food Policy Research Institute, 2018).
26. “Food Security and Covid-19,” *World Bank*, January 31, 2022, https://www.worldbank.org/en/topic/agriculture/brief/food-security-and-covid-19.
27. Ehrlich, *Population Bomb*, 72.
28. Ehrlich, 34.
29. National Academy of Sciences USA, “A Joint Statement by Fifty-Eight of the World’s Scientific Academies” (Paper presented at the Population Summit of the World’s Scientific Academies, New Delhi, India, 1993).
30. Union of Concerned Scientists, *World Scientists’ Warning to Humanity* (Cambridge, Mass.: Union of Concerned Scientists, 1993).
31. William J. Ripple et al., “World Scientists’ Warning to Humanity: A Second Notice,” *BioScience* 67 (2017): 1026–28.

13. Combatting the Forces of the Endarkenment

1. See the Conservative Catholic blog LifeSite on my invite to speak at the Vatican, Pete Baklinski, "Population Controller Who Says All Catholics Are 'Terrorists' Coming to Speak at Vatican," *LifeSite*, February 10, 2017, www.lifesitenews.com/blogs/who-said-this-pope-or-population-controller-thus-you-have-god-fearing-peopl/.
2. Partha Dasgupta, Peter Raven, and Anna McIvor, *Biological Extinction: New Perspectives* (New York: Cambridge University Press, 2019).
3. Jared Diamond, *Collapse: How Societies Choose to Fail or Succeed* (New York: Viking, 2005), 3.
4. Anne and I discussed the antiscience movement in detail a quarter of a century ago in Paul R. Ehrlich and Anne H. Ehrlich, *Betrayal of Science and Reason: How Anti-Environmental Rhetoric Threatens Our Future* (Washington, D.C.: Island Press, 1996). Examples that seemed extreme at the time, such as a mail-order marketer who claimed the human population could grow for billions of years, now seem dwarfed by claims that, for example, wildfires are caused by Jewish space lasers. Jonathan Chait, "GOP Congresswoman Blames Wildfires on Secret Jewish Space Laser," *Intelligencer*, January 28, 2021, https://nymag.com/intelligencer/article/marjorie-taylor-greene-qanon-wildfires-space-laser-rothschild-execute.html.
5. On the concept of God in Universal Unitarianism, see www.uua.org/beliefs/what-we-believe/higher-power.
6. A. E. Michotte, *The Perception of Causality* (New York: Basic Books, 1965).
7. Martin Parker, *Shut Down the Business School: What's Wrong with Management Education* (London: Pluto Press, 2018), 15, 75.
8. Farhad Manjoo, "Coronavirus Is What You Get When You Ignore Science," *New York Times*, March 4, 2020, https://www.nytimes.com/2020/03/04/opinion/coronavirus-science.html.
9. Paul R. Ehrlich and Anne H. Ehrlich, "Returning to Normal? The Historic Roots of the Human Prospect," *BioScience*, in press (2022).
10. Eli B. Cohen and Scott J. Lloyd, "Disciplinary Evolution and the Rise of the Transdiscipline," *Informing Science: The International Journal of an Emerging Transdiscipline*, 17 (2014): 189–215.
11. James Hansen, "Dangerous Scientific Reticence," March 23, 2016, available at www.columbia.edu/~jeh1/mailings/2016/20160323_DangerousReticence.pdf.
12. Corey J. A. Bradshaw et al., "Underestimating the Challenges of Avoiding a Ghastly Future," *Frontiers in Conservation Science* 1 (2021), https://doi.org/10.3389/fcosc.2020.615419.
13. Elizabeth Williams, "Yeap! Finland Will Become the First Country in the World

to Get Rid of All School Subjects," *Curious Mind Magazine*, https://curiousmind magazine.com/goodbye-subjects-finland-taking-revolution-education-step/.

14. While today's level of globalization and population density can spread pandemics faster than the 1918 "Spanish" flu, supply chain problems even in the Covid-19 pandemic suggested the possible great difficulties of dealing with an even more dangerous virus if it transfers to our species from its nonhuman animal host.
15. On the food system, see Sonja J. Vermeulen, Bruce M. Campbell, and John S. I. Ingram, "Climate Change and Food Systems," *Annual Review of Environment and Resources* 37 (2012): 195–222; Andrew J. Challinor et al., "A Meta-Analysis of Crop Yield under Climate Change and Adaptation," *Nature Climate Change* 4 (2014): 287–91.
16. Joel Bakan, *The Corporation: The Pathological Pursuit of Profit and Power*, rev. and expanded ed. (London: Constable, 2005), 256.
17. Joel Bakan, *The New Corporation: How "Good" Corporations Are Bad for Democracy* (New York: Vintage, 2020).
18. There is a literature in which some argue that hunter-gatherer groups were mostly smaller or, conversely, that people may feel comfortable with two hundred or more. Who cares whether the number could instead be seventy-five or two hundred?
19. R. I. M. Dunbar, "Neocortex Size as a Constraint on Group Size in Primates," *Journal of Human Evolution* 20 (1992): 469–93.
20. Bruno Goncalves, Nicola Perra, and Alessandro Vespignani, "Validation of Dunbar's Number in Twitter Conversations," *arXiv preprint arXiv:1105.5170* (2011); Barry Wellman, "Is Dunbar's Number Up?," *British Journal of Psychology* 103 (2012): 174–76; Robin Dunbar, *How Many Friends Does One Person Need? Dunbar's Number and Other Evolutionary Quirks* (London: Faber and Faber, 2010).
21. Paul R. Ehrlich and Daniel T. Blumstein, "The Great Mismatch," *BioScience* 68 (2018): 844–46.

14. The End of *Life*

1. We were able to move in because we had stretched our finances in 1962 with help from Stanford to buy an Eichler tract house. It increased in value more than forty-fold, barely enough to sell it and pay for our small apartment in a facility providing continuing care when it is necessary. It underlined for us once again the inequities within American society just as travel had made us understand international inequities and how lucky we were to be born white and middle class in twentieth-century United States.
2. On the butterfly fishes, see P. R. Ehrlich, F. H. Talbot, B. C. Russell, and G. R. V. Anderson, "The Behaviour of Chaetodontid Fishes with Special Reference to Lorenz' 'Poster Colouration' Hypothesis," *Journal of Zoology* 183 (1977): 213–28.

3. Weston La Barre, *The Human Animal* (Chicago: University of Chicago Press, 1960), 289 (paraphrased).
4. Part of the opening line of Nabokov's own memoir, *Speak, Memory* (London: Victor Gollancz, 1951).

ACKNOWLEDGMENTS

That's it—an edited version of my life and prejudices. Why did I write a memoir? The primary answer is, of course, ego. You must think that your life experiences are either interesting or instructive enough to want to make an account of them available to others. In my case, I think they are both (no one ever accused me of lacking ego). But the real trigger was that, when I turned eighty-two, a friend said he would like to write my biography. He's a good guy and a great writer, and I owe him much for the trigger, but I thought if someone was going to write pleasant lies about me, I was best equipped to do it.

I wrote this account largely chronologically. I kept detailed field notes only once (closest thing to a diary ever), but it was (to me) an important time, when I was in the Arctic in the summer of 1952. I also saved a raft of duplicated letters I wrote to friends and relatives while overseas in 1965–66, before email and cheap international phone calls were available. For other names or dates that I had forgotten or simply wanted confirmation, I've relied where possible on my pilot's log book, pocket schedulers, passports, some of my publications, and Anne's and Lisa's and some friends' memories.

Creating the manuscript has filled the last few years with nostalgia but made me wish I had a full video record of my life and the world that I could have consulted. Then I would have been able to satisfy my curiosity on personal matters that I failed to discover (such as what ever happened to Margot Baker) and alter this memoir in response. If I could really edit the past, a bunch of things would have ended up on the cutting room floor. There would go my regrets like my relationship with my father when he was dying, and the events I wish had never happened, such as the tragedy at Ngorongoro. My big mistakes, like being a lousy father to Lisa when she was a little girl, not learning more math, and not having Anne as an open co-author on *The Population Bomb* would end up there, too.

This project has given me especially great pleasure since it has meant working with Lisa, who served as editor and contributor, and wrote the Foreword. She has suggested a few deletions, all of which were sensible, rearranged passages into more logical sequences, and drafted short pieces where her memory was better than mine. That's where she really starred, since she was so good at adopting my voice that when revising I sometimes couldn't identify the author. We didn't have a single screaming argument.

I owe a huge debt to my editor friend at Yale University Press, Jean Thomson Black, and my long-term other editor friend, Jonathan Cobb, both Tabard Inn 9/11 alumni, for vastly improving my *Life*. They combined to turn my rants into prose, deal with my tendency to try to tell everything I know, and give excellent advice on a wide range of issues. At Yale I was further aided by the highly competent assistance of Amanda Gerstenfeld and Elizabeth Sylvia, who handled complex illustration issues with great skill and sometimes contributed youthful views to an author-editors team that had almost reached middle age. Laura Jones Dooley did a fine and patient job of copy editing, as did Meridith Murray on the index—it was fun working with them.

Throw in critiques by Anne and Lisa, my sister, Sally Kellock, as well as Tim Daniel, Joan Diamond, Jared Diamond, Partha Dasgupta, Mary Ellen Hannibal, Tom Lovejoy, Kirk Smith, and my agent, Eleanor Jackson, and the genius of the late Lee Ross in suggesting topics, Darryl Wheye in helping greatly with the illustrations program, and the efforts of Joyce Ippolito and Yale's production team, and you can see that the book is somewhat a joint enterprise.

A mob of people, including some already mentioned, have over my career served as sources of support, encouragement, ideas, or helpful criticism, especially in reviewing manuscripts—and many I've doubtless neglected to credit earlier in this memoir. In addition, to Paul Growald and Rick Harriman, who worked for me as volunteer administrative assistants long ago, many others—mentors, colleagues, reviewers, secretaries, assistants, students, companions, relatives, and friends—have aided me in diverse ways that have made most of what I have done possible and have given me a great life while doing it. They don't represent my Dunbar's number because most have not formed long-term stable relationships with Anne and me. But of the some 600 people, about 100 to 150 have. Science for me is a social activity. So I give here in alphabetical order a list of those who come to my fevered brain as I finish up the manuscript to acknowledge my debts to them: Jennifer Ackerman, Andy Adler, Susan Alexander, Vladimir Alexandrov, Marcia Allen, John Allman, Angela Amerillo-Suarez, Marty Anderies, Gordon Anderson, Susan Anderson, Tony Angell, Natalie Angier, Oscar Arias, Karole Armitage, Katie Armitage, Ken Armitage, Kevin Armitage, Paul Armsworth, Suzanne Arnold, Ken Arrow, Andrey Avinoff, Bill Baker, Ian Ballantine, Ginger Barber, Ed Barbier, Tony Barnosky, billy barr, Ralph Barr, Scott Barrett, Jack Baughman, Jane Bavelas, Fakhri Bazzaz, Andy Beattie, Jay Beckner, Steve Beissinger, Aviv Bergman, Joe Berry, Laura Berthold, Rosina Bierbaum, Coleen Bilderback, Loy Bilderback, Ian Billick, Helen Bing, Pete Bing, Charles Birch, David Bishop, Jean Thomson Black, Lucy Blake, Arnold Bloom, Dan Blumstein, John Boething, Carol Boggs, Brendan Bohannan, Larry Bond, Tim Bonebrake, Elizabeth Borgese, Wally Bortz, Deane Bowers, Al Bowker, Corey Bradshaw, Karah Bradshaw, Stewart Brand, Kate Brauman, Dennis Breedlove, Margaret Breinholt, Iris Brest, Paul Brest, Win Briggs, Buzz Brock, Berry Brosi, Dave Brower, Bill Brown, Dorothy Brown, Irene Brown, Lester Brown, Pat Browne, Tommy Bruce, Pete Brussard, Otto Buchholz, Barry Bunch, Paul Buneman, Ellyn Bush, Guy Bush, George Burtness, Yvonne Burtness, Bill Calder, Allen Calvin, Em Camin, Joe Camin, Josep Canadell, Paul Cantor, Rusty Cantor, Kathlene Carney, Steve Carpenter, Bob Carr, Helena Carr, Damian Carrington, John Carson, Gerardo Ceballos, Pupa Ceballos, Kai Chan, Stuart Chapin, Val Chase, Nona Chiariello, Jim Chillcott, Bob Cialdini, Ralph Cicerone, Ann Clark, Harry Clench, Jonathan Cobb, Marie Cohen, Ian Common, Larry Condon, Bob Cotsen, Norman Cousins, Earle Cross, Dac Crossley, Mark Cruz, Danny Cullenward, Mike Cullenward, Joe Curley, Gretchen Daily, Scott Daily, Herman Daly, Howell Daly, Ben Dane, Septi Dane, Lisa Daniel, Melissa Daniel, Tim Daniel, Haydi Danielson, Jill Danzig, Aisha Dasgupta, Carol Dasgupta, Partha Dasgupta, Shamik Dasgupta, Tom Davis, Dorothy Decker, Bertrand de Jouvenel, Dave DeSante, Phil DeVries, Aart de Zeeuw, Jared Diamond, Joan Diamond, Nadia Diamond-Smith, Arturo Dirzo, Guille Dirzo, Rodolfo Dirzo, Avinash Dixit, Carl Djerassi, David Dobkin, Jean Doble, Theodosius Dobzhansky, Peter Dolinger, Cyril Dos Passos, John Downey, Susan Drennan, Diane Drobnis, Jack Drury, Ann Duffield, Duff Duffield, Jim Easterbrook, Don Eff, Tom Eisner, Janet Elder, Alfred Emerson, Tom Emmel, Mary Ann Erickson, Wally Falcon, Sylvia Fallon, Jack Farquhar, John Fay, Marc Feldman, Shirley Feldman, Roxy Ferris, Chris Field, Tony Fisher, Tim Flannery, Erica Fleishman, Greg Florant, John Fogg, Luis Folan, Carl Folke, Jane Fonda, E. B. Ford, Jonathan Freedman, Tom Freeman, Luke Frishkoff, Bob Galen, Richard Garbaccio, Dave Gardner, Ross Gelbspan, Murray Gell-Mann, Jim Gere, Amanda Gerstenfeld, John Gifford, Christine Gilbert, Larry Gilbert, Nick Gillham, Pat Gladney, Peter Gleick, Arthur Godfrey, David Goehring, Josh Goldstein, Wally Good, Corey Goodman, Deborah Gordon, Al Gore, Larry Goulder, Judy Gradwohl, Verne Grant, Dick Graves, Teru Graves, Cliff Grobstein, Jack Grove, Nick Haddad, Liz Hadly, Nate Hagens, Winnie Hallwachs, Bill Hammer, Phil Hanawalt, Mary Ellen Hannibal, Ilkka Hanski, Garret Hardin, Dave Hardwick, Pat Harris, John Harte, Julia Harte, Mel Harte, Alan Harvey, Marv Herrington, Ben Haskell, Jean Haskell, Carl Haub, Tyrone Hayes, Geoff Heal, Dave Heckel, Jack Heinz, Teresa Heinz, Craig Heller, Tom Heller, Jessica Hellmann, John Hendrickson, Ana Hera, Rita Hera, Marion Herzstein, Stanley Herzstein, Aileen Hessel, John Hessel, Mary Ellen Hessel, Gail Hewson, Tom Hirschfeld, Richard Hobbs, Annie Holdren, Cheri Holdren, Craig Holdren, Jill Holdren, John Holdren, Karen Holl, Buzz Holling, Dick Holm, Tad Homer-Dixon, Claire Horner-Devine, Sherry Huang, Russ Hulett, Bob Hull, Mary Ann Hurliman, Sam Hurst, Bonnie Inouye, Brian Inouye, Dave Inouye, Yoh Iwasa, Nina Jablonski, Dan Janzen, Chris Johnson, George Johnson, Joan Johnson, Pat Jones, Elizabeth Player Jones, Elena Kahn, Sandra Kahn,

Sumner Kalman, Danny Karp, Bill Kaufman, Ginny Kaufman, Les Kaufman, Dave Keck, Sally Kellock, Henry Kendall, Don Kennedy, Jeanne Kennedy, Page Kennedy, Ann Kinzig, Pat Kirch, Israel Klabin, Richard Klein, Bill Klots, Joan Knoebel, Susan Koret, Jeff Koseff, Claire Kremen, Wally LaBerge, Pat Labine, Eric Lambin, Dick Lamm, Frans Lanting, Gail Lapidus, Alan Launer, Bill Laurence, Cec Law, Josh Lederberg, Huey Lee, Phil Lee, Terry Leighton, Christina Leijonhufvud, David Leinsdorf, Sandy Leinsdorf, Julie Letsinger, David Leventhal, Bruce Levin, Carol Levin, Iris Levin, John Levin, Simon Levin, Karen Levy, Glenda Lewis, Walt Lewis, Dick Lewontin, Sid Liebes, Dave Lincoln, David Lindenmayer, Gort Linsley, Jack Liu, Vanessa Llana, Mary Ann Lloyd, Scott Loarie, Sharon Long, Tom Lovejoy, Amory Lovins, Jane Lubchenco, Gary Luck, Dick Lyman, Robert MacArthur, Karl-Göran Maler, Sally Mallam, Mark Mancall, Mike Mann, Jessica Marden, Jen Martiny, Steve Masley, Pam Matson, Ryuichi Matsuda, Bob May, Judith May, Mike May, Margie Mayfield, Ernst Mayr, Dick Maser, Harley McAdam, Brenda McCall, Don McCammond, Pete McCloskey, Rob McClung, Sue McConnell, Bill McDonough, Steve McKechnie, John McLaughlin, Don McMichael, Bob McNamara, Maureen McReynolds, Chase Mendenhall, Bruce Menge, Adina Merenlender, LuEsther Mertz, Fiorenza Micheli, Charles Michener, Tony Mihelich, Bill Miller, Pat Miller, Andy Moldenke, Ashley Montagu, Jennifer Montgomery, John Montgomery, Nancy Montgomery, Hal Mooney, Sherry Mooney, John Moore, Dean Morrison, Patrice Morrow, Baxter Moyer, Larry Mueller, Gene Munroe, Dennis Murphy, Lisa Murphy, Matt Murphy, Norman Myers, Pete Myers, Sam Myers, Vladimir Nabokov, Shahid Naeem, Shankar Narayen, Roz Naylor, Erica Newman, Peter Newman, Wendy Newport-Smith, Steve Nightingale, Dick Norgaard, Kari Norgaard, Nicki Norman, Elliot Norse, Eddie Novitski, Karine Nyborg, Francois Odendaal, John Ogden, Nancy Ogden, Isobel Olivieri, Bill Olsan, William Ophuls, Paul Opler, Naomi Oreskes, Gordon Orians, Bob Ornstein, Eleanor Ostrom, Jill Otto, Sally Otto, Zhiyun Ouyang, Bob Page, Camille Parmesan, Dennis Parnell, Lynn Pasahow, David Paul, Dan Pauly, Kay Pearse, Gordon Peay, Dave Perkins, Paul Perret, Charles Perrings, Bill Perry, Stuart Pimm, Dennis Pirages, Sue Pirages,

Steve Polasky, Johanna Polsenberg, Lauren Ponisio, Duncan Porter, Hugh Possingham, Sandra Postel, Floyd Preston, June Preston, Bettye Price, Mary Price, Rob Pringle, Robert Proctor, Tim Prout, Graham Pyke, Kilaparti Ramakrishna, Jack Randall, Jai Ranganathan, Jésus Rangel, Pat Raven, Peter Raven, Tamra Raven, George Rawson, Harry Recher, Judy Recher, Bill Rees, James Rehn, Don Reinberg, Carl Reiner, Estelle Reiner, Charlie Remington, Jean Remington, Irwin Remson, Andrew Revkin, Taylor Ricketts, Bob Ricklefs, Fred Rindge, Deborah Rogers, Terry Root, Gene Rosa, Bill Rosenberg, Ellie Rosenberg, Risa Rosenberg, Lee Ross, Joe Rotenberg, Lena Rotenberg, Sonia Rotenberg, Ruth Rothman, Miriam Rothschild, Steve Rottenborn, Joan Roughgarden, Sherry Rowland, Barry Russell, Bill Ryerson, Carl Safina, Oswaldo Sala, Heather Salzman, Jim Salzman, Barbara Sanders, Roger Sant, Vicki Sant, Ben Santer, Santianna, Robert Sapolsky, Adelaída Sarukhán, José Sarukhán, Dennis Saunders, Chuck Savitt, Richard Scheller, Rudolph Schmieder, Steve Schneider, Tom Schoener, Jack Scholer, David Schrier, Rachel Schrier, Hope Schroeder, Jennifer Schroeder, John Schroeder, Pete Seeger, Çağan Şekercioğlu, Judy Senderowitz, Gill Senn, Elton Sette, Sheila Shadwell, Lucy Shapiro, Maggie Sharp, Carla Shatz, Carolyn Sherwood, Ted Shoemaker, Claire Shoens, Dan Simberloff, Bob Simoni, George Simpson, Mike Singer, Tom Sisk, Dick Smith, Kirk Smith, Pip Smith, Peter Sneath, Jorge Soberón, Navjot Sodhi, Bob Sokal, Susan Solomon, Tracy Sonneborn, Michael Soulé, Dick Southwood, Helen Sparrow, Don Stallings, Fred Stanback, Heather Stanford, Rick Stanley, Dave Starrett, Dave Suzuki, Shanna Swan, Kathy Switky, Elizabeth Sylvia, Albert Szent-Györgyi, Joe Szent-Ivany, Alon Tal, Frank Talbot, Sue Talbot, Heather Tallis, Howard Temin, Fred Terman, John Thomas, Sue Thomas, John Thompson, Fred Thorne, Dave Tilman, Michael Tobias, Bettye Toguchi, Miro Torbica, Vanja Torbica, Rex Tugwell, Chris Turnbull, Ted Turner, Julia Tussing, Ted Tussing, Vic Twitty, Álvaro Umaña, Nora Underwood, Bob Usinger, Kyle Van Houtan, Jane Van Zandt, Peggy Vas Dias, Peter Vitousek, Mathis Wackernagel, Bob Wagner, Hal Wagner, Judy Wagner, Dave Wake, Brian Walker, Diana Wall, Nick Waser, Ken Watt, Ward Watt, Alan Weeden, Alan Weisman, Andy Weiss, Stu Weiss, Karen Weissman, Lois Wessells, Norm Wessells, Darryl Wheye, Ray White, Noah Whiteman, Joe

Wible, Jerry Wiesner, Ira Wiggins, David Wilcove, Bruce Wilcox, Jody Wilkerson, Ernest Williams, Kathy Williams, Robyn Williams, Ed Wilson, Kelsey Wirth, Tim Wirth, Wren Wirth, Tom Wisler, Scott Wissinger, Simon Wong, George Woodwell, Patti Wylie, Tasos Xepapadeas, Charley Yanofsky, Andy Yoggy, Jim Young, Ed Zachery, Ben Ziegler, and Jim Zook. A great many others have also helped, and I'm deeply grateful to them as well.

The author and Johnny Carson discuss politics on *The Tonight Show* in 1979. Illustration by Darryl Wheye, who also drew the tiger swallowtail butterfly dinkuses (section breaks).

INDEX

Note: Page numbers in bold indicate figures.